Holt Science & Technology
Short Courses

Teacher Edition WALK-THROUGH

Student Edition CONTENTS IN BRIEF

HOLT, RINEHART AND WINSTON
A Harcourt Education Company
Orlando • **Austin** • New York • San Diego • Toronto • London

Designed to meet the needs of all students

15 Short Courses

Holt Science & Technology: Short Course Series allows you to match your curriculum by choosing from 15 books covering life, earth, and physical sciences. The program reflects current curriculum developments and includes the strongest skills-development strand of any middle school science series. Students of all abilities will develop skills that they can use both in science as well as in other courses.

STUDENTS OF ALL ABILITIES RECEIVE THE READING HELP AND TAILORED INSTRUCTION THEY NEED.

- The *Student Edition* is accessible with a clean, easy-to-follow design and highlighted vocabulary words.
- Inclusion strategies and different learning styles help support all learners.
- Comprehensive Section and Chapter Reviews and Standardized Test Preparation allow students to practice their test-taking skills.
- Reading Comprehension Guide and Guided Reading Audio CDs help students better understand the content.

CROSS-DISCIPLINARY CONNECTIONS LET STUDENTS SEE HOW SCIENCE RELATES TO OTHER DISCIPLINES.

- Mathematics, reading, and writing skills are integrated throughout the program.
- Cross-discipline Connection To features show students how science relates to language arts, social studies, and other sciences.

A FLEXIBLE LABORATORY PROGRAM HELPS STUDENTS BUILD IMPORTANT INQUIRY AND CRITICAL-THINKING SKILLS.

- The laboratory program includes labs in each chapter, labs in the **LabBook** at the end of the text, six different lab books, and **Video Labs.**
- All labs are teacher-tested and rated by difficulty in the *Teacher Edition,* so you can be sure the labs will be appropriate for your students.
- A variety of labs, from **Inquiry Labs** to **Skills Practice Labs,** helps you meet the needs of your curriculum and work within the time constraints of your teaching schedule.

INTEGRATED TECHNOLOGY AND ONLINE RESOURCES EXPAND LEARNING BEYOND CLASSROOM WALLS.

- An **Enhanced Online Edition** or **CD-ROM Version** of the student text lightens your students' load.

- **SciLinks,** a Web service developed and maintained by the National Science Teachers Association (NSTA), contains current prescreened links directly related to the textbook.

- **Brain Food Video Quizzes** on videotape and DVD are game-show style quizzes that assess students' progress and motivate them to study.

- The **One-stop Planner® CD-ROM** with **Exam View® Test Generator** contains all of the resources you need including an *Interactive Teacher Edition,* worksheets, customizable lesson plans, **Holt Calendar Planner,** a powerful test generator, **Lab Materials QuickList Software,** and more.

- Spanish Resources include **Guided Reading Audio CD** in Spanish.

HOLT **CIENCIAS Y TECNOLOGÍA** LOS **ANIMALES**

EcoLabs

HOLT **SCIENCE & TECHNOLOGY**

CHAPTER RESOURCE FILES FOR
Inside the Restless Earth

Skills Worksheets
- Directed Reading A
- Directed Reading B
- Vocabulary & Notes
- Section Reviews
- Chapter Review
- Reinforcement
- Critical Thinking

Assessments
- Section Quizzes
- Chapter Test A
- Chapter Test B
- Chapter Test C
- Performance-Based Assessment
- Standardized Test Preparation

Labs and Activities
- Datasheets for In-Text Labs
- Datasheets for Quick Labs
- Datasheets for LabBook
- Vocabulary Activity
- SciLinks® Activity

Teacher Resources
- Teacher Notes for Performance-Based Assessment
- Lab Notes and Answers
- Answer Keys
- Lesson Plans
- Test Item Listing for ExamView® Test Generator
- Teaching Transparencies
- Chapter Starter Transparencies
- Bellringer Transparencies
- Concept Mapping Transparencies

HOLT **CIENCIAS Y TECNOLOGÍA**

Guided Reading Audio CD Program

Direct read of the student text

INTRODUCCIÓN A LA MATERIA

K

HOLT SCIENCE & TECHNOLOGY

One-Stop Planner®

HOLT RINEHART AND WINSTON

Life Science

A — MICROORGANISMS, FUNGI, AND PLANTS

B — ANIMALS

CHAPTER 1

It's Alive!! Or, Is It?
- Characteristics of living things
- Homeostasis
- Heredity and DNA
- Producers, consumers, and decomposers
- Biomolecules

Animals and Behavior
- Characteristics of animals
- Classification of animals
- Animal behavior
- Hibernation and estivation
- The biological clock
- Animal communication
- Living in groups

CHAPTER 2

Bacteria and Viruses
- Binary fission
- Characteristics of bacteria
- Nitrogen-fixing bacteria
- Antibiotics
- Pathogenic bacteria
- Characteristics of viruses
- Lytic cycle

Invertebrates
- General characteristics of invertebrates
- Types of symmetry
- Characteristics of sponges, cnidarians, arthropods, and echinoderms
- Flatworms versus roundworms
- Types of circulatory systems

CHAPTER 3

Protists and Fungi
- Characteristics of protists
- Types of algae
- Types of protozoa
- Protist reproduction
- Characteristics of fungi and lichens

Fishes, Amphibians, and Reptiles
- Characteristics of vertebrates
- Structure and kinds of fishes
- Development of lungs
- Structure and kinds of amphibians and reptiles
- Function of the amniotic egg

CHAPTER 4

Introduction to Plants
- Characteristics of plants and seeds
- Reproduction and classification
- Angiosperms versus gymnosperms
- Monocots versus dicots
- Structure and functions of roots, stems, leaves, and flowers

Birds and Mammals
- Structure and kinds of birds
- Types of feathers
- Adaptations for flight
- Structure and kinds of mammals
- Function of the placenta

CHAPTER 5

Plant Processes
- Pollination and fertilization
- Dormancy
- Photosynthesis
- Plant tropisms
- Seasonal responses of plants

CHAPTER 6

CHAPTER 7

T4

PROGRAM SCOPE AND SEQUENCE

Selecting the right books for your course is easy. Just review the topics presented in each book to determine the best match to your district curriculum.

C CELLS, HEREDITY, & CLASSIFICATION

Cells: The Basic Units of Life
- Cells, tissues, and organs
- Cell theory
- Surface-to-volume ratio
- Prokaryotic versus eukaryotic cells
- Cell organelles

The Cell in Action
- Diffusion and osmosis
- Passive versus active transport
- Endocytosis versus exocytosis
- Photosynthesis
- Cellular respiration and fermentation
- Cell cycle

Heredity
- Dominant versus recessive traits
- Genes and alleles
- Genotype, phenotype, the Punnett square and probability
- Meiosis
- Determination of sex

Genes and Gene Technology
- Structure of DNA
- Protein synthesis
- Mutations
- Heredity disorders and genetic counseling

The Evolution of Living Things
- Adaptations and species
- Evidence for evolution
- Darwin's work and natural selection
- Formation of new species

The History of Life on Earth
- Geologic time scale and extinctions
- Plate tectonics
- Human evolution

Classification
- Levels of classification
- Cladistic diagrams
- Dichotomous keys
- Characteristics of the six kingdoms

D HUMAN BODY SYSTEMS & HEALTH

Body Organization and Structure
- Homeostasis
- Types of tissue
- Organ systems
- Structure and function of the skeletal system, muscular system, and integumentary system

Circulation and Respiration
- Structure and function of the cardiovascular system, lymphatic system, and respiratory system
- Respiratory disorders

The Digestive and Urinary Systems
- Structure and function of the digestive system
- Structure and function of the urinary system

Communication and Control
- Structure and function of the nervous system and endocrine system
- The senses
- Structure and function of the eye and ear

Reproduction and Development
- Asexual versus sexual reproduction
- Internal versus external fertilization
- Structure and function of the human male and female reproductive systems
- Fertilization, placental development, and embryo growth
- Stages of human life

Body Defenses and Disease
- Types of diseases
- Vaccines and immunity
- Structure and function of the immune system
- Autoimmune diseases, cancer, and AIDS

Staying Healthy
- Nutrition and reading food labels
- Alcohol and drug effects on the body
- Hygiene, exercise, and first aid

E ENVIRONMENTAL SCIENCE

Interactions of Living Things
- Biotic versus abiotic parts of the environment
- Producers, consumers, and decomposers
- Food chains and food webs
- Factors limiting population growth
- Predator-prey relationships
- Symbiosis and coevolution

Cycles in Nature
- Water cycle
- Carbon cycle
- Nitrogen cycle
- Ecological succession

The Earth's Ecosystems
- Kinds of land and water biomes
- Marine ecosystems
- Freshwater ecosystems

Environmental Problems and Solutions
- Types of pollutants
- Types of resources
- Conservation practices
- Species protection

Energy Resources
- Types of resources
- Energy resources and pollution
- Alternative energy resources

Earth Science

H WATER ON EARTH

The Flow of Fresh Water
- Water cycle
- River systems
- Stream erosion
- Life cycle of rivers
- Deposition
- Aquifers, springs, and wells
- Ground water
- Water treatment and pollution

Exploring the Oceans
- Properties and characteristics of the oceans
- Features of the ocean floor
- Ocean ecology
- Ocean resources and pollution

The Movement of Ocean Water
- Types of currents
- Characteristics of waves
- Types of ocean waves
- Tides

I WEATHER AND CLIMATE

The Atmosphere
- Structure of the atmosphere
- Air pressure
- Radiation, convection, and conduction
- Greenhouse effect and global warming
- Characteristics of winds
- Types of winds
- Air pollution

Understanding Weather
- Water cycle
- Humidity
- Types of clouds
- Types of precipitation
- Air masses and fronts
- Storms, tornadoes, and hurricanes
- Weather forecasting
- Weather maps

Climate
- Weather versus climate
- Seasons and latitude
- Prevailing winds
- Earth's biomes
- Earth's climate zones
- Ice ages
- Global warming
- Greenhouse effect

J ASTRONOMY

Studying Space
- Astronomy
- Keeping time
- Types of telescope
- Radioastronomy
- Mapping the stars
- Scales of the universe

Stars, Galaxies, and the Universe
- Composition of stars
- Classification of stars
- Star brightness, distance, and motions
- H-R diagram
- Life cycle of stars
- Types of galaxies
- Theories on the formation of the universe

Formation of the Solar System
- Birth of the solar system
- Structure of the sun
- Fusion
- Earth's structure and atmosphere
- Planetary motion
- Newton's Law of Universal Gravitation

A Family of Planets
- Properties and characteristics of the planets
- Properties and characteristics of moons
- Comets, asteroids, and meteoroids

Exploring Space
- Rocketry and artificial satellites
- Types of Earth orbit
- Space probes and space exploration

Physical Science

	K INTRODUCTION TO MATTER	**L** INTERACTIONS OF MATTER
CHAPTER 1	**The Properties of Matter** • Definition of matter • Mass and weight • Physical and chemical properties • Physical and chemical change • Density	**Chemical Bonding** • Types of chemical bonds • Valence electrons • Ions versus molecules • Crystal lattice
CHAPTER 2	**States of Matter** • States of matter and their properties • Boyle's and Charles's laws • Changes of state	**Chemical Reactions** • Writing chemical formulas and equations • Law of conservation of mass • Types of reactions • Endothermic versus exothermic reactions • Law of conservation of energy • Activation energy • Catalysts and inhibitors
CHAPTER 3	**Elements, Compounds, and Mixtures** • Elements and compounds • Metals, nonmetals, and metalloids (semiconductors) • Properties of mixtures • Properties of solutions, suspensions, and colloids	**Chemical Compounds** • Ionic versus covalent compounds • Acids, bases, and salts • pH • Organic compounds • Biomolecules
CHAPTER 4	**Introduction to Atoms** • Atomic theory • Atomic model and structure • Isotopes • Atomic mass and mass number	**Atomic Energy** • Properties of radioactive substances • Types of decay • Half-life • Fission, fusion, and chain reactions
CHAPTER 5	**The Periodic Table** • Structure of the periodic table • Periodic law • Properties of alkali metals, alkaline-earth metals, halogens, and noble gases	
CHAPTER 6		

M FORCES, MOTION, AND ENERGY

Matter in Motion
- Speed, velocity, and acceleration
- Measuring force
- Friction
- Mass versus weight

Forces in Motion
- Terminal velocity and free fall
- Projectile motion
- Inertia
- Momentum

Forces in Fluids
- Properties in fluids
- Atmospheric pressure
- Density
- Pascal's principle
- Buoyant force
- Archimedes' principle
- Bernoulli's principle

Work and Machines
- Measuring work
- Measuring power
- Types of machines
- Mechanical advantage
- Mechanical efficiency

Energy and Energy Resources
- Forms of energy
- Energy conversions
- Law of conservation of energy
- Energy resources

Heat and Heat Technology
- Heat versus temperature
- Thermal expansion
- Absolute zero
- Conduction, convection, radiation
- Conductors versus insulators
- Specific heat capacity
- Changes of state
- Heat engines
- Thermal pollution

N ELECTRICITY AND MAGNETISM

Introduction to Electricity
- Law of electric charges
- Conduction versus induction
- Static electricity
- Potential difference
- Cells, batteries, and photocells
- Thermocouples
- Voltage, current, and resistance
- Electric power
- Types of circuits

Electromagnetism
- Properties of magnets
- Magnetic force
- Electromagnetism
- Solenoids and electric motors
- Electromagnetic induction
- Generators and transformers

Electronic Technology
- Properties of semiconductors
- Integrated circuits
- Diodes and transistors
- Analog versus digital signals
- Microprocessors
- Features of computers

O SOUND AND LIGHT

The Energy of Waves
- Properties of waves
- Types of waves
- Reflection and refraction
- Diffraction and interference
- Standing waves and resonance

The Nature of Sound
- Properties of sound waves
- Structure of the human ear
- Pitch and the Doppler effect
- Infrasonic versus ultrasonic sound
- Sound reflection and echolocation
- Sound barrier
- Interference, resonance, diffraction, and standing waves
- Sound quality of instruments

The Nature of Light
- Electromagnetic waves
- Electromagnetic spectrum
- Law of reflection
- Absorption and scattering
- Reflection and refraction
- Diffraction and interference

Light and Our World
- Luminosity
- Types of lighting
- Types of mirrors and lenses
- Focal point
- Structure of the human eye
- Lasers and holograms

Program resources make teaching and learning easier.

CHAPTER RESOURCES

A *Chapter Resources book* accompanies each of the 15 *Short Courses*. Here you'll find everything you need to make sure your students are getting the most out of learning science—all in one book.

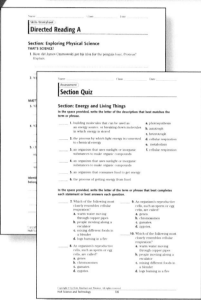

Skills Worksheets
- Directed Reading A: Basic
- Directed Reading B: Special Needs
- Vocabulary and Chapter Summary
- Section Reviews
- Chapter Reviews
- Reinforcement
- Critical Thinking

Labs & Activities
- Datasheets for Chapter Labs
- Datasheets for Quick Labs
- Datasheets for LabBook
- Vocabulary Activity
- SciLinks® Activity

Assessments
- Section Quizzes
- Chapter Tests A: General
- Chapter Tests B: Advanced
- Chapter Tests C: Special Needs
- Performance-Based Assessments
- Standardized Test Preparation

Teacher Resources
- Lab Notes and Answers
- Teacher Notes for Performance-Based Assessment
- Answer Keys
- Lesson Plans
- Test Item Listing for ExamView® Test Generator
- Full-color Teaching Transparencies, plus section Bellringers, Concept Mapping, and Chapter Starter Transparencies.

SPANISH RESOURCES

Spanish materials are available for each *Short Course:*

- *Student Edition*
- **Spanish Resources** booklet contains worksheets and assessments translated into Spanish with an English Answer Key.
- Guided Reading Audio CD Program

ONLINE RESOURCES

- *Enhanced Online Editions* engage students and assist teachers with a host of interactive features that are available anytime and anywhere you can connect to the Internet.
- CNNStudentNews.com provides award-winning news and information for both teachers and students.
- SciLinks—a Web service developed and maintained by the National Science Teachers Association—links you and your students to up-to-date online resources directly related to chapter topics.
- go.hrw.com links you and your students to online chapter activities and resources.
- Current Science articles relate to students' lives.

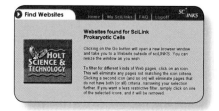

ADDITIONAL LAB AND SKILLS RESOURCES

- *Calculator-Based Labs* incorporates scientific instruments, offering students insight into modern scientific investigation.
- *EcoLabs & Field Activities* develops awareness of the natural world.
- *Holt Science Skills Workshop: Reading in the Content Area* contains exercises that target reading skills key.
- *Inquiry Labs* taps students' natural curiosity and creativity with a focus on the process of discovery.
- *Labs You Can Eat* safely incorporates edible items into the classroom.
- *Long-Term Projects & Research Ideas* extends and enriches lessons.
- *Math Skills for Science* provides additional explanations, examples, and math problems so students can develop their skills.
- *Science Skills Worksheets* helps your students hone important learning skills.
- *Whiz-Bang Demonstrations* gets your students' attention at the beginning of a lesson.

ADDITIONAL RESOURCES

- *Assessment Checklists & Rubrics* gives you guidelines for evaluating students' progress.
- *Holt Anthology of Science Fiction* sparks your students' imaginations with thought-provoking stories.
- *Holt Science Posters* visually reinforces scientific concepts and themes with seven colorful posters including **The Periodic Table of the Elements.**

- *Professional Reference for Teachers* contains professional articles that discuss a variety of topics, such as classroom management.
- *Program Introduction Resource File* explains the program and its features and provides several additional references, including lab safety, scoring rubrics, and more.
- *Science Fair Guide* gives teachers, students, and parents tips for planning and assisting in a science fair.
- *Science Puzzlers, Twisters & Teasers* activities challenge students to think about science concepts in different ways.

TECHNOLOGY RESOURCES

- *CNN Presents Science in the News: Video Library* helps students see the impact of science on their everyday lives with actual news video clips.
  - Multicultural Connections
  - Science, Technology & Society
  - Scientists in Action
  - Eye on the Environment
- *Guided Reading Audio CD Program*, available in English and Spanish, provides students with a direct read of each section.
- *HRW Earth Science Videotape* takes your students on a geology "field trip" with full-motion video.
- *Interactive Explorations CD-ROM Program* develops students' inquiry and decision-making skills as they investigate science phenomena in a virtual lab setting.

- *One-Stop Planner CD-ROM®* organizes everything you need on one disc, including printable worksheets, customizable lesson plans, a powerful test generator, **PowerPoint® Resources, Lab Materials QuickList Software, Holt Calendar Planner, Interactive Teacher Edition,** and more.
- *Science Tutor CD-ROMs* help students practice what they learn with immediate feedback.
- *Lab Videos* make it easier to integrate more experiments into your lessons without the preparation time and costs. Available on DVD and VHS.
- *Brain Food Video Quizzes* are game-show style quizzes that assess students' progress. Available on DVD and VHS.
- *Visual Concepts CD-ROMs* include graphics, animations, and movie clips that demonstrate key chapter concepts.

Science and Math Worksheets

The **Holt Science & Technology** program helps you meet the needs of a wide variety of students, regardless of their skill level. The following pages provide examples of the worksheets available to improve your students' science and math skills whether they already have a strong science and math background or are weak in these areas. Samples of assessment checklists and rubrics are also provided.

In addition to the skills worksheets represented here, **Holt Science & Technology** provides a variety of worksheets that are correlated directly with each chapter of the program. Representations of these worksheets are found at the beginning of each chapter in this *Teacher Edition*.

Many worksheets are also available on the Holt Web site. The address is **go.hrw.com**.

Science Skills Worksheets: Thinking Skills

BEING FLEXIBLE

USING YOUR SENSES

THINKING OBJECTIVELY

UNDERSTANDING BIAS

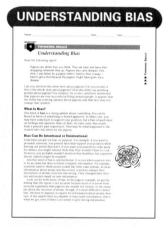

USING LOGIC

BOOSTING YOUR MEMORY

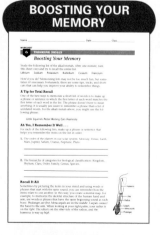

IMPROVING YOUR STUDY HABITS

READING A SCIENCE TEXTBOOK

Science Skills Worksheets: Experimenting Skills

SAFETY RULES!

9 EXPERIMENTING SKILLS
Safety Rules!

DOING A LAB WRITE-UP
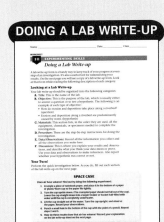

10 EXPERIMENTING SKILLS
Doing a Lab Write-up

UNDERSTANDING VARIABLES
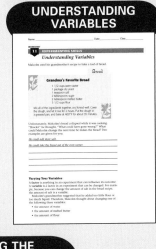

11 EXPERIMENTING SKILLS
Understanding Variables

WORKING WITH HYPOTHESES
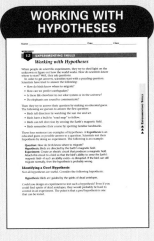

12 EXPERIMENTING SKILLS
Working with Hypotheses

DESIGNING AN EXPERIMENT
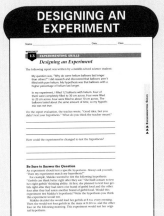

13 EXPERIMENTING SKILLS
Designing an Experiment

USING THE INTERNATIONAL SYSTEM OF UNITS (SI)

14 EXPERIMENTING SKILLS
Using the International System of Units (SI)

MEASURING
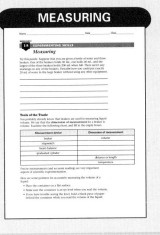

15 EXPERIMENTING SKILLS
Measuring

Science Skills Worksheets: Researching Skills

CHOOSING YOUR TOPIC
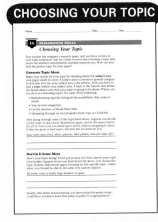

16 RESEARCHING SKILLS
Choosing Your Topic

ORGANIZING YOUR RESEARCH

17 RESEARCHING SKILLS
Organizing Your Research

FINDING USEFUL SOURCES
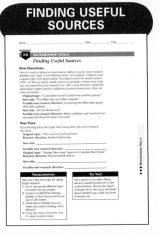

18 RESEARCHING SKILLS
Finding Useful Sources

RESEARCHING ON THE WEB
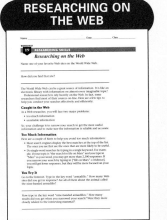

19 RESEARCHING SKILLS
Researching on the Web

Science Skills Worksheets: Researching Skills (continued)

IDENTIFYING BIAS

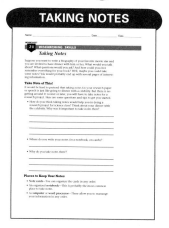

TAKING NOTES

Science Skills Worksheets: Communicating Skills

SCIENCE WRITING

SCIENCE DRAWING

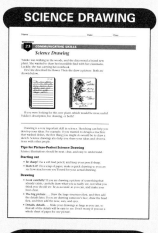

USING MODELS TO COMMUNICATE

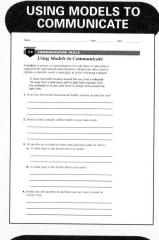

INTRODUCTION TO GRAPHS

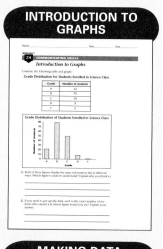

GRASPING GRAPHING

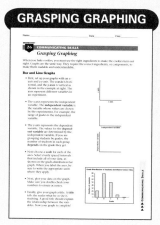

INTERPRETING YOUR DATA

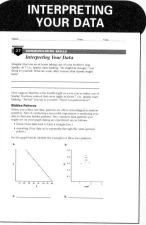

RECOGNIZING BIAS IN GRAPHS

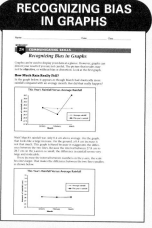

MAKING DATA MEANINGFUL

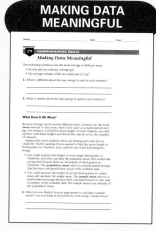

HINTS FOR ORAL PRESENTATIONS

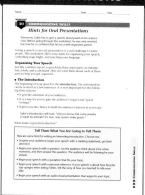

Math Skills for Science

ADDITION AND SUBTRACTION

WORKSHEET 1 — MATH SKILLS
Addition Review

WORKSHEET 2 — MATH SKILLS
Subtraction Review

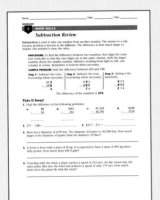

MULTIPLICATION

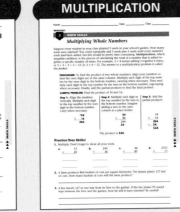

WORKSHEET 3 — MATH SKILLS
Multiplying Whole Numbers

WORKSHEET 4 — MATH SKILLS
A Shortcut for Multiplying Large Numbers

DIVISION

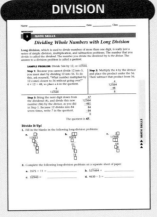

WORKSHEET 5 — MATH SKILLS
Dividing Whole Numbers with Long Division

WORKSHEET 6 — MATH SKILLS
Checking Division with Multiplication

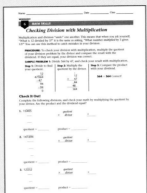

AVERAGES

WORKSHEET 7 — MATH SKILLS
What Is an Average?

WORKSHEET 8 — MATH SKILLS
Average, Mode, and Median

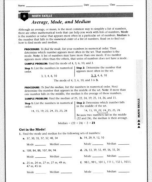

POSITIVE AND NEGATIVE NUMBERS

WORKSHEET 9 — MATH SKILLS
Comparing Integers on a Number Line

WORKSHEET 10 — MATH SKILLS
Arithmetic with Positive and Negative Numbers

FRACTIONS

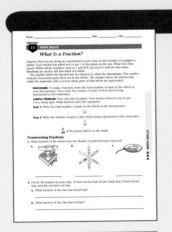

WORKSHEET 11 — MATH SKILLS
What Is a Fraction?

WORKSHEET 12 — MATH SKILLS
Reducing Fractions to Lowest Terms

WORKSHEET 13 — MATH SKILLS
Improper Fractions and Mixed Numbers

WORKSHEET 14 — MATH SKILLS
Adding and Subtracting Fractions

WORKSHEET 15 — MATH SKILLS
Multiplying and Dividing Fractions

Math Skills for Science (continued)

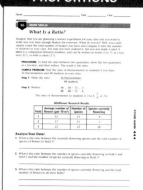

RATIOS AND PROPORTIONS

What Is a Ratio?

Using Proportions and Cross-Multiplication

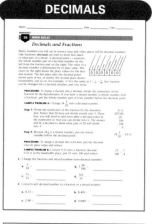

DECIMALS

Decimals and Fractions

Arithmetic with Decimals

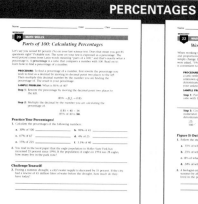

PERCENTAGES

Parts of 100: Calculating Percentages

Working with Percentages and Proportions

Percentages, Fractions, and Decimals

POWERS OF 10

Counting the Zeros

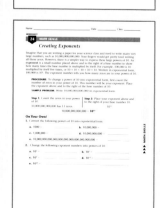

Creating Exponents

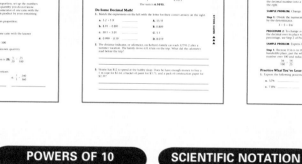

SCIENTIFIC NOTATION

What Is Scientific Notation?

Multiplying and Dividing in Scientific Notation

SI MEASUREMENT AND CONVERSION

What Is SI?

A Formula for SI Catch-up

Math Skills for Science (continued)

GEOMETRY

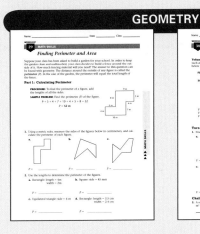

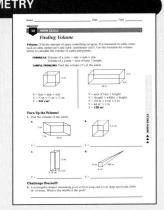

THE UNIT FACTOR AND DIMENSIONAL ANALYSIS

MATH IN SCIENCE: INTEGRATED SCIENCE

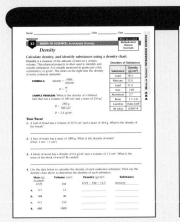

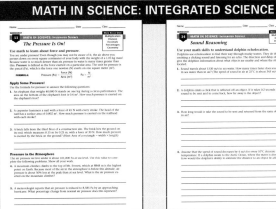

Math Skills for Science (continued)

MATH IN SCIENCE: LIFE SCIENCE

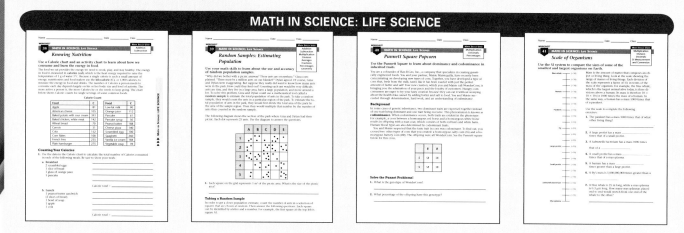

MATH IN SCIENCE: EARTH SCIENCE

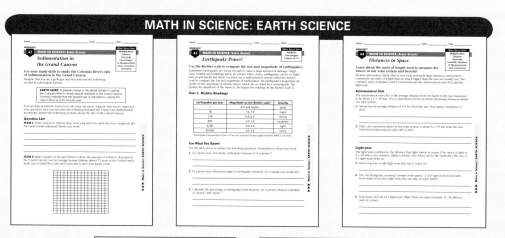

T18

Science and Math Skills Worksheets

MATH IN SCIENCE: PHYSICAL SCIENCE

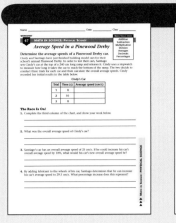
Worksheet 47 — *Average Speed in a Pinewood Derby*

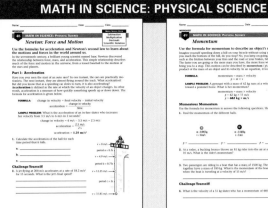
Worksheet 48 — *Newton: Force and Motion*

Worksheet 49 — *Momentum*

Worksheet 50 — *Balancing Chemical Equations*

Worksheet 51 — *Work and Power*

Worksheet 52 — *A Bicycle Trip*

Worksheet 53 — *Mechanical Advantage*

Worksheet 54 — *Color at Light Speed*

Assessment Checklist & Rubrics

The following is just a sample of over 50 checklists and rubrics contained in this booklet.

RUBRICS FOR WRITTEN WORK

RUBRIC FOR EXPERIMENTS

TEACHER EVALUATION OF COOPERATIVE LEARNING

TEACHER EVALUATION OF STUDENT PROGRESS

National Science Education Standards

The following lists show the chapter correlation of *Holt Science & Technology: Inside the Restless Earth* with the *National Science Education Standards* (grades 5–8).

Unifying Concepts and Processes

Standard	Chapter Correlation
Systems, order, and organization Code: UCP 1	Chapter 1 1.2, 1.3 Chapter 2 2.1, 2.2, 2.3, 2.4 Chapter 3 3.2, 3.3, 3.4, 3.5
Evidence, models, and explanation Code: UCP 2	Chapter 2 2.2, 2.3, 2.4 Chapter 3 3.1, 3.2, 3.4 Chapter 4 4.2, 4.3, 4.4 Chapter 5 5.1, 5.3
Change, constancy, and measurement Code: UCP 3	Chapter 3 3.3, 3.4, 3.5 Chapter 5 5.2, 5.3 Chapter 6 6.3
Evolution and equilibrium Code: UCP 4	Chapter 3 3.1, 3.4, 3.5
Form and function Code: UCP 5	Chapter 1 1.1, 1.2, 1.3

Science as Inquiry

Standard	Chapter Correlation
Abilities necessary to do scientific inquiry Code: SAI 1	Chapter 1 1.2, 1.3 Chapter 2 2.1, 2.2, 2.3, 2.4 Chapter 3 3.3, 3.4, 3.5 Chapter 4 4.1, 4.2, 4.3, 4.4 Chapter 5 5.1, 5.2, 5.3 Chapter 6 6.1, 6.3
Understandings about scientific inquiry Code: SAI 2	Chapter 1 1.2 Chapter 2 2.1, 2.2, 2.3, 2.4 Chapter 3 3.3, 3.4, 3.5 Chapter 4 4.1, 4.2, 4.3 Chapter 5 5.1, 5.2, 5.3

Science and Technology

Standard	Chapter Correlation
Understandings about science and technology Code: ST 2	Chapter 2 2.1 Chapter 3 3.3 Chapter 4 4.2, 4.3 Chapter 5 5.1, 5.2, 5.3 Chapter 6 6.2, 6.3

Science in Personal Perspectives

Standard	Chapter Correlation
Personal Health Code: SPSP 1	Chapter 5 5.3
Populations, resources, and environments Code: SPSP 2	Chapter 1 1.3
Natural hazards Code: SPSP 3	Chapter 4 4.3 Chapter 5 5.1, 5.2, 5.3 Chapter 6 6.2
Risks and benefits Code: SPSP 4	Chapter 1 1.3 Chapter 4 4.3 Chapter 5 5.1, 5.2, 5.3 Chapter 6 6.2
Science and technology in society Code: SPSP 5	Chapter 1 1.3 Chapter 2 2.1 Chapter 3 3.1, 3.3, 3.4 Chapter 4 4.2, 4.3 Chapter 5 5.3

History and Nature of Science

Standard	Chapter Correlation
Science as a human endeavor Code: HNS 1	Chapter 2 2.1 Chapter 3 3.1, 3.3 Chapter 4 4.2 Chapter 5 5.2
Nature of science Code: HNS 2	Chapter 3 3.1, 3.2, 3.3, 3.5 Chapter 4 4.2, 4.3 Chapter 5 5.3 Chapter 6 6.1
History of science Code: HNS 3	Chapter 3 3.1, 3.3 Chapter 4 4.2 Chapter 5 5.2

Earth Science Content Standards

Structure of the Earth System

Standard	Chapter Correlation	
The solid earth is layered with a lithosphere; hot, convecting mantle; and dense metallic core. Code: ES 1a	**Chapter 5**	5.1
Lithospheric plates on the scales of continents and oceans constantly move at rates of centimeters per year in response to movements in the mantle. Major geological events, such as earthquakes, volcanic eruptions, and mountain building result from these plate motions. Code: ES 1b	**Chapter 4** **Chapter 5** **Chapter 6**	4.2, 4.3, 4.4 5.1, 5.2, 5.3 6.3
Land forms are the result of a combination of constructive and destructive forces. Constructive forces include crustal deformation, volcanic eruption, and deposition of sediment, while destructive forces include weathering and erosion. Code: ES 1c	**Chapter 2** **Chapter 6**	2.1, 2.2, 2.3, 2.4 6.1, 6.2, 6.3
Some changes in the solid earth can be described as the "rock cycle." Old rocks at the earth's surface weather, forming sediments that are buried, then compacted, heated, and often recrystallized into new rock. Eventually, those new rocks may be brought to the earth's surface by the forces that drive plate motions, and the rock cycle continues. Code: ES 1d	**Chapter 2**	2.1, 2.2, 2.3
Living organisms have played many roles in the earth system, including affecting the composition of the atmosphere, producing some types of rocks, and contributing to the weathering of rocks. Code: ES 1k	**Chapter 2** **Chapter 3**	2.3 3.4

Earth's History

Standard	Chapter Correlation	
The earth processes we see today, including erosion, movement of lithospheric plates, and changes in atmospheric composition, are similar to those that occurred in the past. Earth history is also influenced by occasional catastrophes, such as the impact of an asteroid or comet. Code: ES 2a	**Chapter 3** **Chapter 4**	3.1 4.2, 4.3, 4.4
Fossils provide important evidence of how life and environmental conditions have changed. Code: ES 2b	**Chapter 2** **Chapter 3**	2.3 3.1, 3.2, 3.3, 3.4, 3.5

HOLT SCIENCE & TECHNOLOGY

Inside the Restless Earth

HOLT, RINEHART AND WINSTON

A Harcourt Education Company

Orlando • **Austin** • New York • San Diego • Toronto • London

Acknowledgments

Contributing Authors

Kathleen Meehan Berry
Science Chairman
Canon-McMillan School District
Canonsburg, Pennsylvania

Robert H. Fronk, Ph.D.
Professor
Science and Mathematics Education Department
Florida Institute of Technology
Melbourne, Florida

Peter E. Malin, Ph.D.
Professor of Geology
Division of Earth and Ocean Sciences
Duke University
Durham, North Carolina

Inclusion Specialist

Karen Clay
Inclusion Specialist Consultant
Boston, Massachusetts

Safety Reviewer

Jack Gerlovich, Ph.D.
Associate Professor
School of Education
Drake University
Des Moines, Iowa

Academic Reviewers

Roger J. Cuffey, Ph.D.
Professor of Paleontology
Department of Geosciences
Pennsylvania State University
University Park, Pennsylvania

Turgay Ertekin, Ph.D.
Professor and Chairman of Petroleum and Natural Gas Engineering
Energy and Geo-Environmental Engineering
Pennsylvania State University
University Park, Pennsylvania

Richard N. Hey, Ph.D.
Professor of Geophysics
Department of Geophysics & Planetology
University of Hawaii at Manoa
Honolulu, Hawaii

Ken Hon, Ph.D.
Associate Professor of Volcanology
Geology Department
University of Hawaii at Hilo
Hilo, Hawaii

Susan Hough, Ph.D.
Scientist
United States Geological Survey (USGS)
Pasadena, California

Joel S. Leventhal, Ph.D.
Emeritus Scientist
U.S. Geological Survey
Lakewood, Colorado

Kenneth K. Peace
Manager of Transportation
WestArch Coal, Inc.
St. Louis, Missouri

Kenneth H. Rubin, Ph.D.
Associate Professor
Department of Geology & Geophysics
University of Hawaii at Manoa
Honolulu, Hawaii

Colin D. Sumrall, Ph.D.
Lecturer of Paleontology
Earth and Planetary Sciences
The University of Tennessee
Knoxville, Tennessee

Peter W. Weigand, Ph.D.
Professor Emeritus
Department of Geological Sciences
California State University
Northridge, California

Teacher Reviewers

Diedre S. Adams
Physical Science Instructor
Science Department
West Vigo Middle School
West Terre Haute, Indiana

Laura Buchanan
Science Teacher and Department Chairperson
Corkran Middle School
Glen Burnie, Maryland

Robin K. Clanton
Science Department Head
Berrien Middle School
Nashville, Georgia

Meredith Hanson
Science Teacher
Westside Middle School
Rocky Face, Georgia

James Kerr
Oklahoma Teacher of the Year 2002–2003
Oklahoma State Department of Education
Union Public Schools
Tulsa, Oklahoma

Laura Kitselman
Science Teacher and Coordinator
Loudoun Country Day School
Leesburg, Virginia

Printed in the United States of America

ISBN 0-03-025571-6

4 5 6 7 048 08 07 06 05

F | Inside the Restless Earth

Labs and Activities

How to Use Your Textbook

Your Roadmap for Success with Holt Science and Technology

Reading Warm-Up

A Reading Warm-Up at the beginning of every section provides you with the section's objectives and key terms. The objectives tell you what you'll need to know after you finish reading the section.

Key terms are listed for each section. Learn the definitions of these terms because you will most likely be tested on them. Each key term is highlighted in the text and is defined at point of use and in the margin. You can also use the glossary to locate definitions quickly.

STUDY TIP Reread the objectives and the definitions to the key terms when studying for a test to be sure you know the material.

Get Organized

A Reading Strategy at the beginning of every section provides tips to help you organize and remember the information covered in the section. Keep a science notebook so that you are ready to take notes when your teacher reviews the material in class. Keep your assignments in this notebook so that you can review them when studying for the chapter test.

SECTION 5

READING WARM-UP

Objectives
- Explain how geologic time is recorded in rock layers.
- Identify important dates on the geologic time scale.
- Explain how environmental changes resulted in the extinction of some species.

Terms to Learn

geologic time scale   period
eon   epoch
era   extinction

READING STRATEGY

Brainstorming The key idea of this section is the geologic time scale. Brainstorm words and phrases related to the geologic time scale.

Figure 1 Bones of dinosaurs that lived about 150 million years ago are exposed in the quarry wall at Dinosaur National Monument in Utah.

Time Marches On

How old is the Earth? Well, if the Earth celebrated its birthday every million years, there would be 4,600 candles on its birthday cake! Humans have been around only long enough to light the last candle on the cake.

Try to think of the Earth's history in "fast-forward." If you could watch the Earth change from this perspective, you would see mountains rise up like wrinkles in fabric and quickly wear away. You would see life-forms appear and then go extinct. In this section, you will learn that geologists must "fast-forward" the Earth's history when they write or talk about it. You will also learn about some incredible events in the history of life on Earth.

Geologic Time

Shown in **Figure 1** is the rock wall at the Dinosaur Quarry Visitor Center in Dinosaur National Monument, Utah. Contained within this wall are approximately 1,500 fossil bones that have been excavated by paleontologists. These are the remains of dinosaurs that inhabited the area about 150 million years ago. Granted, 150 million years seems to be an incredibly long period of time. However, in terms of the Earth's history, 150 million years is little more than 3% of the time our planet has existed. It is a little less than 4% of the time represented by the Earth's oldest known rocks.

172

Be Resourceful — Use the Web

SCiLINKS

Internet Connect

boxes in your textbook take you to resources that you can use for science projects, reports, and research papers. Go to scilinks.org, and type in the SciLinks code to get information on a topic.

go.hrw.com

Visit go.hrw.com

Find worksheets, Current Science magazine articles online, and other materials that go with your textbook at **go.hrw.com**. Click on the textbook icon and the table of contents to see all of the resources for each chapter.

Figure 2 Well-preserved plant and animal fossils are common in the Green River formation. Clockwise from the upper right are a fossil leaf, a dragonfly, a fish, and a turtle.

The Rock Record and Geologic Time

One of the best places in North America to see the Earth's history recorded in rock layers is in Grand Canyon National Park. The Colorado River has cut the canyon nearly 2 km deep in some places. Over the course of 6 million years, the river has eroded countless layers of rock. These layers represent almost half, or nearly 2 billion years, of Earth's history.

Reading Check How much geologic time is represented by the rock layers in *Reading Checks*

The Fossil

Figure 2 show formation. T Utah, and O were once p period of m common in the fine-grai delicate struc

The Cenozoic Era—The Age of Mammals

The Cenozoic era, as shown in **Figure 7**, began about 65 million years ago and continues to the present. This era is known as the *Age of Mammals*. During the Mesozoic era, mammals had to compete with dinosaurs and other animals for food and habitat. After the mass extinction at the end of the Mesozoic era, mammals flourished. Unique traits, such as regulating body temperature internally and bearing young that develop inside the mother, may have helped mammals survive the environmental changes that probably caused the extinction of the dinosaurs.

Figure 7 Thousands of species of mammals evolved during the Cenozoic era. This scene shows species from the early Cenozoic era that are now extinct.

SECTION Review

Summary

- The geologic time scale divides Earth's 4.6 billion-year history into distinct intervals of time. Divisions of geologic time include eons, eras, periods, and epochs.
- The boundaries between geologic time intervals represent visible changes that have taken place on Earth.
- The rock and fossil record represents mainly the Phanerozoic eon, which is the eon in which we live.
- At certain times in Earth's history, the number of life-forms has increased or decreased dramatically.

Using Key Terms

1. Use each of the following terms in the same sentence: *era, period,* and *epoch.*

Understanding Key Ideas

2. The unit of geologic time that began 65 million years ago and continues to the present is the
   a. Holocene epoch.
   b. Cenozoic era.
   c. Phanerozoic eon.
   d. Quaternary period.
3. What are the major time intervals represented by the geologic time scale?
4. Explain how geologic time is recorded in rock layers.
5. What kinds of environmental changes cause mass extinctions?

Critical Thinking

6. **Making Inferences** What future event might mark the end of the Cenozoic era?
7. **Identifying Relationships** How might a decrease in competition between species lead to the sudden appearance of many new species?

Interpreting Graphics

8. Look at the illustration below. On the Earth-history clock shown, 1 h equals 383 million years, and 1 min equals 6.4 million years. In millions of years, how much more time is represented by the Proterozoic eon than by the Phanerozoic eon?

Phanerozoic eon   Hadean eon

Proterozoic eon   Archean eon

For a variety of links related to this chapter, go to www.scilinks.org
Topic: Geologic Time
SciLinks code: HSM0668

177

Use the Illustrations and Photos

Art shows complex ideas and processes. Learn to analyze the art so that you better understand the material you read in the text.

Tables and graphs display important information in an organized way to help you see relationships.

A picture is worth a thousand words. Look at the photographs to see relevant examples of science concepts that you are reading about.

Answer the Section Reviews

Section Reviews test your knowledge of the main points of the section. Critical Thinking items challenge you to think about the material in greater depth and to find connections that you infer from the text.

STUDY TIP When you can't answer a question, reread the section. The answer is usually there.

Do Your Homework

Your teacher may assign worksheets to help you understand and remember the material in the chapter.

STUDY TIP Don't try to answer the questions without reading the text and reviewing your class notes. A little preparation up front will make your homework assignments a lot easier. Answering the items in the Chapter Review will help prepare you for the chapter test.

Visit Holt Online Learning

If your teacher gives you a special password to log onto the Holt Online Learning site, you'll find your complete textbook on the Web. In addition, you'll find some great learning tools and practice quizzes. You'll be able to see how well you know the material from your textbook.

Visit CNN Student News

You'll find up-to-date events in science at **cnnstudentnews.com**.

SAFETY FIRST!

Exploring, inventing, and investigating are essential to the study of science. However, these activities can also be dangerous. To make sure that your experiments and explorations are safe, you must be aware of a variety of safety guidelines. You have probably heard of the saying, "It is better to be safe than sorry." This is particularly true in a science classroom where experiments and explorations are being performed. Being uninformed and careless can result in serious injuries. Don't take chances with your own safety or with anyone else's.

The following pages describe important guidelines for staying safe in the science classroom. Your teacher may also have safety guidelines and tips that are specific to your classroom and laboratory. Take the time to be safe.

Safety Rules!

Start Out Right

Always get your teacher's permission before attempting any laboratory exploration. Read the procedures carefully, and pay particular attention to safety information and caution statements. If you are unsure about what a safety symbol means, look it up or ask your teacher. You cannot be too careful when it comes to safety. If an accident does occur, inform your teacher immediately regardless of how minor you think the accident is.

Safety Symbols

All of the experiments and investigations in this book and their related worksheets include important safety symbols to alert you to particular safety concerns. Become familiar with these symbols so that when you see them, you will know what they mean and what to do. It is important that you read this entire safety section to learn about specific dangers in the laboratory.

If you are instructed to note the odor of a substance, wave the fumes toward your nose with your hand. Never put your nose close to the source.

Eye protection

Clothing protection

Hand safety

Heating safety

Electric safety

Chemical safety

Animal safety

Sharp object

Plant safety

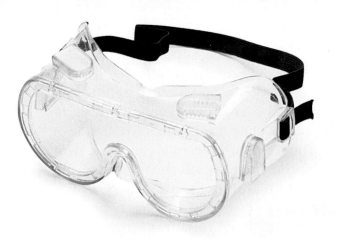

Eye Safety

Wear safety goggles when working around chemicals, acids, bases, or any type of flame or heating device. Wear safety goggles any time there is even the slightest chance that harm could come to your eyes. If any substance gets into your eyes, notify your teacher immediately and flush your eyes with running water for at least 15 minutes. Treat any unknown chemical as if it were a dangerous chemical. Never look directly into the sun. Doing so could cause permanent blindness.

Avoid wearing contact lenses in a laboratory situation. Even if you are wearing safety goggles, chemicals can get between the contact lenses and your eyes. If your doctor requires that you wear contact lenses instead of glasses, wear eye-cup safety goggles in the lab.

Safety Equipment

Know the locations of the nearest fire alarms and any other safety equipment, such as fire blankets and eyewash fountains, as identified by your teacher, and know the procedures for using the equipment.

Neatness

Keep your work area free of all unnecessary books and papers. Tie back long hair, and secure loose sleeves or other loose articles of clothing, such as ties and bows. Remove dangling jewelry. Don't wear open-toed shoes or sandals in the laboratory. Never eat, drink, or apply cosmetics in a laboratory setting. Food, drink, and cosmetics can easily become contaminated with dangerous materials.

Certain hair products (such as aerosol hair spray) are flammable and should not be worn while working near an open flame. Avoid wearing hair spray or hair gel on lab days.

Sharp/Pointed Objects

Use knives and other sharp instruments with extreme care. Never cut objects while holding them in your hands. Place objects on a suitable work surface for cutting.

Be extra careful when using any glassware. When adding a heavy object to a graduated cylinder, tilt the cylinder so that the object slides slowly to the bottom.

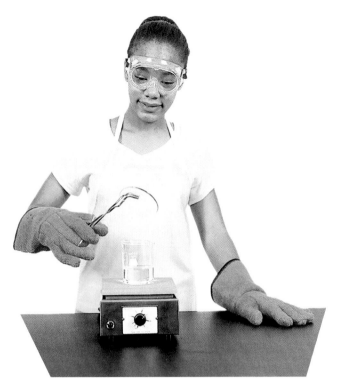

Heat

Wear safety goggles when using a heating device or a flame. Whenever possible, use an electric hot plate as a heat source instead of using an open flame. When heating materials in a test tube, always angle the test tube away from yourself and others. To avoid burns, wear heat-resistant gloves whenever instructed to do so.

Electricity

Be careful with electrical cords. When using a microscope with a lamp, do not place the cord where it could trip someone. Do not let cords hang over a table edge in a way that could cause equipment to fall if the cord is accidentally pulled. Do not use equipment with damaged cords. Be sure that your hands are dry and that the electrical equipment is in the "off" position before plugging it in. Turn off and unplug electrical equipment when you are finished.

Chemicals

Wear safety goggles when handling any potentially dangerous chemicals, acids, or bases. If a chemical is unknown, handle it as you would a dangerous chemical. Wear an apron and protective gloves when you work with acids or bases or whenever you are told to do so. If a spill gets on your skin or clothing, rinse it off immediately with water for at least 5 minutes while calling to your teacher.

Never mix chemicals unless your teacher tells you to do so. Never taste, touch, or smell chemicals unless you are specifically directed to do so. Before working with a flammable liquid or gas, check for the presence of any source of flame, spark, or heat.

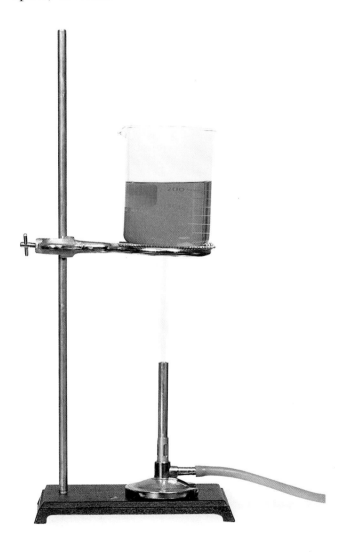

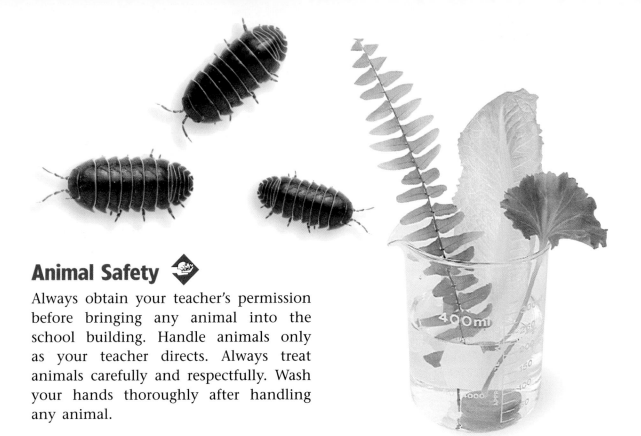

Animal Safety

Always obtain your teacher's permission before bringing any animal into the school building. Handle animals only as your teacher directs. Always treat animals carefully and respectfully. Wash your hands thoroughly after handling any animal.

Plant Safety

Do not eat any part of a plant or plant seed used in the laboratory. Wash your hands thoroughly after handling any part of a plant. When in nature, do not pick any wild plants unless your teacher instructs you to do so.

Glassware

Examine all glassware before use. Be sure that glassware is clean and free of chips and cracks. Report damaged glassware to your teacher. Glass containers used for heating should be made of heat-resistant glass.

Minerals of the Earth's Crust
Chapter Planning Guide

Compression guide:
To shorten instruction because of time limitations, omit the Chapter Lab.

OBJECTIVES	LABS, DEMONSTRATIONS, AND ACTIVITIES	TECHNOLOGY RESOURCES
PACING • 90 min pp. 2–7 **Chapter Opener**	SE **Start-up Activity,** p. 3 GENERAL	OSP **Parent Letter** ■ GENERAL CD **Student Edition on CD-ROM** CD **Guided Reading Audio CD** ■ TR **Chapter Starter Transparency*** VID **Brain Food Video Quiz**
Section 1 What Is a Mineral? • Describe the structure of minerals. • Describe the two major groups of minerals.	TE **Group Activity** Identifying Minerals, p. 4 ◆ GENERAL TE **Group Activity** Mineral Identification, p. 5 GENERAL SE **Science in Action** Math, Social Studies, and Language Arts Activities, pp. 24–25 GENERAL	CRF **Lesson Plans*** TR **Bellringer Transparency*** CD **Science Tutor**
PACING • 90 min pp. 8–11 **Section 2 Identifying Minerals** • Identify seven ways to determine the identity of minerals. • Explain special properties of minerals.	TE **Group Activity** Mineral Classification, p. 8 GENERAL TE **Connection Activity** Real World, p. 9 ◆ GENERAL TE **Demonstration** Applying the Scientific Method, p. 9 GENERAL SE **Quick Lab** Scratch Test, p. 10 GENERAL CRF **Datasheet for Quick Lab*** SE **Skills Practice Lab** Is It Fool's Gold?—A Dense Situation, p. 18 GENERAL CRF **Datasheet for Chapter Lab*** SE **Skills Practice Lab** Mysterious Minerals, p. 180 GENERAL CRF **Datasheet for LabBook***	CRF **Lesson Plans*** TR **Bellringer Transparency*** TR **_LINK TO PHYSICAL SCIENCE_** The Three Major Categories of Elements*** TR **Mohs' Hardness Scale*** TR **Special Properties of Some Minerals*** CRF **SciLinks Activity*** GENERAL VID **Lab Videos for Earth Science** CD **Science Tutor**
PACING • 45 min pp. 12–17 **Section 3 The Formation, Mining, and Use of Minerals** • Describe the environments in which minerals form. • Compare the two types of mining. • Describe two ways to reduce the effects of mining. • Describe different uses for metallic and nonmetallic minerals.	TE **Connection Activity** History, p. 13 GENERAL SE **School-to-Home Activity** Recycling Minerals at Home, p. 15 GENERAL TE **Connection Activity** Life Science, p. 16 GENERAL LB **Long-Term Projects & Research Ideas** What's Yours is Mined* ADVANCED	CRF **Lesson Plans*** TR **Bellringer Transparency*** SE **Internet Activity,** p. 13 GENERAL CD **Science Tutor**

PACING • 90 min

CHAPTER REVIEW, ASSESSMENT, AND STANDARDIZED TEST PREPARATION

CRF **Vocabulary Activity*** GENERAL
SE **Chapter Review,** pp. 20–21 GENERAL
CRF **Chapter Review*** ■ GENERAL
CRF **Chapter Tests A*** ■ GENERAL , **B*** ADVANCED , **C*** SPECIAL NEEDS
SE **Standardized Test Preparation,** pp. 22–23 GENERAL
CRF **Standardized Test Preparation*** GENERAL
CRF **Performance-Based Assessment*** GENERAL
OSP **Test Generator** GENERAL
CRF **Test Item Listing*** GENERAL

Online and Technology Resources

Visit **go.hrw.com** for a variety of free resources related to this textbook. Enter the keyword **HZ5MIN.**

Holt Online Learning

Students can access interactive problem-solving help and active visual concept development with the *Holt Science and Technology* Online Edition available at **www.hrw.com.**

 Guided Reading Audio CD
Also in Spanish

A direct reading of each chapter for auditory learners, reluctant readers, and Spanish-speaking students.

 Science Tutor CD-ROM
Excellent for remediation and test practice.

SKILLS DEVELOPMENT RESOURCES	SECTION REVIEW AND ASSESSMENT	CORRELATIONS
SE Pre-Reading Activity, p. 2 `GENERAL` **OSP** Science Puzzlers, Twisters & Teasers `GENERAL`		National Science Education Standards UCP 5; SAI 1
CRF Directed Reading A* ■ `BASIC`, B* `SPECIAL NEEDS` **CRF** Vocabulary and Section Summary* ■ `GENERAL` **SE** Reading Strategy Paired Summarizing, p. 4 `GENERAL` **SE** Connection to Biology Magnetite, p. 6 `GENERAL` **TE** Inclusion Strategies, p. 6 ◆ **CRF** Reinforcement Worksheet Mystery Mineral* `BASIC` **CRF** Reinforcement Worksheet The Mineral Quiz Show* `BASIC`	**TE** Homework, p. 4 `GENERAL` **SE** Reading Checks, pp. 5, 6 `GENERAL` **TE** Reteaching, p. 6 `BASIC` **TE** Quiz, p. 6 `GENERAL` **TE** Alternative Assessment, p. 6 `GENERAL` **SE** Section Review,* p. 7 `GENERAL` **CRF** Section Quiz* ■ `GENERAL`	UCP 1, 5
CRF Directed Reading A* ■ `BASIC`, B* `GENERAL` **CRF** Vocabulary and Section Summary* ■ `GENERAL` **SE** Reading Strategy Reading Organizer, p. 8 `GENERAL` **MS** Math Skills for Science Percentages, Fractions, and Decimals* `GENERAL` **CRF** Critical Thinking Mineral Hunt* `ADVANCED`	**SE** Reading Checks, pp. 9, 10 `GENERAL` **TE** Reteaching, p. 10 `BASIC` **TE** Quiz, p. 10 `GENERAL` **TE** Alternative Assessment, p. 10 `GENERAL` **SE** Section Review,* p. 11 ■ `GENERAL` **CRF** Section Quiz* ■ `GENERAL`	UCP 1, 5; SAI 1, 2; *LabBook:* SAI 1
CRF Directed Reading A* ■ `BASIC`, B* `SPECIAL NEEDS` **CRF** Vocabulary and Section Summary* ■ `GENERAL` **SE** Reading Strategy Discussion, p. 12 `GENERAL` **SE** Math Practice Surface Coal Mining, p. 14 `GENERAL` **TE** Inclusion Strategies, p. 13	**SE** Reading Checks, pp. 15, 17 `GENERAL` **TE** Reteaching, p. 16 `BASIC` **TE** Quiz, p. 16 `GENERAL` **TE** Alternative Assessment, p. 16 `GENERAL` **SE** Section Review,* p. 17 ■ `GENERAL` **CRF** Section Quiz* ■ `GENERAL`	UCP 5; SAI 1; SPSP 2, 4, 5

One-Stop Planner® CD-ROM

This CD-ROM package includes:
- Lab Materials QuickList Software
- Holt Calendar Planner
- Customizable Lesson Plans
- Printable Worksheets
- ExamView® Test Generator
- Interactive Teacher Edition
- Holt PuzzlePro® Resources
- Holt PowerPoint® Resources

SCLINKS
NSTA

www.scilinks.org

Maintained by the **National Science Teachers Association.** See Chapter Enrichment pages for a complete list of topics.

Current Science®

Check out *Current Science* articles and activities by visiting the HRW Web site at **go.hrw.com.** Just type in the keyword **HZ5CS03T.**

Classroom Videos

- **Lab Videos** demonstrate the chapter lab.
- **Brain Food Video Quizzes** help students review the chapter material.
- **CNN Videos** bring science into your students' daily life.

Visual Resources

CHAPTER STARTER TRANSPARENCY

Imagine . . .

If you owned all of the jewels shown on this page, you would be a millionaire. These precious gems—diamonds, rubies, sapphires, and emeralds—are valued at anywhere from $1,000 to $50,000 per carat (1 carat = 200 mg).

You may not be surprised that precious gems are so expensive. But did you know that the value of these gems has little to do with what they're made of? For example, rubies and sapphires are two varieties of the same mineral that is used to make sandpaper. And diamonds are made of the same material as the graphite in your pencil. Unlike gems,

however, a few handfuls of pencils will not make you rich.

Gems are valuable not because of the elements they contain but because of how their atoms are arranged. Under certain conditions, common atoms can be arranged into rare crystal forms. Gems are rare because the conditions that produce them exist in only a few places in the world. The crystals that form gems are prized for their durability, subtle colors, and translucent quality. When properly cut and polished, like the examples shown above, gems sparkle brilliantly.

BELLRINGER TRANSPARENCIES

Section: What Is a Mineral?
Compare the piece of pencil lead and the diamond in the photograph provided by your teacher. Both substances are composed of carbon. How can the same element form two substances with such different properties? Sand and glass are also composed of the same elements, silicon and oxygen. Can you think of any other substances that are composed of the same elements?

Record your answer in your **science journal.**

Section: Identifying Minerals
How do you describe what you see, feel, and smell? List as many phrases as you can to describe each mineral shown. Organize your phrases into different categories, such as color, shape, and luster. Do any minerals have a specific smell? Use the comparisons to determine whether the samples are actually the same mineral.

Write your responses in your **science journal.**

TEACHING TRANSPARENCIES

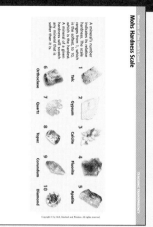

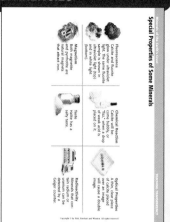

TEACHING TRANSPARENCIES

Chapter: States of Matter

CONCEPT MAPPING TRANSPARENCY

Use the following terms to complete the concept map below:
gems, compounds, atoms, mineral ore, mining, minerals, diamonds

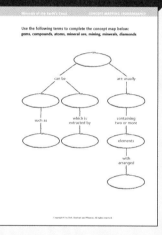

Planning Resources

LESSON PLANS

Lesson Plan SAMPLE

Section: Waves

Pacing
Regular Schedule: with lab(s):2 days without lab(s)2 days
Block Schedule: with lab(s):1 1/2 days without lab(s):1 day

Objectives
1. Relate the seven properties of life to a living organism.
2. Describe seven themes that can help you to organize what you learn about biology.
3. Identify the tiny structures that make up all living organisms.
4. Differentiate between reproduction and heredity and between metabolism and homeostasis.

National Science Education Standards Covered
LSInter4:Cells have particular structures that underlie their functions.
LSMat1: Most cell functions involve chemical reactions.
LSBeh1:Cells store and use information to guide their functions.
UCP1:Cell functions are regulated.
SI1: Cells can differentiate and form complete multicellular organisms.
PS1: Organisms evolve over time.
ESS1: The great diversity of organisms is the result of more than 3.5 billion years of evolution.
ESS2: Natural selection and its evolutionary consequences provide a scientific explanation for the fossil record of ancient life forms as well as for the striking molecular similarities observed among the diverse species of living organisms.
ST1: The millions of different species of plants, animals, and microorganisms that live on Earth today are related by descent from common ancestors.
ST2: The energy for life primarily comes from the sun.
SPSP1: The complexity and organization of organisms accommodates the need for obtaining, transforming, transporting, releasing, and eliminating the matter and energy used to sustain the organism.
SPSP6: As matter and energy flows through different levels of organization of living systems—cells, organs, communities—and between living systems and the physical environment, chemical elements are recombined in different ways.
HNS1: Organisms have behavioral responses to internal changes and to external stimuli.

PARENT LETTER

SAMPLE

Dear Parent,

Your son's or daughter's science class will soon begin exploring the chapter entitled "The World of Physical Science." In this chapter, students will learn about how the scientific method applies to the world of physical science and the role of physical science in the world. By the end of the chapter, students should demonstrate a clear understanding of the chapter's main ideas and be able to discuss the following topics:

1. physical science is the study of energy and matter (Section 1)
2. the role of physical science in the world around them (Section 1)
3. careers that rely on physical science (Section 1)
4. the steps used in the scientific method (Section 2)
5. examples of technology (Section 2)
6. how the scientific method is used to answer questions and solve problems (Section 2)
7. how our knowledge of science changes over time (Section 2)
8. how models represent real objects or systems (Section 3)
9. examples of different ways models are used in science (Section 3)
10. the importance of the International System of Units (Section 4)
11. the appropriate units to use for particular measurements (Section 4)
12. how area and density are derived quantities (Section 4)

Questions to Ask Along the Way

You can help your son or daughter learn about these topics by asking interesting questions such as the following:

• What are some surprising careers that use physical science?
• What is a characteristic of a good hypothesis?
• Where is it a good idea to use a model?
• Why do Americans measure things in terms of inches and feet and meters?

ALSO IN SPANISH

TEST ITEM LISTING

TEST ITEM LISTING
The World of Earth Science SAMPLE

MULTIPLE CHOICE

1. A limitation of models is that
   a. they are large enough to see.
   b. they do not act exactly like the things that they model.
   c. they are smaller than the things that they model.
   d. they model unfamiliar things.
   Answer: B   Difficulty: 1   Section: 3   Objective: 2

2. The length 10 m is equal to
   a. 100 cm.   c. 10,000 mm.
   b. 1,000 cm.   d. Both (b) and (c)
   Answer: B   Difficulty: 1   Section: 3   Objective: 2

3. To be valid, a hypothesis must be
   a. testable.   c. made into a law.
   b. supported by evidence.   d. Both (a) and (b)
   Answer: B   Difficulty: 1   Section: 3   Objective: 2 1

4. The statement "Sheila has a stain on her shirt" is an example of a(n)
   a. law.   c. observation.
   b. hypothesis.   d. prediction.
   Answer: B   Difficulty: 1   Section: 3   Objective: 2

5. A hypothesis is often developed out of
   a. observations.   c. laws.
   b. experiments.   d. Both (a) and (b)
   Answer: B   Difficulty: 1   Section: 3   Objective: 2

6. How many milliliters are in 3.5 kL?
   a. 3,500 mL   c. 3,500,000 mL
   b. 0.0035 mL.   d. 35,000 mL
   Answer: B   Difficulty: 1   Section: 3   Objective: 2

7. A map of Seattle is an example of a
   a. law.   c. model.
   b. theory.   d. unit.
   Answer: B   Difficulty: 1   Section: 3   Objective: 2

8. A lab has the safety icons shown below. These icons mean that you should wear
   a. only safety goggles.   c. safety goggles and a lab apron.
   b. only a lab apron.   d. safety goggles, a lab apron, and gloves.
   Answer: B   Difficulty: 1   Section: 3   Objective: 2

9. The law of conservation of mass says the total mass before a chemical change is
   a. more than the total mass after the change.
   b. less than the total mass after the change.
   c. the same as the total mass after the change.
   d. not the same as the total mass after the change.
   Answer: B   Difficulty: 1   Section: 3   Objective: 2

10. If each of the following areas might you find a geochemist at work?
    a. studying the chemistry of rocks   c. studying fishes
    b. studying forestry   d. studying the atmosphere
    Answer: B   Difficulty: 1   Section: 3   Objective: 2

One-Stop Planner® CD-ROM

This CD-ROM includes all of the resources shown here and the following time-saving tools:

• **Lab Materials QuickList Software**
• **Customizable lesson plans**
• **Holt Calendar Planner**
• **The powerful ExamView® Test Generator**

Meeting Individual Needs

DIRECTED READING A

Skills Worksheet
Directed Reading A   SAMPLE

Section:
THAT'S SCIENCE!
1. How did James Czarnowski get his idea for the penguin boat, Proteus? Explain.

BASIC   ALSO IN SPANISH

DIRECTED READING B

Skills Worksheet
Directed Reading B   SAMPLE

Section:
THAT'S SCIENCE!
1. How did James Czarnowski get his idea for the penguin boat, Proteus? Explain.

2. What is unusual about the way that Proteus moves through the water?

SPECIAL NEEDS   PHYSICAL SCIENCE

VOCABULARY ACTIVITY

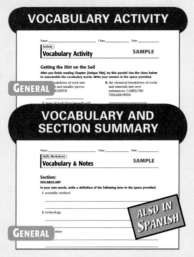

Activity
Vocabulary Activity   SAMPLE

Getting the Dirt on the Soil
After you finish reading Chapter [Unique Title], try this puzzle! Use the clues below to unscramble the vocabulary words. Write your answer in the space provided.

GENERAL

VOCABULARY AND SECTION SUMMARY

Skills Worksheet
Vocabulary & Notes   SAMPLE

Section:
VOCABULARY
In your own words, write a definition of the following term in the space provided.
1. scientific method

2. technology

GENERAL   ALSO IN SPANISH

REINFORCEMENT

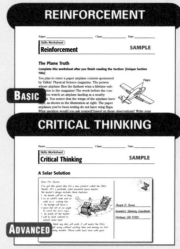

Skills Worksheet
Reinforcement   SAMPLE

The Plane Truth
Complete this worksheet after you finish reading the Section: [Unique Section Title]

BASIC

CRITICAL THINKING

Skills Worksheet
Critical Thinking   SAMPLE

A Solar Solution

ADVANCED

SCILINKS ACTIVITY

Activity
SciLinks Activity   SAMPLE

MARINE ECOSYSTEMS
Go to www.scilinks.com. To find links related to marine ecosystems, type in the keyword HS5690. Then, use the links to answer the questions about marine ecosys-

GENERAL

SCIENCE PUZZLERS, TWISTERS & TEASERS

CHAPTER
3   SCIENCE PUZZLERS, TWISTERS & TEASERS
Minerals of the Earth's Crust

Gem Search
1. The names of six common gemstones are scrambled in the gems below. All of the letters spelling a particular gemstone can be found on gems having the same cut. Unscramble the letters on the similar gems to identify the six gemstones and list them on the spaces provided.

GENERAL

Labs and Activities

LONG-TERM PROJECTS & RESEARCH IDEAS

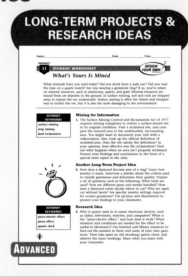

Name ___ Date ___ Class ___
PROJECT
31   STUDENT WORKSHEET
What's Yours Is Mined   DESIGN YOUR OWN

What minerals have you used today? Did you drink from a soda can? Did you read the time on a quartz watch? Are you wearing a gemstone ring? If so, you've relied on mineral resources, such as aluminum, quartz, and gold. Mineral resources are mined from ore deposits in the ground. In surface mining, soil and rock are stripped away to expose the ore underneath. Surface mining is often the fastest and cheapest way to extract the ore, but it is also the most damaging to the environment.

INTERNET KEYWORDS
surface mining
strip mining
land reclamation

Mining for Information
1. The Surface Mining Control and Reclamation Act of 1977 requires mining companies to restore a surface-mined site to its original condition. Visit a reclaimed site, and compare the restored area to the undisturbed, surrounding area. You might want to document your visit with a videocamera. Also, look up the official definition of *reclaimed area*. Does the site satisfy the definition? In your opinion, how effective was the reclamation? Find out what happens when an area isn't properly reclaimed. Present your findings and conclusions in the form of a special news report to the class.

Another Long-Term Project Idea
2. How does a diamond become part of a ring? Learn how jewelry is made. Interview a jeweler about the criteria used to classify gemstones and determine their quality. Prepare a set of questions such as the following: What tools are used? How are different gems and metals handled? How does a diamond cutter decide where to cut? Why are opals cut without facets? Are specific jewelry settings required for certain gemstones? Use pictures and illustrations to present your findings to your classmates.

INTERNET KEYWORDS
piezo-electric effect
piezo effect
quartz clock

Research Idea
3. Why is quartz used in so many electronic devices, such as radios, televisions, watches, and computers? What is the "piezo-electric effect," and how does it work? What elements and conditions are needed for the effect to be useful in electronics? Use Internet and library resources to find out the answers to these and some of your own questions. Then take apart an old (working) quartz clock, and observe the inner workings. Share what you learn with your classmates.

ADVANCED

DATASHEETS FOR QUICK LABS

TEACHER RESOURCE PAGE
Quick Lab
Reaction to Stress   DATASHEET FOR QUICK LAB
SAMPLE

Background
The graph below illustrates changes that occur in the membrane potential of a neuron during an action potential. Use the graph to answer the following questions. Refer to Figure 3 as needed.

DATASHEETS FOR CHAPTER LABS

TEACHER RESOURCE PAGE
Skills Practice Lab
Using Scientific Methods   DATASHEET FOR CHAPTER LAB
SAMPLE

Teacher's Notes
TIME REQUIRED
One 45-minute class period.

DATASHEETS FOR LABBOOK

TEACHER RESOURCE PAGE
Skills Practice Lab
Does It All Add Up?   DATASHEET FOR LABBOOK LAB
SAMPLE

Teacher's Notes
TIME REQUIRED
One 45-minute class period.

Review and Assessments

SECTION QUIZ

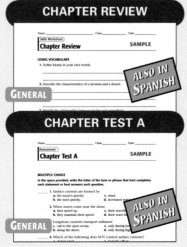

Assessment
Section Quiz   SAMPLE

Section:
In the space provided, write the letter of the description that best matches the term or phrase.
___ 1. building molecules that can be used as an energy source, or breaking down molecules in which energy is stored
___ 2. the process by which light energy is converted to chemical energy
___ 3. an organism that uses sunlight or inorganic substances to make organic compounds

GENERAL   ALSO IN SPANISH

SECTION REVIEW

Skills Worksheet
Section Review   SAMPLE

Section:
KEY TERMS
1. What do paleontologist study?

2. How does a trace fossil differ from petrified wood?

GENERAL   ALSO IN SPANISH

CHAPTER REVIEW

Skills Worksheet
Chapter Review   SAMPLE

USING VOCABULARY
1. Define biome in your own words.

2. Describe the characteristics of a savanna and a desert.

GENERAL   ALSO IN SPANISH

CHAPTER TEST A

Assessment
Chapter Test A   SAMPLE

MULTIPLE CHOICE
In the space provided, write the letter of the term or phrase that best completes each statement or best answers each question.
___ 1. Surface currents are formed by
   a. the moon's gravity.   c. wind.
   b. the sun's gravity.   d. increased water
___ 2. When waves come near the shore,
   a. they speed up.   c. their wave
   b. they maintain their speed. d. their wave
___ 3. Longshore currents transport sediment
   a. out to the open ocean.   c. only during low
   b. along the shore.   d. only during high
___ 4. Which of the following does NOT control surface currents?

GENERAL   ALSO IN SPANISH

CHAPTER TEST B

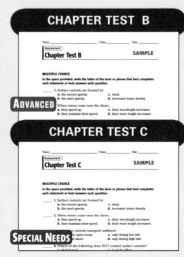

Assessment
Chapter Test B   SAMPLE

MULTIPLE CHOICE
In the space provided, write the letter of the term or phrase that best completes each statement or best answers each question.
___ 1. Surface currents are formed by
   a. the moon's gravity.   c. wind.
   b. the sun's gravity.   d. increased water density.
___ 2. When waves come near the shore,
   a. they speed up.   c. their wavelength increases.
   b. they maintain their speed. d. their wave height increases.

ADVANCED

CHAPTER TEST C

Assessment
Chapter Test C   SAMPLE

MULTIPLE CHOICE
In the space provided, write the letter of the term or phrase that best completes each statement or best answers each question.
___ 1. Surface currents are formed by
   a. the moon's gravity.   c. wind.
   b. the sun's gravity.   d. increased water density.
___ 2. When waves come near the shore,
   a. they speed up.   c. their wavelength increases.
   b. they maintain their speed. d. their wave height increases.
___ 3. Longshore currents transport sediment
   a. out to the open ocean.   c. only during low tide.
   b. along the shore.   d. only during high tide.
___ 4. Which of the following does NOT control surface currents?

SPECIAL NEEDS

STANDARDIZED TEST PREPARATION

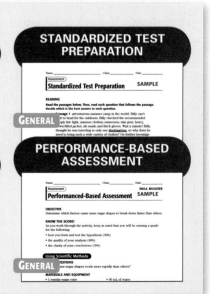

Assessment
Standardized Test Preparation   SAMPLE

READING
Read the passages below. Then, read each question that follows the passage. Decide which is the best answer to each question.

GENERAL

PERFORMANCE-BASED ASSESSMENT

Assessment
Performanced-Based Assessment   SKILL BUILDER
SAMPLE

OBJECTIVE
Determine which factors cause some sugar shapes to break down faster than others.

KNOW THE SCORE!
As you work through the activity below, keep in mind that you will be earning a grade for the following:
• how you form and test the hypothesis (30%)
• the quality of your analysis (40%)
• the clarity of your conclusions (30%)

Using Scientific Methods

MATERIALS AND EQUIPMENT
• 1 regular sugar cube   • 90 mL of water

GENERAL

This Chapter Enrichment provides relevant and interesting information to expand and enhance your presentation of the chapter material.

Section 1

What Is a Mineral?

Crystal Structures

- Minerals are composed of atoms that are arranged in repeating three-dimensional patterns. The basic building block of a mineral crystal is called a unit cell. A *unit cell* is the smallest three-dimensional arrangement of atoms that displays the basic form, or symmetry, of the crystal. Many unit cells stacked together form a crystal. For example, a crystal of halite is composed of unit cells of sodium and chlorine atoms arranged in a unique three-dimensional structure.

The Origins of Mineralogy

- The founder of mineralogy is considered to be Georgius Agricola. His treatise on minerals, *De Re Metallica* (1556), recorded most of what was known about minerals at that time. The science of mineralogy advanced greatly when Romé de l'Isle, a French scientist, proposed the concept of the unit cell in 1772. He argued that the characteristics of mineral crystals could be explained only if they were composed of identical unit cells organized in a predictable way. Crystals are composed of unit cells much like a wall might be composed of bricks. After that discovery, the composition of mineral crystals was actively studied by many scientists.

Industrial Uses of Crystals

- The properties of crystals make crystals useful in many ways. The electronics industry uses quartz in the manufacture of radios, watches, microphones, and sonar transducers. Rubies are used in lasers and as styluses in record players, and diamonds are used in industrial drills and saws.

Is That a Fact!

◆ Currently, about 4,000 minerals have been identified, and 50 to 100 new minerals are discovered each year.

Section 2

Identifying Minerals

Methods of Identifying Minerals

- Scientists usually identify minerals using a petrographic microscope, the hand-specimen method, X-ray diffraction, or an electron microprobe.

  - The hand-specimen method involves determining the color, luster, streak, cleavage, hardness, density, fluorescence, and magnetic qualities of a mineral.

  - When geologists take samples back to the lab, they often use petrographic microscopes to identify minerals. These microscopes make it easier to identify minerals by the optical properties of their crystals.

  - Geologists can analyze minerals at the atomic level by using X-ray diffraction, which measures the way crystal structures diffract X rays. The chemical composition of minerals can also be determined by using an electron microprobe. An electron microprobe produces a beam of electrons that focuses on a sample diameter that may be as small as .001 to .002 mm.

Mohs Hardness Scale

- Friedrich Mohs (1773–1839) was a mineralogist who lived in Vienna, Austria. In 1812, Mohs developed a method for identifying minerals based on their relative hardness. He proposed that a mineral's identity can be determined by comparing the mineral with several minerals of known hardness. A mineral can scratch another mineral of equal or lesser hardness, but it cannot scratch a mineral of greater hardness.

Gemstones

- Of the approximately 4,000 known minerals, only about 100 are cut and polished to become gemstones. One definition of a gemstone is any naturally occurring mineral, rock, or organic material that, when cut and polished, is suitable for use as jewelry.

- Diamond, emerald, ruby, and topaz are usually referred to as precious stones. Amethyst, garnet, and jade are considered semiprecious. Materials such as coral, pearls, and amber are also considered gemstones, even though they form by organic processes.

- Many gems used in jewelry are imitations. For example, glass can be colored green to look like an emerald. Scientists also create some gems artificially. Synthetic rubies, for example, have the same chemical structure as natural rubies. However, a gemologist can identify synthetic rubies by the presence of curved growth striations and air pockets, which do not occur in natural rubies.

Is That a Fact!

- ◆ The Cullinan diamond is the world's largest diamond. It was found in the Premier mine in Pretoria, Transvaal in 1905. Before being cut, the Cullinan weighed 3,106 carats, or a little more than .5 kg.

- ◆ The largest gold nugget ever found was the "Welcome Stranger." It had a mass of 71 kg (156.5 pounds) and was found in Australia on February 5, 1869.

Section 3

The Formation, Mining, and Use of Minerals

Ancient Mines

- The earliest evidence of mining dates to a 43,000-year-old iron mine in South Africa. Early miners were proba-bly interested in the pig-ments associated with iron ores. The earliest metals used by neolithic people were probably gold and copper. Archaeological evidence indicates that the Egyptians mined copper and turquoise around 3400 BCE. Although most of the earliest mining was conducted on the surface, under-ground mining did occur by 1300 BCE in Africa.

Intrusions and Mineral Formation

- Plutons are intrusive bodies of igneous rock that cool beneath the Earth's surface. A large body of exposed intrusive rock (greater than 100 km^2) is called a *batholith*. Large batholiths occur in British Columbia, Alaska, and in the Sierra Nevada.

- A pegmatite is a very coarse-grained intrusive rock formed from the fluid-rich magma that remains after the rest of a pluton has solidified. Pegmatites may contain minerals such as tourmaline, topaz, or beryl.

The Hope Diamond

- The Hope diamond is a 45.5-carat blue diamond owned by the Smithsonian Institution since 1958. The gem was thought to be cursed because it was allegedly stolen from a statue of the Hindu goddess Sita. Misfortune and tragedy seemed to befall those who came in contact with the stone. The fabled gem was originally 112 carats. It was sold to King Louis XIV in 1668, and named the French Blue. The French Blue was stolen in 1792 from Louis XVI and may have been depicted in an 1800 portrait of a Spanish queen. In 1830, a 45.5-carat cut diamond surfaced in London. Experts declared that it was the French Blue recut to hide its identity. The American Henry Hope bought it, and it has since been called the Hope diamond.

Is That a Fact!

- ◆ At 215 m deep and 1.6 km in circumference, the Kimberley Mine in Kimberley, Union of South Africa, is the largest hand-dug excavation in the world.

SciLINKS®

NSTA
Developed and maintained by the
National Science Teachers Association

SciLinks is maintained by the National Science Teachers Association to provide you and your students with interesting, up-to-date links that will enrich your classroom presentation of the chapter.

Visit www.scilinks.org and enter the SciLinks code for more information about the topic listed.

Topic: Gems
SciLinks code: HSM0640

Topic: Mining Minerals
SciLinks code: HSM0968

Topic: Identifying Minerals
SciLinks code: HSM0782

Overview

Tell students that this chapter will help them learn about the minerals found in the rocks of the Earth's crust. The chapter describes the structure of minerals, mineral identification, environments in which minerals form, the mining of minerals, and mineral uses.

Assessing Prior Knowledge

Students should be familiar with the following topics:

• fundamental geologic processes
• the periodic table

Identifying Misconceptions

Before teaching the material in this chapter, make sure that students understand the difference between minerals and rocks. Often, these two words are used interchangeably. Emphasize that minerals are the building blocks of rocks and that different rocks are composed of different minerals or different combinations of minerals. For example, the sedimentary rock limestone is composed mostly of calcium carbonate in the form of the mineral calcite. The igneous rock granite is composed of a combination of the minerals quartz, orthoclase, and mica, and often has accessory minerals.

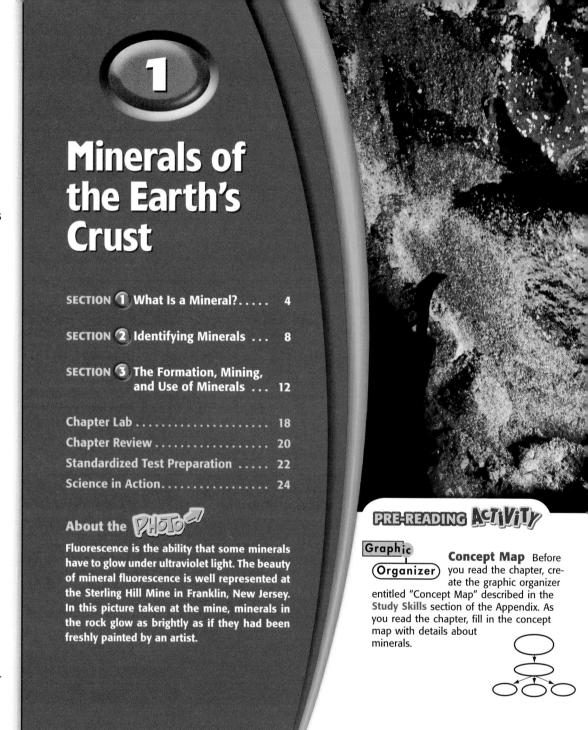

Minerals of the Earth's Crust

About the PHOTO

Fluorescence is the ability that some minerals have to glow under ultraviolet light. The beauty of mineral fluorescence is well represented at the Sterling Hill Mine in Franklin, New Jersey. In this picture taken at the mine, minerals in the rock glow as brightly as if they had been freshly painted by an artist.

PRE-READING ACTIVITY

Graphic Organizer

Concept Map Before you read the chapter, create the graphic organizer entitled "Concept Map" described in the Study Skills section of the Appendix. As you read the chapter, fill in the concept map with details about minerals.

Standards Correlations

National Science Education Standards

The following codes indicate the National Science Education Standards that correlate to this chapter. The full text of the standards is at the front of the book.

Chapter Opener
SAI 1; UCP 5

Section 1 What Is a Mineral?
UCP 1, 5

Section 2 Identifying Minerals
SAI 1; UCP 1, 5; *LabBook:* SAI 1

Section 3 The Formation, Mining, and Use of Minerals
SAI 1; UCP 5; SPSP 2, 4

Chapter Lab
SAI 1, 2

Chapter Review
SAI 1; UCP 1, 5; SPSP 2, 4

Science in Action
HNS 1

Teacher's Notes: Make students aware that most of the materials in the classroom will be made from nonliving things. Exceptions are items that are made of wood or plant fiber and items that are made of plastic, which are made from petroleum. You may want to go further and have students attempt to differentiate between items that are made of metallic minerals and those made of nonmetallic minerals.

Answers

1. Most of the materials in the classroom will most likely be made of nonliving materials. Materials that are made of minerals include graphite in pencils, clay in paper products, metal in desks, gypsum in wallboard, silica in glass, and cement (calcite) in the concrete-slab foundation.

START-UP ACTIVITY

What Is Your Classroom Made Of?

One of the properties of minerals is that minerals are made from nonliving material. Complete the following activity to see if you can determine whether items in your classroom are made from living or nonliving materials.

Procedure

1. On a **sheet of paper,** make two columns. Label one column "Materials made from living things." Label the second column "Materials made from nonliving things."

2. Look around your classroom. Choose a variety of items to put on your list. Some items that you might select are your clothing, your desk, books, notebook paper, pencils, the classroom windows, doors, walls, the ceiling, and the floor.

3. With a partner, discuss each item that you have chosen. Decide into which column each item should be placed. Write down the reason for your decision.

Analysis

1. Are most of the items that you chose made of living or nonliving materials?

Imagine . . .

If you owned all of the jewels shown on this page, you would be a millionaire. These precious gems—diamonds, rubies, sapphires, and emeralds—are valued at anywhere from $1,000 to $50,000 per carat (1 carat = 200 mg).

however, a few handfuls of pencils will not make you rich.
Gems are valuable not because of the elements they contain but because of how their atoms are arranged. Under certain conditions, common atoms can

Chapter Starter Transparency
Use this transparency to help students begin thinking about the diversity of minerals.

CHAPTER RESOURCES

Technology

 Transparencies
• Chapter Starter Transparency

READING SKILLS

Student Edition on CD-ROM

Guided Reading Audio CD
• English or Spanish

Classroom Videos
• Brain Food Video Quiz

Workbooks

Science Puzzlers, Twisters & Teasers
• Minerals of the Earth's Crust GENERAL

Focus

Overview

This section explores the nature of minerals by describing their four characteristics. Students learn that mineral crystals are generated by atomic structures, and they learn how to classify minerals into two major compositional groups—silicates and nonsilicates.

🎙 Bellringer

Display a piece of pencil lead (graphite) and a photograph of a diamond. Explain that both substances are composed of carbon. Ask students to brainstorm how two substances with such different properties can form from atoms of the same element.

Motivate

Group ActiViTy — GENERAL

Identifying Minerals Place an assortment of objects on a table. Possibilities include a piece of wood, a fossil, a piece of bone, a piece of granite, and a quartz crystal. Organize the class into groups of two or three students. Tell the students to examine the objects and to determine which ones are minerals by using the four questions in **Figure 1** on this page. **LS** Logical/Verbal

What Is a Mineral?

You may think that all minerals look like gems. But, in fact, most minerals look more like rocks. Does this mean that minerals are the same as rocks? Well, not really. So, what's the difference?

For one thing, rocks are made of minerals, but minerals are not made of rocks. A **mineral** is a naturally formed, inorganic solid that has a definite crystalline structure.

Mineral Structure

By answering the four questions in **Figure 1,** you can tell whether an object is a mineral. If you cannot answer "yes" to all four questions, you don't have a mineral. Three of the four questions may be easy to answer. The question about crystalline structure may be more difficult. To understand what crystalline structure is, you need to know a little about the elements that make up a mineral. **Elements** are pure substances that cannot be broken down into simpler substances by ordinary chemical means. All minerals contain one or more of the 92 naturally occurring elements.

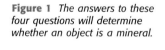

Does it have a crystalline structure? Minerals are crystals, which have a repeating inner structure that is often reflected in the shape of the crystal. Minerals generally have the same chemical composition throughout.

Is it nonliving material? A mineral is inorganic, meaning it isn't made of living things.

Is it a solid? Minerals can't be gases or liquids.

Is it formed in nature? Crystalline materials made by people aren't classified as minerals.

Figure 1 *The answers to these four questions will determine whether an object is a mineral.*

CHAPTER RESOURCES

Chapter Resource File

- **Lesson Plan**
- **Directed Reading A** BASIC
- **Directed Reading B** SPECIAL NEEDS

Technology

Transparencies
- Bellringer

Homework — GENERAL

At Home with Minerals Ask students to find four items in their home that are derived from minerals. Have them add labels to identify the minerals that are contained in different products. Have students share their findings with the class. (Examples include table salt, which is composed of halite; pencil lead, which is composed of graphite; and cooking pots, which are composed of iron, copper, or aluminum.) **LS** Visual

Atoms and Compounds

Each element is made of only one kind of atom. An *atom* is the smallest part of an element that has all the properties of that element. Like other substances, minerals are made up of atoms of one or more elements.

Most minerals are made of compounds of several different elements. A **compound** is a substance made of two or more elements that have been chemically joined, or bonded. Halite, NaCl, for example, is a compound of sodium, Na, and chlorine, Cl, as shown in **Figure 2**. A few minerals, such as gold and silver, are composed of only one element. A mineral that is composed of only one element is called a *native element*.

✓ **Reading Check** How does a compound differ from an element? (*See the Appendix for answers to Reading Checks.*)

Crystals

Solid, geometric forms of minerals produced by a repeating pattern of atoms that is present throughout the mineral are called **crystals.** A crystal's shape is determined by the arrangement of the atoms within the crystal. The arrangement of atoms in turn is determined by the kinds of atoms that make up the mineral. Each mineral has a definite crystalline structure. All minerals can be grouped into crystal classes according to the kinds of crystals they form. **Figure 3** shows how the atomic structure of gold gives rise to cubic crystals.

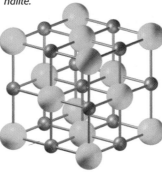

Figure 2 *When atoms of sodium (purple) and chlorine (green) join, they form a compound commonly known as rock salt, or the mineral halite.*

mineral a naturally formed, inorganic solid that has a definite crystalline structure

element a substance that cannot be separated or broken down into simpler substances by chemical means

compound a substance made up of atoms of two or more different elements joined by chemical bonds

crystal a solid whose atoms, ions, or molecules are arranged in a definite pattern

---

Figure 3	**Composition of the Mineral Gold**

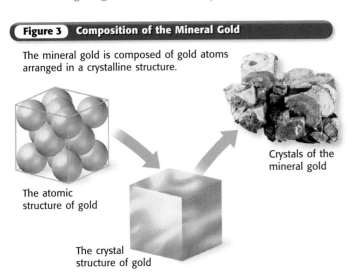

The mineral gold is composed of gold atoms arranged in a crystalline structure.

The atomic structure of gold

The crystal structure of gold

Crystals of the mineral gold

MISCONCEPTION ALERT

Crystal Form and Mineral Identification
In much the same way that color is a deceptive guide to identifying minerals, crystal form is often a misleading physical property. The unit cells of halite and gold are shown in **Figure 2** and **Figure 3**. When different unit cells are combined, however, they can generate crystal forms that look nothing like their atomic structure. A large variety of complex crystal shapes can be generated by starting with a simple polyhedron, such as a cube. For example, the mineral fluorite belongs in the isometric (cubic) class but commonly forms octahedral-shaped crystals.

Reteaching ——— BASIC

Elements and Compounds Have students prepare a set of cards for 10 common minerals. Give students the chemical formula for each mineral, and have them write the chemical formula next to the mineral name. This exercise will reinforce the difference between minerals that are composed of a single element and minerals that are composed of multiple elements. **LS** **Visual**

Quiz ——— GENERAL

1. What is a mineral? (a naturally formed, inorganic solid that has a crystalline structure)

2. What does a crystal's shape depend on? (the arrangement of the atoms within the crystal)

Alternative Assessment ——— GENERAL

Classifying Minerals Write the following mineral-group names on the board: silicates, native elements, carbonates, halides, oxides, sulfates, and sulfides. Have students match the following items with the mineral group from which they are derived: a copper penny (native elements); cement (carbonates); rock salt (halides); toothpaste (sulfates); batteries (sulfides); sand (silicates). **LS** **Logical**

Answer to Reading Check

Answers may vary. Silicate minerals contain a combination of silicon and oxygen; nonsilicate minerals do not contain a combination of silicon and oxygen.

CONNECTION TO Biology

WRITING SKILL **Magnetite** The mineral magnetite has a special property—it is magnetic. Scientists have found that some animals' brains contain magnetite. And scientists have shown that certain fish can sense magnetic fields because of the magnetite in the brains of these fish. The magnetite gives the fish a sense of direction. Using the Internet or another source, research other animals that have magnetite in their brains. Summarize your findings in a short essay.

silicate mineral a mineral that contains a combination of silicon, oxygen, and one or more metals

nonsilicate mineral a mineral that does not contain compounds of silicon and oxygen

Two Groups of Minerals

The most common classification of minerals is based on chemical composition. Minerals are divided into two groups based on their chemical composition. These groups are the silicate minerals and the nonsilicate minerals.

Silicate Minerals

Silicon and oxygen are the two most common elements in the Earth's crust. Minerals that contain a combination of these two elements are called **silicate minerals.** Silicate minerals make up more than 90% of the Earth's crust. The rest of the Earth's crust is made up of nonsilicate minerals. Silicon and oxygen usually combine with other elements, such as aluminum, iron, magnesium, and potassium, to make up silicate minerals. Some of the more common silicate minerals are shown in **Figure 4.**

Nonsilicate Minerals

Minerals that do not contain a combination of the elements silicon and oxygen form a group called the **nonsilicate minerals.** Some of these minerals are made up of elements such as carbon, oxygen, fluorine, and sulfur. **Figure 5** on the following page shows the most important classes of nonsilicate minerals.

✓ **Reading Check** How do silicate minerals differ from nonsilicate minerals?

Figure 4 **Common Silicate Minerals**

Quartz is the basic building block of many rocks.

Feldspar minerals are the main component of most rocks on the Earth's surface.

Mica minerals separate easily into sheets when they break. Biotite is one of several kinds of mica.

INCLUSION Strategies

• *Learning Disabilities*
• *Developmentally Delayed*

Organize students into pairs or groups of three. Give each group some common mineral samples. Pass out paint sample strips from a hardware store, and have students identify each mineral's color. Students should record their observations in their **science journal.** Next, hand out materials that serve as examples of luster. A candle could demonstrate waxy luster, and a jar top is an example of metallic luster. Have students use these examples to determine the luster of each mineral sample. The teams should perform all of the mineral tests in a similar way and share their findings with the class. **LS** **Visual/Kinesthetic**   English Language Learners

Figure 5 **Classes of Nonsilicate Minerals**

Native elements are minerals that are composed of only one element. Some examples are copper, Cu, gold, Au, and silver, Ag. Native elements are used in communications and electronics equipment.

Copper

Oxides are compounds that form when an element, such as aluminum or iron, combines chemically with oxygen. Oxide minerals are used to make abrasives, aircraft parts, and paint.

Corundum

Carbonates are minerals that contain combinations of carbon and oxygen in their chemical structure. We use carbonate minerals in cement, building stones, and fireworks.

Calcite

Sulfates are minerals that contain sulfur and oxygen, SO$_4$. Sulfates are used in cosmetics, toothpaste, cement, and paint.

Gypsum

Halides are compounds that form when fluorine, chlorine, iodine, or bromine combine with sodium, potassium, or calcium. Halide minerals are used in the chemical industry and in detergents.

Fluorite

Sulfides are minerals that contain one or more elements, such as lead, iron, or nickel, combined with sulfur. Sulfide minerals are used to make batteries, medicines, and electronic parts.

Galena

SECTION Review

Summary

- A mineral is a naturally formed, inorganic solid that has a definite crystalline structure.
- Minerals may be either elements or compounds.
- Mineral crystals are solid, geometric forms that are produced by a repeating pattern of atoms.
- Minerals are classified as either silicate minerals or nonsilicate minerals based on the elements of which they are composed.

Using Key Terms

1. In your own words, write a definition for each of the following terms: *element, compound,* and *mineral*.

Understanding Key Ideas

2. Which of the following minerals is a nonsilicate mineral?
   a. mica
   b. quartz
   c. gypsum
   d. feldspar

3. What is a crystal, and what determines a crystal's shape?

4. Describe the two major groups of minerals.

Math Skills

5. If there are approximately 3,600 known minerals and about 20 of the minerals are native elements, what percentage of all minerals are native elements?

Critical Thinking

6. **Applying Concepts** Explain why each of the following is not considered a mineral: water, oxygen, honey, and teeth.

7. **Applying Concepts** Explain why scientists consider ice to be a mineral.

8. **Making Comparisons** In what ways are sulfate and sulfide minerals the same. In what ways are they different?

CHAPTER RESOURCES

Chapter Resource File

- **Section Quiz** GENERAL
- **Section Review** GENERAL
- **Vocabulary and Section Summary** GENERAL
- **Reinforcement Worksheet** BASIC

Answers to Section Review

1. Sample answer: Pure substances that cannot be broken down into simpler substances are called elements. Compounds are two or more elements bonded together. A mineral is a naturally formed, inorganic solid that has a crystalline structure.

2. c

3. A crystal is a solid, geometric form of mineral produced by a repeating pattern of atoms that is present throughout the mineral. The shape of a crystal is determined by the arrangement of atoms within the crystal.

4. The two major groups of minerals are silicate and nonsilicate minerals. Silicate minerals contain a combination of silicon and oxygen. Nonsilicate minerals do not contain a combination of silicon and oxygen.

5. $20 \div 3,600 \times 100 = .55\%$

6. Water is not a mineral because it does not have a crystalline structure and it is a liquid, not a solid. Oxygen is not a mineral because oxygen atoms by themselves do not have a crystalline structure. Teeth are not minerals because they are living parts of your body. Honey is not a mineral because it is made of organic substances.

7. Ice is considered to be a mineral because it is a solid, it is a non-living material, it is formed in nature, and it has a definite crystalline structure.

8. Sulfate minerals are similar to sulfide minerals because both contain the element sulfur. Sulfate minerals and sulfide minerals are different because sulfide minerals contain one or more elements combined with sulfur, whereas sulfate minerals contain one or more elements combined with sulfur and oxygen.

Focus

Overview

In this section, students will learn common techniques used to identify minerals. They will also examine some of the interesting properties of minerals, such as fluorescence, radioactivity, and magnetism.

Bellringer

Show students a variety of mineral samples. Have students list as many phrases as they can to describe each sample. Have students organize these phrases into categories. Students can use these categories to determine whether or not each sample is a different mineral.

Motivate

Group ACTiViTY — GENERAL

Mineral Classification Have students develop a classification system for minerals based on observable physical properties. Give groups a variety of minerals or photographs of minerals. Students should create a classification system based on observable differences and similarities between the samples. After the groups have developed a classification system, give them several new samples. Have them place the samples in their classification scheme.
LS Visual/Logical

luster the way in which a mineral reflects light

Identifying Minerals

If you closed your eyes and tasted different foods, you could probably determine what the foods are by noting properties such as saltiness or sweetness. You can also determine the identity of a mineral by noting different properties.

In this section, you will learn about the properties that will help you identify minerals.

Color

The same mineral can come in a variety of colors. For example, in its purest state quartz is clear. Samples of quartz that contain various types of and various amounts of impurities, however, can be a variety of colors.

Besides impurities, other factors can change the appearance of minerals. The mineral pyrite, often called fool's gold, normally has a golden color. But if pyrite is exposed to air and water for a long period, it can turn brown or black. Because of factors such as impurities, color usually is not the best way to identify a mineral.

Luster

The way a surface reflects light is called **luster.** When you say an object is shiny or dull, you are describing its luster. Minerals have metallic, submetallic, or nonmetallic luster. If a mineral is shiny, it has a metallic luster. If the mineral is dull, its luster is either submetallic or nonmetallic. The different types of lusters are shown in **Figure 1.**

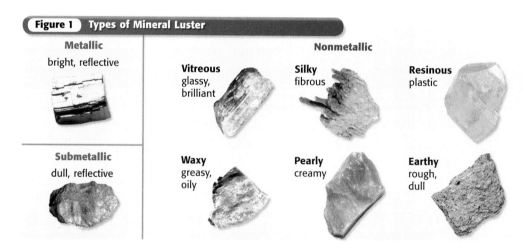

Figure 1   Types of Mineral Luster

Metallic
bright, reflective

Submetallic
dull, reflective

Nonmetallic

Vitreous
glassy, brilliant

Waxy
greasy, oily

Silky
fibrous

Pearly
creamy

Resinous
plastic

Earthy
rough, dull

CHAPTER RESOURCES

Chapter Resource File

- **Lesson Plan**
- **Directed Reading A** BASIC
- **Directed Reading B** SPECIAL NEEDS

Technology

Transparencies
- Bellringer
- *LINK TO PHYSICAL SCIENCE* The Three Major Categories of Elements

WEIRD SCIENCE

How can you tell a real diamond from a fake? A gem specialist uses specialized tools to distinguish real diamonds from impostors. But there are some tests that even an untrained person can conduct. One of the simplest tests is to try to pick up the stone in question with a moistened fingertip. Diamonds can be picked up this way; most other stones cannot.

Streak

The color of a mineral in powdered form is called the mineral's **streak.** A mineral's streak can be found by rubbing the mineral against a piece of unglazed porcelain called a *streak plate*. The mark left on the streak plate is the streak. The streak is a thin layer of powdered mineral. The color of a mineral's streak is not always the same as the color of the mineral sample. The difference between color and streak is shown in **Figure 2.** Unlike the surface of a mineral sample, the streak is not affected by air or water. For this reason, using streak is more reliable than using color in identifying a mineral.

Reading Check Why is using streak more reliable in identifying a mineral than using color is? (*See the Appendix for answers to Reading Checks.*)

Cleavage and Fracture

Different types of minerals break in different ways. The way a mineral breaks is determined by the arrangement of its atoms. **Cleavage** is the tendency of some minerals to break along smooth, flat surfaces. **Figure 3** shows the cleavage patterns of the minerals mica and halite.

Fracture is the tendency of some minerals to break unevenly along curved or irregular surfaces. One type of fracture is shown in **Figure 4.**

Figure 2 *The color of the mineral hematite may vary, but hematite's streak is always red-brown.*

streak the color of the powder of a mineral

cleavage the splitting of a mineral along smooth, flat surfaces

fracture the manner in which a mineral breaks along either curved or irregular surfaces

Figure 3 *Cleavage varies with mineral type.*

Mica breaks easily into distinct sheets. ▶

Halite breaks at 90° angles in three directions. ▼

Figure 4 *This sample of quartz shows a curved fracture pattern called* conchoidal fracture *(kahn KOYD uhl FRAK chuhr).*

Answer to Reading Check

A mineral's streak is not affected by air or water, but a mineral's color may be affected by air or water.

CONNECTION ACTIVITY

Real World — GENERAL

Class Visit Invite a jeweler to visit the class, and ask the jeweler to explain how gemstones are made into jewelry. The jeweler could bring in visual aids to help students understand how gems are located, mined, and prepared for commercial use. **LS Visual**

Mnemonics Have students create a mnemonic device that will help them learn the Mohs hardness scale. One example is **T**errible **G**iants **C**an **F**ind **A**lligators **O**r **Q**uaint **T**igers **C**onveniently **D**igestible. This will help students remember the minerals in order of hardness: talc, gypsum, calcite, fluorite, apatite, orthoclase, quartz, topaz, corundum, and diamond. **LS** Auditory

Quiz — GENERAL

1. Why is color not always a reliable way of identifying a mineral? (Factors such as weathering and the inclusion of impurities can affect the mineral's color.)

2. What property do minerals that glow under ultraviolet light display? (fluorescence)

Alternative Assessment — GENERAL

Mineral Identification Cards
Have students prepare mineral identification cards for some of the most common minerals. They can list the words color, luster, hardness, streak, cleavage and fracture, and density on each card. For each card, ask them to fill in the properties of a common mineral. Students should write the name of the mineral on the back of the card and use the cards as study aids or assessment tools. **LS** Visual

Figure 5 Mohs Hardness Scale

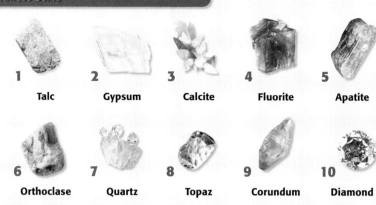

A mineral's number indicates its relative hardness. The scale ranges from 1, which is the softest, to 10, which is the hardest. A mineral of a given hardness will scratch any mineral that is softer than it is.

1 Talc
2 Gypsum
3 Calcite
4 Fluorite
5 Apatite
6 Orthoclase
7 Quartz
8 Topaz
9 Corundum
10 Diamond

hardness a measure of the ability of a mineral to resist scratching

density the ratio of the mass of a substance to the volume of the substance

Scratch Test

1. You will need a **penny,** a **pencil,** and your **fingernail.** Which one of these three materials is the hardest?

2. Use your fingernail to try to scratch the graphite at the tip of a pencil.

3. Now try to scratch the penny with your fingernail.

4. Rank the three materials in order from softest to hardest.

Hardness

A mineral's resistance to being scratched is called **hardness.** To determine the hardness of minerals, scientists use *Mohs hardness scale,* shown in **Figure 5.** Notice that talc has a rating of 1 and diamond has a rating of 10. The greater a mineral's resistance to being scratched is, the higher the mineral's rating is. To identify a mineral by using Mohs scale, try to scratch the surface of a mineral with the edge of one of the 10 reference minerals. If the reference mineral scratches your mineral, the reference mineral is harder than your mineral.

✓ **Reading Check** How would you determine the hardness of an unidentified mineral sample?

Density

If you pick up a golf ball and a table-tennis ball, which will feel heavier? Although the balls are of similar size, the golf ball will feel heavier because it is denser. **Density** is the measure of how much matter is in a given amount of space. In other words, density is a ratio of an object's mass to its volume. Density is usually measured in grams per cubic centimeter. Because water has a density of 1 g/cm^3, it is used as a reference point for other substances. The ratio of an object's density to the density of water is called the object's *specific gravity.* The specific gravity of gold, for example, is 19. So, gold has a density of 19 g/cm^3. In other words, there is 19 times more matter in 1 cm^3 of gold than in 1 cm^3 of water.

Answer to Reading Check

Scratch the mineral with a series of 10 reference minerals. If the reference mineral scratches the unidentified mineral, the reference mineral is harder than the unidentified mineral.

MATERIALS

FOR EACH GROUP
• pencil
• penny

Answers

4. The penny is the hardest material of the three, followed by the fingernail and then the graphite.

Special Properties

Some properties are particular to only a few types of minerals. The properties shown in **Figure 6** can help you quickly identify the minerals shown. To identify some properties, however, you will need specialized equipment.

Figure 6 Special Properties of Some Minerals

  Fluorescence Calcite and fluorite glow under ultraviolet light. The same fluorite sample is shown in ultraviolet light (top) and in white light (bottom).

 Chemical Reaction Calcite will become bubbly, or "fizz," when a drop of weak acid is placed on it.

 Optical Properties A thin, clear piece of calcite placed over an image will cause a double image.

 Magnetism Both magnetite and pyrrhotite are natural magnets that attract iron.

 Taste Halite has a salty taste.

Radioactivity Minerals that contain radium or uranium can be detected by a Geiger counter.

SECTION Review

Summary

- Properties that can be used to identify minerals are color, luster, streak, cleavage, fracture, hardness, and density.
- Some minerals can be identified by special properties they have, such as taste, magnetism, fluorescence, radioactivity, chemical reaction, and optical properties.

Using Key Terms

1. Use each of the following terms in a separate sentence: *luster, streak,* and *cleavage.*

Understanding Key Ideas

2. Which of the following properties of minerals is expressed in numbers?
   a. fracture
   b. cleavage
   c. hardness
   d. streak

3. How do you determine a mineral's streak?

4. Briefly describe the special properties of minerals.

Math Skills

5. If a mineral has a specific gravity of 5.5, how much more matter is there in 1 cm^3 of this mineral than in 1 cm^3 of water?

Critical Thinking

6. **Applying Concepts** What properties would you use to determine whether two mineral samples are different minerals?

7. **Applying Concepts** If a mineral scratches calcite but is scratched by apatite, what is the mineral's hardness?

8. **Analyzing Methods** What would be the easiest way to identify calcite?

For a variety of links related to this chapter, go to www.scilinks.org

Topic: Identifying Minerals
SciLinks code: HSM0782

SCILINKS®

NSTA
Developed and maintained by the National Science Teachers Association

Answers to Section Review

1. Sample answer: Luster is the way the surface of a mineral reflects light. Streak is the thin layer of powder that a mineral leaves when rubbed against a streak plate. If a mineral has cleavage, it breaks along flat surfaces.

2. c

3. The streak of a mineral is determined by rubbing the mineral against a streak plate. The thin layer of powder left on the streak plate is the mineral's streak.

4. The special properties of minerals include fluorescence (glowing under ultraviolet light), chemical reaction, optical properties (such as producing a double image), magnetism, taste, and radioactivity.

5. There is 5.5 times more matter in 1 cm^3 of this mineral than in 1 cm^3 of water.

6. Properties that would be useful to determine whether two mineral samples are different include color, luster, streak, cleavage and fracture, hardness, density, or any of the special properties listed in the text.

7. The hardness would be 4 on the Mohs hardness scale.

8. The easiest way to identify calcite would be to place a drop of weak acid on the sample to see if the acid produces bubbles.

CHAPTER RESOURCES

Chapter Resource File

- Section Quiz **GENERAL**
- Section Review **GENERAL**
- Vocabulary and Section Summary **GENERAL**
- Datasheet for Quick Lab
- SciLinks Activity **GENERAL**
- Critical Thinking **ADVANCED**

Technology

Transparencies
- Mohs Hardness Scale
- Special Properties of Some Minerals

Overview

This section discusses how minerals form deep within Earth's crust and how they form at or close to the Earth's surface. Students will learn about different techniques used to mine minerals. This section concludes with a discussion of the value of mineral resources and the importance of environmentally responsible mining and reclamation.

 Bellringer

Show students a mineral resource map of your state. Have students locate mines that are closest to where they live and discuss the mineral commodities that are mined at these locations.

Motivate

Discussion ——— GENERAL

Simulating a Gold Rush To simulate the excitement of the gold rush of 1849, make up a flyer that tells of a rich gold deposit found in a nearby area. Make copies, and pass them out to students. Have students discuss their reactions to such an announcement. Then, discuss the chaotic enthusiasm of the gold rush. Note that from 1848 to 1860, the population in California grew from 14,000 to 380,000 people! **Visual/Verbal**

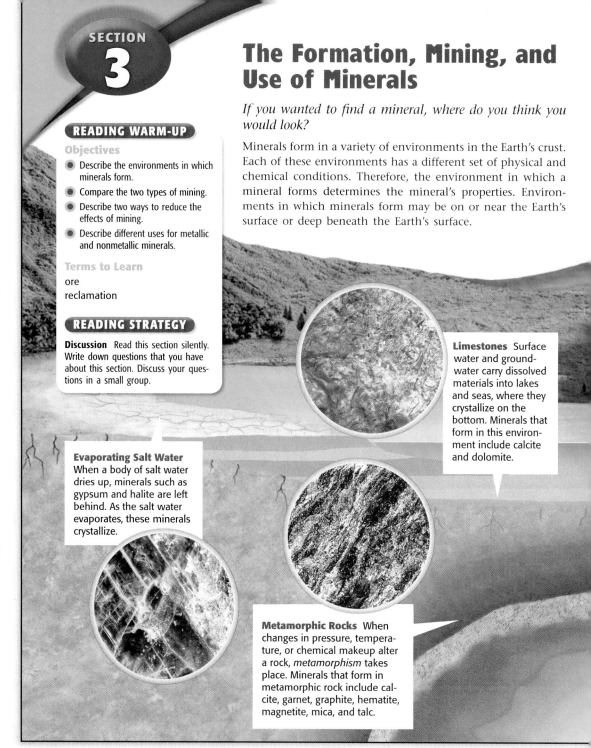

The Formation, Mining, and Use of Minerals

If you wanted to find a mineral, where do you think you would look?

Minerals form in a variety of environments in the Earth's crust. Each of these environments has a different set of physical and chemical conditions. Therefore, the environment in which a mineral forms determines the mineral's properties. Environments in which minerals form may be on or near the Earth's surface or deep beneath the Earth's surface.

READING WARM-UP

Objectives
- Describe the environments in which minerals form.
- Compare the two types of mining.
- Describe two ways to reduce the effects of mining.
- Describe different uses for metallic and nonmetallic minerals.

Terms to Learn
ore
reclamation

READING STRATEGY

Discussion Read this section silently. Write down questions that you have about this section. Discuss your questions in a small group.

Limestones Surface water and groundwater carry dissolved materials into lakes and seas, where they crystallize on the bottom. Minerals that form in this environment include calcite and dolomite.

Evaporating Salt Water When a body of salt water dries up, minerals such as gypsum and halite are left behind. As the salt water evaporates, these minerals crystallize.

Metamorphic Rocks When changes in pressure, temperature, or chemical makeup alter a rock, *metamorphism* takes place. Minerals that form in metamorphic rock include calcite, garnet, graphite, hematite, magnetite, mica, and talc.

CHAPTER RESOURCES

Chapter Resource File
- Lesson Plan
- Directed Reading A **BASIC**
- Directed Reading B **SPECIAL NEEDS**

Technology

Transparencies
- Bellringer

WEIRD SCIENCE

Some of the greatest untapped sources of minerals are hydrothermal vents deep under the sea. These hydrothermal vents are called *black smokers* because they spew out hot, mineral-rich water that is almost black. As the hot water mixes with the cool ocean water, minerals crystallize on the ocean floor. But no one has found an economical way to mine them yet.

INTERNET ACTIVITY

For another activity related to this chapter, go to go.hrw.com and type in the keyword **HZ5MINW**.

Hot-Water Solutions
Groundwater works its way downward and is heated by magma. It then reacts with minerals to form a hot liquid solution. Dissolved metals and other elements crystallize out of the hot fluid to form new minerals. Gold, copper, sulfur, pyrite, and galena form in such hot-water environments.

Pegmatites As magma moves upward, it can form teardrop-shaped bodies called *pegmatites.* The mineral crystals in pegmatites become extremely large, sometimes growing to several meters across! Many gemstones, such as topaz and tourmaline, form in pegmatites.

Plutons As magma rises upward through the crust, it sometimes stops moving before it reaches the surface and cools slowly, forming millions of mineral crystals. Eventually, the entire magma body solidifies to form a *pluton.* Mica, feldspar, magnetite, and quartz are some of the minerals that form from magma.

Teach

CONNECTION ACTIVITY
History ————————— GENERAL

The History of Mining Communities

Encourage students to learn more about the social and environmental effects of mining by having each student create a scrapbook detailing the history of a mining community. Students should research the history of a community from the discovery of ore to the present. Students' scrapbooks should include drawings and photographs showing changes in the community as well as text describing the history of the area. Have students focus on the types of ore extracted, the use and value of the ore in the world market, and the impact mining has had on the people and environment of the area. Possible communities include the following: Bodie, California; Calico, California; Johannesburg, California; Randsburg, California; Bullfrog, Nevada; Goldfield, Nevada; Manhattan, Nevada; Rhyolite, Nevada; Tonopah, Nevada; Silver City, Utah; Bisbee, Arizona; Gleeson, Arizona; Silverbell, Arizona; Tombstone, Arizona; Kelly, New Mexico; Terlingua, Texas; Leadville, Colorado; Butte, Montana; and the Yanomami Indian tribes of Brazil and Venezuela. Have students share their scrapbooks with the class. **LS** Visual/Intrapersonal

INCLUSION Strategies

- *Learning Disabled*
- *Attention Deficit Disorder*
- *Behavior Control Issues*

Organize students into small teams to play a mineral quiz game. Each team should choose a category that relates to a heading in the section and write five questions and answers for the category on separate index cards. The difficulty and point value of the questions should increase incrementally. Review each team's questions and answers before you start the game. If a team cannot answer a question, the team should work with another team to answer the question. If teams cooperate, they should share the points earned. When the game is over, hand out a review sheet that contains the questions and answers. **LS** Interpersonal

English Language Learners

Debate ———————— GENERAL

Surface Versus Subsurface Mining Tell the class that both surface and subsurface mining have positive and negative aspects. Divide the class into two groups. Assign each group a type of mining, and ask the students in the groups to list the advantages of their type of mining. Also have the groups list the disadvantages of the other group's type of mining. Then, have the groups debate their points. (Some advantages of surface mining include that miners are safer when working above ground and have easier access to ore. On the other hand, surface mining alters the landscape and has a greater potential for contaminating the environment. Subsurface mining does not necessarily affect the landscape, and with this type of mining, it is easier to contain potentially harmful wastes. However, subsurface mining has a greater potential for miners to be trapped underground and has the possibility of underground fires and explosions.) Ask each student to write a brief summary of his or her team's viewpoint. Students should include reasons they personally agree or disagree with the opinion. **LS** Verbal/Interpersonal Co-op Learning

Surface Coal Mining
Producing 1 metric ton of coal requires that up to 30 metric tons of earth be removed first. Some surface coal mines produce up to 50,000 metric tons of coal per day. How many metric tons of earth might have to be removed in order to mine 50,000 metric tons of coal?

ore a natural material whose concentration of economically valuable minerals is high enough for the material to be mined profitably

Mining

Many kinds of rocks and minerals must be mined to extract the valuable elements they contain. Geologists use the term **ore** to describe a mineral deposit large enough and pure enough to be mined for profit. Rocks and minerals are removed from the ground by one of two methods—surface mining or subsurface mining. The method miners choose depends on how close to the surface or how far down in the Earth the mineral is located.

Surface Mining

When mineral deposits are located at or near the surface of the Earth, surface-mining methods are used to remove the minerals. Types of surface mines include open pits, surface coal mines, and quarries.

Open-pit mining is used to remove large, near-surface deposits of economically important minerals such as gold and copper. As shown in **Figure 1,** ore is mined downward, layer by layer, in an open-pit mine. Explosives are often used to break up the ore. The ore is then loaded into haul trucks and transported from the mine for processing. Quarries are open pits that are used to mine building stone, crushed rock, sand, and gravel. Coal that is near the surface is removed by surface coal mining. Surface coal mining is sometimes known as strip mining because the coal is removed in strips that may be as wide as 50 m and as long as 1 km.

Figure 1 *In open-pit mines, the ore is mined downward in layers. The stair-step excavation of the walls keeps the sides of the mine from collapsing. Giant haul trucks (inset) are used to transport ore from the mine.*

Cultural Awareness GENERAL

The Empire of Great Zimbabwe The mining of gold, copper, and iron in southeastern Africa helped build the empire of Great Zimbabwe, which arose during the mid-thirteenth century and lasted until about the middle of the fifteenth century. Invite students to find out more about mining techniques in Great Zimbabwe and about the Karanga people who ruled the empire. **LS** Logical

Mining on Other Planets Some scientists speculate that there are valuable deposits of minerals on other bodies in our solar system. Ask students to think about what issues should be considered before staking claims and mining other planets.

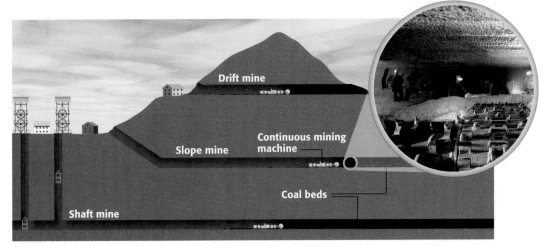

Figure 2 *Subsurface mining is the removal of minerals or other materials from deep within the Earth. Passageways must be dug underground to reach the ore. Machines such as continuous mining machines (inset) are used to mine ore in subsurface mines.*

Subsurface Mining

Subsurface mining methods are used when mineral deposits are located too deep within the Earth to be surface mined. Subsurface mining often requires that passageways be dug into the Earth to reach the ore. As shown in **Figure 2,** these passageways may be dug horizontally or at an angle. If a mineral deposit extends deep within the Earth, however, a vertical shaft is sunk. This shaft may connect a number of passageways that intersect the ore at different levels.

 Reading Check Compare surface and subsurface mining.
(See the Appendix for answers to Reading Checks.)

Responsible Mining

Mining gives us the minerals we need, but it may also create problems. Mining can destroy or disturb the habitats of plants and animals. Also, the waste products from a mine may get into water sources, which pollutes surface water and groundwater.

Mine Reclamation

One way to reduce the potential harmful effects of mining is to return the land to its original state after the mining is completed. The process by which land used for mining is returned to its original state or better is called **reclamation.** Reclamation of mined public and private land has been required by law since the mid-1970s. Another way to reduce the effects of mining is to reduce our need for minerals. We reduce our need for minerals by recycling many of the mineral products that we currently use, such as aluminum.

reclamation the process of returning land to its original condition after mining is completed

SCHOOL to HOME

Recycling Minerals at Home

With your parent, locate products in your home that are made of minerals. Decide which of these products could be recycled. In your **science journal,** make a list of the products that could be recycled to save minerals.

ACTIVITY

Concept Mapping Have students make a concept map in their **science journal** of one mining process discussed in this section. Make sure students include each step in the mining process. The first step should be the search for mineral or ore deposits. The final step should include information about the products that are manufactured from the mineral and information about the cleanup of the mine wastes. **LS** Visual

Quiz — GENERAL

1. List three minerals that form in metamorphic rock. (sample answers: garnet, mica, and talc)

2. What is ore? (mineral deposits large enough and pure enough to be mined for profit)

3. How can mining cause water pollution? (The waste products from a mine can introduce toxic concentrations of elements into rivers, lakes, and groundwater.)

Alternative Assessment — GENERAL

Designing a Spacecraft Tell students to design a spacecraft that will carry astronauts to another planet in our solar system. Have students create a diagram of their spacecraft that includes labels that indicate the minerals used to make the spacecraft. **LS** Logical

Table 1	Common Uses of Minerals
Mineral	**Uses**
Copper	electrical wire, plumbing, coins
Diamond	jewelry, cutting tools, drill bits
Galena	batteries, ammunition
Gibbsite	cans, foil, appliances, utensils
Gold	jewelry, computers, spacecraft, dentistry
Gypsum	wallboards, plaster, cement
Halite	nutrition, highway de-icer, water softener
Quartz	glass, computer chips
Silver	photography, electronics products, jewelry
Sphalerite	jet aircraft, spacecraft, paints

The Use of Minerals

As shown in **Table 1,** some minerals are of major economic and industrial importance. Some minerals can be used just as they are. Other minerals must be processed to get the element or elements that the minerals contain. **Figure 3** shows some processed minerals used to make the parts of a bicycle.

Metallic Minerals

Some minerals are metallic. Metallic minerals have shiny surfaces, do not let light pass through them, and are good conductors of heat and electricity. Metallic minerals can be processed into metals that are strong and do not rust. Other metals can be pounded or pressed into various shapes or stretched thinly without breaking. These properties make metals desirable for use in aircraft, automobiles, computers, communications and electronic equipment, and spacecraft. Examples of metallic minerals that have many industrial uses are gold, silver, and copper.

Nonmetallic Minerals

Other minerals are nonmetals. Nonmetallic minerals have shiny or dull surfaces, may let light pass through them, and are good insulators of electricity. Nonmetallic minerals are some of the most widely used minerals in industry. For example, calcite is a major component of concrete, which is used in building roads, buildings, bridges, and other structures. Industrial sand and gravel, or silica, have uses that range from glassmaking to producing computer chips.

Figure 3 Some Materials Used in the Parts of a Bicycle

Handlebars titanium from ilmenite

Frame aluminum from bauxite

Spokes iron from magnetite

Pedals beryllium from beryl

CONNECTION ACTIVITY Life Science — GENERAL

The SEAM Project The Surface Environment and Mining (SEAM) program was established by the U.S. Forest Service in 1973 to address the issue of land reclamation in the wake of mining operations. Since then, this highly successful program has returned vast areas of land formerly used for mining to its original condition. The most recent SEAM projects can be researched on the Internet. To research local reclamation efforts, students could contact mining companies and local conservation groups listed in the phone directory. **LS** Logical

Gemstones

Some nonmetallic minerals, called *gemstones*, are highly valued for their beauty and rarity rather than for their usefulness. Important gemstones include diamond, ruby, sapphire, emerald, aquamarine, topaz, and tourmaline. An example of a diamond is shown in **Figure 4.** Color is the most important characteristic of a gemstone. The more attractive the color is, the more valuable the gem is. Gemstones must also be durable. That is, they must be hard enough to be cut and polished. The mass of a gemstone is expressed in a unit known as a *carat*. One carat is equal to 200 mg.

☑ **Reading Check** In your own words, define the term *gemstone*.

Figure 4 *The Cullinan diamond, at the center of this scepter, is part of the largest diamond ever found.*

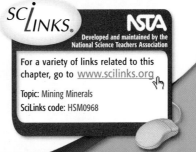

SECTION Review

Summary

- Environments in which minerals form may be located at or near the Earth's surface or deep below the surface.
- The two types of mining are surface mining and subsurface mining.
- Two ways to reduce the effects of mining are the reclamation of mined land and the recycling of mineral products.
- Some metallic and nonmetallic minerals have many important economic and industrial uses.

Using Key Terms

Complete each of the following sentences by choosing the correct term from the word bank.

ore   reclamation

1. _____ is the process of returning land to its original condition after mining is completed.

2. _____ is the term used to describe a mineral deposit that is large enough and pure enough to be mined for profit.

Understanding Key Ideas

3. Which of the following conditions is NOT important in the formation of minerals?

   a. presence of groundwater

   b. evaporation

   c. volcanic activity

   d. wind

4. What are the two main types of mining, and how do they differ?

5. List some uses of metallic minerals.

6. List some uses of nonmetallic minerals.

Math Skills

7. A diamond cutter has a raw diamond that weighs 19.5 carats and from which two 5-carat diamonds will be cut. How much did the raw diamond weigh in milligrams? How much will each of the two cut diamonds weigh in milligrams?

Critical Thinking

8. **Analyzing Ideas** How does reclamation protect the environment around a mine?

9. **Applying Concepts** Suppose you find a mineral crystal that is as tall as you are. What kinds of environmental factors would cause such a crystal to form?

SCILINKS

NSTA
Developed and maintained by the National Science Teachers Association

For a variety of links related to this chapter, go to www.scilinks.org

Topic: Mining Minerals
SciLinks code: HSM0968

CHAPTER RESOURCES

Chapter Resource File

- **Section Quiz** GENERAL
- **Section Review** GENERAL
- **Vocabulary and Section Summary** GENERAL

Is It Fool's Gold? A Dense Situation

Teacher's Notes

Time Required
One 45-minute class period

Lab Ratings

EASY ————————————→ HARD

Teacher Prep 🔺🔺
Student Set-Up 🔺🔺🔺
Concept Level 🔺🔺
Clean Up 🔺🔺

MATERIALS

Materials listed on the student page are sufficient for a group of 2 to 4 students. If your mineral samples are small, the change in volume may be difficult to detect. In that case, replace the beaker in steps 7–10 with a graduated cylinder.

Safety Caution

Remind students to review all safety cautions and icons before beginning this lab activity.

Preparation Notes

Students may need to review the concepts of density and specific gravity prior to performing this activity.

Is It Fool's Gold? A Dense Situation

Have you heard of fool's gold? Maybe you've seen a piece of it. This mineral is actually pyrite, and it was often passed off as real gold. However, there are simple tests that you can do to keep from being tricked. Minerals can be identified by their properties. Some properties, such as color, vary from sample to sample. Other properties, such as density and specific gravity, remain consistent across samples. In this activity, you will try to verify the identity of some mineral samples.

Ask a Question

❶ How can I determine if an unknown mineral is not gold or silver?

Form a Hypothesis

❷ Write a hypothesis that is a possible answer to the question above. Explain your reasoning.

Test the Hypothesis

❸ Copy the data table. Use it to record your observations.

OBJECTIVES

Calculate the density and specific gravity of a mineral.

Explain how density and specific gravity can be used to identify a mineral specimen.

MATERIALS

- balance
- beaker, 400 mL
- galena sample
- pyrite sample
- ring stand
- spring scale
- string
- water, 400 mL

SAFETY

Galena

Pyrite

Observation Chart		
Measurement	**Galena**	**Pyrite**
Mass in air (g)		
Weight in air (N)		
Volume of mineral (mL)	DO NOT WRITE IN BOOK	
Weight in water (N)		

❹ Find the mass of each sample by laying the mineral on the balance. Record the mass of each sample in your data table.

❺ Attach the spring scale to the ring stand.

❻ Tie a string around the sample of galena, and leave a loop at the loose end. Suspend the galena from the spring scale, and find its mass and weight in air. Do not remove the sample from the spring scale yet. Enter these data in your data table.

Norman Holcomb
Marion Local Schools
Maria Stein, Ohio

CHAPTER RESOURCES
Chapter Resource File
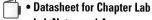 • Datasheet for Chapter Lab
• Lab Notes and Answers
Technology
💾 Classroom Videos
• Lab Video
LabBook
• Mysterious Minerals

7 Fill a beaker halfway with water. Record the beginning volume of water in your data table.

8 Carefully lift the beaker around the galena until the mineral is completely submerged. Be careful not to splash any water out of the beaker! Do not allow the mineral to touch the beaker.

9 Record the new volume and weight in your data table.

10 Subtract the original volume of water from the new volume to find the amount of water displaced by the mineral. This is the volume of the mineral sample itself. Record this value in your data table.

11 Repeat steps 6–10 for the sample of pyrite.

Analyze the Results

1 **Constructing Tables** Copy the data table below. (Note: 1 mL = 1 cm³)

Density Data Table

Mineral	Density (g/cm³)	Specific gravity
Silver	10.5	10.5
Galena	DO NOT WRITE IN BOOK	
Pyrite		
Gold	19.0	19.0

2 **Organizing Data** Use the following equations to calculate the density and specific gravity of each mineral, and record your answers in your data table.

$$density = \frac{mass\ in\ air}{volume}$$

$$specific\ gravity = \frac{weight\ in\ air}{weight\ in\ air - weight\ in\ water}$$

Draw Conclusions

3 **Drawing Conclusions** The density of pure gold is 19 g/cm³. How can you use this information to prove that your sample of pyrite is not gold?

4 **Drawing Conclusions** The density of pure silver is 10.5 g/cm³. How can you use this information to prove that your sample of galena is not silver?

5 **Applying Conclusions** If you found a gold-colored nugget, how could you find out if the nugget was real gold or fool's gold?

CHAPTER RESOURCES

Workbooks

Long-Term Projects & Research Ideas
• What's Yours Is Mined **ADVANCED**

Analyze the Results

2.

Mineral	Density (g/cm³)	Specific gravity
Silver	10.5	10.5
Galena	7.4 to 7.6	7.4 to 7.6
Pyrite	5.0	5.0
Gold	19.0	19.0

Lab Notes

• Density is conventionally described as g/cm³, not g/mL.

• Because specific gravity is the ratio of a substance's density to the density of water (1 g/cm³), the value will be the same for density. The difference is that specific gravity is a number, and density is a number with the units grams per cubic centimeter (g/cm³).

• Because of impurities, the density of some minerals is given in ranges. The density of pure gold is 19.0 g/cm³; lower numbers indicate the presence of impurities. The density of pure silver is 10.5 g/cm³; depending on impurities, that number can be higher or lower.

• Ideally, the values for specific gravity and density obtained in this lab will be identical. Discrepancies will likely result from differences in precision. Students should learn that all scientific measurements involve some margin of error.

Draw Conclusions

3. Because the density of the sample is not 19.0 g/cm³, the sample is not gold.

4. Because the density of the sample is not 10.5 g/cm³, the sample is not pure silver. (The sample could contain silver mixed with other minerals.)

5. Sample answer: You could find the density and specific gravity of the nugget. If it was pure gold, the density would be 19.0 g/cm³ and the specific gravity would be 19.0, but you would have to perform more tests. If the sample had a density of 5.0 g/cm³ and a specific gravity of 5.0, then it would likely be pyrite (fool's gold).

Chapter Review

Assignment Guide

Section	Questions
1	1, 4, 6, 8, 12, 19
2	2, 5, 7, 16, 18–20, 22–25
3	9–11, 13–15, 21
1 and 3	3

ANSWERS

Using Key Terms

1. Sample answer: An element is a pure substance that cannot be broken into simpler substances by normal chemical means. A compound is a substance made of two or more bonded elements. A mineral is an inorganic solid that formed naturally and has a crystalline structure.

2. Sample answer: Streak is the color of a mineral in powdered form. The color of a mineral may change due to air or water, but the mineral's streak is always the same.

3. Sample answer: A mineral is a naturally formed, inorganic solid with a crystalline structure. An ore is a deposit of minerals that is large enough and pure enough to be mined for a profit.

4. Sample answer: Silicate minerals contain compounds of silicon and oxygen; nonsilicate minerals do not contain compounds of silicon and oxygen.

USING KEY TERMS

1 Use each of the following terms in a separate sentence: *element*, *compound*, and *mineral*.

For each pair of terms, explain how the meanings of the terms differ.

2 *color* and *streak*

3 *mineral* and *ore*

4 *silicate mineral* and *nonsilicate mineral*

UNDERSTANDING KEY IDEAS

Multiple Choice

5 Which of the following properties of minerals does Mohs scale measure?
  a. luster
  b. hardness
  c. density
  d. streak

6 Pure substances that cannot be broken down into simpler substances by ordinary chemical means are called
  a. molecules.
  b. elements.
  c. compounds.
  d. crystals.

7 Which of the following properties is considered a special property that applies to only a few minerals?
  a. luster
  b. hardness
  c. taste
  d. density

8 Silicate minerals contain a combination of the elements
  a. sulfur and oxygen.
  b. carbon and oxygen.
  c. iron and oxygen.
  d. silicon and oxygen.

9 The process by which land used for mining is returned to its original state is called
  a. recycling.
  b. regeneration.
  c. reclamation.
  d. renovation.

10 Which of the following minerals is an example of a gemstone?
  a. mica
  b. diamond
  c. gypsum
  d. copper

Short Answer

11 Compare surface and subsurface mining.

12 Explain the four characteristics of a mineral.

13 Describe two environments in which minerals form.

14 List two uses for metallic minerals and two uses for nonmetallic minerals.

15 Describe two ways to reduce the effects of mining.

16 Describe three special properties of minerals.

Understanding Key Ideas

  5. b
  6. b
  7. c
  8. d
  9. c
  10. b
  11. Surface mining is used to mine mineral deposits that are at or near the Earth's surface. Subsurface mining is used to mine mineral deposits that are too deep in the Earth to be surface mined.

  12. A mineral is inorganic, meaning its origin is not living things. A mineral is a solid, not a liquid or gas. A mineral is formed in nature and is not made by people. A mineral has a crystalline structure and has the same chemical structure throughout.

  13. Sample answer: Two environments in which minerals form are plutons, in which a magma body solidifies before it reaches the Earth's surface, and hot-water solutions, from which dissolved metals and other elements crystallize out of a hot fluid to form minerals.

CRITICAL THINKING

17. Concept Mapping Use the following terms to create a concept map: *minerals, calcite, silicate minerals, gypsum, carbonates, nonsilicate minerals, quartz,* and *sulfates*.

18. Making Inferences Imagine that you are trying to determine the identity of a mineral. You decide to do a streak test. You rub the mineral across the streak plate, but the mineral does not leave a streak. Has your test failed? Explain your answer.

19. Applying Concepts Why would cleavage be important to gem cutters, who cut and shape gemstones?

20. Applying Concepts Imagine that you work at a jeweler's shop and someone brings in some gold nuggets for sale. You are not sure if the nuggets are real gold. Which identification tests would help you decide whether the nuggets are gold?

21. Identifying Relationships Suppose you are in a desert. You are walking across the floor of a dry lake, and you see crusts of cubic halite crystals. How do you suppose the halite crystals formed? Explain your answer.

INTERPRETING GRAPHICS

The table below shows the temperatures at which various minerals melt. Use the table below to answer the questions that follow.

Melting Points of Various Minerals

Mineral	Melting Point (°C)
Mercury	−39
Sulfur	+113
Halite	801
Silver	961
Gold	1,062
Copper	1,083
Pyrite	1,171
Fluorite	1,360
Quartz	1,710
Zircon	2,500

22. According to the table, what is the approximate difference in temperature between the melting points of the mineral that has the lowest melting point and the mineral that has the highest melting point?

23. Which of the minerals listed in the table do you think is a liquid at room temperature?

24. Pyrite is often called *fool's gold*. Using the information in the table, how could you determine if a mineral sample is pyrite or gold?

25. Convert the melting points of the minerals shown in the table from degrees Celsius to degrees Fahrenheit. Use the formula °F = (9/5 × °C) + 32.

---

16. Sample answer: chemical reaction: some minerals, such as calcite, bubble when a drop of weak acid is placed on them; fluorescence: some minerals glow under ultraviolet light; radioactivity: minerals that contain radium or uranium can be detected by a Geiger counter

Critical Thinking

17. An answer to this exercise can be found at the end of this book.

18. No, the test was successful. I learned that the unknown mineral has no streak and that the mineral is harder than the streak plate. This clue will help me identify the mineral.

19. Sample answer: Gem cutters can cut along cleavage surfaces to shape gemstones. Gem cutters also want to avoid cutting across cleavage surfaces.

20. Students should suggest performing several tests to see whether the mineral is gold. Gold is very dense and soft, so one would start with density and hardness tests.

21. Sample answer: Because halite is salt (sodium chloride), the crusts of halite crystals formed when a body of salt water evaporated and left the halite behind.

Interpreting Graphics

22. The difference between the highest and lowest melting points is 2,539°C, the difference between the melting points of mercury and zircon. (2,500°C − −39°C = 2,539°C)

23. Mercury would be a liquid at room temperature because its melting point is −39°C.

24. Pyrite has a higher melting point than gold does (1,171°C > 1,062°C).

25. mercury: −38°F; sulfur: 235°F; halite: 1,474°F; silver: 1,762°F; gold: 1,944°F; copper: 1,981°F; pyrite: 2,140°F; fluorite: 2,480°F; quartz: 3,110°F; zircon: 4,532°F (Answers are rounded.)

---

14. Sample answer: Metallic minerals such as gold are used in the manufacture of computers and spacecraft. Nonmetallic minerals such as quartz are used to manufacture computer chips and glass.

15. Two ways to reduce the effects of mining are the reclamation of mined land and the recycling of mineral products.

CHAPTER RESOURCES

Chapter Resource File

- **Chapter Review** GENERAL
- **Chapter Test A** GENERAL
- **Chapter Test B** ADVANCED
- **Chapter Test C** SPECIAL NEEDS
- **Vocabulary Activity** GENERAL

Workbooks

Study Guide
- Assessment resources are also available in Spanish.

Standardized Test Preparation

Teacher's Note

To provide practice under more realistic testing conditions, give students 20 minutes to answer all of the questions in this Standardized Test Preparation.

MISCONCEPTION ALERT

Answers to the standardized test preparation can help you identify student misconceptions and misunderstandings.

READING

Passage 1

1. D

2. H

3. A

✚ TEST DOCTOR

Question 2: Answer H is correct. Because the ancient copper miners traded copper and these artifacts appear to be widespread across North America, answers F and I are incorrect. Rock was heated, not cooled, to make the copper easier to extract. Therefore, answer G is incorrect.

READING

Read each of the passages below. Then, answer the questions that follow each passage.

Passage 1 In North America, copper was mined at least 6,700 years ago by the ancestors of the Native Americans who live on Michigan's upper peninsula. Much of this mining took place on Isle Royale, an island in Lake Superior. These <u>ancient</u> people removed copper from the rock by using stone hammers and wedges. The rock was sometimes heated first to make breaking it up easier. Copper that was mined was used to make jewelry, tools, weapons, fish hooks, and other objects. These objects were often marked with designs. The Lake Superior copper was traded over long distances along ancient trade routes. Copper objects have been found in Ohio, Florida, the Southwest, and the Northwest.

1. In the passage, what does *ancient* mean?
  A young
  B future
  C modern
  D early

2. According to the passage, what did the ancient copper miners do?
  F They mined copper in Ohio, Florida, the Southwest, and the Northwest.
  G They mined copper by cooling the rock in which the copper was found.
  H They mined copper by using stone tools.
  I They mined copper for their use only.

3. Which of the following statements is a fact according to the passage?
  A Copper could be shaped into different objects.
  B Copper was unknown outside of Michigan's upper peninsula.
  C Copper could be mined easily from the rock in which it was found.
  D Copper could not be marked with designs.

Passage 2 Most mineral names end in *-ite*. The <u>practice</u> of so naming minerals dates back to the ancient Romans and Greeks, who added *-ites* and *-itis* to common words to indicate a color, a use, or the chemistry of a mineral. More recently, mineral names have been used to honor people, such as scientists, mineral collectors, and even rulers of countries. Other minerals have been named after the place where they were discovered. These place names include mines, quarries, hills, mountains, towns, regions, and even countries. Finally, some minerals have been named after gods in Greek, Roman, and Scandinavian mythology.

1. In the passage, what does *practice* mean?
  A skill
  B custom
  C profession
  D use

2. According to the passage, the ancient Greeks and Romans did not name minerals after what?
  F colors
  G chemical properties
  H people
  I uses

3. Which of the following statements is a fact according to the passage?
  A Minerals are sometimes named for the country in which they are discovered.
  B Minerals are never named after their collectors.
  C All mineral names end in *-ite*.
  D All of the known minerals were named by the Greeks and Romans.

Passage 2

1. B

2. H

3. A

✚ TEST DOCTOR

Question 3: Answer A is correct. Answer B is incorrect, because modern practice includes naming minerals after people. Because most, but not all, mineral names end in *-ite,* answer C is incorrect. Answer D is incorrect, because it is clear that the practice of naming minerals has continued since the time of the ancient Greeks and Romans.

A sample of feldspar was analyzed to find out what it was made of. The graph below shows the results of the analysis. Use the graph below to answer the questions that follow.

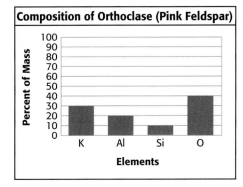

Composition of Orthoclase (Pink Feldspar)

1. The sample consists of four elements: potassium, K, aluminum, Al, silicon, Si, and oxygen, O. Which element makes up the largest percentage of your sample?

   A potassium
   B aluminum
   C silicon
   D oxygen

2. Silicate minerals, such as feldspar, contain a combination of silicon and oxygen. What percentage of your sample is composed of silicon and oxygen combined?

   F 30%
   G 40%
   H 50%
   I 70%

3. If your sample has a mass of 10 g, how many grams of oxygen does it contain?

   A 1 g
   B 2 g
   C 4 g
   D 8 g

4. Your sample of orthoclase has a hardness of 6. Which of the following minerals will scratch your sample?

   F gypsum
   G corundum
   H calcite
   I apatite

MATH

Read each question below, and choose the best answer.

1. Gold classified as 24-karat is 100% gold. Gold classified as 18-karat is 18 parts gold and 6 parts another, similar metal. The gold is therefore 18/24, or 3/4, pure. What is the percentage of pure gold in 18-karat gold?

   A 10%
   B 25%
   C 50%
   D 75%

2. Gold's specific gravity is 19. Pyrite's specific gravity is 5. What is the difference in the specific gravities of gold and pyrite?

   F 8 g/cm^3
   G 10 g/cm^3
   H 12 g/cm^3
   I 14 g/cm^3

3. In a quartz crystal, there is one silicon atom for every two oxygen atoms. So, the ratio of silicon atoms to oxygen atoms is 1:2. If there were 8 million oxygen atoms in a sample of quartz, how many silicon atoms would there be in the sample?

   A 2 million
   B 4 million
   C 8 million
   D 16 million

Standardized Test Preparation

1. D
2. H
3. C
4. G

TEST DOCTOR

Question 4: Answer G is correct. Corundum has a hardness of 7, which is greater than 6. Gypsum, calcite, and apatite all have hardnesses less than 6, so answers F, H, and I are incorrect.

MATH

1. D
2. I
3. B

TEST DOCTOR

Question 3: Answer B is correct. In the mineral quartz, the ratio of silicon atoms to oxygen atoms is 1:2. Therefore, there are twice as many oxygen atoms as silicon atoms in a sample of quartz. Inversely, there are half as many silicon atoms as oxygen atoms in a sample of quartz. If there are 8 million oxygen atoms in a sample of quartz, then there are half as many, or 4 million, silicon atoms in the sample. Students who misread the question and reverse the ratio of silicon atoms to oxygen atoms might incorrectly answer D.

Science in Action

Science Fiction

Background

Few people have had as long-lasting an impact on science fiction as Jack Williamson. This story, "The Metal Man," was first published in 1928—over 70 years ago! Although it was his very first short story, it is still a classic. Since then, Williamson has written dozens of science fiction novels, short-stories, other novels, and books about writing. The term *science fiction* did not exist when Williamson began writing. Known as one of the great pioneers of science fiction, Williamson was the first to write about antimatter. And, he coined the terms *terraform* (in 1941) and *genetic engineering* (in 1951). Williamson is also credited for making science fiction a field worthy of literary attention. For this accomplishment, Williamson has received several awards. In 1976, he became the second person to win the Grand Nebula Award. In 1994, he earned a lifetime achievement award from World Fantasy.

Science Fiction

"The Metal Man" by Jack Williamson

In a dark, dusty corner of Tyburn College Museum stands a life-sized statue of a man. Except for its strange greenish color, the statue looks quite ordinary. But if you look closely, you will see the perfect detail of the hair and skin. On the statue's chest, you will also see a strange mark—a dark crimson shape with six sides. No one knows how the statue ended up in the dark corner. But most people in Tyburn believe that the metal man is, or once was, Professor Thomas Kelvin of Tyburn College's geology department. Read for yourself the strange story of Professor Kelvin and the Metal Man, which is in the *Holt Anthology of Science Fiction.*

Language Arts ACTIVITY

WRITING SKILL Read "The Metal Man" by Jack Williamson. Write a short essay explaining how the ideas in the story are related to what you are learning.

Weird Science

Wieliczka Salt Mine

Imagine an underground city that is made entirely of salt. Within the city are churches, chapels, rooms of many kinds, and salt lakes. Sculptures of biblical scenes, saints, and famous historical figures carved from salt are found throughout the city. Even chandeliers of salt hang from the ceilings. Such a city is located 16 km southeast of Krakow, Poland, inside the Wieliczka (VEE uh LEETS kuh) Salt Mine. As the mine grew over the past 700 years, it turned into an elaborate underground city. Miners constructed chapels to patron saints so they could pray for a safe day in the mine. Miners also developed superstitions about the mine. So, images that were meant to bring good luck were carved in salt. In 1978, the mine was added to UNESCO's list of endangered world heritage sites. Many of the sculptures in the mine have begun to dissolve because of the humidity in the air. Efforts to save the treasures in the mine from further damage were begun in 1996.

Social Studies ACTIVITY

WRITING SKILL Research some aspect of the role of salt in human history. For example, subjects might include the Saharan and Tibetan salt trade or the use of salt as a form of money in ancient Poland. Report your findings in a one-page essay.

Answer to Language Arts Activity

Have students present short essays on "The Metal Man" in front of the class.

Answer to Social Studies Activity

Answers may vary.

People in Science

Jamie Hill

The Emerald Man Jamie Hill was raised in the Brushy Mountains of North Carolina. While growing up, Hill gained firsthand knowledge of the fabulous green crystals that could be found in the mountains. These green crystals were emeralds. Emerald is the green variety of the silicate mineral beryl and is a valuable gemstone. Emerald crystals form in pockets, or openings, in rock known as *pegmatite*.

Since 1985, Hill has been searching for pockets containing emeralds in rock near the small town of Hiddenite, North Carolina. He has been amazingly successful. Hill has discovered some spectacular emerald crystals. The largest of these crystals weighs 858 carats and is on display at the North Carolina Museum of Natural Science. Estimates of the total value of the emeralds that Hill has discovered so far are well in the millions of dollars. Hill's discoveries have made him a celebrity, and he has appeared both on national TV and in magazines.

Math ACTIVITY

An emerald discovered by Jamie Hill in 1999 was cut into a 7.85-carat stone that sold for $64,000 per carat. What was the total value of the cut stone?

Answer to Math Activity

$64,000 × 7.85 = $502,400

Weird Science

Background

On September 9, 1978, the Wieliczka Salt Mine was entered into UNESCO's 1st World List of Cultural and Natural Heritage. An important reason for the mine's inclusion in the list was the fact that the mine illustrates most of the stages of the development of mining technology over time. This developmental progression began in the Middle Ages, when salt was obtained from brine springs by the process of heating the brine and vaporizing the water. During the 14th and early 15th centuries, technological developments included the sinking of shafts and the use of pulley systems to transport salt to the surface. By the mid-15th century, horse gear was used to transport salt to the surface. In the 18th century, steam lifts began to be used for transporting salt. Similarly, the excavation of the salt progressed from the use of simple hand-tools to hand drills and then to pneumatic drills.

People in Science

Teaching Strategy— BASIC

Have students research minerals that can be found in the area in which they live. This information may be obtained from the United States Geological Survey or from a state entity, such as a state bureau of mines and geology. Have students put together a mineral list and, if possible, locations where specific minerals might be found.

If the option is practical, you may wish to lead the class on a rock hunt around the schoolyard. Have students discuss which minerals they think make up the rocks they found.

Rocks: Mineral Mixtures
Chapter Planning Guide

Compression guide:
To shorten instruction because of time limitations, omit the Chapter Lab.

OBJECTIVES	LABS, DEMONSTRATIONS, AND ACTIVITIES	TECHNOLOGY RESOURCES
PACING • 90 min pp. 26–35 **Chapter Opener**	SE **Start-up Activity**, p. 27 ◆ `GENERAL`	OSP **Parent Letter** ■ `GENERAL` CD **Student Edition on CD-ROM** CD **Guided Reading Audio CD** ■ TR **Chapter Starter Transparency*** VID **Brain Food Video Quiz**
Section 1 The Rock Cycle • Describe two ways rocks have been used by humans. • Describe four processes that shape Earth's features. • Describe how each type of rock changes into another type as it moves through the rock cycle. • List two characteristics of rock that are used to help classify it.	TE **Group Activity** Rates of Weathering, p. 29 `GENERAL` TE **Activity** Rock Dictionary, p. 31 `BASIC` TE **Connection Activity** Language Arts, p. 31 `BASIC` TE **Group Activity** Describing Rocks, p. 33 `BASIC` LB **Labs You Can Eat** Famous Rock Groups* ◆ `GENERAL` LB **Calculator-Based Labs** A Hot and Cool Lab ◆ `ADVANCED`	CRF **Lesson Plans*** TR **Bellringer Transparency*** TR The Rock Cycle* TR ***LINK TO LIFE SCIENCE*** The Water Cycle* CD **Science Tutor**
PACING • 45 min pp. 36–39 **Section 2 Igneous Rock** • Describe three ways that igneous rock forms. • Explain how the cooling rate of magma affects the texture of igneous rock. • Distinguish between igneous rock that cools within Earth's crust and igneous rock that cools at Earth's surface.	SE **Science in Action** Math, Social Studies, and Language Arts Activities, pp. 56–57 `GENERAL` SE **Skills Practice Lab** Crystal Growth, p. 182 ◆ `GENERAL`	CRF **Lesson Plans*** TR **Bellringer Transparency*** TR Intrusive Igneous Rock Bodies* SE **Internet Activity**, p. 38 `GENERAL` CD **Science Tutor**
PACING • 45 min pp. 40–43 **Section 3 Sedimentary Rock** • Describe the origin of sedimentary rock. • Describe the three main categories of sedimentary rock. • Describe three types of sedimentary structures.	TE **Demonstration** Dissolution of Minerals, p. 40 `GENERAL` SE **Connection to Language Arts** Salty Expressions, p. 41 `GENERAL` TE **Activity** Sedimentary Rock, p. 41 `BASIC` TE **Connection Activity** Real World, p. 42 `GENERAL` SE **Skills Practice Lab** Let's Get Sedimental, p. 50 ◆ `GENERAL` LB **Whiz-Bang Demonstrations** Settling Down* ◆ `BASIC`	CRF **Lesson Plans*** TR **Bellringer Transparency*** VID **Lab Videos for Earth Science** CD **Science Tutor**
PACING • 45 min pp. 44–49 **Section 4 Metamorphic Rock** • Describe two ways a rock can undergo metamorphism. • Explain how the mineral composition of rock changes as the rocks undergo metamorphism. • Describe the difference between foliated and nonfoliated metamorphic rock. • Explain how metamorphic rock structures are related to deformation.	TE **Activity** Modeling Metamorphism, p. 44 `GENERAL` SE **Quick Lab** Stretching Out, p. 45 `GENERAL` SE **School-to-Home Activity** Making a Rock Collection, p. 46 `GENERAL` TE **Connection Activity** Real World, p. 47 `ADVANCED` SE **Connection to Biology** Metamorphosis, p. 48 `GENERAL` SE **Model-Making Lab** Metamorphic Mash, p. 185 ◆ `GENERAL` LB **Long-Term Projects & Research Ideas** Home-Grown Crystals* `ADVANCED`	CRF **Lesson Plans*** TR **Bellringer Transparency*** TR Regional and Contact Metamorphism* CD **Interactive Explorations CD-ROM** "Rock On!"* `GENERAL` CD **Science Tutor**

PACING • 90 min

CHAPTER REVIEW, ASSESSMENT, AND STANDARDIZED TEST PREPARATION

CRF **Vocabulary Activity*** `GENERAL`
SE **Chapter Review**, pp. 52–53 `GENERAL`
CRF **Chapter Review*** ■ `GENERAL`
CRF **Chapter Tests A*** ■ `GENERAL`, **B*** `ADVANCED`, **C*** `SPECIAL NEEDS`
SE **Standardized Test Preparation**, pp. 54–55 `GENERAL`
CRF **Standardized Test Preparation*** `GENERAL`
CRF **Performance-Based Assessment*** `GENERAL`
OSP **Test Generator** `GENERAL`
CRF **Test Item Listing*** `GENERAL`

Online and Technology Resources

Visit **go.hrw.com** for a variety of free resources related to this textbook. Enter the keyword **HZ5RCK**.

Holt Online Learning

Students can access interactive problem-solving help and active visual concept development with the *Holt Science and Technology* Online Edition available at **www.hrw.com**.

 Guided Reading Audio CD Also in Spanish

A direct reading of each chapter for auditory learners, reluctant readers, and Spanish-speaking students.

 Science Tutor CD-ROM

Excellent for remediation and test practice.

SKILLS DEVELOPMENT RESOURCES	SECTION REVIEW AND ASSESSMENT	CORRELATIONS
SE **Pre-Reading Activity,** p. 26 `GENERAL` OSP **Science Puzzlers, Twisters & Teasers*** `GENERAL`		National Science Education Standards SAI 1, 2
CRF **Directed Reading A*** ■ `BASIC`, **B*** `SPECIAL NEEDS` CRF **Vocabulary and Section Summary*** ■ `GENERAL` SE **Reading Strategy** Reading Organizer, p. 28 `GENERAL` TE **Inclusion Strategies,** p. 30 ◆ SE **Math Practice** What's In It?, p. 33 `GENERAL` MS **Math Skills for Science** Parts of 100: Calculating Percentages* `GENERAL` CRF **SciLinks Activity,** The Rock Cycle* `GENERAL`	SE **Reading Checks,** pp. 28, 32, 33, 34 `GENERAL` TE **Homework,** p. 31 `GENERAL` TE **Reteaching,** p. 34 `BASIC` TE **Quiz,** p. 34 `GENERAL` TE **Alternative Assessment,** p. 34 `GENERAL` SE **Section Review,*** p. 35 ■ `GENERAL` CRF **Section Quiz*** ■ `GENERAL`	UCP 1; SAI 1, 2; ST 2; SPSP 5; HNS 1; ES 1c, 1d
CRF **Directed Reading A*** ■ `BASIC`, **B*** `SPECIAL NEEDS` CRF **Vocabulary and Section Summary*** ■ `GENERAL` SE **Reading Strategy** Reading Organizer, p. 36 `GENERAL`	SE **Reading Checks,** pp. 37, 39 `GENERAL` TE **Reteaching,** p. 38 `BASIC` TE **Quiz,** p. 38 `GENERAL` TE **Alternative Assessment,** p. 38 `GENERAL` TE **Homework,** p. 38 `ADVANCED` SE **Section Review,*** p. 39 ■ `GENERAL` CRF **Section Quiz*** ■ `GENERAL`	UCP 1, 2; SAI 1, 2; ES 1c, 1d; *LabBook:* SAI 1, 2
CRF **Directed Reading A*** ■ `BASIC`, **B*** `SPECIAL NEEDS` CRF **Vocabulary and Section Summary*** ■ `GENERAL` SE **Reading Strategy** Reading Organizer, p. 40 `GENERAL`	SE **Reading Checks,** pp. 41, 43 `GENERAL` TE **Reteaching,** p. 42 `BASIC` TE **Quiz,** p. 42 `GENERAL` TE **Alternative Assessment,** p. 42 `GENERAL` SE **Section Review,*** p. 43 ■ `GENERAL` CRF **Section Quiz*** ■ `GENERAL`	UCP 1, 2; SAI 1, 2; ES 1c, 1d, 1k, 2b; *Chapter Lab:* SAI 1, 2
CRF **Directed Reading A*** ■ `BASIC`, **B*** `SPECIAL NEEDS` CRF **Vocabulary and Section Summary*** ■ `GENERAL` SE **Reading Strategy** Discussion, p. 44 `GENERAL` TE **Inclusion Strategies,** p. 47 MS **Math Skills for Science** The Unit Factor and Dimensional Analysis* `GENERAL` CRF **Reinforcement Worksheet** What Is It?* `BASIC` CRF **Critical Thinking** Between a Rock and a Hard Place* `ADVANCED`	SE **Reading Checks,** pp. 45, 46, 49 `GENERAL` TE **Homework,** p. 46 `GENERAL` TE **Reteaching,** p. 48 `BASIC` TE **Quiz,** p. 48 `GENERAL` TE **Alternative Assessment,** p. 48 `GENERAL` TE **Homework,** p. 48 `ADVANCED` SE **Section Review,*** p. 49 ■ `GENERAL` CRF **Section Quiz*** ■ `GENERAL`	UCP 1, 2; SAI 1, 2; ES 1c; *LabBook:* SAI 1, 2

One-Stop Planner® CD-ROM

This CD-ROM package includes:
- Lab Materials QuickList Software
- Holt Calendar Planner
- Customizable Lesson Plans
- Printable Worksheets
- ExamView® Test Generator
- Interactive Teacher Edition
- Holt PuzzlePro® Resources
- Holt PowerPoint® Resources

SCILINKS.
NSTA

www.scilinks.org

Maintained by the **National Science Teachers Association.** See Chapter Enrichment pages for a complete list of topics.

Current Science®

Check out **Current Science** articles and activities by visiting the HRW Web site at **go.hrw.com.** Just type in the keyword **HZ5CS04T.**

Classroom Videos

- **Lab Videos** demonstrate the chapter lab.
- **Brain Food Video Quizzes** help students review the chapter material.
- **CNN Videos** bring science into your students' daily life.

Visual Resources

CHAPTER STARTER TRANSPARENCY

Rocks: Mineral Mixtures — CHAPTER STARTER

Imagine . . .

Imagine that you are an architect who has just been hired to design an amphitheater. The client wants the amphitheater to be big enough to host large concerts. In fact, she wants the amphitheater to seat an audience of 9,200. The client also wants excellent acoustics (sound qualities), and she wants it without a roof so the guests can enjoy the open air. She also wants the audience to be awed by two red sandstone formations that will tower 122 m above the stage.

You think about the design and come back with a plan that requires a minimum of 400 billion metric tons of red sandstone for the walls and floor. You also estimate that it will take about 12 million years to create. Sound ridiculous? Well, such an amphitheater actually exists.

Welcome to the Red Rocks Amphitheater just outside of Denver,

Colorado. As you can see, this amphitheater was created by the forces of nature rather than by human hands. The amphitheater is a perfect place for a rock concert, and it is also a good place to start thinking about rocks. For example, what exactly is a rock? And how are rocks important to the study of Earth science? You will be able to answer these questions as you read this chapter.

BELLRINGER TRANSPARENCIES

Rocks: Mineral Mixtures — BELLRINGER TRANSPARENCY

Section: The Rock Cycle

Many of us work hard to recycle the items we use in our daily lives to reduce the impact we have on the environment. In a way, the Earth also recycles through the rock cycle. Can you imagine what rock might look like through each stage of the rock cycle? How long do you think it takes to recycle a soda can? What about a piece of granite?

Record your thoughts in your **science journal**.

Section: Igneous Rock

Do you think rocks that cooled and solidified from lava on Earth's surface would look different from those that cooled and solidified from magma inside the Earth? To answer this question, ask yourself how the Hawaiian Islands differ from the Rocky Mountains.

Explain your answer in your **science journal**.

TEACHING TRANSPARENCIES

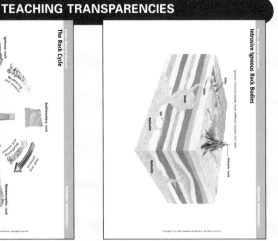

The Rock Cycle

Intrusive Igneous Rock Bodies

TEACHING TRANSPARENCIES

Regional and Contact Metamorphism

The Digestive System of a Bird

LINK TO LIFE SCIENCE

Chapter: Birds and Mammals

CONCEPT MAPPING TRANSPARENCY

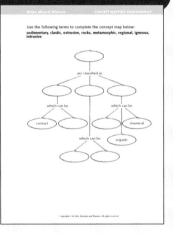

Use the following terms to complete the concept map below:
sedimentary, clastic, extrusive, rocks, metamorphic, regional, igneous, intrusive

Planning Resources

LESSON PLANS

Lesson Plan SAMPLE

Section: Waves

Pacing
Regular Schedule: with lab(s)2 days without lab(s)2 days
Block Schedule: with lab(s) 1 1/2 days without lab(s)1 day

Objectives
1. Relate the seven properties of life to a living organism.
2. Describe seven themes that can help you to organize what you learn about biology.
3. Identify the tiny structures that make up all living organisms.
4. Differentiate between reproduction and heredity and between metabolism and homeostasis.

National Science Education Standards Covered
LSInter6:Cells have particular structures that underlie their functions.
LSMat1:Most cell functions involve chemical reactions.
LSBeh1:Cells store and use information to guide their functions.
UCP1:Cell functions are regulated.
SI1: Cells can differentiate and form complete multicellular organisms.
PS1: Species evolve over time.
ESS1: The great diversity of organisms is the result of more than 3.5 billion years of evolution.
ESS2: Natural selection and its evolutionary consequences provide a scientific explanation for the fossil record of ancient life forms as well as for the striking molecular similarities observed among the diverse species of living organisms.
ST1: The millions of different species of plants, animals, and microorganisms that live on Earth today are related by descent from common ancestors.
ST2: The energy for life primarily comes from the sun.
SPSP5: The complexity and organization of organisms accommodates the need for obtaining, transforming, transporting, releasing, and eliminating the matter and energy used to sustain the organism.
SPSP6: As matter and energy flows through different levels of organization of living systems—cells, organs, communities—and between living systems and the physical environment, chemical elements are recombined in different ways.
HNS1: Organisms have behavioral responses to internal changes and to external stimuli.

PARENT LETTER

SAMPLE

Dear Parent,

Your son's or daughter's science class will soon begin exploring the chapter entitled "The World of Physical Science." In this chapter, students will learn about how the scientific method applies to the world of physical science and the role of physical science in the world. By the end of the chapter, students should demonstrate a clear understanding of the chapter's main ideas and be able to discuss the following topics:

1. physical science is the study of energy and matter (Section 1)
2. the role of physical science in the world around them (Section 1)
3. careers that rely on physical science (Section 1)
4. the steps used in the scientific method (Section 2)
5. examples of technology (Section 2)
6. how the scientific method is used to answer questions and solve problems (Section 2)
7. how our knowledge of science changes over time (Section 2)
8. how models represent real objects or systems (Section 3)
9. examples of different ways models are used in science (Section 3)
10. the importance of the International System of Units (Section 4)
11. the appropriate units to use for particular measurements (Section 4)
12. how area and density are derived quantities (Section 4)

Questions to Ask Along the Way

You can help your son or daughter learn about these topics by asking interesting questions such as the following:

• What are some surprising careers that use physical science?
• What is a characteristic of a good hypothesis?
• When is it a good idea to use a model?
• Why do Americans measure things in terms of inches and yards and meters?

ALSO IN SPANISH

TEST ITEM LISTING

TEST ITEM LISTING
The World of Earth Science SAMPLE

MULTIPLE CHOICE

1. A limitation of models is that
   a. they are large enough to see.
   b. they do not act exactly like the things that they model.
   c. they are smaller than the things that they model.
   d. they model unfamiliar things.
   Answer: B   Difficulty: 1   Section: 3   Objective: 2

2. The length 10 m is equal to
   a. 100 cm.   c. 10,000 mm.
   b. 1,000 cm.   d. Both (b) and (c)
   Answer: B   Difficulty: 1   Section: 3   Objective: 2

3. To be valid, a hypothesis must be
   a. testable   c. made into a law
   b. supported by evidence   d. Both (a) and (b)
   Answer: D   Difficulty: 1   Section: 2   Objective: 2 1

4. The statement "Sheila has a stain on her shirt" is an example of a(n)
   a. law   c. observation
   b. hypothesis.   d. prediction
   Answer: B   Difficulty: 1   Section: 3   Objective: 2

5. How many milliliters are in 3.5 kL?
   a. 3,500 mL   c. 3,500,000 mL
   b. 0.0035 mL   d. 35,000 mL
   Answer: C   Difficulty: 1   Section: 3   Objective: 2

7. A map of Seattle is an example of a
   a. law   c. model
   b. theory   d. unit
   Answer: C   Difficulty: 1   Section: 3   Objective: 2

8. A lab has the safety icons shown below. These icons mean that you should wear
   a. only safety goggles   c. safety goggles and a lab apron
   b. only a lab apron   d. safety goggles, a lab apron, and gloves
   Answer: B   Difficulty: 1   Section: 5   Objective: 3

9. The law of conservation of mass says that total mass before a chemical change is
   a. more than the total mass after the change
   b. less than the total mass after the change
   c. the same as the total mass after the change
   d. not the same as the total mass after the change
   Answer: C   Difficulty: 1   Section: 3   Objective: 2

10. In which of the following areas might you find a geochemist at work?
    a. studying the chemistry of rocks   c. studying lakes
    b. studying forests   d. studying the atmosphere
    Answer: A   Difficulty: 1   Section: 3   Objective: 2

One-Stop Planner® CD-ROM

This CD-ROM includes all of the resources shown here and the following time-saving tools:

• *Lab Materials QuickList Software*
• *Customizable lesson plans*
• *Holt Calendar Planner*
• *The powerful ExamView® Test Generator*

Meeting Individual Needs

DIRECTED READING A

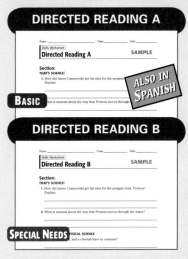

Skills Worksheet
Directed Reading A SAMPLE

Section:
THAT'S SCIENCE!

1. How did James Czarnowski get his idea for the penguin boat? Explain.

ALSO IN SPANISH

BASIC

2. What is unusual about the way that Proteus moves through

DIRECTED READING B

Skills Worksheet
Directed Reading B SAMPLE

Section:
THAT'S SCIENCE!

1. How did James Czarnowski get his idea for the penguin boat, Proteus? Explain.

2. What is unusual about the way that Proteus moves through the water?

SPECIAL NEEDS PHYSICAL SCIENCE

3. and a cheetah have in common?

VOCABULARY ACTIVITY

Activity
Vocabulary Activity SAMPLE

Getting the Dirt on the Soil

After you finish reading Chapter: [Unique Title], try this puzzle! Use the clues below to unscramble the vocabulary words. Write your answer in the spaces provided.

breakdowns of rock into ... smaller pieces:
NGNETH

layers of rock lying beneath soil:

5. the chemical breakdowns of rocks and minerals into new substances: CAMILCHE THEAIRGWEN

GENERAL

VOCABULARY AND SECTION SUMMARY

Skills Worksheet
Vocabulary & Notes SAMPLE

Section:
VOCABULARY

In your own words, write a definition of the following term in the space provided.

1. scientific method

2. technology

ALSO IN SPANISH

GENERAL

REINFORCEMENT

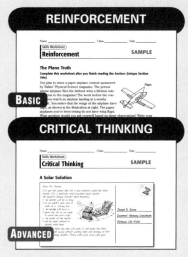

Skills Worksheet
Reinforcement SAMPLE

The Plane Truth

Complete this worksheet after you finish reading the Section: [Unique Section Title]

You plan to enter a paper airplane contest sponsored by Talkin' Physical Science magazine. The person whose airplane flies the farthest wins a lifetime subscription to the magazine! The week before the contest, you watch as the wings of the airplane have flaps, as shown in the illustration at right. The paper airplanes you've been testing do not have wing flaps.

What question would you ask yourself based on these observations? Write your

BASIC

CRITICAL THINKING

Skills Worksheet
Critical Thinking SAMPLE

A Solar Solution

[handwritten letter illustration]

ADVANCED

SCILINKS ACTIVITY

Activity
SciLinks Activity SAMPLE

MARINE ECOSYSTEMS

Go to www.scilinks.org. To find links related to marine ecosystems, type in the keyword HI 5450. Then, use the links to answer the questions about marine ecosystems.

Topic: Reproductive System
SciLinks code: HL5450

percentage of the Earth's surface is covered by water?

GENERAL

SCIENCE PUZZLERS, TWISTERS & TEASERS

CHAPTER
4 SCIENCE PUZZLERS, TWISTERS & TEASERS
Rocks: Mineral Mixtures

Cooking up Classifications

You've entered your geological kitchen. Now you are ready to whip up some recipes involving rocks. Along with the more "usual" ingredients, your cupboards hold the following: calcite, quartz, and feldspar. Decide which recipes you have the proper ingredients for. If you can't make something, explain why not.

Can you make

a. Limestone pie?

b. Granite casserole?

GENERAL cookies?

Labs and Activities

LONG-TERM PROJECTS & RESEARCH IDEAS

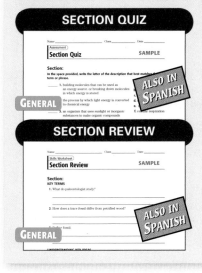

Name _____ Date _____ Class _____
PROJECT
32 STUDENT WORKSHEET DESIGN YOUR OWN
Home-Grown Crystals

Peter Rogue: Hello, and welcome to this week's edition of *In Your Garden*. Today we're interviewing that world-famous gardener Ms. Mary Contrary. So, Mary, how does your garden grow?

Mary: My garden grows best with table salt, ammonia, charcoal . . .

Peter Rogue: Wait a minute! What kind of flowers are you growing?

Mary: Flowers? I'm not growing flowers. I'm growing a crystal garden. With the right procedure, my household ingredients will become a beautiful stack of crystals. I can even change their appearance by changing their growing environment!

MATERIALS
- tray
- 2 small, disposable plastic or plastic foam bowls
- 150 g of charcoal
- 5 mL liquid bluing
- water
- table salt
- ammonia
- laundry bluing
- food coloring (3 different colors)
- dishwashing gloves

Grow Your Own Crystal Garden

1. Use the materials listed at left, and follow the steps below to make a colorful crystal garden. Document your crystal growth with daily sketches or photos.

Day 1: Put on the dishwashing gloves. Put all the charcoal in one bowl. Sprinkle 15 mL of water, 15 mL of salt, and 15 mL of laundry bluing over the charcoal. Do not stir.

Add several drops of food coloring to this mixture. Do not stir. Leave the bowl overnight in a place where it will remain undisturbed.

Day 2: Sprinkle 15 mL of salt over the mixture.

Day 3: In the second bowl, mix a solution of 15 mL each of salt, laundry bluing, water, and ammonia. Pour the solution around, not over, the charcoal in the first bowl.

Check the progress of your crystals daily. When crystal formation slows, repeat the step for Day 3. You may repeat this step as many times as you wish to create more crystals.

Consider the following questions:
- How do your crystals differ from naturally formed crystals?
- Can you make the crystals grow faster? How?
- How does the growing surface affect crystal growth?
- Can you get the crystals to grow in different angles?
Make a poster display of your findings. Be sure to include your photos or sketches.

EARTH SCIENCE

ADVANCED

WHIZ-BANG DEMONSTRATIONS

DEMO
17 TEACHER-LED DEMONSTRATION MAKING MODELS
Settling Down

Purpose
Students learn about the formation of sedimentary rocks.

Time Required
5–10 minutes

Lab Ratings

MATERIALS

2. Fill the beaker approximately halfway with water. Add a mixture of sand, pebbles, and soil to the water.

3. Stir vigorously, and then let the mixture stand until the particles settle.

Discussion
- Ask students to describe what happened. (The particles in the mixture settled in layers, or became stratified, with the largest particles at the bottom of the beaker.)
- Ask students to explain how this demonstration simulates a river. (As a river flows, it picks up and transports sediments. The heaviest particles settle to the bottom of the

BASIC

LABS YOU CAN EAT

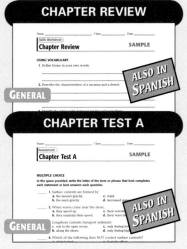

Name _____ Date _____ Class _____
LAB
11 STUDENT WORKSHEET MAKING MODELS
Famous Rock Groups

When is a rock a liquid? When it melts, of course! But melting is just one part of the rock cycle.

A rock can follow many paths in the rock cycle. For example, a molten rock cools and hardens to form igneous rock. Mechanical weathering or erosion can later break the rock down into tiny particles. These particles build up in layers to form sedimentary rock. As the layers accumulate, their weight adds pressure to compress the rock below to create metamorphic rock. When the temperature and pressure become great enough, the metamorphic rock melts. The cycle can then continue on the same pathway or a completely different

activity, you will get a chance to make a tasty ... one pathway through the rock cycle.

MATERIALS Objective

GENERAL

CALCULATOR-BASED LABS

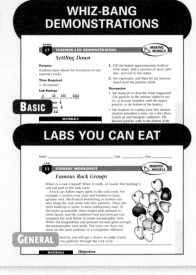

Name _____ Date _____ Class _____
LAB
2 STUDENT WORKSHEET DISCOVERY LAB
A Hot and Cool Lab

GRADE 6

When you add energy to a substance through heating, does the substance's temperature always go up? When you remove energy from a substance through cooling, does the substance's temperature always go down? In this lab, you'll investigate these important questions with a very common substance—water.

Part A: Boiling Water
Make a Prediction

1. What happens to the temperature of boiling water when you continue to add energy through heating?

Procedure

2. Fill the beaker about one-third to one-half full with water.

3. Put on heat-resistant gloves. Turn on the hot plate, and put the beaker on the burner.

Caution: Use extreme care when working near a hot plate. Do not touch the hot plate even when it is turned off. It could still be very hot.

4. Set up the calculator and LabPro or CBL 2 for data collection with the temperature probe by completing the following steps.

a. Plug the temperature probe into channel 1 (CH 1) of the LabPro or CBL 2 interface. Connect the graphing calculator by plugging the black link cable into the base of the temperature probe and LabPro or CBL 2 interface. Firmly press in the cable ends.

b. Turn on the graphing calculator, and start the DataMate program. Press ENTER to reset the program. If the calculator displays a temperature probe in CH 1, proceed directly to step 5. If it does not, continue with this step to set up your sensor manually.

c. Select SETUP from the main screen.

d. Press ▶ to select CH 1.

e. Select TEMPERATURE from the SELECT SENSOR menu. Select the temperature probe you are using (in degrees Celsius) from the TEMPERATURE menu.

f. Select OK to return to the main screen.

MATERIALS
Part A
- 250 mL or 400 mL beaker
- water
- heat-resistant gloves
- hot plate
- LabPro or CBL 2 interface
- TI graphing calculator
- DataMate program
- black calculator link cable
- temperature probe
Part B
- 10 mL graduated cylinder
- water
- large coffee can
- crushed ice
- rock salt
- wire-loop stirring device
- LabPro or CBL 2 interface
- TI graphing calculator
- DataMate program
- black calculator link cable
- temperature probe

ADVANCED

DATASHEETS FOR QUICK LABS

TEACHER RESOURCE PAGE
Quick Lab
Reaction to Stress DATASHEET FOR QUICK LAB SAMPLE

Background
The graph below illustrates changes that occur in the membrane potential of a neuron during an action potential. Use the graph to answer the following questions. Refer to Figure 3 on page

DATASHEETS FOR CHAPTER LABS

TEACHER RESOURCE PAGE
Skills Practice Lab
Using Scientific Methods DATASHEET FOR CHAPTER LAB SAMPLE

Teacher's Notes
TIME REQUIRED
One 45-minute class period.

DATASHEETS FOR LABBOOK

TEACHER RESOURCE PAGE
Skills Practice Lab
Does It All Add Up? DATASHEET FOR LABBOOK LAB SAMPLE

Teacher's Notes
TIME REQUIRED
One 45-minute class period.

Review and Assessments

SECTION QUIZ

Assessment
Section Quiz SAMPLE

Section:
In the space provided, write the letter of the description that best matches the term or phrase.

_____ 1. building molecules that can be used as an energy source or breaking down molecules in which energy is stored

_____ 2. the process by which light energy is converted to chemical energy

_____ 3. an organism that uses sunlight or inorganic substances to make organic compounds

ALSO IN SPANISH

a. cellular respiration

GENERAL

SECTION REVIEW

Skills Worksheet
Section Review SAMPLE

Section:
KEY TERMS

1. What do paleontologist study?

2. How does a trace fossil differ from petrified wood?

3. fossil

ALSO IN SPANISH

GENERAL UNDERSTANDING KEY IDEAS

CHAPTER REVIEW

Skills Worksheet
Chapter Review SAMPLE

USING VOCABULARY

1. Define biome in your own words.

2. Describe the characteristics of a savanna and a desert.

3. Identify the relationship between tundra and permafrost

ALSO IN SPANISH

GENERAL

CHAPTER TEST A

Assessment
Chapter Test A SAMPLE

MULTIPLE CHOICE

In the space provided, write the letter of the term or phrase that best completes each statement or best answers each question.

_____ 1. Surface currents are formed by
a. the moon's gravity.   c. wind.
b. the sun's gravity.   d. increased water density.

_____ 2. When waves come near the shore,
a. they speed up.   c. their wavelength increases.
b. they maintain their speed.   d. their wave height increases.

Longshore currents transport sediment
3. out to the open ocean.   c. only during low tide.
along the shore.   d. only during high tide.

4. Which of the following does NOT control surface currents?

ALSO IN SPANISH

GENERAL

CHAPTER TEST B

Assessment
Chapter Test B SAMPLE

MULTIPLE CHOICE

In the space provided, write the letter of the term or phrase that best completes each statement or best answers each question.

_____ 1. Surface currents are formed by
a. the moon's gravity.   c. wind.
b. the sun's gravity.   d. increased water density.

When waves come near the shore,
a. they speed up.   c. their wavelength increases.
b. they maintain their speed.   d. their wave height increases.

ADVANCED

CHAPTER TEST C

Assessment
Chapter Test C SAMPLE

MULTIPLE CHOICE

In the space provided, write the letter of the term or phrase that best completes each statement or best answers each question.

_____ 1. Surface currents are formed by
a. the moon's gravity.   c. wind.
b. the sun's gravity.   d. increased water density.

_____ 2. When waves come near the shore,
a. they speed up.   c. their wavelength increases.
b. they maintain their speed.   d. their wave height increases.

currents transport sediment
open ocean.   c. only during low tide.
shore.   d. only during high tide.

Which of the following does NOT control surface currents?

SPECIAL NEEDS

STANDARDIZED TEST PREPARATION

Assessment
Standardized Test Preparation SAMPLE

READING
Read the passages below. Then, read each question that follows the passage. Decide which is the best answer to each question.

Passage 1 adventurous summer camp in the world. Billy was ready for the outdoors. Billy checked the recommended supply list: light, summer clothes, sunscreen, rain gear, heavy, snow-filled jacket, ski mask; and thick gloves. Wait a minute! Billy thought he was traveling to only one destination, so why does he need to bring such a wide variety of clothes? On further investiga-

GENERAL

PERFORMANCE-BASED ASSESSMENT

Assessment
Performance-Based Assessment SKILL BUILDER SAMPLE

OBJECTIVE
Determine which factors cause some sugar shapes to break down faster than others.

KNOW THE SCORE!
As you work through the activity, keep in mind that you will be earning a grade for the following:
- how you form and test the hypothesis (30%)
- the clarity of your analysis (40%)
- the clarity of your conclusions (30%)

Using Scientific Methods
QUESTIONS

MATERIALS AND EQUIPMENT
- 1 regular sugar cube   • 90 mL of water

GENERAL

This Chapter Enrichment provides relevant and interesting information to expand and enhance your presentation of the chapter material.

Section 1

The Rock Cycle

Rock Composition

- This chapter focuses on the mineral composition of rock, not its bulk composition. These are two very different means of measuring rock composition.

- The *mineral composition* of a rock refers to the proportions of the different minerals in the rock and is usually expressed in percentages by volume. Even coal, a sedimentary rock made of organic matter, contains clay minerals or pyrite.

- The *bulk composition* of a rock is the sum of the different elements that make up the rock and is usually expressed in percentages by weight. Mineral composition is affected by bulk composition.

Is That a Fact!

- ◆ Although rocks contain many elements, the rocks in Earth's crust are nearly 94% oxygen by number of atoms.

- ◆ Approximately 92% of the Earth's crust is igneous and metamorphic rock.

- ◆ Although sedimentary rock makes up about 8% of the Earth's crust, it is spread thinly over much of the planet's surface. Sedimentary rock covers 75% of the Earth's continental surfaces!

Section 2

Igneous Rock

The Great Dike of Zimbabwe

- Dikes can range in width from a few millimeters to many kilometers. The Great Dike of Zimbabwe, in Africa, is the largest known dike on Earth. It has an average width of 6 to 8 km and extends for almost 500 km across Zimbabwe.

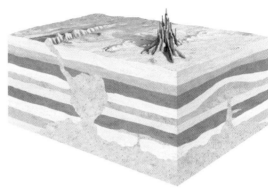

Pumice

- Some magmas contain dissolved gases, such as carbon dioxide. When these gases come out of magma in the form of small bubbles, the magma greatly increases its volume, causing an enormous buildup of pressure. This can result in an explosive volcanic eruption. The result can be a frothy-looking rock called *pumice*. Pumice is full of small holes, called *vesicles,* where the trapped gases used to be. Depending on how much space is taken up by vesicles, some types of pumice can float in water!

Is That a Fact!

- ◆ Igneous rocks that form deep underground are called plutonic rocks, after Pluto, the god of the underworld in Roman mythology. Volcanic rocks are named after Vulcan, the Roman god of metalworking and fire.

- ◆ Although many people think of lava as a thin and runny liquid, lava flows are often quite viscous. Usually, the temperature has cooled enough for crystals to begin forming, which can give lava a consistency similar to that of thick oatmeal.

Section 3

Sedimentary Rock

Working with Clay

- Clay is composed primarily of silicate minerals. Clays are easy to work with when they are wet because the tiny plate-shaped silicate crystals are surrounded by water molecules. As the water evaporates, the silicates are cemented into place, and the clay becomes brittle and difficult to work with.

Is That a Fact!

- ◆ Bentonite, a form of clay composed of very fine silicate crystals, has a wide variety of industrial applications. Some forms of bentonite can expand as much as 300% when mixed with water. Bentonite is used to make cat litter, to line artificial ponds, to remove impurities from wines and juices, to treat wastewater, and in a variety of applications for oil drilling.

Section 4

Metamorphic Rock

Metamorphosis in a Lab

- Geologists can estimate the temperature and pressure that metamorphosed a rock by simulating the process of metamorphosis in a laboratory. When geologists know the chemical composition of certain minerals within a rock, they can subject a similar compound to a range of temperatures and pressures. By observing the laboratory results, they can make predictions about how similar materials behave in metamorphic environments. Geologists can determine the temperature at which metamorphism occurred within 20°C and the pressure within a fraction of a kilobar.

Carrara Marble

- In the mountains around Carrara, Italy, a marble prized for its purity and beauty has been quarried for at least 2,000 years. Its whiteness is due to the lack of organic materials in the limestone from which it recrystallized. Carrara marble was used in the interior of the Pantheon, in Rome. It is also found in the Leaning Tower of Pisa, in the pavement of Saint Peter's Basilica, in Vatican City, and in the Kennedy Center, in Washington, D.C.

Is That a Fact!

- ◆ Metamorphic rocks are a challenge to study because they form within a wide range of temperature and pressure. Scientists must distinguish between the geologic history of the metamorphic rock and the history of the igneous, sedimentary, or previously metamorphosed rocks it formed from. For the same reason, however, metamorphic rocks offer many important clues about tectonic activity in the Earth's past.

- ◆ Metamorphism occurs quickly at high temperatures, but it also occurs at temperatures that are surprisingly low. For example, clay minerals in mudstone and shale can begin to metamorphose at temperatures as low as 50°C! This reaction, however, takes many millions of years to occur.

 NSTA
Developed and maintained by the National Science Teachers Association

SciLinks is maintained by the National Science Teachers Association to provide you and your students with interesting, up-to-date links that will enrich your classroom presentation of the chapter.

Visit www.scilinks.org and enter the SciLinks code for more information about the topic listed.

Topic: Composition of Rock
SciLinks code: HSM0327

Topic: Igneous Rock
SciLinks code: HSM0783

Topic: Sedimentary Rock
SciLinks code: HSM1365

Topic: Metamorphic Rock
SciLinks code: HSM0949

Overview

Tell students that this chapter will teach them about the rock cycle. They will learn about igneous, sedimentary, and metamorphic rocks. Students will find out how each rock type is formed and how each rock type is classified.

Assessing Prior Knowledge

Students should be familiar with the following topics:

• mineral environments

Identifying Misconceptions

Students may not realize that rock, like other substances on Earth, is part of a cycle. Within this cycle, a variety of geological processes act on rock to change and ultimately recycle it. These processes occur on the Earth's surface, in the shallow subsurface, or deep within the Earth and may be continuous or occur in a series of steps. The time in which processes act to change or recycle rock often happen over millions or tens of millions of years.

Rocks: Mineral Mixtures

About the PHOTO

Irish legend claims that the mythical hero Finn MacCool built the Giant's Causeway, shown here. But this rock formation is the result of the cooling of huge amounts of molten rock. As the molten rock cooled, it formed tall pillars separated by cracks called *columnar joints*.

PRE-READING ACTIVITY

Graphic Organizer

Spider Map Before you read the chapter, create the graphic organizer entitled "Spider Map" described in the **Study Skills** section of the Appendix. Label the circle "Rock." Create a leg for each of the sections in this chapter. As you read the chapter, fill in the map with details about the material presented in each section of the chapter.

Standards Correlations

National Science Education Standards

The following codes indicate the National Science Education Standards that correlate to this chapter. The full text of the standards is at the front of the book.

Chapter Opener
SAI 1, 2

Section 1 The Rock Cycle
ES 1c, 1d; HNS 1; SAI 1, 2; SPSP 5; ST 2; UCP 1

Section 2 Igneous Rock
ES 1c, 1d; SAI 1, 2; UCP 1, 2; LabBook: SAI 1, 2

Section 3 Sedimentary Rock
ES 1c, 1d, 1k, 2b; SAI 1, 2: UCP 1, 2

Section 4 Metamorphic Rock
ES 1c; SAI 1, 2; UCP 1, 2; LabBook: SAI 1, 2

Chapter Lab
SAI 1, 2

Chapter Review
ES 1c, 1d, 2b; HNS 1; SAI 1, 2; SPSP 5; ST 2; UCP 1, 2

Science in Action
ES 1c, 2a; HNS 1, 2, 3; SAI 1, 2; SPSP 3, 5; ST 2

Answers

1. Answers may vary. Sample answer: I sorted the objects by color, size, and composition.

2. Answers may vary. Sample answer: Yes, there were objects that could fit into more than one group. I solved this problem by deciding which characteristics were more important and then sorting the object into a corresponding group.

3. Answers may vary. Accept all reasonable responses. Students may mention color, texture, composition, and hardness.

START-UP ACTIVITY

Classifying Objects

Scientists use the physical and chemical properties of rocks to classify rocks. Classifying objects such as rocks requires looking at many properties. Do this exercise for some classification practice.

Procedure

1. Your teacher will give you a **bag** containing **several objects.** Examine the objects, and note features such as size, color, shape, texture, smell, and any unique properties.

2. Develop three different ways to sort these objects.

3. Create a chart that organizes objects by properties.

Analysis

1. What properties did you use to sort the items?

2. Were there any objects that could fit into more than one group? How did you solve this problem?

3. Which properties might you use to classify rocks? Explain your answer.

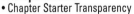
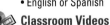

Chapter Starter Transparency
Use this transparency to help students begin thinking about the importance of rock to human societies.

CHAPTER RESOURCES

Technology

Transparencies
- Chapter Starter Transparency

READING SKILLS

Student Edition on CD-ROM

Guided Reading Audio CD
- English or Spanish

Classroom Videos
- Brain Food Video Quiz

Workbooks

Science Puzzlers, Twisters & Teasers
- Rocks: Mineral Mixtures GENERAL

Focus

Overview

This section introduces the rock cycle and the processes that shape the surface of the Earth. The processes of weathering, erosion, deposition, uplift, melting, cooling, and metamorphism are explained, in the context of the rock cycle.

Bellringer

Pose the following questions to students:

• How can rock be recycled?

• How long would recycling a rock take?

• What would the rock look like before, during, and after the process of recycling?

Motivate

Discussion —— GENERAL

Geologic Time Some students may not realize how long changes in the rock cycle take. The processes that shape rock can take millions to tens of millions of years. Discuss the geologic time scale with students to give them a perspective of how long the Earth has existed and how long these processes have been affecting the Earth.

LS Logical

The Rock Cycle

You know that paper, plastic, and aluminum can be recycled. But did you know that the Earth also recycles? And one of the things that Earth recycles is rock.

Scientists define **rock** as a naturally occurring solid mixture of one or more minerals and organic matter. It may be hard to believe, but rocks are always changing. The continual process by which new rock forms from old rock material is called the **rock cycle.**

The Value of Rock

Rock has been an important natural resource as long as humans have existed. Early humans used rocks as hammers to make other tools. They discovered that they could make arrowheads, spear points, knives, and scrapers by carefully shaping rocks such as chert and obsidian.

Rock has also been used for centuries to make buildings, monuments, and roads. **Figure 1** shows how rock has been used as a construction material by both ancient and modern civilizations. Buildings have been made out of granite, limestone, marble, sandstone, slate, and other rocks. Modern buildings also contain concrete and plaster, in which rock is an important ingredient.

✓ Reading Check Name some types of rock that have been used to construct buildings. (*See the Appendix for answers to Reading Checks.*)

Figure 1 *The ancient Egyptians used a sedimentary rock called limestone to construct the pyramids at Giza (left). Granite, an igneous rock, was used to construct the Texas state capitol building in Austin (right).*

CHAPTER RESOURCES

Chapter Resource File

 • Lesson Plan
• Directed Reading A **BASIC**
• Directed Reading B **SPECIAL NEEDS**

Technology

 Transparencies
• Bellringer

Answer to Reading Check

Types of rock that have been used by humans to construct buildings include granite, limestone, marble, sandstone, and slate.

Processes That Shape the Earth

Certain geological processes make and destroy rock. These processes shape the features of our planet. These processes also influence the type of rock that is found in a certain area of Earth's surface.

Weathering, Erosion, and Deposition

The process in which water, wind, ice, and heat break down rock is called *weathering*. Weathering is important because it breaks down rock into fragments. These rock and mineral fragments are the sediment of which much sedimentary rock is made.

The process by which sediment is removed from its source is called **erosion.** Water, wind, ice, and gravity can erode and move sediments and cause them to collect. **Figure 2** shows an example of the way land looks after weathering and erosion.

The process in which sediment moved by erosion is dropped and comes to rest is called **deposition.** Sediment is deposited in bodies of water and other low-lying areas. In those places, sediment may be pressed and cemented together by minerals dissolved in water to form sedimentary rock.

Heat and Pressure

Sedimentary rock made of sediment can also form when buried sediment is squeezed by the weight of overlying layers of sediment. If the temperature and pressure are high enough at the bottom of the sediment, the rock can change into metamorphic rock. In some cases, the rock gets hot enough to melt. This melting creates the magma that eventually cools to form igneous rock.

How the Cycle Continues

Buried rock is exposed at the Earth's surface by a combination of uplift and erosion. *Uplift* is movement within the Earth that causes rocks inside the Earth to be moved to the Earth's surface. When uplifted rock reaches the Earth's surface, weathering, erosion, and deposition begin.

rock a naturally occurring solid mixture of one or more minerals or organic matter

rock cycle the series of processes in which a rock forms, changes from one type to another, is destroyed, and forms again by geological processes

erosion the process by which wind, water, ice, or gravity transports soil and sediment from one location to another

deposition the process in which material is laid down

Figure 2 *Bryce Canyon, in Utah, is an excellent example of how the processes of weathering and erosion shape the face of our planet.*

Using the Figure—GENERAL

Diagramming the Rock Cycle Ask students to use the information in the rock-cycle illustration to draw a diagram of the rock cycle in their **science journal.** The first step in the illustration is the formation of sedimentary rock; ask students to begin their rock cycle with a different step. Encourage them to write a descriptive caption for every stage of the rock cycle. **LS Visual**

MISCONCEPTION ///ALERT\\\

Rock Cycle Misconceptions
Rocks rarely undergo the complete process shown in the rock-cycle diagram. Sedimentary rocks can become igneous rocks, and metamorphic rocks can become sedimentary rocks. Also, some students may not realize the length of time it takes for changes to occur in the rock cycle. The process shown in the diagram can take millions to tens of millions of years.

Illustrating the Rock Cycle

You have learned about various geological processes, such as weathering, erosion, heat, and pressure, that create and destroy rock. The diagram on these two pages illustrates one way that sand grains can change as different geological processes act on them. In the following steps, you will see how these processes change the original sand grains into sedimentary rock, metamorphic rock, and igneous rock.

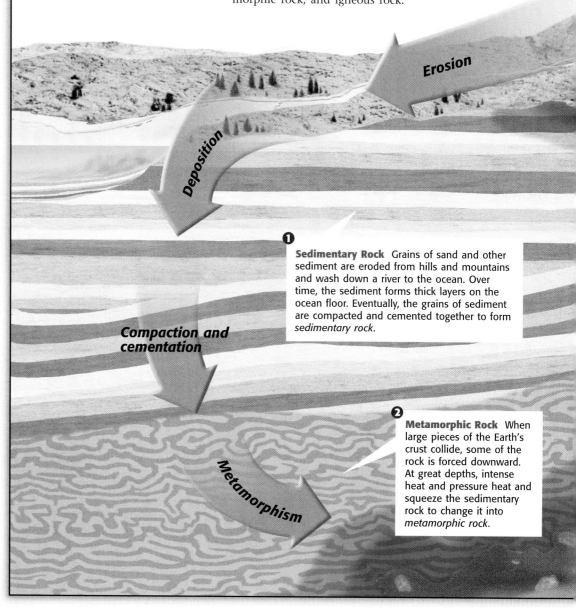

Erosion

Deposition

Compaction and cementation

Metamorphism

❶ Sedimentary Rock Grains of sand and other sediment are eroded from hills and mountains and wash down a river to the ocean. Over time, the sediment forms thick layers on the ocean floor. Eventually, the grains of sediment are compacted and cemented together to form *sedimentary rock*.

❷ Metamorphic Rock When large pieces of the Earth's crust collide, some of the rock is forced downward. At great depths, intense heat and pressure heat and squeeze the sedimentary rock to change it into *metamorphic rock*.

INCLUSION Strategies

- *Learning Disabled*
- *Attention Deficit Disorder*
- *Hearing Impaired*

Groups will use different foods to model sedimentary, metamorphic, and igneous rocks and minerals. Have real rock samples available (enough for each group). Organize students into groups of three or four students. Give students a chocolate-chip cookie to model granite (igneous), a sugar cube to model marble (metamorphic), a brownie to model shale (sedimentary), a magnifying glass, a large sheet of paper, and magic markers. Ask students to describe and sketch their three samples. To describe each sample, students should note the sample's texture, color, and composition. On the board, compile descriptions for each "rock" from each group. Pass real rock samples to each group, and have the groups match their samples to the real rocks. **LS Visual**

English Language Learners

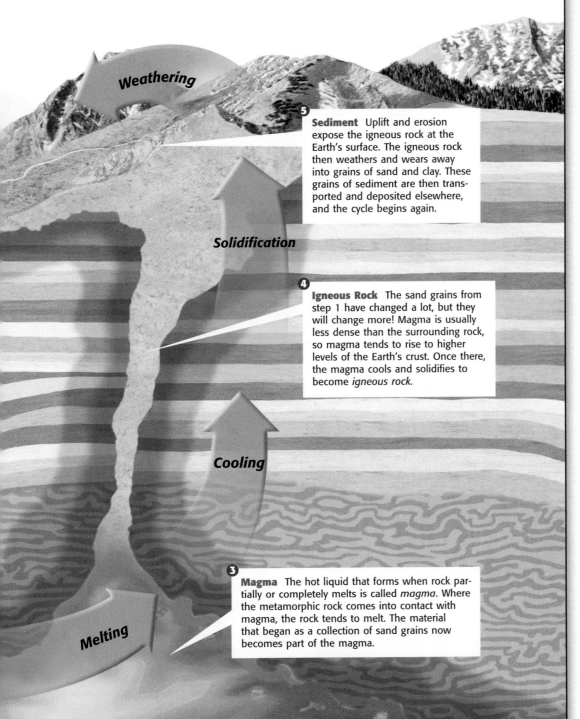

Weathering

Sediment Uplift and erosion expose the igneous rock at the Earth's surface. The igneous rock then weathers and wears away into grains of sand and clay. These grains of sediment are then transported and deposited elsewhere, and the cycle begins again. **5**

Solidification

Igneous Rock The sand grains from step 1 have changed a lot, but they will change more! Magma is usually less dense than the surrounding rock, so magma tends to rise to higher levels of the Earth's crust. Once there, the magma cools and solidifies to become *igneous rock*. **4**

Cooling

Magma The hot liquid that forms when rock partially or completely melts is called *magma*. Where the metamorphic rock comes into contact with magma, the rock tends to melt. The material that began as a collection of sand grains now becomes part of the magma. **3**

Melting

Is That a Fact!

Geologists can use the Earth's magnetic field to determine the approximate age of rocks. They examine both igneous and sedimentary rocks to determine the pattern of magnetic reversals. When these rocks form, the magnetic minerals they contain orient with the direction of the Earth's magnetic field. The pattern of magnetic reversals allows scientists to date the rock layers.

Teach, continued

Cultural Awareness GENERAL

Avicenna The Persian scholar Avicenna (980–1037) contributed immensely to our knowledge of medicine, astronomy, mathematics, and geology. In the *Book of Minerals,* he described how rivers and seas laid down sediment that eventually became rock. Avicenna's theories contributed to the foundations of Western geology. Many of his controversial ideas did not gain acceptance in Europe until the 1600s. Encourage students to learn more about Avicenna. Have them come to class as Avicenna and act out his life story. **LS** Logical

CONNECTION to Environmental Science — ADVANCED

Cycles in Nature Many important substances on Earth follow cycles. Examples include water, carbon, and rock. Use the teaching transparency entitled "The Water Cycle" to lead a discussion about the ways that the water cycle and the rock cycle interact with each other. **LS** Visual

---

Figure 3 The Rock Cycle

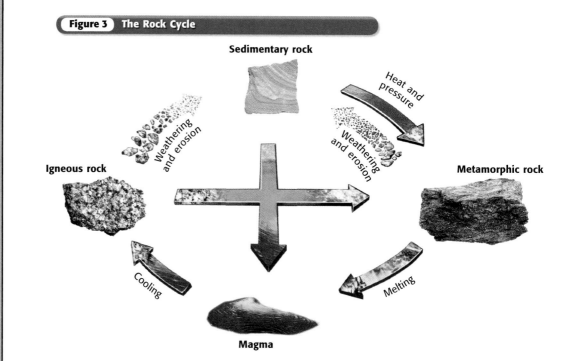

Round and Round It Goes

You have seen how different geological processes can change rock. Each rock type can change into one of the three types of rock. For example, igneous rock can change into sedimentary rock, metamorphic rock, or even back into igneous rock. This cycle, in which rock is changed by geological processes into different types of rock, is known as the rock cycle.

Rocks may follow various pathways in the rock cycle. As one rock type is changed to another type, several variables, including time, heat, pressure, weathering, and erosion may alter a rock's identity. The location of a rock determines which natural forces will have the biggest impact on the process of change. For example, rock at the Earth's surface is primarily affected by forces of weathering and erosion, whereas deep inside the Earth, rocks change because of extreme heat and pressure. **Figure 3** shows the different ways rock may change when it goes through the rock cycle and the different forces that affect rock during the cycle.

Reading Check What processes change rock deep within the Earth?

CHAPTER RESOURCES

Technology

Transparencies
• *LINK TO LIFE SCIENCE* The Water Cycle

Workbooks

Math Skills for Science
• Percentages GENERAL

Answer to Reading Check
Rock within the Earth is affected by temperature and pressure.

Rock Classification

You have already learned that scientists divide all rock into three main classes based on how the rock formed: igneous, sedimentary, and metamorphic. But did you know that each class of rock can be divided further? These divisions are also based on differences in the way rocks form. For example, all igneous rock forms when magma cools and solidifies. But some igneous rocks form when magma cools *on* the Earth's surface, and others form when magma cools *beneath* the surface. Therefore, igneous rock can be divided again based on how and where it forms. Sedimentary and metamorphic rocks are also divided into groups. How do scientists know how to classify rocks? They study rocks in detail using two important criteria—composition and texture.

Composition

The minerals a rock contains determine the **composition** of that rock, as shown in **Figure 4**. For example, a rock made of mostly the mineral quartz will have a composition very similar to that of quartz. But a rock made of 50% quartz and 50% feldspar will have a very different composition than quartz does.

Reading Check What determines a rock's composition?

composition the chemical makeup of a rock; describes either the minerals or other materials in the rock

The composition of a rock depends on the minerals the rock contains.

Limestone — 95% Calcite, 5% Aragonite

Granite — 10% Biotite mica, 35% Quartz, 55% Feldspar

MATH PRACTICE

What's in It?

Assume that a granite sample you are studying is made of 30% quartz and 55% feldspar by volume. The rest is made of biotite mica. What percentage of the sample is biotite mica?

Answer to Math Practice

100% of rock − (30% quartz + 55% feldspar) = 15% biotite mica

Group ACTIVITY — BASIC

Describing Rocks Organize the class into small groups. Give each group samples of sandstone, limestone, and conglomerate. Number the samples. Provide a magnifying lens, a mineral identification key, a small dental pick, and paper towels (to capture any pieces of rock that break off during the activity). Write the following instructions on the board:

1. Describe the color and texture of each rock.

2. Using your unaided eye, examine the grains that make up each rock. Describe what you see.

3. Using the magnifying lens, try to identify the mineral composition of each rock.

4. Use the dental pick to test how well each rock is cemented, and record what you discover.

5. Classify each rock by grain size as fine grained, medium grained, or coarse grained.

After groups have analyzed the rocks, have group members discuss their findings. **English Language Learners**
LS Logical/Kinesthetic

CONNECTION to Math — GENERAL

Percentages A percentage is a ratio that is expressed in terms of hundredths. When analyzing pure substances, percentage composition remains the same at any mass. For example, in terms of atomic mass, the percentage of oxygen by weight in water is 88.8%, whether you are describing a single raindrop or an entire ocean. **LS Logical**

Answer to Reading Check

The minerals that a rock contains determine a rock's composition.

Diagramming the Rock Cycle
Have students create a diagram of the processes that shape Earth's surface. The diagram should be a simplified version of the rock cycle. The diagram should include the processes of weathering, erosion, deposition, and uplift. **LS** Visual

Quiz — GENERAL

1. List four processes that change rock from one type to another. (weathering, changes in pressure, melting, and cooling)

2. What are the three main classes of rock? (igneous, sedimentary, and metamorphic)

3. How is a brick similar to a metamorphic rock? (Bricks are made from clay and then baked to become strong and resistant to weathering. Bricks are "metamorphosed" by high temperatures.)

Alternative Assessment — GENERAL

Rock Cycle Skit Have students write a skit portraying the rock cycle. Roles can include the minerals that make up rock and the forces that affect them. To represent the forces—heat, pressure, erosion, and weathering—suggest that students create special costumes. **LS** Kinesthetic

Figure 5 Three Examples of Sedimentary Rock Texture

Fine-grained

Siltstone

Medium-grained

Sandstone

Coarse-grained

Conglomerate

texture the quality of a rock that is based on the sizes, shapes, and positions of the rock's grains

Texture

The size, shape, and positions of the grains that make up a rock determine a rock's **texture**. Sedimentary rock can have a fine-grained, medium-grained, or coarse-grained texture, depending on the size of the grains that make up the rock. Three samples of textures are shown in **Figure 5**. The texture of igneous rock can be fine-grained or coarse-grained, depending on how much time magma has to cool. Based on the degree of temperature and pressure a rock is exposed to, metamorphic rock can also have a fine-grained or coarse-grained texture.

The texture of a rock can provide clues as to how and where the rock formed. Look at the rocks shown in **Figure 6**. The rocks look different because they formed in very different ways. The texture of a rock can reveal the process that formed it.

Reading Check Give three examples of sedimentary rock textures.

Figure 6 Texture and Rock Formation

Basalt, a fine-grained igneous rock, forms when lava that erupts onto Earth's surface cools rapidly.

Sandstone, a medium-grained sedimentary rock, forms when sand grains deposited in dunes, on beaches, or on the ocean floor are buried and cemented.

Answer to Reading Check
Fine-grained rocks are made of small grains, such as silt or clay particles. Medium-grained rocks are made of medium-sized grains, such as sand. Coarse-grained rocks are made of large grains, such as pebbles.

Summary

- Rock has been an important natural resource for as long as humans have existed. Early humans used rock to make tools. Ancient and modern civilizations have used rock as a construction material.

- Weathering, erosion, deposition, and uplift are all processes that shape the surface features of the Earth.

- The rock cycle is the continual process by which new rock forms from old rock material.

- The sequence of events in the rock cycle depends on processes, such as weathering, erosion, deposition, pressure, and heat, that change the rock material.

- Composition and texture are two characteristics that scientists use to classify rocks.

- The composition of a rock is determined by the minerals that make up the rock.

- The texture of a rock is determined by the size, shape, and positions of the grains that make up the rock.

Using Key Terms

Complete each of the following sentences by choosing the correct term from the word bank.

rock	composition
rock cycle	texture

1. The minerals that a rock is made of determine the ___ of that rock.

2. ___ is a naturally occurring, solid mixture of crystals of one or more minerals.

Understanding Key Ideas

3. Sediments are transported or moved from their original source by a process called
   a. deposition.
   b. erosion.
   c. uplift.
   d. weathering.

4. Describe two ways that rocks have been used by humans.

5. Name four processes that change rock inside the Earth.

6. Describe four processes that shape Earth's surface.

7. Give an example of how texture can provide clues as to how and where a rock formed.

Critical Thinking

8. **Making Comparisons** Explain the difference between texture and composition.

9. **Analyzing Processes** Explain how rock is continually recycled in the rock cycle.

Interpreting Graphics

10. Look at the table below. Sandstone is a type of sedimentary rock. If you had a sample of sandstone that had an average particle size of 2 mm, what texture would your sandstone have?

Classification of Clastic Sedimentary Rocks	
Texture	**Particle size**
coarse grained	> 2 mm
medium grained	0.06 to 2 mm
fine grained	< 0.06 mm

For a variety of links related to this chapter, go to www.scilinks.org

Topic: Composition of Rock
SciLinks code: HSM0327

CHAPTER RESOURCES

Chapter Resource File

- Section Quiz GENERAL
- Section Review GENERAL
- Vocabulary and Section Summary GENERAL

Answers to Section Review

1. composition

2. Rock

3. b

4. Rocks have been used by humans to make tools and weapons and to construct buildings.

5. Four processes that change rock inside the Earth are compaction and cementation, metamorphism, melting, and cooling.

6. Weathering is the process by which water, wind, ice, and heat break down rock. Erosion is the process by which sediment is removed from its source. Deposition is the process by which sediment moved by erosion is laid down. Uplift is the process by which rock within the Earth moves to Earth's surface.

7. Answers may vary. Sample answer: Fine grains in an igneous rock indicate that the rock cooled quickly, which means it was likely to have formed at Earth's surface.

8. Composition is the percent of elements that make up a rock. Texture is a quality of a rock that is based on the size, shape, and position of its grains.

9. Answers may vary. Sample answer: Rock is continually recycled by different processes in the rock cycle. Melting of sedimentary, metamorphic, or igneous rock creates new igneous rock. The weathering, erosion, deposition, burial, compression, and cementation of igneous, metamorphic, or sedimentary rock creates new sedimentary rock. Igneous, sedimentary, or metamorphic rock that is subjected to increased heat and pressure can be metamorphosed.

10. a medium-grained texture

Overview

This section discusses the formation of igneous rock from the cooling of magma. Students learn about the difference between intrusive and extrusive igneous rock. Students also learn about the difference between felsic and mafic igneous rock and how the rate of cooling affects the texture of igneous rock.

🎙️ Bellringer

Pose the following question to students: "Do you think rocks that cooled and solidified from lava on Earth's surface would look different from those that cooled and solidified from magma inside the Earth? Why?"

Discussion ——— GENERAL

Volcanoes Ask students to discuss how volcanoes affect people. Discuss eruptions, lava flows, and ash clouds. Then, ask students about the benefits of volcanoes. Explain that lava and magma form land. Explain that volcanic soil is some of the most fertile soil in the world, which is why many populations are willing to live alongside potentially dangerous volcanoes. **LS Logical**

Igneous Rock

Where do igneous rocks come from? Here's a hint: The word igneous *comes from a Latin word that means "fire."*

Igneous rock forms when hot, liquid rock, or *magma*, cools and solidifies. The type of igneous rock that forms depends on the composition of the magma and the amount of time it takes the magma to cool.

Origins of Igneous Rock

Igneous rock begins as magma. As shown in **Figure 1,** there are three ways magma can form: when rock is heated, when pressure is released, or when rock changes composition.

When magma cools enough, it solidifies to form igneous rock. Magma solidifies in much the same way that water freezes. But there are also differences between the way magma freezes and the way water freezes. One main difference is that water freezes at 0°C. Magma freezes between 700°C and 1,250°C. Also, liquid magma is a complex mixture containing many melted minerals. Because these minerals have different melting points, some minerals in the magma will freeze or become solid before other minerals do.

Figure 1 The Formation of Magma

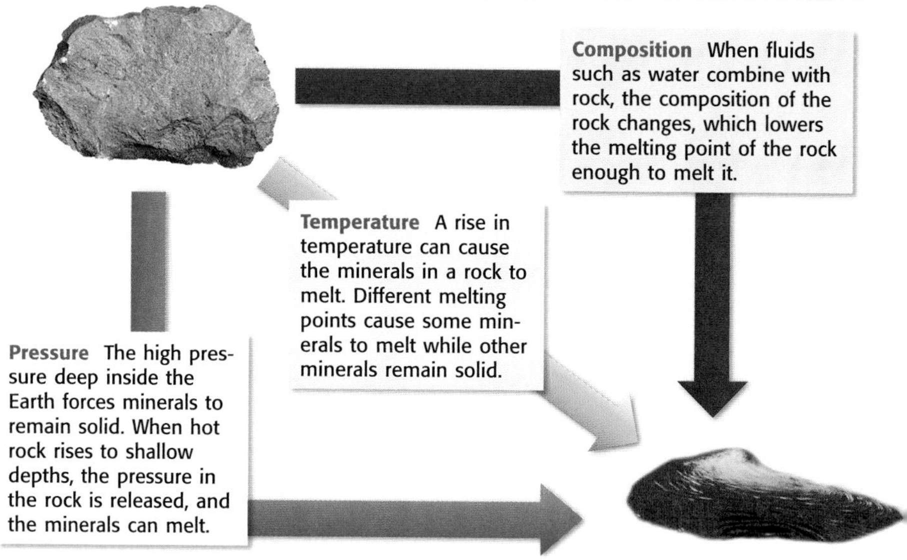

Composition When fluids such as water combine with rock, the composition of the rock changes, which lowers the melting point of the rock enough to melt it.

Temperature A rise in temperature can cause the minerals in a rock to melt. Different melting points cause some minerals to melt while other minerals remain solid.

Pressure The high pressure deep inside the Earth forces minerals to remain solid. When hot rock rises to shallow depths, the pressure in the rock is released, and the minerals can melt.

⚛️ WEIRD SCIENCE

Surtsey is a volcanic island south of Iceland that people actually saw being born! In 1963, fishermen saw jets of spray, steam, and lava shooting more than 30 m out of the ocean. One month later, the volcano broke through the surface to form an island. By the time the eruptions ended, Surtsey covered an area of approximately 2.8 km².

Figure 2 Igneous Rock Texture

	Coarse-grained	Fine-grained
Felsic	Granite	Rhyolite
Mafic	Gabbro	Basalt

Composition and Texture of Igneous Rock

Look at the rocks in **Figure 2.** All of the rocks are igneous rocks even though they look different from one another. These rocks differ from one another in what they are made of and how fast they cooled.

The light-colored rocks are less dense than the dark-colored rocks are. The light-colored rocks are rich in elements such as aluminum, potassium, silicon, and sodium. These rocks are called *felsic rocks.* The dark-colored rocks, called *mafic rocks,* are rich in calcium, iron, and magnesium, and poor in silicon.

Figure 3 shows what happens to magma when it cools at different rates. The longer it takes for the magma or lava to cool, the more time mineral crystals have to grow. The more time the crystals have to grow, the larger the crystals are and the coarser the texture of the resulting igneous rock is.

In contrast, the less time magma takes to cool, the less time crystals have to grow. Therefore, the rock that is formed will be fine grained. Fine-grained igneous rock contains very small crystals, or if the cooling is very rapid, it contains no crystals.

Reading Check Explain the difference between felsic rock and mafic rock. (*See the Appendix for answers to Reading Checks.*)

Figure 3 *The amount of time it takes for magma or lava to cool determines the texture of igneous rock.*

Fast-cooling lava

Fine-grained igneous rock

Magma

Slow-cooling magma

Coarse-grained igneous rock

Answer to Reading Check

Felsic rocks are light-colored igneous rocks rich in aluminum, potassium, silicon, and sodium. Mafic rocks are dark-colored igneous rocks rich in calcium, iron, and magnesium.

Teach

Using the Figure — BASIC

Making Inferences Have students rank the rocks shown in **Figure 2** by how fast they cooled. Tell students to pay careful attention to the grain size of each rock. (From fastest cooled to slowest cooled, the rocks are basalt, rhyolite, gabbro, and granite.) **LS** Visual/Logical

CONNECTION to Life Science — ADVANCED

Life Along a Rift Until 1977, biologists thought few life-forms lived at ocean depths where sunlight does not reach. When scientists in the submersible *Alvin* explored the bottom of a deep ocean trench called the Galápagos Rift, they discovered structures called black smokers that release dissolved mineral compounds and heat the water. Scientists were amazed to discover an entire ecosystem that did not depend on photosynthesis for energy. This discovery has led some scientists to speculate that life may also have originated in the outer solar system—particularly in the oceans that may exist under the surface of Europa, one of Jupiter's moons. Have students research the bizarre life-forms that scientists found living around black smokers. **LS** Logical

Is That a Fact!

The Deccan Traps of India Between 68 and 64 million years ago, a hot spot under western India erupted over 1 million km^3 of basaltic lava. These lava flows, called the Deccan Traps, are more than 2 km thick in some places. Mathematicians calculate that if the lava from the eruptions in western India were spread evenly over the entire Earth, it would cover the Earth with a layer more than 2 m thick!

INTERNET ACTIVITY

For another activity related to this chapter, go to **go.hrw.com** and type in the keyword **HZ5RCKW.**

intrusive igneous rock rock formed from the cooling and solidification of magma beneath the Earth's surface

Figure 4 *Igneous intrusive bodies have different shapes and sizes.*

Igneous Rock Formations

Igneous rock formations are located above and below the surface of the Earth. You may be familiar with igneous rock formations that were caused by lava cooling on the Earth's surface, such as volcanoes. But not all magma reaches the surface. Some magma cools and solidifies deep within the Earth's crust.

Intrusive Igneous Rock

When magma *intrudes,* or pushes, into surrounding rock below the Earth's surface and cools, the rock that forms is called **intrusive igneous rock.** Intrusive igneous rock usually has a coarse-grained texture because it is well insulated by surrounding rock and cools very slowly. The minerals that form are large, visible crystals.

Masses of intrusive igneous rock are named for their size and shape. Common intrusive shapes are shown in **Figure 4.** *Plutons* are large, irregular-shaped intrusive bodies. The largest of all igneous intrusions are *batholiths.* *Stocks* are intrusive bodies that are exposed over smaller areas than batholiths. Sheetlike intrusions that cut across previous rock units are called *dikes,* whereas *sills* are sheetlike intrusions that are oriented parallel to previous rock units.

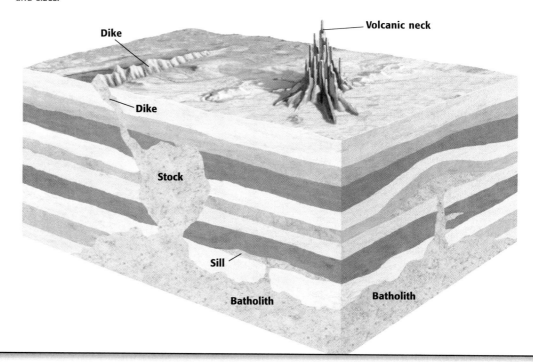

Dike, Dike, Volcanic neck, Stock, Sill, Batholith, Batholith

Extrusive Igneous Rock

Igneous rock that forms from magma that erupts, or extrudes, onto the Earth's surface is called **extrusive igneous rock.** Extrusive rock is common around volcanoes. It cools quickly on the surface and contains very small crystals or no crystals.

When lava erupts from a volcano, a *lava flow* forms. **Figure 5** shows an active lava flow. Lava does not always flow from volcanoes. Sometimes lava erupts and flows from long cracks in the Earth's crust called *fissures*. Lava flows from fissures on the ocean floor at places where tension is causing the ocean floor to be pulled apart. This lava cools to form new ocean floor. When a large amount of lava flows out of fissures onto land, the lava can cover a large area and form a plain called a *lava plateau*. Pre-existing landforms are often buried by these lava flows.

Reading Check How does new ocean floor form?

Figure 5 *An active lava flow is shown in this photo. When exposed to Earth's surface conditions, lava quickly cools and solidifies to form a fine-grained igneous rock.*

extrusive igneous rock rock that forms as a result of volcanic activity at or near the Earth's surface

---

SECTION Review

Summary

- Igneous rock forms when magma cools and hardens.
- The texture of igneous rock is determined by the rate at which the rock cools.
- Igneous rock that solidifies at Earth's surface is extrusive. Igneous rock that solidifies within Earth's surface is intrusive.
- Shapes of common igneous intrusive bodies include batholiths, stocks, sills, and dikes.

Using Key Terms

1. In your own words, write a definition for each of the following terms: *intrusive igneous rock* and *extrusive igneous rock*.

Understanding Key Ideas

2. ___ is an example of a coarse-grained, felsic, igneous rock.
   a. Basalt
   b. Gabbro
   c. Granite
   d. Rhyolite

3. Explain three ways in which magma can form.

4. What determines the texture of igneous rocks?

Math Skills

5. The summit of a granite batholith has an elevation of 1,825 ft. What is the height of the batholith in meters?

Critical Thinking

6. **Making Comparisons** Dikes and sills are both types of igneous intrusive bodies. What is the difference between a dike and a sill?

7. **Predicting Consequences** An igneous rock forms from slow-cooling magma deep beneath the surface of the Earth. What type of texture is this rock most likely to have? Explain.

Answer to Reading Check

New sea floor forms when lava that flows from fissures on the ocean floor cools and hardens.

Focus

Overview

This section explores how sedimentary rock forms and how it accumulates in layers, or strata. Students distinguish between clastic, chemical, and organic sedimentary rocks and learn how each rock type forms.

Bellringer

Ask students to write about how layers in sedimentary rock are like the rings in a tree. How are they different? What information can geologists infer by examining sedimentary layers?

Motivate

Demonstration —— GENERAL

Dissolution of Minerals Limestone forms when calcium carbonate crystallizes out of ocean water. Students may not believe that water contains the chemical components of dissolved minerals. If you live in an area with hard water, have students observe ice melting in warm water. After the ice melts, there is a layer of fluffy calcium carbonate that forms at the bottom of the glass. If you live in an area with soft water, make hard water by dissolving a little baking soda and calcium chloride in water. Then, freeze the water into ice cubes. Use these ice cubes for the demonstration. **Visual**

READING WARM-UP

Objectives

- Describe the origin of sedimentary rock.
- Describe the three main categories of sedimentary rock.
- Describe three types of sedimentary structures.

Terms to Learn

strata
stratification

READING STRATEGY

Reading Organizer As you read this section, create an outline of this section. Use the headings from the section in your outline.

Figure 1 *The red sandstone "monuments" for which Monument Valley in Arizona has been named are the products of millions of years of erosion.*

Sedimentary Rock

Have you ever tried to build a sand castle at the beach? Did you ever wonder where the sand came from?

Sand is a product of weathering, which breaks rock into pieces. Over time, sand grains may be compacted, or compressed, and then cemented together to form a rock called *sandstone*. Sandstone is just one of many types of sedimentary rock.

Origins of Sedimentary Rock

Wind, water, ice, sunlight, and gravity all cause rock to physically weather into fragments. Through the process of erosion, these rock and mineral fragments, called *sediment*, are moved from one place to another. Eventually, the sediment is deposited in layers. As new layers of sediment are deposited, they cover older layers. Older layers become compacted. Dissolved minerals, such as calcite and quartz, separate from water that passes through the sediment to form a natural cement that binds the rock and mineral fragments together into sedimentary rock.

Sedimentary rock forms at or near the Earth's surface. It forms without the heat and pressure that are involved in the formation of igneous and metamorphic rocks.

The most noticeable feature of sedimentary rock is its layers, or **strata**. A single, horizontal layer of rock is sometimes visible for many miles. Road cuts are good places to observe strata. **Figure 1** shows the spectacular views that sedimentary rock formations carved by erosion can provide.

CHAPTER RESOURCES

Chapter Resource File

- Lesson Plan
- Directed Reading A **BASIC**
- Directed Reading B **SPECIAL NEEDS**

Technology

- Transparencies
  - Bellringer

WEIRD SCIENCE

The Bonneville Salt Flats, in Utah, are the remnants of a vast lake called Lake Bonneville. After the last ice age, most of the lake drained quickly, but much of the remaining water slowly evaporated, which left behind the salt flats. The Great Salt Lake is the largest of the lakes left after Lake Bonneville evaporated.

Figure 2 Classification of Clastic Sedimentary Rock

Conglomerate Sandstone Siltstone Shale

Coarse grained ◄————————————————► Fine grained

Composition of Sedimentary Rock

Sedimentary rock is classified by the way it forms. *Clastic sedimentary rock* forms when rock or mineral fragments, called *clasts*, are cemented together. *Chemical sedimentary rock* forms when minerals crystallize out of a solution, such as sea water, to become rock. *Organic sedimentary rock* forms from the remains of once-living plants and animals.

Clastic Sedimentary Rock

Clastic sedimentary rock is made of fragments of rocks cemented together by a mineral such as calcite or quartz. **Figure 2** shows how clastic sedimentary rock is classified according to the size of the fragments from which the rock is made. Clastic sedimentary rocks can have coarse-grained, medium-grained, or fine-grained textures.

Chemical Sedimentary Rock

Chemical sedimentary rock forms from solutions of dissolved minerals and water. As rainwater slowly makes its way to the ocean, it dissolves some of the rock material it passes through. Some of this dissolved material eventually crystallizes and forms the minerals that make up chemical sedimentary rock. Halite, one type of chemical sedimentary rock, is made of sodium chloride, NaCl, or table salt. Halite forms when sodium ions and chlorine ions in shallow bodies of water become so concentrated that halite crystallizes from solution.

✔ **Reading Check** How does a chemical sedimentary rock such as halite form? (*See the Appendix for answers to Reading Checks.*)

strata layers of rock (singular, *stratum*)

CONNECTION TO Language Arts

WRITING SKILL **Salty Expressions** The word salt is used in many expressions in the English language. Some common examples include "the salt of the earth," "taken with a grain of salt," not worth his salt," "the salt of truth," "rubbing salt into a wound," and "old salt." Use the Internet or another source to research one these expressions. In your research, attempt to find the origin of the expression. Write a short paragraph that summarizes what you found.

Answer to Reading Check

Halite forms when sodium ions and chlorine ions in shallow bodies of water become so concentrated that halite crystallizes from solution.

ACTIVITY ——— BASIC

writing **Sedimentary Rock** Organize students into three groups to investigate sandstone, shale, and limestone. The first group should work together to learn how the rocks form. The second group should investigate how the rocks are used in industry, architecture, or the arts. The third group should investigate rock formations that have become tourist attractions. Members of each group should prepare exhibits, posters, or models to demonstrate what they have learned. **LS** Logical/Visual Co-op Learning

CONNECTION to Life Science ——— BASIC

Calcium Carbonate Critters Calcium carbonate is an important compound for many different animals. Many mollusks remove calcium and carbonate from sea water and combine them in special tissues that then harden to form a calcium carbonate shell. When the mollusk dies, its shell either dissolves back into the water or becomes part of the sediment on the bottom of the ocean. If the shell is part of deposited sediment, it may become a fossil. Have students research a fossil locality in their state (for example, the Mazon Creek deposits, in Illinois) to learn more about fossils. **LS** Logical

Creating a Diagram Have students select one of the three types of sedimentary rock. Ask students to create a diagram that illustrates all of the processes that occur in the formation of the rock type they have selected. **LS Visual**

Quiz — GENERAL

1. How does halite form? (It forms when sodium ions and chlorine ions become so concentrated in ocean water that halite crystallizes out of the water.)

2. What is stratification, and why is it important to Earth scientists? (Stratification is the layering of rock. It is important because it records many events in Earth's history, as well as erosion and deposition rates.)

Alternative Assessment — GENERAL

Depositional Environments
To review sedimentary rock formation, have students draw a picture of an environment that shows where the sediments come from and where they are deposited. A second drawing should show what the environment might look like millions of years later after sedimentary rock has formed. **LS Visual**

Figure 3 Ocean animals called coral *create huge deposits of limestone. As they die, their skeletons collect on the ocean floor.*

Organic Sedimentary Rock

Most limestone forms from the remains, or *fossils*, of animals that once lived in the ocean. For example, some limestone is made of the skeletons of tiny organisms called *coral*. Coral are very small, but they live in huge colonies called *reefs*, shown in **Figure 3**. Over time, the skeletons of these sea animals, which are made of calcium carbonate, collect on the ocean floor. These animal remains eventually become cemented together to form *fossiliferous limestone* (FAH suhl IF uhr uhs LIEM STOHN).

Corals are not the only animals whose remains are found in fossiliferous limestone. The shells of mollusks, such as clams and oysters, commonly form fossiliferous limestone. An example of fossiliferous limestone that contains mollusks is shown in **Figure 4**.

Another type of organic sedimentary rock is *coal*. Coal forms underground when partially decomposed plant material is buried beneath sediment and is changed into coal by increasing heat and pressure. This process occurs over millions of years.

Figure 4 The Formation of Organic Sedimentary Rock

Marine organisms, such as brachiopods, get the calcium carbonate for their shells from ocean water. When these organisms die, their shells collect on the ocean floor and eventually form fossiliferous limestone (inset). Over time, huge rock formations that contain the remains of large numbers of organisms, such as brachiopods, form.

CONNECTION ACTiViTy
Real World — GENERAL

Uses of Organic Sedimentary Rock
Chalk is a sedimentary rock formed from the shells of tiny marine creatures, including diatoms. The shells of diatoms contain silica, which can be used as an abrasive to clean teeth. Have students divide into groups and research other uses of organic sedimentary rock. Have each group prepare a class presentation in which they discuss the benefits and ingredients of a product made from sedimentary rock. **LS Logical**

Is That a Fact!
The Great Barrier Reef, a long coral reef that lies off the northeastern coast of Australia, is the most massive structure ever built by living creatures. It is more than 2,000 km long and covers an area of 207,000 km².

Sedimentary Rock Structures

Many features can tell you about the way sedimentary rock formed. The most important feature of sedimentary rock is stratification. **Stratification** is the process in which sedimentary rocks are arranged in layers. Strata differ from one another depending on the kind, size, and color of their sediment.

Sedimentary rocks sometimes record the motion of wind and water waves on lakes, oceans, rivers, and sand dunes in features called *ripple marks*, as shown in **Figure 5.** Structures called *mud cracks* form when fine-grained sediments at the bottom of a shallow body of water are exposed to the air and dry out. Mud cracks indicate the location of an ancient lake, stream, or ocean shoreline. Even raindrop impressions can be preserved in fine-grained sediments, as small pits with raised rims.

Reading Check What are ripple marks?

Figure 5 *These ripple marks were made by flowing water and were preserved when the sediments became sedimentary rock. Ripple marks can also form from the action of wind.*

stratification the process in which sedimentary rocks are arranged in layers

---

SECTION Review

Summary

- Sedimentary rock forms at or near the Earth's surface.
- Clastic sedimentary rock forms when rock or mineral fragments are cemented together.
- Chemical sedimentary rock forms from solutions of dissolved minerals and water.
- Organic limestone forms from the remains of plants and animals.
- Sedimentary structures include ripple marks, mud cracks, and raindrop impressions.

Using Key Terms

1. In your own words, write a definition for each of the following terms: *strata* and *stratification*.

Understanding Key Ideas

2. Which of the following is an organic sedimentary rock?
   a. chemical limestone
   b. shale
   c. fossiliferous limestone
   d. conglomerate

3. Explain the process by which clastic sedimentary rock forms.

4. Describe the three main categories of sedimentary rock.

Math Skills

5. A layer of a sedimentary rock is 2 m thick. How many years did it take for this layer to form if an average of 4 mm of sediment accumulated per year?

Critical Thinking

6. **Identifying Relationships** Rocks are classified based on texture and composition. Which of these two properties would be more important for classifying clastic sedimentary rock?

7. **Analyzing Processes** Why do you think raindrop impressions are more likely to be preserved in fine-grained sedimentary rock rather than in coarse-grained sedimentary rock?

SCLINKS.

NSTA
Developed and maintained by the National Science Teachers Association

For a variety of links related to this chapter, go to www.scilinks.org

Topic: Sedimentary Rock
SciLinks code: HSM1365

Answer to Reading Check

Ripple marks are the marks left by wind and water waves on lakes, seas, rivers, and sand dunes.

CHAPTER RESOURCES

Chapter Resource File

- • Section Quiz GENERAL
- • Section Review GENERAL
- • Vocabulary and Section Summary GENERAL

Focus

Overview

This section examines what happens when rock metamorphoses. Changes in heat or pressure can alter a rock's chemical nature and physical structure. Students will learn how different types of metamorphism cause changes in rock texture.

 Bellringer

Ask students to write a brief description of how cookies are made. Ask them to consider how the mixture of raw ingredients is like sedimentary rock. Ask them to describe how cookie dough metamorphoses when it is baked in an oven.

Motivate

ACTiViTY————— GENERAL

Modeling Metamorphism

Provide each student with pieces of red, yellow, green, and purple modeling clay. Have students flatten each piece, pile the pieces on top of each other, and press down on them firmly. Then, have students push inward on opposite sides of the stack or pull the stack gently so that the clay doesn't break apart. Explain that they will be learning how intense pressure and heat can cause rock to behave in similar ways. **LS** Visual/Kinesthetic

READING WARM-UP

Objectives

● Describe two ways a rock can undergo metamorphism.

● Explain how the mineral composition of rocks changes as the rocks undergo metamorphism.

● Describe the difference between foliated and nonfoliated metamorphic rock.

● Explain how metamorphic rock structures are related to deformation.

Terms to Learn

foliated
nonfoliated

READING STRATEGY

Discussion Read this section silently. Write down questions that you have about this section. Discuss your questions in a small group.

Metamorphic Rock

Have you ever watched a caterpillar change into a butterfly? Some caterpillars go through a biological process called metamorphosis in which they completely change their shape.

Rocks can also go through a process called *metamorphism.* The word *metamorphism* comes from the Greek words *meta,* which means "changed," and *morphos,* which means "shape." Metamorphic rocks are rocks in which the structure, texture, or composition of the rock have changed. All three types of rock can be changed by heat, pressure, or a combination of both.

Origins of Metamorphic Rock

The texture or mineral composition of a rock can change when its surroundings change. If the temperature or pressure of the new environment is different from the one in which the rock formed, the rock will undergo metamorphism.

The temperature at which most metamorphism occurs ranges from 50°C to 1,000°C. However, the metamorphism of some rocks takes place at temperatures above 1,000°C. It seems that at these temperatures the rock would melt, but this is not true of metamorphic rock. It is the depth and pressure at which metamorphic rocks form that allows the rock to heat to this temperature and maintain its solid nature. Most metamorphic change takes place at depths greater than 2 km. But at depths greater than 16 km, the pressure can be 4,000 times greater than the pressure of the atmosphere at Earth's surface.

Large movements within the crust of the Earth cause additional pressure to be exerted on a rock during metamorphism. This pressure can cause the mineral grains in rock to align themselves in certain directions. The alignment of mineral grains into parallel bands is shown in the metamorphic rock in **Figure 1.**

Figure 1 *This metamorphic rock is an example of how mineral grains were aligned into distinct bands when the rock underwent metamorphism.*

CHAPTER RESOURCES

Chapter Resource File

 • Lesson Plan
• Directed Reading A BASIC
• Directed Reading B SPECIAL NEEDS

Technology

 Transparencies
• Bellringer
• Regional and Contact Metamorphism

WEIRD SCIENCE

When rocks metamorphose under high temperature and pressure, they become plastic and can be easily deformed. It is not unusual for spherical pebbles in a conglomerate to be stretched into ellipses more than 30 times their original diameter!

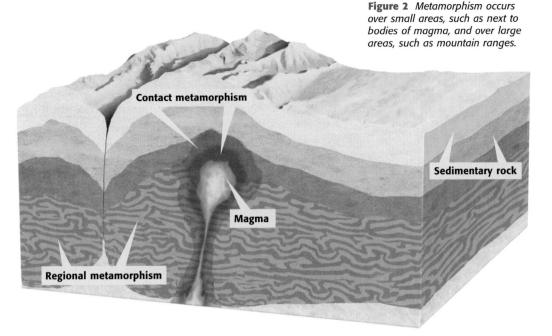

Contact metamorphism

Sedimentary rock

Magma

Regional metamorphism

Contact Metamorphism

One way rock can undergo metamorphism is by being heated by nearby magma. When magma moves through the crust, the magma heats the surrounding rock and changes it. Some minerals in the surrounding rock are changed into other minerals by this increase in temperature. The greatest change takes place where magma comes into direct contact with the surrounding rock. The effect of heat on rock gradually decreases as the rock's distance from the magma increases and as temperature decreases. *Contact metamorphism* occurs near igneous intrusions, as shown in **Figure 2.**

Regional Metamorphism

When pressure builds up in rock that is buried deep below other rock formations or when large pieces of the Earth's crust collide with each other, *regional metamorphism* occurs. The increased pressure and temperature causes rock to become deformed and chemically changed. Unlike contact metamorphism, which happens near bodies of magma, regional metamorphism occurs over thousands of cubic kilometers deep within Earth's crust. Rocks that have undergone regional metamorphism are found beneath most continental rock formations.

Reading Check Explain how and where regional metamorphism takes place. (*See the Appendix for answers to Reading Checks.*)

Answer to Reading Check

Regional metamorphism occurs when pressure builds up in rock that is buried deep below other rock formations or when large pieces of the Earth's crust collide. The increased pressure can cause thousands of square miles of rock to become deformed and chemically changed.

Stretching Out

1. Sketch the crystals in granite rock on a **piece of paper** with a **black-ink pen.** Be sure to include the outline of the rock, and fill it in with different crystal shapes.

2. Flatten some **plastic play putty** over your drawing, and slowly peel it off.

3. After making sure that the outline of your granite has been transferred to the putty, squeeze and stretch the putty. What happened to the crystals in the granite? What happened to the granite?

Is That a Fact!

The largest expanse of exposed metamorphic rock in the world is the Canadian Shield, a huge horseshoe-shaped region encircling Hudson Bay. Covering about half of Canada, it is about 4,586,900 km² and is the source of more than 70% of the minerals mined in Canada.

Metamorphic Minerals
Several types of minerals found in metamorphic rock, such as garnet, tourmaline, and serpentine, are used in sculpture and in jewelry making. Encourage students to choose one of these minerals, research it, and create a poster illustrating how it forms and what its uses are. **LS Visual**

MISCONCEPTION
///ALERT

Heat and Temperature Heat and temperature are not the same thing. Heat is the transfer of thermal energy from one object to another. Temperature is a measure of how hot (or cold) something is. Temperature is not a form of energy. When a rock comes into contact with magma, thermal energy is transferred from the magma to the rock because the magma is at a higher temperature than the rock. As a result, the temperature of the rock increases while the temperature of the magma decreases. But heating a rock does not always raise its temperature. If the rock is already so hot that it is on the verge of melting, additional heat will cause the rock to melt (and change state), but will not change the rock's temperature.

Figure 3 *The minerals calcite, quartz, and hematite combine and recrystallize to form the metamorphic mineral garnet.*

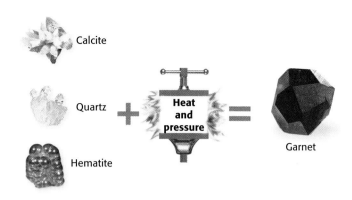

SCHOOL to HOME

Making a Rock Collection
With a parent, try to collect a sample of each class of rock described in this chapter. You may wish to collect rocks from road cuts or simply collect pebbles from your garden or driveway. Try to collect samples that show the composition and texture of each rock. Classify the rocks in your collection, and bring it to class. With other members of the class, discuss your rock samples and see if they are accurately identified.

Figure 4 *Scientists can understand a metamorphic rock's history by observing the minerals the rock contains. For example, a metamorphic rock that contains garnet formed at a greater depth and under greater heat and pressure than a rock that contains only chlorite.*

Composition of Metamorphic Rock

Metamorphism occurs when temperature and pressure inside the Earth's crust change. Minerals that were present in the rock when it formed may not be stable in the new temperature and pressure conditions. The original minerals change into minerals that are more stable in these new conditions. Look at **Figure 3** to see an example of how this change happens.

Many of these new minerals form only in metamorphic rock. As shown in **Figure 4,** some metamorphic minerals form only at certain temperatures and pressures. These minerals, known as *index minerals,* are used to estimate the temperature, depth, and pressure at which a rock undergoes metamorphism. Index minerals include biotite mica, chlorite, garnet, kyanite, muscovite mica, sillimanite, and staurolite.

✓ Reading Check What is an index mineral?

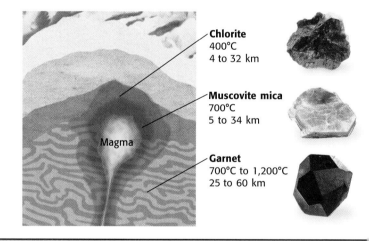

Chlorite
400°C
4 to 32 km

Muscovite mica
700°C
5 to 34 km

Garnet
700°C to 1,200°C
25 to 60 km

Magma

Answer to Reading Check
An index mineral is a metamorphic mineral that forms only at certain temperatures and pressures and therefore can be used by scientists to estimate the temperature, pressure, and depth at which a rock undergoes metamorphosis.

Homework ───── GENERAL

Making Models Have students make a model cross section of the Earth's crust. The model should include materials that represent magma, contact and regional metamorphic rocks, and sedimentary strata. **LS Kinesthetic/Visual**   English Language Learners

---

Textures of Metamorphic Rock

You have learned that texture helps scientists classify igneous and sedimentary rock. The same is true of metamorphic rock. All metamorphic rock has one of two textures—foliated or nonfoliated. Take a closer look at each of these types of metamorphic rock to find out how each type forms.

Foliated Metamorphic Rock

The texture of metamorphic rock in which the mineral grains are arranged in planes or bands is called **foliated.** Foliated metamorphic rock usually contains aligned grains of flat minerals, such as biotite mica or chlorite. Look at **Figure 5.** Shale is a sedimentary rock made of layers of clay minerals. When shale is exposed to slight heat and pressure, the clay minerals change into mica minerals. The shale becomes a foliated metamorphic rock called *slate*.

Metamorphic rocks can become other metamorphic rocks if the environment changes again. If slate is exposed to more heat and pressure, the slate can change into rock called *phyllite*. When phyllite is exposed to heat and pressure, it can change into *schist*.

If metamorphism continues, the arrangement of minerals in the rock changes. More heat and pressure cause minerals to separate into distinct bands in a metamorphic rock called *gneiss* (NIES).

foliated the texture of metamorphic rock in which the mineral grains are arranged in planes or bands

Sedimentary shale

Slate

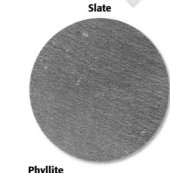

Phyllite

Figure 5 *The effects of metamorphism depend on the heat and pressure applied to the rock. Here you can see what happens to shale, a sedimentary rock, when it is exposed to more and more heat and pressure.*

Schist

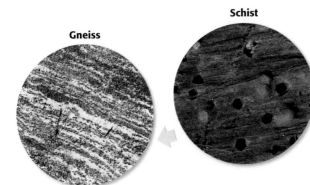

Gneiss

Creating an Outline Have students select a type of foliated or nonfoliated metamorphic rock. Ask students to create an outline of the steps that occur in the formation of the rock. Some students may want to write their outline in the form of a recipe for making a metamorphic rock. **LS** Logical

Quiz — GENERAL

1. Why is marble considered a nonfoliated metamorphic rock? (Its mineral grains are not arranged in planes or bands.)

2. What does the composition of a metamorphic rock tell you about the rock's origin and formation? (Different metamorphic minerals indicate the temperature and pressure conditions that existed when the rock formed.)

Alternative Assessment — GENERAL

Preparing a Lesson Have students prepare a lesson about this chapter to present to a second-grade class. They will need to prepare vocabulary lists, illustrations, and worksheets to help the younger students understand the types of rock, the uses of rock, and the way rocks form. **LS** Logical/Visual

---

CONNECTION TO Biology

WRITING SKILL **Metamorphosis** The term *metamorphosis* means "change in form." When some animals undergo a dramatic change in the shape of their body, they are said to have undergone a metamorphosis. As part of their natural life cycle, moths and butterflies go through four stages. After they hatch from an egg, they are in the larval stage in the form of a caterpillar. In the next stage, they build a cocoon or become a chrysalis. This stage is called the *pupal stage*. They finally emerge into the adult stage of their life, in which they have wings, antennae, and legs! Research other animals that undergo a metamorphosis, and summarize your findings in a short essay.

nonfoliated the texture of metamorphic rock in which the mineral grains are not arranged in planes or bands

---

Nonfoliated Metamorphic Rock

The texture of metamorphic rock in which the mineral grains are not arranged in planes or bands is called **nonfoliated**. Notice that the rocks shown in **Figure 6** do not have mineral grains that are aligned. This lack of aligned mineral grains is the reason these rocks are called *nonfoliated rocks*.

Nonfoliated rocks are commonly made of one or only a few minerals. During metamorphism, the crystals of these minerals may change in size or the mineral may change in composition in a process called *recrystallization*. The quartzite and marble shown in **Figure 6** are examples of sedimentary rocks that have recrystallized during metamorphism.

Quartz sandstone is a sedimentary rock made of quartz sand grains that have been cemented together. When quartz sandstone is exposed to the heat and pressure, the spaces between the sand grains disappear as the grains recrystallize to form quartzite. Quartzite has a shiny, glittery appearance. Like quartz sandstone, it is made of quartz. But during recrystallization, the mineral grains have grown larger than the original grains in the sandstone.

When limestone undergoes metamorphism, the same process that happened to the quartz happens to the calcite, and the limestone becomes marble. The calcite crystals in the marble are larger than the calcite grains in the original limestone.

Figure 6 **Two Examples of Nonfoliated Metamorphic Rock**

Marble and quartzite are nonfoliated metamorphic rocks. As you can see in the views through a microscope, the mineral crystals are not well aligned.

Marble

Quartzite

Homework — ADVANCED

Investigate Your Area Have students look at stone buildings and houses around their town. Ask students to identify the rock used in construction as igneous, sedimentary, or metamorphic. Ask students to consider the following questions: Which rock type was most commonly used? Which rock type was used least? Why was a specific rock type used for a particular application? Encourage students to find out the origin of rock used in buildings in your community. **LS** Visual

Metamorphic Rock Structures

Like igneous and sedimentary rock, metamorphic rock also has features that tell you about its history. In metamorphic rocks, these features are caused by deformation. *Deformation* is a change in the shape of a rock caused by a force placed on it. These forces may cause a rock to be squeezed or stretched.

Folds, or bends, in metamorphic rock are structures that indicate that a rock has been deformed. Some folds are not visible to the naked eye. But, as shown in **Figure 7,** some folds may be kilometers or even hundreds of kilometers in size.

✓ Reading Check How are metamorphic rock structures related to deformation?

Figure 7 *These large folds occur in metamorphosed sedimentary rock along Saglet Fiord in Labrador, Canada.*

SECTION Review

Summary

- Metamorphic rocks are rocks in which the structure, texture, or composition has changed.
- Two ways rocks can undergo metamorphism are by contact metamorphism and regional metamorphism.
- As rocks undergo metamorphism, the original minerals in a rock change into new minerals that are more stable in new pressure and temperature conditions.
- Foliated metamorphic rock has mineral crystals aligned in planes or bands, whereas nonfoliated rocks have unaligned mineral crystals.
- Metamorphic rock structures are caused by deformation.

Using Key Terms

1. In your own words, define the following terms: *foliated* and *nonfoliated*.

Understanding Key Ideas

2. Which of the following is not a type of foliated metamorphic rock?
   a. gneiss
   b. slate
   c. marble
   d. schist

3. Explain the difference between contact metamorphism and regional metamorphism.

4. Explain how index minerals allow a scientist to understand the history of a metamorphic rock.

Math Skills

5. For every 3.3 km a rock is buried, the pressure placed upon it increases 0.1 gigapascal (100 million pascals). If rock undergoing metamorphosis is buried at 16 km, what is the pressure placed on that rock? (Hint: The pressure at Earth's surface is .101 gigapascal.)

Critical Thinking

6. **Making Inferences** If you had two metamorphic rocks, one that has garnet crystals and the other that has chlorite crystals, which one could have formed at a deeper level in the Earth's crust? Explain your answer.

7. **Applying Concepts** Which do you think would be easier to break, a foliated rock, such as slate, or a nonfoliated rock, such as quartzite? Explain.

8. **Analyzing Processes** A mountain range is located at a boundary where two tectonic plates are colliding. Would most of the metamorphic rock in the mountain range be a product of contact metamorphism or regional metamorphism? Explain.

For a variety of links related to this chapter, go to www.scilinks.org

Topic: Metamorphic Rock
SciLinks code: HSM0949

Answer to Reading Check

Deformation causes metamorphic structures such as folds.

CHAPTER RESOURCES

Chapter Resource File

- Section Quiz GENERAL
- Section Review GENERAL
- Vocabulary and Section Summary GENERAL
- Reinforcement Worksheet BASIC
- Critical Thinking ADVANCED

Technology

- Interactive Explorations CD-ROM
  - "Rock On!" GENERAL

Answers to Section Review

1. Sample answer: Foliated metamorphic rock consists of minerals that are arranged in planes or bands. The minerals in nonfoliated metamorphic rock do not appear to be arranged in a pattern.

2. c

3. Contact metamorphism is a type of metamorphism that occurs near igneous intrusions, where magma comes into direct contact with surrounding rock. Regional metamorphism is a type of metamorphism that occurs when large pieces of Earth's crust collide, causing rock to become deformed and chemically changed over large areas.

4. Because index minerals form only at certain temperatures and pressures, index minerals indicate the temperature, pressure, and depth at which a rock metamorphosed.

5. 16 km ÷ 3.3 km = 4.84 km × 0.1 gigapascal = 0.484 gigapascal + .101 gigapascal (atmospheric pressure) = .585 gigapascal

6. The rock with garnet crystals would probably have formed deeper in the Earth because the mineral garnet forms at a higher temperature and higher pressure than the mineral chlorite.

7. Because the grains in a foliated metamorphic rock are arranged in parallel bands, foliated metamorphic rock would be easier to break than a nonfoliated metamorphic rock.

8. Rock becomes deformed and chemically changed over large areas of Earth's crust by increases in temperature and pressure that occur when tectonic plates collide. Therefore, most of the rock in the mountain range would be the product of regional metamorphism.

Let's Get Sedimental

Teacher's Notes

Time Required

Two 45-minute class periods

Lab Ratings

EASY ——————————→ HARD

Teacher Prep 🧪

Student Set-Up 🧪🧪

Concept Level 🧪🧪

Clean Up 🧪🧪

MATERIALS

The materials listed are enough for a group of three or four students. You may substitute smaller plastic bottles. The amount of sand, gravel, and soil depends on the size of the jar. Each group will need enough of these materials to fill the bottle two-thirds full with a mixture of sand, gravel, and soil.

Safety Caution

Students should be extremely careful when cutting the sides from the plastic bottles.

Preparation Notes

If the students use larger plastic bottles, the sediment may take several days to dry completely. It may be a good idea to ask the students to follow steps 1–5 as an introduction to the chapter. The class can then finish the procedure when the sediment has dried.

Lab Notes

This lab illustrates the sedimentary (depositional) process of sorting. When sediment is suspended in water, the largest, heaviest particles will settle out first, followed by the finer, lighter particles. This process can allow scientists and students studying sedimentary rock layers to determine the original orientation of the rock.

OBJECTIVES

Model the process of sedimentation.

Determine whether sedimentary rock layers are undisturbed.

MATERIALS

- clay
- dropper pipet
- gravel
- magnifying lens
- mixing bowl, 2 qt
- sand
- scissors
- soda bottle with a cap, plastic, 2 L
- soil, clay rich, if available
- water

SAFETY

Let's Get Sedimental

How do we determine if sedimentary rock layers are undisturbed? The best way to do this is to be sure that fine-grained sediments near the top of a layer lie above coarse-grained sediments near the bottom of the layer. This lab activity will show you how to read rock features that will help you distinguish individual sedimentary rock layers. Then, you can look for the features in real rock layers.

Procedure

1. In a mixing bowl, thoroughly mix the sand, gravel, and soil. Fill the soda bottle about one-third full of the mixture.

2. Add water to the soda bottle until the bottle is two-thirds full. Twist the cap back onto the bottle, and shake the bottle vigorously until all of the sediment is mixed in the rapidly moving water.

3. Place the bottle on a tabletop. Using the scissors, carefully cut the top off the bottle a few centimeters above the water, as shown. The open bottle will allow water to evaporate.

4. Immediately after you set the bottle on the tabletop, describe what you see from above and through the sides of the bottle.

5. Do not disturb the container. Allow the water to evaporate. (You may speed up the process by carefully using the dropper pipet to siphon off some of the clear water after you allow the container to sit for at least 24 hours.) You may also set the bottle in the sun or under a desk lamp to speed up evaporation.

6. After the sediment has dried and hardened, describe its surface.

7. Carefully lay the container on its side, and cut a wide, vertical strip of plastic down the length of the bottle to expose the sediments in the container. You may find it easier if you place pieces of clay on either side of the container to stabilize it. (If the bottle is clear along its length, this step may not be required.)

8. Brush away the loose material from the sediment, and gently blow on the surface until it is clean. Examine the surface, and record your observations.

Analyze the Results

1 **Identifying Patterns** Do you see anything through the side of the bottle that could help you determine if a sedimentary rock is undisturbed? Explain your answer.

2 **Identifying Patterns** Can you observe a pattern of deposition? If so, describe the pattern of deposition of sediment that you observe from top to bottom.

3 **Explaining Events** Explain how these features might be used to identify the top of a sedimentary layer in real rock and to decide if the layer has been disturbed.

4 **Identifying Patterns** Do you see any structures through the side of the bottle that might indicate which direction is up, such as a change in particle density or size?

5 **Identifying Patterns** Use the magnifying lens to examine the boundaries between the gravel, sand, and silt. Do the size of the particles and the type of sediment change dramatically in each layer?

Draw Conclusions

6 **Making Predictions** Imagine that a layer was deposited directly above the sediment in your bottle. Describe the composition of this new layer. Will it have the same composition as the mixture in steps 1–5 in the Procedure?

> ### Applying Your Data
>
> With your class or with a parent, visit an outcrop of sedimentary rock. Apply the information that you have learned in this lab to see if you can determine whether the sedimentary rock layers are disturbed or undisturbed.

Analyze the Results

1. Answers may vary. Students should understand that the finest sediments should be at the top. This sequence can indicate the top of a layer in a sedimentary outcrop. If the layers are not in this order, the rock may have been disturbed.

2. Students should indicate that in the sorting process, gravel settled out first, followed by sand, and then soil.

3. If features that geologists expect to find only in the top layer are found elsewhere, this finding indicates that the column has been disturbed. Geologists carefully study the layers for these features so that they can determine the original order of the layers.

4. Each layer should show finer particles at the top. This pattern can be seen only from the side.

5. Students should see the same grading effect at the boundaries. The changes within each layer will be gradual, but the changes between layers may be more dramatic.

Draw Conclusions

6. If sediment having the same particle sizes as the mixture in steps 1-5 is deposited on top of the sediment in the bottle, the new layer should have the same composition as the layer in the bottle.

CHAPTER RESOURCES

Workbooks

- **Whiz-Bang Demonstrations**
  - Settling Down **BASIC**
- **Labs You Can Eat**
  - Famous Rock Groups **GENERAL**
- **Long-Term Projects & Research Ideas**
  - Home-Grown Crystals **ADVANCED**
- **Calculator-Based Labs**
  - A Hot and Cool Lab **ADVANCED**

CLASSROOM TESTED & APPROVED

Helen Schiller
Northwood Middle School
Taylors, South Carolina

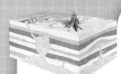

Chapter Review

Chapter Review

Assignment Guide

SECTION	QUESTIONS
1	1, 2, 10, 12, 15–16, 21–25
2	5, 7, 8, 11, 19
3	4, 6
4	3, 9, 13–14, 18, 20
2, 3, and 4	17

ANSWERS

Using Key Terms

1. Sample answer: The rock cycle is the process in which one rock type changes into another rock type. In this process, rock is continuously recycled.
2. texture
3. Foliated
4. stratification
5. Extrusive igneous rock

Understanding Key Ideas

6. c
7. d
8. c
9. b
10. b
11. d
12. Scientists use differences in composition, or the minerals a rock is made up of, to classify rock. Scientists use differences in texture—the sizes, shapes, and positions of the grains a rock is made up of—to further classify rocks.

USING KEY TERMS

1 In your own words, write a definition for the term *rock cycle*.

Complete each of the following sentences by choosing the correct term from the word bank.

stratification   foliated
extrusive igneous rock   texture

2 The ___ of a rock is determined by the sizes, shapes, and positions of the minerals the rock contains.

3 ___ metamorphic rock contains minerals that are arranged in plates or bands.

4 The most characteristic property of sedimentary rock is ___.

5 ___ forms plains called *lava plateaus*.

UNDERSTANDING KEY IDEAS

Multiple Choice

6 Sedimentary rock is classified into all of the following main categories except
  a. clastic sedimentary rock.
  b. chemical sedimentary rock.
  c. nonfoliated sedimentary rock.
  d. organic sedimentary rock.

7 An igneous rock that cools very slowly has a ___ texture.
  a. foliated
  b. fine-grained
  c. nonfoliated
  d. coarse-grained

8 Igneous rock forms when
  a. minerals crystallize from a solution.
  b. sand grains are cemented together.
  c. magma cools and solidifies.
  d. mineral grains in a rock recrystallize.

9 A ___ is a common structure found in metamorphic rock.
  a. ripple mark   **c.** sill
  b. fold   **d.** layer

10 The process in which sediment is removed from its source and transported is called
  a. deposition.   **c.** weathering.
  b. erosion.   **d.** uplift.

11 Mafic rocks are
  a. light-colored rocks rich in calcium, iron, and magnesium.
  b. dark-colored rocks rich in aluminum, potassium, silica, and sodium.
  c. light-colored rocks rich in aluminum, potassium, silica, and sodium.
  d. dark-colored rocks rich in calcium, iron, and magnesium.

Short Answer

12 Explain how composition and texture are used by scientists to classify rocks.

13 Describe two ways a rock can undergo metamorphism.

14 Explain why some minerals only occur in metamorphic rocks.

15 Describe how each type of rock changes as it moves through the rock cycle.

13. Two ways in which a rock can undergo metamorphism is by contact metamorphism and regional metamorphism. Contact metamorphism occurs near igneous intrusions, where magma comes in direct contact with the surrounding rock. Regional metamorphism occurs when pressure builds up in deep rock or when large pieces of Earth's crust collide, deforming and chemically changing rock over large areas.

14. Some minerals can form only at specific pressures and temperatures present during metamorphism.

15. Sample answer: When rocks are buried, they are heated and squeezed to create metamorphic rock. Sometimes, the heat is enough to melt the rock and create magma, which cools to form igneous rock. Buried rocks are uplifted, and when rocks at the Earth's surface are eroded, sediments are created. These sediments are buried and later harden into sedimentary rock.

16 Describe two ways rocks were used by early humans and ancient civilizations.

17 **Concept Mapping** Use the following terms to construct a concept map: *rocks, metamorphic, sedimentary, igneous, foliated, nonfoliated, organic, clastic, chemical, intrusive,* and *extrusive.*

18 **Making Inferences** If you were looking for fossils in the rocks around your home and the rock type that was closest to your home was metamorphic, do you think that you would find many fossils? Explain your answer.

19 **Applying Concepts** Imagine that you want to quarry, or mine, granite. You have all of the equipment, but you have two pieces of land to choose from. One area has a granite batholith underneath it. The other has a granite sill. If both intrusive bodies are at the same depth, which one would be the better choice for you to quarry? Explain your answer.

20 **Applying Concepts** The sedimentary rock coquina is made up of pieces of seashells. Which of the three kinds of sedimentary rock could coquina be? Explain your answer.

21 **Analyzing Processes** If a rock is buried deep inside the Earth, which geological processes cannot change the rock? Explain your answer.

INTERPRETING GRAPHICS

The bar graph below shows the percentage of minerals by mass that compose a sample of granite. Use the graph below to answer the questions that follow.

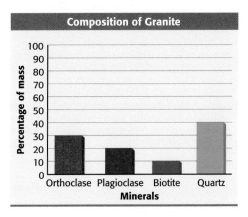

Composition of Granite

22 Your rock sample is made of four minerals. What percentage of each mineral makes up your sample?

23 Both plagioclase and orthoclase are feldspar minerals. What percentage of the minerals in your sample of granite are not feldspar minerals?

24 If your rock sample has a mass of 10 g, how many grams of quartz does it contain?

25 Use paper, a compass, and a protractor or a computer to make a pie chart. Show the percentage of each of the four minerals your sample of granite contains. (Look in the Appendix of this book for help on making a pie chart.)

16. Two ways rocks were used by early humans and ancient civilizations were as tools and as building materials.

Critical Thinking

17. 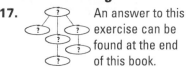 An answer to this exercise can be found at the end of this book.

18. You would not find many—or any—fossils where you live because fossils are usually found in sedimentary rock, not metamorphic rock. (Occasionally, fossils are preserved in metamorphic rock that was once sedimentary rock.)

19. The property with the batholith would be a better buy because batholiths are much bigger than sills.

20. The seashells that make up coquina are made up of the remains of once-living organisms, so coquina is an organic sedimentary rock. (The shells are technically clasts, because they are particles that have been deposited.)

21. A rock buried deep beneath the surface cannot be changed by weathering and erosion, which are geological processes that change Earth's surface features.

Interpreting Graphics

22. orthoclase = 30%, plagioclase = 20%, biotite = 10%, quartz = 40%

23. plagioclase + orthoclase = 30% + 20% = 50%
100% − 50% = 50%
Fifty percent of the minerals in the granite are not feldspars.

24. $10 \text{ g} \times 0.40 = 4 \text{ g}$

25. Accept all reasonable responses. Charts should show the correct percentages of the minerals.

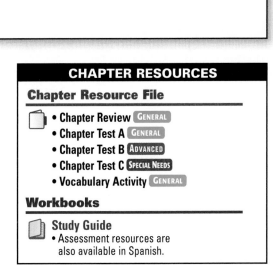

CHAPTER RESOURCES

Chapter Resource File

- **Chapter Review** GENERAL
- **Chapter Test A** GENERAL
- **Chapter Test B** ADVANCED
- **Chapter Test C** SPECIAL NEEDS
- **Vocabulary Activity** GENERAL

Workbooks

Study Guide
- Assessment resources are also available in Spanish.

Teacher's Note

To provide practice under more realistic testing conditions, give students 20 minutes to answer all of the questions in this Standardized Test Preparation.

MISCONCEPTION
///ALERT

Answers to the standardized test preparation can help you identify student misconceptions and misunderstandings.

Passage 1

1. D
2. G
3. B

Question 3: The correct answer is B. Some students who have not read the passage carefully may choose answer D. Although this statement is correct, it is not the main idea of the passage, which is elucidated in the opening sentence.

READING

Read each of the passages below. Then, answer the questions that follow each passage.

Passage 1 The texture and composition of a rock can provide good clues about how and where the rock formed. Scientists use both texture and composition to understand the <u>origin</u> and history of rocks. For example, marble is a rock that is made when limestone is metamorphosed. Only limestone contains the mineral—calcite—that can change into marble. Therefore, wherever scientists find marble, they know the sediment that created the original limestone was deposited in a warm ocean or lake environment.

1. In the passage, what does the word *origin* mean?
   A size or appearance
   B age
   C location or surroundings
   D source or formation

2. Based on the passage, what can the reader conclude?
   F Marble is a sedimentary rock.
   G Limestone is created by sediments deposited in warm ocean or lake environments.
   H Marble is a rock that is made when sandstone has undergone metamorphism.
   I In identifying a rock, the texture of a rock is more important than the composition of the rock.

3. What is the main idea of the passage?
   A Scientists believe marble is the most important rock type to study.
   B Scientists study the composition and texture of a rock to determine how the rock formed and what happened after it formed.
   C Some sediments are deposited in warm oceans and lakes.
   D When limestone undergoes metamorphism, it creates marble.

Passage 2 Fulgurites are a rare type of natural glass found in areas that have quartz-rich sediments, such as beaches and deserts. A <u>tubular</u> fulgurite forms when a lightning bolt strikes material such as sand and melts the quartz into a liquid. The liquid quartz cools and solidifies quickly, and a thin, glassy tube is left behind. Fulgurites usually have a rough outer surface and a smooth inner surface. Underground, a fulgurite may be shaped like the roots of a tree. The fulgurite branches out with many arms that trace the zigzag path of the lightning bolt. Some fulgurites are as short as your little finger, but others stretch 20 m into the ground.

1. In the passage, what does the word *tubular* mean?
   A flat and sharp
   B round and long
   C funnel shaped
   D pyramid shaped

2. From the information in the passage, what can the reader conclude?
   F Fulgurites are formed above ground.
   G Sand contains a large amount of quartz.
   H Fulgurites are most often very small.
   I Fulgurites are easy to find in sandy places.

3. Which of the following statements best describes a fulgurite?
   A Fulgurites are frozen lightning bolts.
   B Fulgurites are rootlike rocks.
   C Fulgurites are glassy tubes found in deserts.
   D Fulgurites are natural glass tubes formed by lightning bolts.

Passage 2

1. B
2. G
3. D

Question 2: The correct answer is G. Some students who have not read the passage carefully may choose answer F. Although lightning strikes the ground surface, the vast majority of a fulgurite is located underground, which gives little or no evidence of its existence.

Question 3: The correct answer is D. Some students may choose answer C. Although this answer may appear correct, it does not contain the necessary modifier *natural*, nor does it describe how fulgurites form.

Use the diagram below to answer the questions that follow.

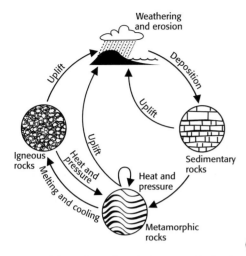

Weathering and erosion

Deposition

Uplift

Uplift

Uplift

Heat and pressure

Melting and cooling

Igneous rocks

Heat and pressure

Sedimentary rocks

Metamorphic rocks

1. According to the rock cycle diagram, which of the following statements is true?

A Only sedimentary rock gets weathered and eroded.

B Sedimentary rocks are made from metamorphic, igneous, and sedimentary rock fragments and minerals.

C Heat and pressure create igneous rocks.

D Metamorphic rocks are created by melting and cooling.

2. A rock exists at the surface of the Earth. What would be the next step in the rock cycle?

F cooling

G weathering

H melting

I metamorphism

3. Which of the following processes brings rocks to Earth's surface, where they can be eroded?

A burial

B deposition

C uplift

D weathering

4. Which of the following is the best summary of the rock cycle?

F Each type of rock gets melted. Then the magma turns into igneous, sedimentary, and metamorphic rock.

G Magma cools to form igneous rock. Then, the igneous rock becomes sedimentary rock. Sedimentary rock is heated and forms metamorphic rock. Metamorphic rock melts to form magma.

H All three rock types weather to create sedimentary rock. All three rock types melt to form magma. Magma forms igneous rock. All three types of rock form metamorphic rock because of heat and pressure.

I Igneous rock is weathered to create sedimentary rock. Sedimentary rock is melted to form igneous rock. Metamorphic rock is weathered to form igneous rock.

Read each question below, and choose the best answer.

1. Eric has 25 rocks he has collected as a science project for class. Nine rocks are sedimentary, 10 are igneous, and 6 are metamorphic. If Eric chooses a rock at random, what is the probability that he will choose an igneous rock?

A 1/2

B 2/5

C 3/8

D 1/15

2. At a mineral and fossil show, Elizabeth bought two quartz crystals that cost $2.00 each and four trilobite fossils that cost $3.50 each. Which equation can be used to describe c, the total cost of her purchase?

F $c = (2 \times 4) + (2.00 \times 3.50)$

G $c = (2 \times 2.00) + (4 \times 3.50)$

H $c = (4 \times 2.00) + (2 \times 3.50)$

I $c = (2 + 2.00) + (4 + 3.50)$

1. B

2. G

3. C

4. H

✚ TEST DOCTOR

Question 1: The correct answer is B. Some students may select answer A, incorrectly believing that sedimentary rock forms during the processes of weathering and erosion rather than as a result of it.

Question 4: The correct answer is H. Answers F, G, and I incorrectly describe one or more processes that are part of the rock cycle. (Helpful hint: When describing the rock cycle to students, make them aware that the three classes of rock can be involved in each process in the cycle.)

1. B

2. G

✚ TEST DOCTOR

Question 2: The correct answer is G. Answer F incorrectly multiplies the numbers of objects with each other and the prices with each other, then adds the totals together. Answer H incorrectly matches the prices with the objects and adds the totals together. Answer I incorrectly adds the number of objects to the prices.

Standardized Test Preparation

CHAPTER RESOURCES

Chapter Resource File

📁 • Standardized Test Preparation GENERAL

State Resources

🗺️ For specific resources for your state, visit **go.hrw.com** and type in the keyword **HSMSTR**.

Science, Technology, and Society

Background

Archaeologists estimate that Easter Island was first settled sometime between 400 CE and 700 CE. The first inhabitants arrived from Polynesia. This was confirmed in 1994, when DNA extracted from 12 Easter Island skeletons was found to be Polynesian. Either Tahiti or the Marquesas islands, which had been reached by Melanesian seafarers by at least 300 CE, were the most likely starting point for these voyages.

Scientific Discoveries

Background

Sixty-five million years ago, an asteroid at least 10 km wide struck the Earth near Yucatán, Mexico. Some scientists think the collision caused the extinction of approximately 15% to 20% of life on Earth, including the dinosaurs. Today, the crater is buried beneath 1,100 m of limestone, so there are few clues to the crater's existence. As scientists drilled into the impact site, they found mineral evidence of shock metamorphism. They confirmed that rocks in the area had been subjected to a high-pressure event.

Science in Action

Science, Technology, and Society

The Moai of Easter Island

Easter island is located in the Pacific Ocean more than 3,200 km from the coast of Chile. The island is home to mysterious statues that were carved from volcanic ash. The statues, called *moai*, have human heads and large torsos. The average moai weighs 14 tons and is more than 4.5 m tall, though some are as tall as 10 m! Altogether, 887 moai have been discovered. How old are the moai? Scientists believe that the moai were built between 500 and 1,000 years ago. What purpose did moai serve for their creators? The moai may have been religious symbols or gods.

Social Studies ACTIVITY

WRITING SKILL Research another ancient society or civilization, such as the ancient Egyptians, who are believed to have used stone to construct monuments to their gods or to important people. Report your findings in a short essay.

Scientific Discoveries

Shock Metamorphism

When a large asteroid, meteoroid, or comet collides with the Earth, extremely high temperatures and pressures are created in Earth's surface rock. These high pressures and temperatures cause minerals in the surface rock to shatter and recrystallize. The new minerals that result from this recrystallization cannot be created under any other conditions. This process is called *shock metamorphism*.

When large objects from space collide with the Earth, craters are formed by the impact. However, impact craters are not always easy to find on Earth. Scientists use shock metamorphism as a clue to locate ancient impact craters.

Language Arts ACTIVITY

WRITING SKILL The impact site caused by the asteroid strike in the Yucatán 65 million years ago has been named the Chicxulub (cheeks OO loob) structure. Research the origin of the name Chicxulub, and report your findings in a short paper.

Answer to Social Studies Activity

Have students report their findings to the class. While reporting their findings, students should pinpoint the location of the monuments they are discussing on a world map.

Answer to Language Arts Activity

Hold a short discussion with the class about the meaning of the name *Chicxulub* (in the local Mayan dialect, *Chicxulub* means "the devil's tail") and the importance of the Chicxulub impact structure. While doing so, point out the location of the Chicxulub impact site on a map. You may also want to discuss other large North American impact structures, such as Sudbury in Ontario, Canada, Manicouagan in Quebec, Canada, and the impact structure in Chesapeake Bay, in Virginia, USA.

Robert L. Folk

Petrologist For Dr. Robert Folk, the study of rock takes place on the microscopic level. Dr. Folk is searching for tiny life-forms he has named nannobacteria, or dwarf bacteria, in rock. *Nannobacteria* may also be spelled *nanobacteria*. Because nannobacteria are so incredibly small, only 0.05 to 0.2 μm in diameter, Folk must use an extremely powerful 100,000× microscope, called a *scanning electron microscope,* to see the shape of the bacteria in rock. Folk's research had already led him to discover that a certain type of Italian limestone is produced by bacteria. The bacteria were consuming the minerals, and the waste of the bacteria was forming the limestone. Further research led Folk to the discovery of the tiny nannobacteria. The spherical or oval-shaped nannobacteria appeared as chains and grapelike clusters. From his research, Folk hypothesized that nannobacteria are responsible for many inorganic reactions that occur in rock. Many scientists are skeptical of Folk's nannobacteria. Some skeptics believe that the tiny size of nannobacteria makes the bacteria simply too small to contain the chemistry of life. Others believe that nannobacteria actually represent structures that do not come from living things.

Math ACTIVITY

If a nannobacterium is 1/10 the length, 1/10 the width, and 1/10 the height of an ordinary bacterium, how many nannobacteria can fit within an ordinary bacterium? (Hint: Draw block diagrams of both a nannobacterium and an ordinary bacterium.)

go.hrw.com

To learn more about these Science in Action topics, visit go.hrw.com and type in the keyword HZ5RCKF.

Current Science

Check out Current Science® articles related to this chapter by visiting go.hrw.com. Just type in the keyword HZ5CS04.

Answer to Math Activity

$10 \times 10 \times 10 = 10^3 = 1{,}000$ nannobacteria can fit within a normal bacterium.

Careers
Background
Dr. Robert L. Folk is currently Professor Emeritus in the Department of Geology at the University of Texas at Austin, where he taught sedimentary geology from 1953 to 1988. His classification system of sediments, proposed in 1954, is still used by some sedimentary petrologists. In 1962, Dr. Folk's *The Classification of Sedimentary Rocks* was published. This work is considered a classic text in the field of sedimentary petrology. Dr. Folk was the recipient of the Twenhofel Medal for excellence in sedimentary petrology in 1979 and was awarded the Penrose Medal in 2000 for outstanding original contributions or achievements that mark a major advance in the science of geology. In addition, Dr. Folk has received two national teaching awards. In 1980, he first became interested in the role of bacteria in forming materials, and, in 1990, he discovered the first mineralized nannobacteria. Dr. Folk's research involving nannobacteria is still very controversial.

MISCONCEPTION ALERT

Nannobacteria or Nanobacteria? In 1988, the term *nanobacteria* was first applied to the controversial microscopic spheres and rods that Dr. Folk is studying. Since the first use of term, *nanobacteria* (with the prefix *nano-*) has become the preferred spelling of the term in the scientific literature. Dr. Folk prefers to spell the same term *nannobacteria* (with the prefix *nanno-*). His contention is that this is the preferred geological spelling. In point of fact, both prefixes come from the Greek *nannos,* meaning "dwarf."

The Rock and Fossil Record
Chapter Planning Guide

Compression guide:
To shorten instruction because of time limitations, omit Section 1.

OBJECTIVES	LABS, DEMONSTRATIONS, AND ACTIVITIES	TECHNOLOGY RESOURCES
PACING • 90 min pp. 58–63 **Chapter Opener**	**SE** Start-up Activity, p. 59 `GENERAL`	**OSP** Parent Letter ■ `GENERAL` **CD** Student Edition on CD-ROM **CD** Guided Reading Audio CD ■ **CRF** Chapter Starter Transparency* **VID** Brain Food Video Quiz
Section 1 Earth's Story and Those Who First Listened • Compare uniformitarianism and catastrophism. • Describe how the science of geology has changed over the past 200 years. • Explain the role of paleontology in the study of Earth's history.	**TE** Activity Debate Posters, p. 60 `GENERAL` **SE** Connection to Biology Darwin and Lyell, p. 61 `GENERAL` **TE** Connection Activity Language Arts, p. 61 `GENERAL` **LB** Inquiry Labs A Penny for Your Thoughts* `GENERAL`	**CRF** Lesson Plans* **TR** Bellringer Transparency* **TR** Hutton and the Principle of Uniformitarianism* **CD** Science Tutor
PACING • 45 min pp. 64–69 **Section 2 Relative Dating: Which Came First?** • Explain how relative dating is used in geology. • Explain the principle of superposition. • Describe how the geologic column is used in relative dating. • Identify two events and two features that disrupt rock layers. • Explain how physical features are used to determine relative ages.	**TE** Demonstration Superposition, p. 64 `GENERAL` **TE** Activity Modeling Faults and Intrusions, p. 66 ◆ `GENERAL` **TE** Group Activity Field Trip, p. 66 **TE** Activity Unconformities, p. 67 `BASIC` **SE** Skills Practice Lab How Do You Stack Up?, p. 86 ◆ `GENERAL`	**CRF** Lesson Plans* **TR** Bellringer Transparency* **TR** Constructing the Geologic Column* **VID** Lab Videos for Earth Science **CD** Science Tutor
PACING • 45 min pp. 70–73 **Section 3 Absolute Dating: A Measure of Time** • Describe how radioactive decay occurs. • Explain how radioactive decay relates to radiometric dating. • Identify four types of radiometric dating. • Determine the best type of radiometric dating to use to date an object.	**TE** Activity Absolute Dating Skit, p. 70 `GENERAL` **TE** Connection Activity Math, p. 70 `GENERAL` **LB** Long-Term Projects & Research Ideas The Hard Rock Chronicles* `ADVANCED` **LB** Labs You Can Eat Geopancakes* `BASIC`	**CRF** Lesson Plans* **TR** Bellringer Transparency* **TR** *LINK TO PHYSICAL SCIENCE* Radioactive Decay and Half-Life* **CD** Science Tutor
PACING • 45 min pp. 74–79 **Section 4 Looking at Fossils** • Describe five ways that different types of fossils form. • List three types of fossils that are not part of organisms. • Explain how fossils can be used to determine the history of changes in environments and organisms. • Explain how index fossils can be used to date rock layers.	**TE** Group Activity Carbon Impressions, p. 74 ◆ `GENERAL` **SE** Connection to Environmental Science Preservation in Ice, p. 75 `GENERAL` **TE** Activity Making Fossils, p. 75 ◆ `GENERAL` **TE** Group Activity Imagining Environmental Change, p. 77 `GENERAL` **SE** Quick Lab Make a Fossil, p. 77 ◆ `GENERAL` **SE** School-to-Home Activity Fossil Hunt, p. 78 `GENERAL`	**CRF** Lesson Plans* **TR** Bellringer Transparency* **CD** Science Tutor
PACING • 45 min pp. 80–85 **Section 5 Time Marches On** • Explain how geologic time is recorded in rock layers. • Identify important dates on the geologic time scale. • Explain how environmental changes resulted in the extinction of some species.	**TE** Connection Activity Math, p. 80 `GENERAL` **TE** Activity Learning About the Eons, p. 81 `BASIC` **TE** Connection Activity Language Arts, p. 82 `GENERAL` **TE** Activity Prehistoric Illustrations, p. 84 `ADVANCED` **LB** EcoLabs & Field Activities Rock of Ages* `ADVANCED` **SE** Science in Action Math, Social Studies, and Language Arts Activities, p. 82 `GENERAL`	**CRF** Lesson Plans* **TR** Bellringer Transparency* **TR** The Geologic Time Scale* **SE** Internet Activity, p. 81 `GENERAL` **CRF** SciLinks Activity* `GENERAL` **CD** Science Tutor

PACING • 90 min

CHAPTER REVIEW, ASSESSMENT, AND STANDARDIZED TEST PREPARATION

CRF Vocabulary Activity* `GENERAL`
SE Chapter Review, pp. 88–89 `GENERAL`
CRF Chapter Review* ■ `GENERAL`
CRF Chapter Tests A* ■ `GENERAL`, B* `ADVANCED`, C* `SPECIAL NEEDS`
SE Standardized Test Preparation, pp. 90–91 `GENERAL`
CRF Standardized Test Preparation* `GENERAL`
CRF Performance-Based Assessment* `GENERAL`
OSP Test Generator `GENERAL`
CRF Test Item Listing* `GENERAL`

Online and Technology Resources

Visit **go.hrw.com** for a variety of free resources related to this textbook. Enter the keyword **HZ5FOS**.

Holt Online Learning
Students can access interactive problem-solving help and active visual concept development with the *Holt Science and Technology* Online Edition available at **www.hrw.com**.

 Guided Reading Audio CD
Also in Spanish
A direct reading of each chapter for auditory learners, reluctant readers, and Spanish-speaking students.

 Science Tutor CD-ROM
Excellent for remediation and test practice.

SKILLS DEVELOPMENT RESOURCES	SECTION REVIEW AND ASSESSMENT	CORRELATIONS
SE Pre-Reading Activity, p. 58 `GENERAL` **OSP** Science Puzzlers, Twisters & Teasers* `GENERAL`		National Science Education Standards SAI 1, 2
CRF Directed Reading A* ■ `BASIC`, B* `SPECIAL NEEDS` **CRF** Vocabulary and Section Summary* ■ `GENERAL` **SE** Reading Strategy Reading Organizer, p. 60 `GENERAL`	**SE** Reading Checks, pp. 61, 62 `GENERAL` **TE** Reteaching, p. 62 `BASIC` **TE** Quiz, p. 62 `GENERAL` **TE** Alternative Assessment, p. 62 `GENERAL` **SE** Section Review,* p. 63 ■ `GENERAL` **CRF** Section Quiz* ■ `GENERAL`	UCP 2, 4; SAI 1, 2; SPSP 5; HNS 1, 2, 3; ES 2a
CRF Directed Reading A* ■ `BASIC`, B* `SPECIAL NEEDS` **CRF** Vocabulary and Section Summary* ■ `GENERAL` **SE** Reading Strategy Reading Organizer, p. 64 `GENERAL` **TE** Reading Strategy Prediction Guide, p. 66 `BASIC` **CRF** Reinforcement Worksheet A Geologic Column Sandwich* `GENERAL`	**SE** Reading Checks, pp. 65, 67, 68 `GENERAL` **TE** Reteaching, p. 68 `BASIC` **TE** Quiz, p. 68 `GENERAL` **TE** Alternative Assessment, p. 68 `GENERAL` **SE** Section Review,* p. 69 ■ `GENERAL` **CRF** Section Quiz* ■ `GENERAL`	UCP 1, 2; HNS 2; ES 2b
CRF Directed Reading A* ■ `BASIC`, B* `SPECIAL NEEDS` **CRF** Vocabulary and Section Summary* ■ `GENERAL` **SE** Reading Strategy Reading Organizer, p. 70 `GENERAL` **TE** Reading Strategy Activity, p. 71 `GENERAL` **TE** Inclusion Strategies, p. 71	**SE** Reading Checks, pp. 71, 72 `GENERAL` **TE** Reteaching, p. 72 `BASIC` **TE** Quiz, p. 72 `GENERAL` **TE** Alternative Assessment, p. 72 `GENERAL` **SE** Section Review,* p. 73 ■ `GENERAL` **CRF** Section Quiz* ■ `GENERAL`	UCP 1, 3; SAI 1, 2; ST 2; SPSP 5; HNS 1, 2, 3; ES 2b
CRF Directed Reading A* ■ `BASIC`, B* `SPECIAL NEEDS` **CRF** Vocabulary and Section Summary* ■ `GENERAL` **SE** Reading Strategy Reading Organizer, p. 74 `GENERAL` **TE** Reading Strategy Activity, p. 75 `GENERAL` **CRF** Critical Thinking Adiós Alamosaurus* `ADVANCED`	**SE** Reading Checks, pp. 74, 76, 78, 79 `GENERAL` **TE** Homework, p. 77 `GENERAL` **TE** Reteaching, p. 78 `BASIC` **TE** Quiz, p. 78 `GENERAL` **TE** Alternative Assessment, p. 78 `ADVANCED` **TE** Homework, p. 78 `GENERAL` **SE** Section Review,* p. 79 ■ `GENERAL` **CRF** Section Quiz* ■ `GENERAL`	UCP 1, 2, 3, 4; SAI 1, 2; SPSP 5; ES 1k, 2b
CRF Directed Reading A* ■ `BASIC`, B* `SPECIAL NEEDS` **CRF** Vocabulary and Section Summary* ■ `GENERAL` **SE** Reading Strategy Brainstorming, p. 80 `GENERAL` **TE** Reading Strategy Mnemonics, p. 82 `GENERAL` **TE** Inclusion Strategies, p. 83	**SE** Reading Checks, pp. 81, 82, 84 `GENERAL` **TE** Homework, p. 81 `ADVANCED` **TE** Reteaching, p. 84 `BASIC` **TE** Quiz, p. 84 `GENERAL` **TE** Alternative Assessment, p. 84 `GENERAL` **SE** Section Review,* p. 85 ■ `GENERAL` **TE** Homework, p. 85 `GENERAL` **CRF** Section Quiz* ■ `GENERAL`	UCP 1, 3; SAI 1, 2; ES 2b

One-Stop Planner® CD-ROM

This CD-ROM package includes:
- Lab Materials QuickList Software
- Holt Calendar Planner
- Customizable Lesson Plans
- Printable Worksheets
- ExamView® Test Generator
- Interactive Teacher Edition
- Holt PuzzlePro® Resources
- Holt PowerPoint® Resources

SCiLINKS. NSTA

www.scilinks.org

Maintained by the **National Science Teachers Association.** See Chapter Enrichment pages for a complete list of topics.

Current Science®

Check out **Current Science** articles and activities by visiting the HRW Web site at **go.hrw.com.** Just type in the keyword **HZ5CS06T.**

Classroom Videos

- **Lab Videos** demonstrate the chapter lab.
- **Brain Food Video Quizzes** help students review the chapter material.
- **CNN Videos** bring science into your students' daily life.

Visual Resources

CHAPTER STARTER TRANSPARENCY

The Rock and Fossil Record — CHAPTER STARTER

What a Find!

Imagine that you are a scientist looking for fossils. You are climbing up a sandstone cliff in unexplored mountains in North Africa. The sun is scorching. The temperature is 120°F in the shade. You see a tooth in the 90-million-year-old rock. It looks like a shark's tooth, but it is more than 12 cm long! You dig around the tooth and discover that it is attached to a huge skull. Eventually, you uncover the entire skull, which contains a full set of these ferocious teeth. The skull measures about 1.6 m in length, which is about the height of a refrigerator. You realize that this skull with savage teeth belonged to a large dinosaur.

You take the skull back to your lab to study it more closely. Given the size of the skull, you decide the skeleton of the animal it came from must have been about 14 m long—about as big as a school bus. That's even larger than *Tyrannosaurus rex!* This 90-million-year-old giant you have found most likely chased other dinosaurs by running on large, powerful hind legs, and its blade-like teeth meant certain death for its prey. You have discovered a vicious predator from the past!

BELLRINGER TRANSPARENCIES

The Rock and Fossil Record — BELLRINGER TRANSPARENCY

Section: Earth's Story and Those Who First Listened
"The Present Is the Key to the Past." This phrase was the cornerstone of the uniformitarianist theory developed by geologist James Hutton in the late 1700s.

Write a few sentences in your **science journal** about how studying the present could reveal the story of Earth's history. Use sketches to illustrate processes that occurred millions of years ago that you can still see today.

Section: Relative Dating: Which Came First?
Arrange the following sentences in a logical order to make a short story:
I stood in the checkout line.
I selected two apples.
I walked home from the store.
I gave the cashier money.
I went to the store.
The cashier gave me change.
I was hungry.

Write your story in your **science journal.**

TEACHING TRANSPARENCIES

Hutton and the Principle of Uniformitarianism

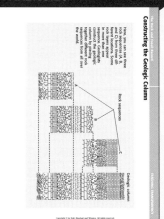

Constructing the Geologic Column

TEACHING TRANSPARENCIES

The Geologic Time Scale

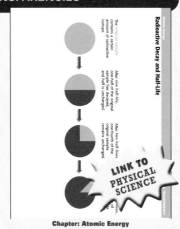

Radioactive Decay and Half-Life

The *original sample* contains a certain amount of radioactive isotope.

After one half-life, one-half of the original sample has decayed, and half is unchanged.

After two half-lives, one-fourth of the original sample remains unchanged.

LINK TO PHYSICAL SCIENCE

Chapter: Atomic Energy

CONCEPT MAPPING TRANSPARENCY

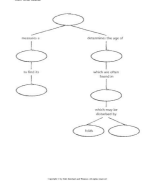

The Rock and Fossil Record — CONCEPT MAPPING TRANSPARENCY

Use the following terms to complete the concept map below:
sedimentary rocks, radioactive isotope, fossils, absolute dating, half-life, faults

---

Planning Resources

LESSON PLANS

Lesson Plan — SAMPLE

Section: Waves

Pacing
Regular Schedule: with lab(s):2 days / without lab(s):2 days
Block Schedule: with lab(s):1 1/2 days / without lab(s):1 day

Objectives
1. Relate the seven properties of life to a living organism.
2. Describe seven themes that can help you to organize what you learn about biology.
3. Identify the tiny structures that make up all living organisms.
4. Differentiate between reproduction and heredity and between metabolism and homeostasis.

National Science Education Standards Covered
LSInter6:Cells have particular structures that underlie their functions.
LSMat1:Most cell functions involve chemical reactions.
LSBeh1:Cells store and use information to guide their functions.
UCP1:Cell functions are regulated.
SI1: Cells can differentiate and form complete multicellular organisms.
PS1: Species evolve over time.
ESS1: The great diversity of organisms is the result of more than 3.5 billion years of evolution.
ESS2: Natural selection and its evolutionary consequences provide a scientific explanation for the fossil record of ancient life forms as well as for the striking molecular similarities observed among the diverse species of living organisms.
ST1: The millions of different species of plants, animals, and microorganisms that live on Earth today are related by descent from common ancestors.
ST2: The energy for life primarily comes from the sun.
SPSP1: The complexity and organization of organisms accommodates the need for obtaining, transforming, transporting, releasing, and eliminating the matter and energy used to sustain the organism.
SPSP6: As matter and energy flows through different levels of organization of living systems—cells, organs, communities—and between living systems and the physical environment, chemical elements are recombined in different ways.
HNS1: Organisms have behavioral responses to internal and external stimuli.

PARENT LETTER

SAMPLE

Dear Parent,

Your son's or daughter's science class will soon begin exploring the chapter entitled "The World of Physical Science." In this chapter, students will learn about how the scientific method applies to the world of physical science and the role of physical science in the world. By the end of the chapter, students should demonstrate a clear understanding of the chapter's main ideas and be able to discuss the following topics:

1. physical science as the study of energy and matter (Section 1)
2. the role of physical science in the world around them (Section 1)
3. careers that rely on physical science (Section 1)
4. the steps used in the scientific method (Section 2)
5. examples of technology (Section 2)
6. how the scientific method is used to answer questions and solve problems (Section 2)
7. how our knowledge of science changes over time (Section 2)
8. how models represent real objects or systems (Section 3)
9. examples of different ways models are used in science (Section 3)
10. the importance of the International System of Units (Section 4)
11. the appropriate units to use for particular measurements (Section 4)
12. how area and density are derived quantities (Section 4)

Questions to Ask Along the Way

You can help your son or daughter learn about these topics by asking interesting questions, such as the following:

- What are some surprising careers that use physical science?
- What is a characteristic of a good hypothesis?
- When is it a good idea to use a model?
- Why do Americans measure things in terms of inches and yards and meters?

ALSO IN SPANISH

TEST ITEM LISTING

TEST ITEM LISTING
The World of Earth Science — SAMPLE

MULTIPLE CHOICE

1. A limitation of models is that
   a. they are large enough to see.
   b. they do not act exactly like the things that they model.
   c. they are smaller than the things that they model.
   d. they model unfamiliar things.
   Answer: B   Difficulty: 1   Section: 3   Objective: 2

2. The length 10 m is equal to
   a. 100 cm.   c. 10,000 mm.
   b. 1,000 cm.   d. Both (b) and (c)
   Answer: B   Difficulty: 1   Section: 3   Objective: 2

3. To be valid, a hypothesis must be
   a. testable   c. made into a law
   b. supported by evidence   d. Both (a) and (b)
   Answer: B   Difficulty: 1   Section: 1   Objective: 2 1

4. The statement "Neila has a stain on her shirt" is an example of a(n)
   a. law.   c. observation.
   b. hypothesis.   d. prediction.
   Answer: C   Difficulty: 1   Section: 2   Objective: 2

5. A hypothesis is often developed out of
   a. observations.   c. laws.
   b. experiments.   d. Both (a) and (b)
   Answer: B   Difficulty: 1   Section: 3   Objective: 2

6. How many milliliters are in 3.5 kL?
   a. 3,500 mL   c. 3,500,000 mL
   b. 0.0035 mL   d. 35,000 mL
   Answer: C   Difficulty: 1   Section: 3   Objective: 2

7. A map of Seattle is an example of a
   a. law.   c. model.
   b. theory.   d. unit.
   Answer: B   Difficulty: 1   Section: 3   Objective: 2

8. A lab has the safety icons shown below. These icons mean that you should wear
   a. only safety goggles.   c. safety goggles and a lab apron.
   b. only a lab apron.   d. safety goggles, a lab apron, and gloves.
   Answer: B   Difficulty: 1   Section: 3   Objective: 2

9. The law of conservation of mass says the for al mass before a chemical change is
   a. more than the total mass after the change.
   b. less than the total mass after the change.
   c. the same as the total mass after the change.
   d. not the same as the total mass after the change.
   Answer: C   Difficulty: 1   Section: 3   Objective: 2

10. In which of the following areas might you find a geochemist at work?
    a. studying the chemistry of rocks   c. studying fishes
    b. studying forestry   d. studying the atmosphere
    Answer: B   Difficulty: 1   Section: 3   Objective: 2

One-Stop Planner® CD-ROM

This CD-ROM includes all of the resources shown here and the following time-saving tools:

- *Lab Materials QuickList Software*
- *Customizable lesson plans*
- *Holt Calendar Planner*
- *The powerful ExamView® Test Generator*

Meeting Individual Needs

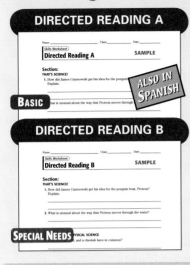

DIRECTED READING A
Skills Worksheet — Directed Reading A — SAMPLE
BASIC — ALSO IN SPANISH

DIRECTED READING B
Skills Worksheet — Directed Reading B — SAMPLE
SPECIAL NEEDS

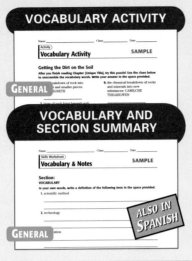

VOCABULARY ACTIVITY
Activity — Vocabulary Activity — SAMPLE
Getting the Dirt on the Soil
GENERAL

VOCABULARY AND SECTION SUMMARY
Skills Worksheet — Vocabulary & Notes — SAMPLE
GENERAL — ALSO IN SPANISH

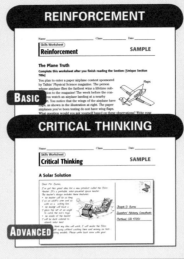

REINFORCEMENT
Skills Worksheet — Reinforcement — SAMPLE
The Plane Truth
BASIC

CRITICAL THINKING
Skills Worksheet — Critical Thinking — SAMPLE
A Solar Solution
ADVANCED

SCILINKS ACTIVITY
Activity — SciLinks Activity — SAMPLE
MARINE ECOSYSTEMS
GENERAL

SCIENCE PUZZLERS, TWISTERS & TEASERS
The Rock and Fossil Record
Anagrams
GENERAL

Labs and Activities

ECOLABS & FIELD ACTIVITIES
Rock of Ages
ADVANCED

LONG-TERM PROJECTS & RESEARCH IDEAS
The Hard Rock Chronicles
ADVANCED

LABS YOU CAN EAT
GeoPancakes
BASIC

INQUIRY LABS
A Penny for Your Thoughts
GENERAL

DATASHEETS FOR QUICK LABS
Reaction to Stress — SAMPLE

DATASHEETS FOR CHAPTER LABS
Using Scientific Methods — SAMPLE

DATASHEETS FOR LABBOOK
Does It All Add Up? — SAMPLE

Review and Assessments

SECTION QUIZ
Assessment — Section Quiz — SAMPLE
GENERAL — ALSO IN SPANISH

SECTION REVIEW
Skills Worksheet — Section Review — SAMPLE
GENERAL

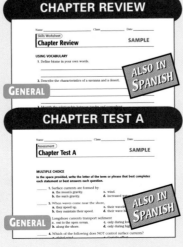

CHAPTER REVIEW
Skills Worksheet — Chapter Review — SAMPLE
GENERAL — ALSO IN SPANISH

CHAPTER TEST A
Assessment — Chapter Test A — SAMPLE
GENERAL — ALSO IN SPANISH

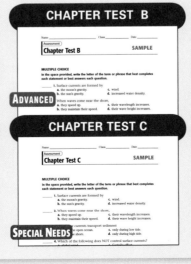

CHAPTER TEST B
Assessment — Chapter Test B — SAMPLE
ADVANCED

CHAPTER TEST C
Assessment — Chapter Test C — SAMPLE
SPECIAL NEEDS

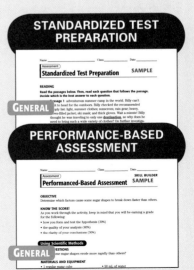

STANDARDIZED TEST PREPARATION
Assessment — Standardized Test Preparation — SAMPLE
GENERAL

PERFORMANCE-BASED ASSESSMENT
Assessment — Performanced-Based Assessment — SAMPLE
GENERAL

This Chapter Enrichment provides relevant and interesting information to expand and enhance your presentation of the chapter material.

Section 1

Earth's Story and Those Who First Listened

Actualism

- Although James Hutton was the first to introduce the principles of uniformitarianism, he is considered an actualist, not a strict uniformitarianist. He recognized that while many geologic processes happen slowly, some catastrophic events do play a role in the formation of the Earth. Today, geologists accept actualism as a more logical explanation of Earth's history.

Section 2

Relative Dating: Which Came First?

Nicolaus Steno

- Credit for discovering the principles of superposition and original horizontality is given to Niels Stensen (also known as Nicolaus Steno), born in Denmark in 1638. Though originally trained in anatomy and medicine, Steno became interested in geology while serving as the house physician to Grand Duke Ferdinand II of Tuscany. During this period, Steno made significant geologic discoveries. In addition to establishing the principles of superposition and original horizontality, Steno was one of the first Western scientists to argue that fossils are organic.

Section 3

Absolute Dating: A Measure of Time

Marie and Pierre Curie

- The Curies met in spring 1894 while Marie was studying mathematics and physics at the Sorbonne, in Paris. They married in 1895 and worked together in Pierre's laboratory. Marie began work on her doctoral thesis shortly after 1896, the year Henri Becquerel discovered that a strange radiation was emitted by uranium. Marie continued Becquerel's work, obtained her doctorate on radioactive substances in 1903, and won the Nobel Prize for physics with her husband and Becquerel.

- In 1906, Pierre Curie was killed in a wagon accident in Paris. Marie Curie was grief-stricken and dedicated the rest of her life to the work she and her husband had begun. She headed his laboratory at the Sorbonne and became the first woman lecturer at the university. In 1911, Marie received her second Nobel Prize, this time in chemistry for isolating pure radium. She died on July 4, 1934, of leukemia, which was probably caused by her prolonged exposure to radiation.

Radiometric Age-Dating

- The work of Becquerel and the Curies eventually changed the fields of archeology, geology, and paleontology. Before their work, geologists were restricted to using relative methods of dating when trying to determine the age of rocks and minerals. However, after scientists discovered that radioactive elements decay at a constant rate, physicists used this rate to calculate the ages of the rocks that contain these elements.

Section 4

Looking at Fossils
Prehistoric Weevil DNA

- In 1993, research in fossil DNA took a tremendous leap forward when Dr. George Poinar, of the University of California at Berkeley, successfully extracted fragmented DNA from the tissue of a weevil that is 125 million years old and was encased in amber found in Lebanon. In almost all fossils, the DNA has decayed and can no longer be analyzed.

Coelacanths: Living Fossils

- Coelacanths are large, carnivorous, lobe-finned fish. Their fossil record dates back to more than 350 million years ago and, until the 20th century, they were believed to have become extinct about 65 million years ago. In 1938, Marjorie Courtenay-Latimer, a museum curator in a small port village near Cape Town, South Africa, noticed an unusual blue-finned fish among the day's catch at the local docks—it was a coelacanth! A second coelacanth was recovered in 1952 by anglers, again off the African coast. Scientists believe that only a small number of the fish still survive, and in 1995, researchers declared the animal to be in danger of extinction.

- In 1998, Dr. Mark Erdmann confirmed at least two coelacanth specimens from North Sulawesi, Indonesia, 10,000 km from the African coast. The coelacanths were discovered living in volcanic caves below sea level.

Is That a Fact!

◆ The largest coprolite ever found is a mound of feces that is 65 million years old and was probably left by a *Tyrannosaurus rex*. It is 43 cm across and 15 cm high.

Section 5

Time Marches On
Life in the Precambrian Era

- The period of time from the formation of Earth 4.6 billion years ago to 543 million years ago is called the Precambrian era. Until the discovery of soft-bodied organisms in Australia in 1947, paleontologists believed that only single-celled microorganisms and blue-green algae lived during this period. Now scientists know that a wide variety of animals resembling jellyfish, annelids, and even arthropods evolved in Precambrian seas between 590 million and 700 million years ago. These animals are so far the oldest known multicellular organisms, although traces of possibly earlier ones date back to 1.2 billion years.

Overview

Tell students that this chapter will help them learn about the history of the Earth. The chapter describes ways in which scientists use the rock and fossil record to decipher Earth's history.

Assessing Prior Knowledge

Students should be familiar with the following topics:

- basic geological processes
- the classification of life

Identifying Misconceptions

When students think of fossils, they probably think of body fossils—the hard parts of organisms most commonly preserved in rock. Make students aware that organisms can also be preserved in such substances as amber, asphalt, and ice, some of which may preserve soft tissues. The soft tissues of plants and animals can also be replaced by minerals, but this replacement rarely happens. Also inform students that the tracks, trails, and burrows made by organisms are considered fossils.

3

The Rock and Fossil Record

About the PHOTO

This extremely well preserved crocodile fossil has been out of water for 49 million years. Its skeleton was collected in an abandoned mine pit in Messel, Germany.

PRE-READING ACTIVITY

FOLDNOTES **Layered Book** Before you read the chapter, create the FoldNote entitled "Layered Book" described in the **Study Skills** section of the Appendix. Label the tabs of the layered book with "Earth's history," "Relative dating," "Absolute dating," "Fossils," and "Geologic time." As you read the chapter, write information you learn about each category under the appropriate tab.

Standards Correlations

National Science Education Standards

The following codes indicate the National Science Education Standards that correlate to this chapter. The full text of the standards is in the front of the book.

Chapter Opener
SAI 1, 2

Section 1 Earth's Story and Those Who First Listened
UCP 2, 4; SAI 1, 2; SPSP 5; HNS 1, 2, 3; ES 2a

Section 2 Relative Dating: Which Came First?
UCP 1, 2; HNS 2; ES 2b

Section 3 Absolute Dating: A Measure of Time
UCP 1, 3; SAI 1, 2; ST 2; SPSP 5; HNS 1, 2, 3; ES 2b

Section 4 Looking at Fossils
UCP 1, 2, 3, 4; SAI 1, 2; SPSP 5; ES 1k, 2b

Section 5 Time Marches On
UCP 1, 3; SAI 1, 2; HNS 2; ES 2b

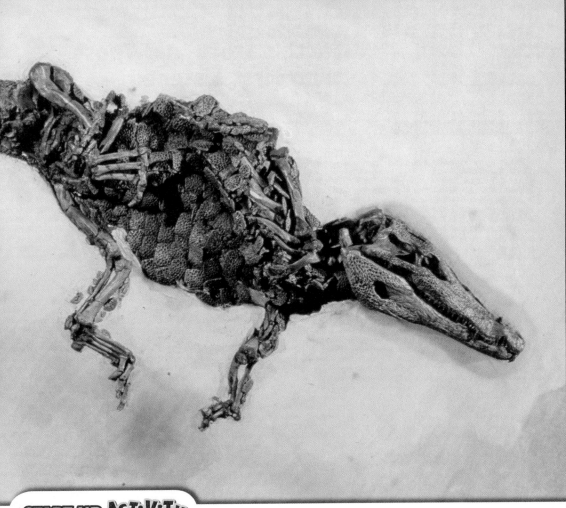

Answers

1. Sample answer: Textures and shapes were useful in identifying the model fossils. Small details, colors, and the internal structure of the objects were not preserved.

2. Sample answer: Scientists carefully study fossil remains to determine the characteristics of the organism that became fossilized.

START-UP ACTIVITY

Making Fossils

How do scientists learn from fossils? In this activity, you will study "fossils" and identify the object that made each.

Procedure

1. You and three or four of your classmates will be given **several pieces** of **modeling clay** and a **paper sack** containing a few **small objects.**

2. Press each object firmly into a piece of clay. Try to leave a "fossil" imprint showing as much detail as possible.

3. After you have made an imprint of each object, exchange your model fossils with another group.

4. On a **sheet of paper,** describe the fossils you have received. List as many details as possible. What patterns and textures do you observe?

5. Work as a group to identify each fossil, and check your results. Were you right?

Analysis

1. What kinds of details were important in identifying your fossils? What kinds of details were not preserved in the imprints? For example, can you tell the materials from which the objects are made or their color?

2. Explain how scientists follow similar methods when studying fossils.

Chapter Lab
SAI 1, 2

Chapter Review
UCP 1, 2, 3, 4; ST 2; HNS 2; ES 1k, 2a, 2b

Science in Action
UCP 2, 3, 4, 5; ST 2; SPSP 5; HNS 1, 2, 3; ES 2b

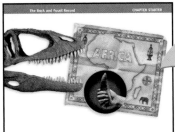

The Rock and Fossil Record   CHAPTER STARTER

What a Find!

Imagine that you are a scientist looking for fossils. You are climbing up a sandstone cliff in unexplored mountains in North Africa. The sun is scorching. The temperature is 120°F in the shade. You see a tooth in the 90-million-year-old rock. It looks like a shark's tooth, but it is more than 12 cm long! You dig around the tooth and discover that it is attached to a huge skull. Eventually, you uncover

You take the skull back to your lab to study it more closely. Given the size of the skull, you decide the skeleton of the animal it came from must have been about 14 m long—about as big as a school bus. That's even larger than *Tyrannosaurus rex!* This 90-million-year-old giant you have found most likely chased other dinosaurs by running on large, powerful hind legs, and its blade-

Chapter Starter Transparency
Use this transparency to help students begin thinking about the excitement of discovering and studying fossils.

CHAPTER RESOURCES

Technology

 Transparencies
- Chapter Starter Transparency   READING SKILLS

Student Edition on CD-ROM

Guided Reading Audio CD
- English or Spanish

Classroom Videos
- Brain Food Video Quiz

Workbooks

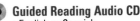 **Science Puzzlers, Twisters & Teasers**
- The Rock and Fossil Record   GENERAL

Focus

Overview

In this section, students will explore the origins of modern geology by comparing and contrasting uniformitarianism and catastrophism. Students will learn that modern geology is a synthesis of both theories and that the forces that shaped the Earth around them are still at work today.

◉ Bellringer

On the board, write the following: "The present is the key to the past." Tell students that this phrase was the cornerstone of the uniformitarianist theory. Have students write a few sentences about how studying the present could reveal the story of Earth's history.

Motivate

ACTIVITY ——————— GENERAL

Debate Posters Have students design a poster announcing a debate between a catastrophist and a uniformitarian. Encourage students to use phrases and illustrations that would attract supporters from both sides. Have them summarize the major points of both sides, and display the finished posters in the classroom. **LS Visual** — English Language Learners

Objectives

◉ Compare uniformitarianism and catastrophism.

◉ Describe how the science of geology has changed over the past 200 years.

◉ Explain the role of paleontology in the study of Earth's history.

Terms to Learn

uniformitarianism
catastrophism
paleontology

READING STRATEGY

Reading Organizer As you read this section, make a table comparing uniformitarianism and catastrophism.

Earth's Story and Those Who First Listened

How do mountains form? How is new rock created? How old is the Earth? Have you ever asked these questions? Nearly 250 years ago, a Scottish farmer and scientist named James Hutton did.

Searching for answers to his questions, Hutton spent more than 30 years studying rock formations in Scotland and England. His observations led to the foundation of modern geology.

The Principle of Uniformitarianism

In 1788, James Hutton collected his notes and wrote *Theory of the Earth.* In *Theory of the Earth,* he stated that the key to understanding Earth's history was all around us. In other words, processes that we observe today—such as erosion and deposition—remain uniform, or do not change, over time. This assumption is now called uniformitarianism. **Uniformitarianism** is the idea that the same geologic processes shaping the Earth today have been at work throughout Earth's history. **Figure 1** shows how Hutton developed the idea of uniformitarianism.

Figure 1 *Hutton observed gradual, uniform geologic change.*

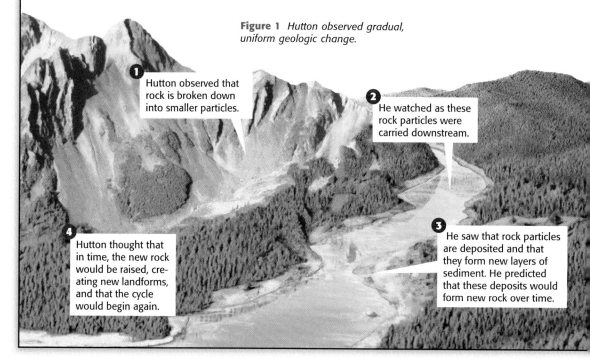

1 Hutton observed that rock is broken down into smaller particles.

2 He watched as these rock particles were carried downstream.

3 He saw that rock particles are deposited and that they form new layers of sediment. He predicted that these deposits would form new rock over time.

4 Hutton thought that in time, the new rock would be raised, creating new landforms, and that the cycle would begin again.

CHAPTER RESOURCES

Chapter Resource File

- Lesson Plan
- Directed Reading A **BASIC**
- Directed Reading B **SPECIAL NEEDS**

Technology

- Transparencies
  • Bellringer
  • Hutton and the Principle of Uniformitarianism

Is That a Fact!

James Hutton's colleague, Sir James Hall, dramatically demonstrated Hutton's theories by melting rock in a furnace and letting it cool, which showed how the rock changed from one form to another form. This demonstration struck a major blow against the catastrophists.

Figure 2 *This photograph shows Siccar Point on the coast of Scotland. Siccar Point is one of the places where Hutton observed results of geologic processes that would lead him to form his principle of uniformitarianism.*

Uniformitarianism Versus Catastrophism

Hutton's theories sparked a scientific debate by suggesting that Earth was much older than previously thought. In Hutton's time, most people thought that Earth was only a few thousand years old. A few thousand years was not nearly enough time for the gradual geologic processes that Hutton described to have shaped our planet. The rocks that he observed at Siccar Point, shown in **Figure 2,** were deposited and folded, indicating a long geological history. To explain Earth's history, most scientists supported catastrophism. **Catastrophism** is the principle that states that all geologic change occurs suddenly. Supporters of catastrophism thought that Earth's features, such as its mountains, canyons, and seas, formed during rare, sudden events called *catastrophes.* These unpredictable events caused rapid geologic change over large areas—sometimes even globally.

✓ *Reading Check* **According to catastrophists, what was the rate of geologic change?** (*See the Appendix for answers to Reading Checks.*)

A Victory for Uniformitarianism

Despite Hutton's work, catastrophism remained geology's guiding principle for decades. Only after the work of British geologist Charles Lyell did people seriously consider uniformitarianism as geology's guiding principle.

From 1830 to 1833, Lyell published three volumes, collectively titled *Principles of Geology,* in which he reintroduced uniformitarianism. Armed with Hutton's notes and new evidence of his own, Lyell successfully challenged the principle of catastrophism. Lyell saw no reason to doubt that major geologic change happened at the same rate in the past as it happens in the present—gradually.

uniformitarianism a principle that states that geologic processes that occurred in the past can be explained by current geologic processes

catastrophism a principle that states that geologic change occurs suddenly

CONNECTION TO Biology

WRITING SKILL **Darwin and Lyell** The theory of evolution was developed soon after Lyell introduced his ideas, which was no coincidence. Lyell and Charles Darwin were good friends, and their talks greatly influenced Darwin's theories. Similar to uniformitarianism, Darwin's theory of evolution proposes that changes in species occur gradually over long periods of time. Write a short essay comparing uniformitarianism and evolution.

Uniformitarianism Versus Catastrophism Ask students to engage in a debate that might have taken place between James Hutton and the catastrophists. Emphasize to students representing the catastrophists that the catastrophists' argument had a strong theological base and was the accepted geologic theory of the time. Help students imagine the opposition Hutton probably faced when he introduced his ideas. Students can advertise their debates with the posters they made in the Activity entitled "Debate Posters" under the Motivate head. **LS** Interpersonal

CONNECTION ACTIVITY
Language Arts ── **GENERAL**

A Conversation Between Darwin and Lyell Although Charles Darwin and Charles Lyell were avid correspondents and good friends, they did not agree on everything. Darwin was quick to accept the principle of uniformitarianism; he read Lyell's *Principles of Geology* before his famous 1831 voyage on HMS *Beagle.* However, Lyell did not readily embrace Darwin's theories of natural selection. It was not until much later in life that Charles Lyell vigorously supported Darwin's ideas. Ask students to write a script for a conversation that the two scientists might have had. Have them imagine that Darwin has just returned from his journey aboard the HMS *Beagle.* Ask students what questions might Darwin and Lyell have exchanged. Students can present the conversations as short skits. **LS** Verbal

Answer to Connection to Biology
Student essays should include the idea that changes due to uniformitarianism or evolution may occur over very long periods of time.

Answer to Reading Check
Catastrophists believed that all geologic change occurs rapidly.

Close

Reteaching — BASIC

Summarizing Modern Geology
Have students write a one-paragraph essay that explains how modern geology incorporates catastrophism and uniformitarianism. **LS** Verbal

Quiz — GENERAL

1. What is catastrophism? (Catastrophism is the idea that geologic change occurred suddenly as a result of infrequent, disastrous events.)

2. Describe uniformitarianism. (Uniformitarianism is the principle that the Earth has been shaped by gradual changes throughout history and is shaped by gradual changes that are still occurring today.)

Alternative Assessment — GENERAL

Writing **Addressing Mr. Hutton or Mr. Lyell** Have students write a letter to Charles Lyell or James Hutton. The letter should explain why the student agrees or disagrees with the scientist's theories. Suggest that students end the letter with at least two questions that they would like to ask the scientist. Have students exchange letters and answer each other's questions. **LS** Verbal/Interpersonal

Modern Geology—A Happy Medium

During the late 20th century, scientists such as Stephen J. Gould challenged Lyell's uniformitarianism. They believed that catastrophes do, at times, play an important role in shaping Earth's history.

Today, scientists realize that neither uniformitarianism nor catastrophism accounts for all geologic change throughout Earth's history. Although most geologic change is gradual and uniform, catastrophes that cause geologic change have occurred during Earth's long history. For example, huge craters have been found where asteroids and comets are thought to have struck Earth in the past. Some scientists think one such asteroid strike, approximately 65 million years ago, may have caused the dinosaurs to become extinct. **Figure 3** is an imaginary re-creation of the asteroid strike that is thought to have caused the extinction of the dinosaurs. The impact of this asteroid is thought to have thrown debris into the atmosphere. The debris spread around the entire planet and rained down on Earth for decades. This global debris cloud may have blocked the sun's rays, causing major changes in the global climate that doomed the dinosaurs.

✓ Reading Check How can a catastrophe affect life on Earth?

Figure 3 *Today, scientists think that sudden events are responsible for some changes during Earth's past. An asteroid hitting Earth, for example, may have led to the extinction of the dinosaurs about 65 million years ago.*

Answer to Reading Check
A global catastrophe can cause the extinction of species.

Paleontology—The Study of Past Life

The history of the Earth would be incomplete without a knowledge of the organisms that have inhabited our planet and the conditions under which they lived. The science involved with the study of past life is called **paleontology.** Scientists who study this life are called *paleontologists.* The data paleontologists use are fossils. Fossils are the remains of organisms preserved by geologic processes. Some paleontologists specialize in the study of particular organisms. Invertebrate paleontologists study animals without backbones, whereas vertebrate paleontologists, such as the scientist in **Figure 4,** study animals with backbones. Paleobotanists study fossils of plants. Other paleontologists reconstruct past ecosystems, study the traces left behind by animals, and piece together the conditions under which fossils were formed. As you see, the study of past life is as varied and complex as Earth's history itself.

Figure 4 *Edwin Colbert was a 20th-century vertebrate paleontologist who made important contributions to the study of dinosaurs.*

paleontology the scientific study of fossils

Answers to Section Review

1. Sample answer: Uniformitarianism is the idea that the same gradual, uniform geologic processes that shape the Earth today have been at work throughout Earth's history. Catastrophism is the idea that all geologic processes that have shaped the Earth throughout Earth's history have been sudden and catastrophic. Paleontology is the scientific study of the history of life using the remains of organisms preserved by geologic processes.

2. d

3. The principle of uniformitarianism states that all geologic processes that shape the Earth are gradual and uniform. The principle of catastrophism states that all geologic processes that shape the Earth are sudden and catastrophic.

4. Catastrophism dominated geologic thinking until it was replaced by Hutton and Lyell's theories of uniformitarianism in the 1800s. Modern geology is based on uniformitarianism, but modern geology recognizes the role of catastrophism in geologic history.

5. Sample answer: One example of catastrophic global change would be a global climate change caused by an asteroid striking Earth.

6. Vertebrate paleontologists study fossils of animals that have backbones. Invertebrate paleontologists study fossils of animals that do not have backbones. Paleobotanists study plant fossils.

7. *area* = $\pi(85 \text{ km})^2$
3.1416 $\times$ 85 km $\times$ 85 km = 22,698 km^2

8. Uniformitarianism is considered to be the foundation of modern geology because most geologic change is gradual and uniform rather than sudden and catastrophic.

9. Answers may vary. An example of a recent catastrophe is the eruption of Mount Pinatubo in the Philippines in 1991.

SECTION Review

Summary

- Uniformitarianism assumes that geologic change is gradual. Catastrophism is based on the idea that geologic change is sudden.

- Modern geology is based on the idea that gradual geologic change is interrupted by catastrophes.

- Using fossils to study past life is called *paleontology.*

Using Key Terms

1. Use each of the following terms in a separate sentence: *uniformitarianism, catastrophism,* and *paleontology.*

Understanding Key Ideas

2. Which of the following words describes change according to the principle of uniformitarianism?
   a. sudden
   b. rare
   c. global
   d. gradual

3. What is the difference between uniformitarianism and catastrophism?

4. Describe how the science of geology has changed.

5. Give one example of catastrophic global change.

6. Describe the work of three types of paleontologists.

Math Skills

7. An impact crater left by an asteroid strike has a radius of 85 km. What is the area of the crater? (Hint: The area of a circle is πr^2.)

Critical Thinking

8. **Analyzing Ideas** Why is uniformitarianism considered to be the foundation of modern geology?

9. **Applying Concepts** Give an example of a type of recent catastrophe.

SCiLINKS.

NSTA
Developed and maintained by the National Science Teachers Association

For a variety of links related to this chapter, go to www.scilinks.org

Topic: Earth's Story
SciLinks code: HSM0450

CHAPTER RESOURCES

Chapter Resource File

- **Section Quiz** `GENERAL`
- **Section Review** `GENERAL`
- **Vocabulary and Section Summary** `GENERAL`

Focus

Overview

In this section, students learn about relative dating techniques and how the geologic column is used to determine the sequence of rock formations.

🎙 Bellringer

Ask students to arrange the following sentences in a logical order to make a short story:

1. I stood in the checkout line.
2. I selected two apples.
3. I walked home from the store.
4. I gave the cashier money.
5. I went to the store.
6. The cashier gave me change.
7. I was hungry.

(7, 5, 2, 1, 4, 6, 3)

Motivate

Demonstration — GENERAL

Superposition Stack several books on your desk. Tell students that the books represent layers of rock that were deposited at different times. Ask students which layer is the oldest. (the one on the bottom) Ask which rock layer is the youngest. (the one on top) Ask students to explain their answers, and tell them that they have just applied a basic geologic concept—the principle of superposition.

 Visual

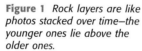
READING WARM-UP

Objectives

● Explain how relative dating is used in geology.

● Explain the principle of superposition.

● Describe how the geologic column is used in relative dating.

● Identify two events and two features that disrupt rock layers.

● Explain how physical features are used to determine relative ages.

Terms to Learn

relative dating
superposition
geologic column
unconformity

READING STRATEGY

Reading Organizer As you read this section, create an outline of the section. Use the headings from the section in your outline.

Relative Dating: Which Came First?

Imagine that you are a detective investigating a crime scene. What is the first thing you would do?

You might begin by dusting the scene for fingerprints or by searching for witnesses. As a detective, you must figure out the sequence of events that took place before you reached the crime scene.

Geologists have a similar goal when investigating the Earth. They try to determine the order in which events have happened during Earth's history. But instead of relying on fingerprints and witnesses, geologists rely on rocks and fossils to help them in their investigation. Determining whether an object or event is older or younger than other objects or events is called **relative dating.**

The Principle of Superposition

Suppose that you have an older brother who takes a lot of photographs of your family and piles them in a box. Over the years, he keeps adding new photographs to the top of the stack. Think about the family history recorded in those photos. Where are the oldest photographs—the ones taken when you were a baby? Where are the most recent photographs—those taken last week?

Layers of sedimentary rock, such as the ones shown in **Figure 1,** are like stacked photographs. As you move from top to bottom, the layers are older. The principle that states that younger rocks lie above older rocks in undisturbed sequences is called **superposition.**

Figure 1 *Rock layers are like photos stacked over time—the younger ones lie above the older ones.*

CHAPTER RESOURCES

Chapter Resource File

• Lesson Plan
• Directed Reading A **BASIC**
• Directed Reading B **SPECIAL NEEDS**

Technology

Transparencies
• Bellringer
• Constructing the Geologic Column

Disturbing Forces

Not all rock sequences are arranged with the oldest layers on the bottom and the youngest layers on top. Some rock sequences are disturbed by forces within the Earth. These forces can push other rocks into a sequence, tilt or fold rock layers, and break sequences into movable parts. Sometimes, geologists even find rock sequences that are upside down! The disruptions of rock sequences pose a challenge to geologists trying to determine the relative ages of rocks. Fortunately, geologists can get help from a very valuable tool—the geologic column.

The Geologic Column

To make their job easier, geologists combine data from all the known undisturbed rock sequences around the world. From this information, geologists create the geologic column, as illustrated in **Figure 2.** The **geologic column** is an ideal sequence of rock layers that contains all the known fossils and rock formations on Earth, arranged from oldest to youngest.

Geologists rely on the geologic column to interpret rock sequences. Geologists also use the geologic column to identify the layers in puzzling rock sequences.

Reading Check List two ways in which geologists use the geologic column. (*See the Appendix for answers to Reading Checks.*)

relative dating any method of determining whether an event or object is older or younger than other events or objects

superposition a principle that states that younger rocks lie above older rocks if the layers have not been disturbed

geologic column an arrangement of rock layers in which the oldest rocks are at the bottom

---

Figure 2 **Constructing the Geologic Column**

Here, you can see three rock sequences (A, B, and C) from three different locations. Some rock layers appear in more than one sequence. Geologists construct the geologic column by piecing together different rock sequences from all over the world.

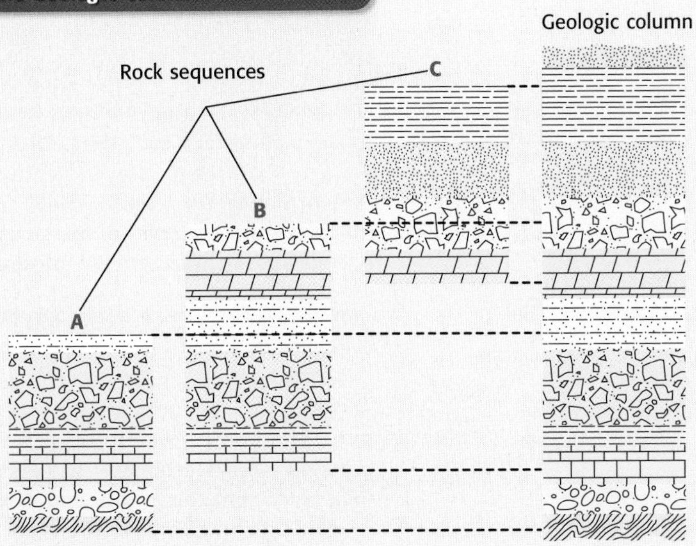

Rock sequences

Geologic column

Teach

Using the Figure— BASIC
Geologic Column Practice
The geologic column is an easy concept for students to understand if they get some hands-on practice. Before the lesson, you may wish to make photocopies of **Figure 2.** Cut out the columns, and have students work independently to piece them together correctly. **English Language Learners**
LS Visual/Logical

MISCONCEPTION ALERT

The Geologic Column
Students may think that there is a place on Earth that has a continuous sequence of all the rocks formed throughout history. Emphasize to students that no single location on Earth has a continuous sequence of all of the rocks formed throughout geologic history. The geologic column is an idealized sequence of rock layers that have formed around the world since the Earth formed. The geologic column was first pieced together in the mid-19th century, and it is continually being revised as geologists map more of the Earth's rock layers.

Answer to Reading Check
Geologists use the geologic column to interpret rock sequences and to identify layers in puzzling rock sequences.

Prediction Guide As students explore this section, ask them to answer the following questions:

- If a fault is observed in rock layers, are the rock layers or is the fault older? (the layers)

- If rock layers are deposited horizontally but you see them sharply tilted, did the deposition happen first or did the tilting happen first? (the deposition)

LS Logical

ACTIVITY — GENERAL

Modeling Faults and Intrusions
Show how intrusions and faults disturb rock layers by doing this simple demonstration. Glue several different-colored sponges together to form a model rock sequence. To show a fault, make a straight, diagonal cut through all of the sponge layers. Demonstrate fault movement by sliding the two sponge sections alongside each other. Have students work together to demonstrate intrusions, folding, and tilting. As an extension, have students create a permanent display by gluing their examples to a piece of poster board. **LS** Visual

Figure 3 How Rock Layers Become Disturbed

Fault A *fault* is a break in the Earth's crust along which blocks of the crust slide relative to one another.

Intrusion An *intrusion* is molten rock from the Earth's interior that squeezes into existing rock and cools.

Folding *Folding* occurs when rock layers bend and buckle from Earth's internal forces.

Tilting *Tilting* occurs when internal forces in the Earth slant rock layers.

Disturbed Rock Layers

Geologists often find features that cut across existing layers of rock. Geologists use the relationships between rock layers and the features that cut across them to assign relative ages to the features and the layers. They know that the features are younger than the rock layers because the rock layers had to be present before the features could cut across them. Faults and intrusions are examples of features that cut across rock layers. A fault and an intrusion are illustrated in **Figure 3.**

Events That Disturb Rock Layers

Geologists assume that the way sediment is deposited to form rock layers—in horizontal layers—has not changed over time. According to this principle, if rock layers are not horizontal, something must have disturbed them after they formed. This principle allows geologists to determine the relative ages of rock layers and the events that disturbed them.

Folding and tilting are two types of events that disturb rock layers. These events are always younger than the rock layers they affect. The results of folding and tilting are shown in **Figure 3.**

MISCONCEPTION ///ALERT\\\

Intrusions Students may think that intrusions are vertical penetrations of rock layers. Point out to students that magma, like water, always follows the path of least resistance. Often, intrusions occur at angles or horizontally, between rock layers.

Group ACTIVITY — GENERAL

Field Trip Arrange a field trip to a local area that has exposed rock strata. If possible, contact a geologist from a local university or a museum to accompany the group. In small groups, have students try to locate unconformities and explain the origins of the unconformities. Encourage students to make drawings of the rock formations that they observe, and have them label the features that are described in this chapter. **LS** Visual

Gaps in the Record—Unconformities

Faults, intrusions, and the effects of folding and tilting can make dating rock layers a challenge. Sometimes, layers of rock are missing altogether, creating a gap in the geologic record. To think of this another way, let's say that you stack your newspapers every day after reading them. Now, let's suppose you want to look at a paper you read 10 days ago. You know that the paper should be 10 papers deep in the stack. But when you look, the paper is not there. What happened? Perhaps you forgot to put the paper in the stack. Now, imagine a missing rock layer instead of a missing newspaper.

Missing Evidence

Missing rock layers create breaks in rock-layer sequences called unconformities. An **unconformity** is a surface that represents a missing part of the geologic column. Unconformities also represent missing time—time that was not recorded in layers of rock. When geologists find an unconformity, they must question whether the "missing layer" was never present or whether it was somehow removed. **Figure 4** shows how *nondeposition*, or the stoppage of deposition when a supply of sediment is cut off, and *erosion* create unconformities.

unconformity a break in the geologic record created when rock layers are eroded or when sediment is not deposited for a long period of time

✔️ **Reading Check** Define the term unconformity.

Figure 4 **How Unconformities Are Created**

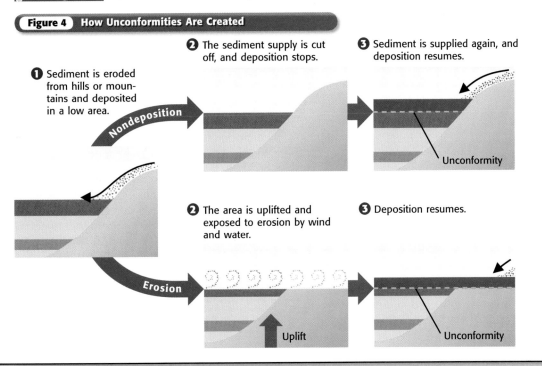

① Sediment is eroded from hills or mountains and deposited in a low area.

Nondeposition

② The sediment supply is cut off, and deposition stops.

③ Sediment is supplied again, and deposition resumes.

Unconformity

Erosion

② The area is uplifted and exposed to erosion by wind and water.

Uplift

③ Deposition resumes.

Unconformity

Answer to Reading Check

An unconformity is a surface that represents a missing part of the geologic column.

Is That a Fact!

Unconformities can represent a short gap or a very long gap in the geologic record. The time gap can be as little as a few hundred years or as much as several billion years. Geologists must analyze many different variables to determine the amount of time an unconformity represents.

Using the Figure—**ADVANCED**

Geologic History Comic Strip
Have students study **Figure 4** and then work independently to create a comic strip that continues the sequence of images in the figure. Students can illustrate geologic events such as intrusions, tilting, folding, faulting, volcanic deposition, or unconformities. Have students share their illustrations with the class and explain the geologic history of their comic strip.
LS Visual

ACTiViTY ————— **BASIC**

Unconformities On the board or overhead projector, use different colors to create a rock formation that consists of five rock layers, an angular unconformity, a nonconformity, and two different fossils located in different layers. Ask students the following:

• Where is the angular unconformity and the nonconformity? How are they different? (An angular unconformity exists between layers that were tilted and horizontal rock layers. The nonconformity is found where nonlayered rock has eroded and where sedimentary rock has been deposited on its surface.)

• Partially erase the top layer of rock; then add two more layers of deposition. Ask students to name this type of unconformity. (disconformity)
LS Visual

Reteaching —

Unconformity Review Have students draw a diagram of each type of unconformity on a separate index card. Students can also depict folds, faults, tilting, and intrusions on separate index cards. Have students exchange cards and then try to guess the geologic concept shown on each card. Students can use the index cards as study aids. **LS** Visual

Quiz — GENERAL

1. What is an unconformity? Name some types of unconformities. (Unconformities are gaps in an area's geologic column. Examples include disconformities, nonconformities, and angular unconformities.)

2. If a folded outcrop features an undeformed intrusion that is interrupted by faulting, in what order did the folding, the faulting, and the intrusion occur? (folding, intrusion, faulting)

Alternative Assessment — GENERAL

Making Models Have students draw and label disconformities, nonconformities, and angular unconformities in their **science journal.** Ask them to identify the youngest and the oldest rocks and include examples of intrusions, folds, and faults. **LS** Visual

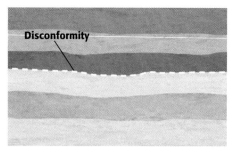

Figure 5 *A disconformity exists where part of a sequence of parallel rock layers is missing.*

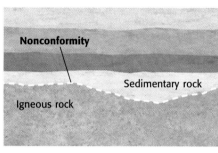

Figure 6 *A nonconformity exists where sedimentary rock layers lie on top of an eroded surface of nonlayered igneous or metamorphic rock.*

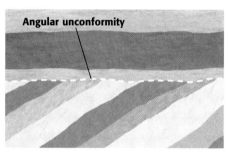

Figure 7 *An angular unconformity exists between horizontal rock layers and rock layers that are tilted or folded.*

Types of Unconformities

Most unconformities form by both erosion and nondeposition. But other factors can complicate matters. To simplify the study of unconformities, geologists place them into three major categories: disconformities, nonconformities, and angular unconformities. The three diagrams at left illustrate these three categories.

Disconformities

The most common type of unconformity is a disconformity, which is illustrated in **Figure 5.** *Disconformities* are found where part of a sequence of parallel rock layers is missing. A disconformity can form in the following way. A sequence of rock layers is uplifted. Younger layers at the top of the sequence are removed by erosion, and the eroded material is deposited elsewhere. At some future time, deposition resumes, and sediment buries the old erosion surface. The disconformity that results shows where erosion has taken place and rock layers are missing. A disconformity represents thousands to many millions of years of missing time.

Nonconformities

A nonconformity is illustrated in **Figure 6.** *Nonconformities* are found where horizontal sedimentary rock layers lie on top of an eroded surface of older intrusive igneous or metamorphic rock. Intrusive igneous and metamorphic rocks form deep within the Earth. When these rocks are raised to Earth's surface, they are eroded. Deposition causes the erosion surface to be buried. Nonconformities represent millions of years of missing time.

Angular Unconformities

An angular unconformity is shown in **Figure 7.** *Angular unconformities* are found between horizontal layers of sedimentary rock and layers of rock that have been tilted or folded. The tilted or folded layers were eroded before horizontal layers formed above them. Angular unconformities represent millions of years of missing time.

✓ Reading Check Describe each of the three major categories of unconformities.

Answer to Reading Check

A disconformity is found where part of a sequence of parallel rock layers is missing. A nonconformity is found where horizontal sedimentary rock layers lie on top of an eroded surface of igneous or metamorphic rock. Angular unconformities are found between horizontal sedimentary rock layers and rock layers that have been tilted or folded.

Rock-Layer Puzzles

Geologists often find rock-layer sequences that have been affected by more than one of the events and features mentioned in this section. For example, as shown in **Figure 8,** intrusions may squeeze into rock layers that contain an unconformity. Determining the order of events that led to such a sequence is like piecing together a jigsaw puzzle. Geologists must use their knowledge of the events that disturb or remove rock-layer sequences to help piece together the history of Earth as told by the rock record.

Figure 8 *Rock-layer sequences are often disturbed by more than one rock-disturbing feature.*

SECTION Review

Summary

- Geologists use relative dating to determine the order in which events happen.
- The principle of superposition states that in undisturbed rock sequences, younger layers lie above older layers.
- Folding and tilting are two events that disturb rock layers. Faults and intrusions are two features that disturb rock layers.
- The known rock and fossil record is indicated by the geologic column.
- Geologists examine the relationships between rock layers and the structures that cut across them in order to determine relative ages.

Using Key Terms

1. In your own words, write a definition for each of the following terms: *relative dating, superposition,* and *geologic column.*

Understanding Key Ideas

2. Molten rock that squeezes into existing rock and cools is called a(n)
   a. fold.
   b. fault.
   c. intrusion.
   d. unconformity.

3. List two events and two features that can disturb rock-layer sequences.

4. Explain how physical features are used to determine relative ages.

Critical Thinking

5. **Analyzing Concepts** Is there a place on Earth that has all the layers of the geologic column? Explain.

6. **Analyzing Ideas** Disconformities are hard to recognize because all of the layers are horizontal. How does a geologist know when he or she is looking at a disconformity?

Interpreting Graphics

Use the illustration below to answer the question that follows.

7. If the top rock layer were eroded and deposition later resumed, what type of unconformity would mark the boundary between older rock layers and the newly deposited rock layers?

SCI LINKS® NSTA
Developed and maintained by the National Science Teachers Association

For a variety of links related to this chapter, go to www.scilinks.org

Topic: Relative Dating
SciLinks code: HSM1288

CHAPTER RESOURCES

Chapter Resource File

- Section Quiz GENERAL
- Section Review GENERAL
- Vocabulary and Section Summary GENERAL
- Reinforcement Worksheet BASIC

Focus

Overview

This section explains how absolute dating can be used to determine the actual age of a fossil or a rock. Students will be able to explain the nature of radioactive decay and describe how radiometric dating measures the radioactive decay of different isotopes to calculate the age of the parent material.

🎙️ Bellringer

Ask students to write a short paragraph explaining why geologists use both absolute and relative dating to interpret the past.

Motivate

ACTiViTY ———— GENERAL

Absolute Dating Skit Ask two students to be the geologists in this activity. The rest of the class will be radioactive isotopes in a newly formed rock sample. Tell the isotopes to stand up and that they have a half-life of 1 min. Have the geologists go outside the classroom and wait. After 1 min, tell half of the isotopes to sit down. Continue this pattern until one student remains standing. Ask the geologists to determine the age of the sample based on the number of original isotopes and the length of a half-life. **LS** Visual/Logical

---

READING WARM-UP

Objectives
- Describe how radioactive decay occurs.
- Explain how radioactive decay relates to radiometric dating.
- Identify four types of radiometric dating.
- Determine the best type of radiometric dating to use to date an object.

Terms to Learn
absolute dating
isotope
radioactive decay
radiometric dating
half-life

READING STRATEGY

Reading Organizer As you read this section, make a concept map by using the terms above.

Absolute Dating: A Measure of Time

Have you ever heard the expression "turning back the clock"? With the discovery of the natural decay of uranium in 1896, French physicist Henri Becquerel provided a means of doing just that. Scientists could use radioactive elements as clocks to measure geologic time.

The process of establishing the age of an object by determining the number of years it has existed is called **absolute dating.** In this section, you will learn about radiometric dating, which is the most common method of absolute dating.

Radioactive Decay

To determine the absolute ages of fossils and rocks, scientists analyze isotopes of radioactive elements. Atoms of the same element that have the same number of protons but have different numbers of neutrons are called **isotopes.** Most isotopes are stable, meaning that they stay in their original form. But some isotopes are unstable. Scientists call unstable isotopes *radioactive*. Radioactive isotopes tend to break down into stable isotopes of the same or other elements in a process called **radioactive decay. Figure 1** shows an example of how radioactive decay occurs. Because radioactive decay occurs at a steady rate, scientists can use the relative amounts of stable and unstable isotopes present in an object to determine the object's age.

Figure 1 Radioactive Decay

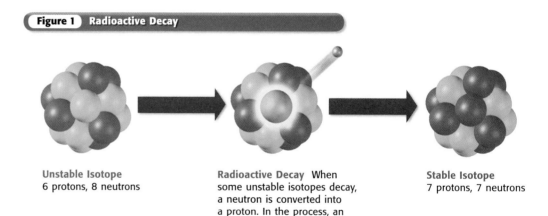

Unstable Isotope
6 protons, 8 neutrons

Radioactive Decay When some unstable isotopes decay, a neutron is converted into a proton. In the process, an electron is released.

Stable Isotope
7 protons, 7 neutrons

CHAPTER RESOURCES

Chapter Resource File

- Lesson Plan
- Directed Reading A BASIC
- Directed Reading B SPECIAL NEEDS

Technology

- Transparencies
  - Bellringer
  - *LINK TO PHYSICAL SCIENCE* Radioactive Decay and Half-Life

---

CONNECTION ACTiViTY
Math ———————— GENERAL

Calculating Half-Life To help students understand the concept of a half-life, use the transparency entitled "Radioactive Decay and Half-Life." Then, assess the comprehension of the students by asking them to calculate how old an object is when 1/4, 1/8, 1/32, and 1/64 of its carbon-14 remains. The half-life for carbon-14 is 5,730 years. (11,460 years; 17,190 years; 28,650 years; 34,380 years) **LS** Logical

Dating Rocks—How Does It Work?

In the process of radioactive decay, an unstable radioactive isotope of one element breaks down into a stable isotope. The stable isotope may be of the same element or, more commonly, a different element. The unstable radioactive isotope is called the *parent isotope*. The stable isotope produced by the radioactive decay of the parent isotope is called the *daughter isotope*. The radioactive decay of a parent isotope into a stable daughter isotope can occur in a single step or a series of steps. In either case, the rate of decay is constant. Therefore, to date rock, scientists compare the amount of parent material with the amount of daughter material. The more daughter material there is, the older the rock is.

Radiometric Dating

If you know the rate of decay for a radioactive element in a rock, you can figure out the absolute age of the rock. Determining the absolute age of a sample, based on the ratio of parent material to daughter material, is called **radiometric dating.** For example, let's say that a rock sample contains an isotope with a half-life of 10,000 years. A **half-life** is the time that it takes one-half of a radioactive sample to decay. So, for this rock sample, in 10,000 years, half the parent material will have decayed and become daughter material. You analyze the sample and find equal amounts of parent material and daughter material. This means that half the original radioactive isotope has decayed and that the sample must be about 10,000 years old.

What if one-fourth of your sample is parent material and three-fourths is daughter material? You would know that it took 10,000 years for half the original sample to decay and another 10,000 years for half of what remained to decay. The age of your sample would be $2 \times 10,000$, or 20,000, years. **Figure 2** shows how this steady decay happens.

 Reading Check What is a half-life? (*See the Appendix for answers to Reading Checks.*)

absolute dating any method of measuring the age of an event or object in years

isotope an atom that has the same number of protons (or the same atomic number) as other atoms of the same element do but that has a different number of neutrons (and thus a different atomic mass)

radioactive decay the process in which a radioactive isotope tends to break down into a stable isotope of the same element or another element

radiometric dating a method of determining the age of an object by estimating the relative percentages of a radioactive (parent) isotope and a stable (daughter) isotope

half-life the time needed for half of a sample of a radioactive substance to undergo radioactive decay

Figure 2 *After every half-life, the amount of parent material decreases by one-half.*

| 1/1 | 1/2 | 1/4 | 1/8 | 1/16 |
| 0 years | 10,000 years | 20,000 years | 30,000 years | 40,000 years |

INCLUSION Strategies

• *Learning Disabled*
• *Hearing Impaired*

Organize students into groups of three to five students. Give each group a stopwatch, a sheet of ruled notebook paper, and scissors. Tell students that this activity will simulate the radioactive decay of a substance. Begin by asking groups to record the time in their **science journal.** Instruct them to wait 1 min and then cut the paper in half. Have them select one piece, and set the other piece aside. Have students wait another minute and then cut the selected piece in half and select one piece. Students should continue this exercise until nine 1-min intervals have elapsed. Ask each group to estimate the age of the paper (10 min). Extra credit may be given to students who can tell you how old the paper is if 1 min represents 100 years (1,000 years). Have them share their answers with the class. **LS** Kinesthetic

Reteaching — BASIC

Modeling Have students use two different colors of modeling clay to construct the nuclei of other unstable isotopes. Ask students to identify the protons and neutrons in each model. Discuss the difference between atomic mass and atomic number. Ask students to identify isotopes of the same element, and help them explain radioactive decay by using their model.

LS Logical/Kinesthetic

Quiz — GENERAL

1. When using the carbon-14 dating method, which sample would be older, a sample with a ratio of carbon-14 to carbon-12 of 2 to 1 or a sample with a ratio of 3 to 1? (the sample with a 2 to 1 ratio)

2. What is a half-life? (the time it takes for one-half of a radioactive isotope to decay)

Alternative Assessment — GENERAL

Absolute Dating Display three images of fossils. Tell students that the first fossil is about 30,000 years old, the second is about 1 million years old, and the last came from the Paleozoic era, around 400 million years ago. Ask students to describe how they would determine the absolute age of each fossil.

LS Verbal

Answer to Reading Check

strontium-87

Figure 3 *This burial mound at Effigy Mounds resembles a snake.*

Types of Radiometric Dating

Imagine traveling back through the centuries to a time before Columbus arrived in America. You are standing along the bluffs of what will one day be called the Mississippi River. You see dozens of people building large mounds. Who are these people, and what are they building?

The people you saw in your time travel were Native Americans, and the structures they were building were burial mounds. The area you imagined is now an archaeological site called Effigy Mounds National Monument. **Figure 3** shows one of these mounds.

According to archaeologists, people lived at Effigy Mounds from 2,500 years ago to 600 years ago. How do archaeologists know these dates? They have dated bones and other objects in the mounds by using radiometric dating. Scientists use different radiometric-dating techniques based on the estimated age of an object. As you read on, think about how the half-life of an isotope relates to the age of the object being dated. Which technique would you use to date the burial mounds?

Potassium-Argon Method

One isotope that is used for radiometric dating is potassium-40. Potassium-40 has a half-life of 1.3 billion years, and it decays to argon and calcium. Geologists measure argon as the daughter material. This method is used mainly to date rocks older than 100,000 years.

Uranium-Lead Method

Uranium-238 is a radioactive isotope that decays in a series of steps to lead-206. The half-life of uranium-238 is 4.5 billion years. The older the rock is, the more daughter material (lead-206) there will be in the rock. Uranium-lead dating can be used for rocks more than 10 million years old. Younger rocks do not contain enough daughter material to be accurately measured by this method.

Rubidium-Strontium Method

Through radioactive decay, the unstable parent isotope rubidium-87 forms the stable daughter isotope strontium-87. The half-life of rubidium-87 is 49 billion years. This method is used to date rocks older than 10 million years.

✓ Reading Check What is the daughter isotope of rubidium-87?

MISCONCEPTION ///ALERT\\\\

Atomic Decay Students may think that atomic decay is similar to other types of organic decay that they know about. Explain that some elements have forms called *isotopes*. Some isotopes have unstable atomic nuclei that tend to change, or decay. The chance that an atom will decay at any given moment is very small, but that chance is constant. Unstable atoms do not "wear out" or "grow old." From the moment these atoms form to the moment they decay, they always have the same probability of decaying. For example, every potassium-40 atom in a sample has a 50:50 chance of decaying during the course of 1.3 billion years. After 1.3 billion years, half the K-40 atoms will have decayed. Every unstable isotope has a characteristic half-life. Some half-lives are only a ten-thousandth of a second!

Carbon-14 Method

The element carbon is normally found in three forms, the stable isotopes carbon-12 and carbon-13 and the radioactive isotope carbon-14. These carbon isotopes combine with oxygen to form the gas carbon dioxide, which is taken in by plants during photosynthesis. As long as a plant is alive, new carbon dioxide with a constant carbon-14 to carbon-12 ratio is continually taken in. Animals that eat plants contain the same ratio of carbon isotopes.

Once a plant or an animal dies, however, no new carbon is taken in. The amount of carbon-14 begins to decrease as the plant or animal decays, and the ratio of carbon-14 to carbon-12 decreases. This decrease can be measured in a laboratory, such as the one shown in **Figure 4.** Because the half-life of carbon-14 is only 5,730 years, this dating method is used mainly for dating things that lived within the last 50,000 years.

Figure 4 *Some samples containing carbon must be cleaned and burned before their age can be determined.*

SECTION Review

Summary

- During radioactive decay, an unstable isotope decays at a constant rate and becomes a stable isotope of the same or a different element.
- Radiometric dating, based on the ratio of parent to daughter material, is used to determine the absolute age of a sample.
- Methods of radiometric dating include potassium-argon, uranium-lead, rubidium-strontium, and carbon-14 dating.

Using Key Terms

1. Use each of the following terms in a separate sentence: *absolute dating, isotope,* and *half-life.*

Understanding Key Ideas

2. Rubidium-87 has a half-life of
   - **a.** 5,730 years.
   - **b.** 4.5 billion years.
   - **c.** 49 billion years.
   - **d.** 1.3 billion years.

3. Explain how radioactive decay occurs.

4. How does radioactive decay relate to radiometric dating?

5. List four types of radiometric dating.

Math Skills

6. A radioactive isotope has a half-life of 1.3 billion years. After 3.9 billion years, how much of the parent material will be left?

Critical Thinking

7. **Analyzing Methods** Explain why radioactive decay must be constant in order for radiometric dating to be accurate.

8. **Applying Concepts** Which radiometric-dating method would be most appropriate for dating artifacts found at Effigy Mounds? Explain.

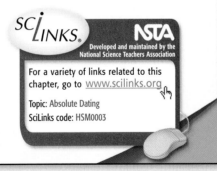

SCiLINKS®

NSTA
Developed and maintained by the
National Science Teachers Association

For a variety of links related to this chapter, go to www.scilinks.org

Topic: Absolute Dating
SciLinks code: HSM0003

CHAPTER RESOURCES

Chapter Resource File

- Section Quiz GENERAL
- Section Review GENERAL
- Vocabulary and Section Summary GENERAL

Answers to Section Review

1. Sample answers: Absolute dating is the process of establishing the age of an object by determining the number of years it has existed. An isotope is an atom that has the same number of protons as other atoms of the same element but has a different number of neutrons. A half-life is the time it takes one-half of a radioactive sample to decay.

2. c

3. Radioactive decay occurs as a radioactive isotope breaks down into a stable isotope. This change happens as the isotope loses an electron and a neutron becomes a proton.

4. Radioactive decay occurs at a constant rate. By determining the ratio between the parent material and the daughter material in an object, scientists can determine how old an object is.

5. potassium-argon, uranium-lead, strontium-rubidium, and carbon-14

6. One-eighth of the parent material will be left. After one half-life, 1/2 of the sample is left. After two half-lives, 1/4 of the sample is left. After three half-lives, 1/8 of the sample is left.

7. If decay rates were inconsistent, scientists would not have a specific half-life number to compare with an object's ratio of parent material to daughter material. Therefore, a precise age could never be determined.

8. Carbon-14 would be the best method to date artifacts from Effigy Mounds. This method is best because carbon-14 has a relatively short half-life of 5,730 years.

Focus

Overview

This section describes the formation and preservation of fossils. Students will learn how fossils are used to interpret the past and to date rock layers.

 Bellringer

Ask students to write a few sentences to describe the fossil record of their own lives that might be found 65 million years from now. Tell students that fossils must be naturally preserved.

Motivate

Group ActiViTy — GENERAL

Carbon Impressions Carbon impressions of plants can form when the plants are buried in sediment. As plants decay, a thin film of carbon is left behind. Have students work in groups to make carbon "fossil" imprints. Using plaster of Paris, have students place a flat leaf on the plaster surface. Then, after the plaster has dried, they should cover it with a second layer of plaster. When the plaster has dried, have students split the layers apart. Have students observe the leaf impression. Have them note that a bit of the leaf material sticks to the impression made in the hard material. **LS** Visual/Kinesthetic

READING WARM-UP

Objectives

- Describe five ways that different types of fossils form.
- List three types of fossils that are not part of organisms.
- Explain how fossils can be used to determine the history of changes in environments and organisms.
- Explain how index fossils can be used to date rock layers.

Terms to Learn

fossil
trace fossil
mold
cast
index fossil

READING STRATEGY

Reading Organizer As you read this section, create an outline of the section. Use the headings from this section in your outline.

Looking at Fossils

Descending from the top of a ridge in the badlands of Argentina, your expedition team suddenly stops. You look down and realize that you are walking on eggshells— dinosaur eggshells!

A paleontologist named Luis Chiappe had this experience. He had found an enormous dinosaur nesting ground.

Fossilized Organisms

The remains or physical evidence of an organism preserved by geologic processes is called a **fossil.** Fossils are most often preserved in sedimentary rock. But as you will see, other materials can also preserve evidence of past life.

Fossils in Rocks

When an organism dies, it either immediately begins to decay or is consumed by other organisms. Sometimes, however, organisms are quickly buried by sediment when they die. The sediment slows down decay. Hard parts of organisms, such as shells and bones, are more resistant to decay than soft tissues are. So, when sediments become rock, the hard parts of animals are much more commonly preserved than are soft tissues.

Fossils in Amber

Imagine that an insect is caught in soft, sticky tree sap. Suppose that the insect gets covered by more sap, which quickly hardens and preserves the insect inside. Hardened tree sap is called *amber*. Some of our best insect fossils are found in amber, as shown in **Figure 1.** Frogs and lizards have also been found in amber.

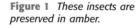 **Reading Check** Describe how organisms are preserved in amber. (*See the Appendix for answers to Reading Checks.*)

Figure 1 *These insects are preserved in amber.*

CHAPTER RESOURCES

Chapter Resource File

- Lesson Plan
- Directed Reading A BASIC
- Directed Reading B SPECIAL NEEDS

Technology

- Transparencies
  - Bellringer

Answer to Reading Check

An organism is caught in soft, sticky tree sap, which hardens and preserves the organism.

Figure 2 *Scientist Vladimir Eisner studies the upper molars of a 20,000-year-old woolly mammoth found in Siberia, Russia. The almost perfectly preserved male mammoth was excavated from a block of ice in October 1999.*

Petrifaction

Another way that organisms are preserved is by petrifaction. *Petrifaction* is a process in which minerals replace an organism's tissues. One form of petrifaction is called *permineralization*. *Permineralization* is a process in which the pore space in an organism's hard tissue—for example, bone or wood—is filled up with mineral. Another form of petrifaction is called *replacement,* a process in which the organism's tissues are completely replaced by minerals. For example, in some specimens of petrified wood, all of the wood has been replaced by minerals.

Fossils in Asphalt

There are places where asphalt wells up at the Earth's surface in thick, sticky pools. The La Brea asphalt deposits in Los Angeles, California, for example, are at least 38,000 years old. These pools of thick, sticky asphalt have trapped and preserved many kinds of organisms for the past 38,000 years. From these fossils, scientists have learned about the past environment in southern California.

Frozen Fossils

In October 1999, scientists removed a 20,000-year-old woolly mammoth frozen in the Siberian tundra. The remains of this mammoth are shown in **Figure 2.** Woolly mammoths, relatives of modern elephants, became extinct approximately 10,000 years ago. Because cold temperatures slow down decay, many types of frozen fossils are preserved from the last ice age. Scientists hope to find out more about the mammoth and the environment in which it lived.

fossil the remains or physical evidence of an organism preserved by geological processes

CONNECTION TO Environmental Science

WRITING SKILL **Preservation in Ice** Subfreezing climates contain almost no decomposing bacteria. The well-preserved body of John Torrington, a member of an expedition that explored the Northwest Passage in Canada in the 1840s, was uncovered in 1984. His body appeared much as it did at the time he died, more than 160 years earlier. Research another well-preserved discovery, and write a report for your class.

Teach

📖 READING STRATEGY — GENERAL

Writing **Activity** Ask students to write short paragraphs exploring possible scenarios for each type of fossilization described in this section. Encourage students to illustrate each scenario and to include details of the paleo-environment at the time of fossilization. **English Language Learners**
LS Logical/Visual

ACTIVITY — GENERAL

Making Fossils Distribute the following materials to groups of students: several leaves or small shells, a small amount of petroleum jelly, plaster of Paris, water, waxed paper, a square of heavy cardboard, and a milk carton. Have each group fill the carton halfway with plaster. Have groups add some water, and stir the mixture to form a smooth, thick paste. Have students pour the plaster mixture onto the cardboard square covered by waxed paper. Then, have them coat the leaves or the shells with petroleum jelly, and place the items jelly side down into the plaster. Have students allow the plaster to dry for 24 h before removing the leaves or the shells. Groups may wish to create a fossil record of a mystery environment. Have students exchange and interpret records of other groups. **LS Kinesthetic/Visual**

MISCONCEPTION ALERT

Rancho La Brea Asphalt Pits Students may refer to the Rancho La Brea asphalt pits in Los Angeles, California, as tar pits. Explain to students that the material seeping to the surface is asphalt, not tar. Asphalt is a type of bitumen found in a natural state or obtained by evaporating petroleum. Tar is obtained by the distillation of coal, wood, or shale.

Amateur Fossil Collecting
Have students debate the pros and cons of amateur fossil collecting. They should understand that amateur fossil collectors have made some amazing discoveries and have helped to advance the field of paleontology. On the other hand, amateur fossil collectors have lost important information by improperly removing fossils, by not recording data about locations or associated fossils, and by failing to donate specimens to research institutions for study. Point out that it is illegal to collect fossils from state or national parks without a permit that allows you to do so. It is also illegal to remove vertebrate fossils from public lands without a permit. Have students conclude the debate by writing a handbook for amateur fossil collectors.
LS Interpersonal

Answer to Reading Check
A mold is a cavity in rock where a plant or an animal was buried. A cast is an object created when sediment fills a mold and becomes rock.

Figure 3 *These dinosaur tracks are located in Arizona. They leave a trace of a dinosaur that had longer legs than humans do.*

trace fossil a fossilized mark that is formed in soft sediment by the movement of an animal

mold a mark or cavity made in a sedimentary surface by a shell or other body

cast a type of fossil that forms when sediments fill in the cavity left by a decomposed organism

Figure 4 *This photograph shows two molds from an ammonite. The image on the left is the internal mold of the ammonite, which formed when sediment filled the ammonite's shell, which later dissolved away. The image on the right is the external mold of the ammonite, which preserves the external features of the shell.*

Other Types of Fossils

Besides their hard parts—and in rare cases their soft parts—do organisms leave behind any other clues about their existence? What other evidence of past life do paleontologists look for?

Trace Fossils

Any naturally preserved evidence of animal activity is called a **trace fossil.** Tracks like the ones shown in **Figure 3** are a fascinating example of a trace fossil. These fossils form when animal footprints fill with sediment and are preserved in rock. Tracks reveal a lot about the animal that made them, including how big it was and how fast it was moving. Parallel trackways showing dinosaurs moving in the same direction have led paleontologists to hypothesize that dinosaurs moved in herds.

Burrows are another trace fossil. Burrows are shelters made by animals, such as clams, that bury in sediment. Like tracks, burrows are preserved when they are filled in with sediment and buried quickly. A *coprolite* (KAHP roh LIET), a third type of trace fossil, is preserved animal dung.

Molds and Casts

Molds and casts are two more examples of fossils. A cavity in rock where a plant or animal was buried is called a **mold.** A **cast** is an object created when sediment fills a mold and becomes rock. A cast shows what the outside of the organism looked like. **Figure 4** shows two types of molds from the same organism—and internal mold and an external mold.

✔ **Reading Check** How are a cast and a mold different?

Museum Displays Many people assume that when they see dinosaur bones in a museum, they are looking at the actual bones that made up the dinosaur. In older museums, this may be the case. However, point out that many newer museums do not display the actual fossilized dinosaur bones. They make casts of the bones. Using the casts, they make fiberglass reproductions of the bones. The fiberglass bones are much lighter than the original bones and can stand without support.

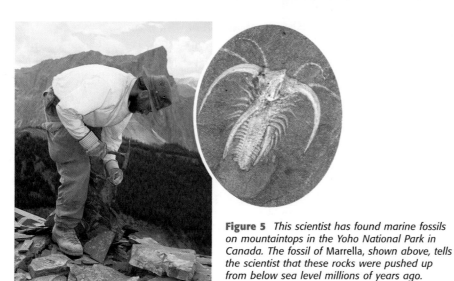

Figure 5 *This scientist has found marine fossils on mountaintops in the Yoho National Park in Canada. The fossil of* Marrella, *shown above, tells the scientist that these rocks were pushed up from below sea level millions of years ago.*

Using Fossils to Interpret the Past

Think about your favorite outdoor place. Now, imagine that you are a paleontologist at the same site 65 million years from now. What types of fossils would you dig up? Based on the fossils you found, how would you reconstruct this place?

The Information in the Fossil Record

The fossil record offers only a rough sketch of the history of life on Earth. Some parts of this history are more complete than others. For example, scientists know more about organisms that had hard body parts than about organisms that had soft body parts. Scientists also know more about organisms that lived in environments that favored fossilization. The fossil record is incomplete because most organisms never became fossils. And of course, many fossils have yet to be discovered.

History of Environmental Changes

Would you expect to find marine fossils on the mountaintop shown in **Figure 5**? The presence of marine fossils means that the rocks of these mountaintops in Canada formed in a totally different environment—at the bottom of an ocean.

The fossil record reveals a history of environmental change. For example, marine fossils help scientists reconstruct ancient coastlines and the deepening and shallowing of ancient seas. Using the fossils of plants and land animals, scientists can reconstruct past climates. They can tell whether the climate in an area was cooler or wetter than it is at present.

Make a Fossil

1. Find a **common object,** such as a shell, a button, or a pencil, to use to make a mold. Keep the object hidden from your classmates.

2. To create a mold, press the items down into **modeling clay** in a **shallow pan or tray.**

3. Trade your tray with a classmate's tray, and try to identify the item that made the mold.

4. Describe how a cast could be formed from your mold.

Reteaching — BASIC

Section Review Have students write two questions for each heading in the section. Then, have students exchange questions and attempt to answer the questions. **LS** Verbal

Quiz — GENERAL

1. Would a shark tooth make a good index fossil? Why or why not? (A shark tooth could make an excellent index fossil if the shark tooth came from a shark that lived during a relatively short, well-defined geologic time span.)

2. Why do the frigid temperatures of Siberia and the sticky asphalt of the La Brea tar pits preserve fossils well? (Both environments slow down the decay of an organism and help preserve it.)

Alternative Assessment — ADVANCED

How-To Guide Have students prepare a how-to guide for the fossilization processes described in this section. Students should imagine that they are teaching an untrained person how to preserve an organism using sedimentation, amber, tar, ice, and petrifaction. Emphasize that this assignment should read like a recipe, so details are important.
LS Intrapersonal

SCHOOL to HOME

Fossil Hunt
Go on a fossil hunt with your family. Find out what kinds of rocks in your local area might contain fossils. Take pictures or draw sketches of your trip and any fossils that you find.

ACTIVITY

index fossil a fossil that is found in the rock layers of only one geologic age and that is used to establish the age of the rock layers

History of Changing Organisms

By studying the relationships between fossils, scientists can interpret how life has changed over time. For example, older rock layers contain organisms that often differ from the organisms found in younger rock layers.

Only a small fraction of the organisms that have existed in Earth's history have been fossilized. Because the fossil record is incomplete, it does not provide paleontologists with a continuous record of change. Instead, they look for similarities between fossils, or between fossilized organisms and their closest living relatives, and try to fill in the blanks in the fossil record.

✓ Reading Check How do paleontologists fill in missing information about changes in organisms in the fossil record?

Using Fossils to Date Rocks

Scientists have found that particular types of fossils appear only in certain layers of rock. By dating the rock layers above and below these fossils, scientists can determine the time span in which the organisms that formed the fossils lived. If a type of organism existed for only a short period of time, its fossils would show up in a limited range of rock layers. These types of fossils are called index fossils. **Index fossils** are fossils of organisms that lived during a relatively short, well-defined geologic time span.

Ammonites

To be considered an index fossil, a fossil must be found in rock layers throughout the world. One example of an index fossil is the fossil of a genus of ammonites (AM uh NIETS) called *Tropites*, shown in **Figure 6**. *Tropites* was a marine mollusk similar to a modern squid. It lived in a coiled shell. *Tropites* lived between 230 million and 208 million years ago and is an index fossil for that period of time.

Figure 6 *Tropites is a genus of coiled ammonites. Tropites existed for only about 20 million years, which makes this genus a good index fossil.*

Homework — GENERAL

Modern Index Fossils Which organisms would make good index fossils for marking the end of the 21st century? Have students research species that have become extinct during the last 100 years and illustrate what the fossils of these species might look like.
LS Logical

Answer to Reading Check

To fill in missing information about changes in organisms in the fossil record, paleontologists look for similarities between fossilized organisms or between fossilized organisms and their closest living relatives.

Trilobites

Fossils of a genus of trilobites (TRIE loh BIETS) called *Phacops* are another example of an index fossil. Trilobites are extinct. Their closest living relative is the horseshoe crab. Through the dating of rock, paleontologists have determined that *Phacops* lived approximately 400 million years ago. So, when scientists find *Phacops* in rock layers anywhere on Earth, they assume that these rock layers are also approximately 400 million years old. An example of a *Phacops* fossil is shown in **Figure 7**.

Reading Check Explain how fossils of *Phacops* can be used to establish the age of rock layers.

Figure 7 *Paleontologists assume that any rock layer containing a fossil of the trilobite* Phacops *is about 400 million years old.*

SECTION Review

Summary

- Fossils are the remains or physical evidence of an organism preserved by geologic processes.

- Fossils can be preserved in rock, amber, asphalt, and ice and by petrifaction.

- Trace fossils are any naturally preserved evidence of animal activity. Tracks, burrows, and coprolites are examples of trace fossils.

- Scientists study fossils to determine how environments and organisms have changed over time.

- An index fossil is a fossil of an organism that lived during a relatively short, well-defined time span. Index fossils can be used to establish the age of rock layers.

Using Key Terms

Complete each of the following sentences by choosing the correct term from the word bank.

cast	index fossils
mold	trace fossils

1. A ___ is a cavity in rock where a plant or animal was buried.

2. ___ can be used to establish the age of rock layers.

Understanding Key Ideas

3. Fossils are most often preserved in
   a. ice.
   b. amber.
   c. asphalt.
   d. rock.

4. Describe three types of trace fossils.

5. Explain how an index fossil can be used to date rock.

6. Explain why the fossil record contains an incomplete record of the history of life on Earth.

7. Explain how fossils can be used to determine the history of changes in environments and organisms.

Math Skills

8. If a scientist finds the remains of a plant between a rock layer that contains 400 million–year-old *Phacops* fossils and a rock layer that contains 230 million–year-old *Tropites* fossils, how old could the plant fossil be?

Critical Thinking

9. **Making Inferences** If you find rock layers containing fish fossils in a desert, what can you infer about the history of the desert?

10. **Identifying Bias** Because information in the fossil record is incomplete, scientists are left with certain biases concerning fossil preservation. Explain two of these biases.

SCILINKS® **NSTA**
Developed and maintained by the National Science Teachers Association

For a variety of links related to this chapter, go to www.scilinks.org

Topic: Looking at Fossils
SciLinks code: HSM0886

Focus

Overview

In this section, students will be introduced to the geologic time scale. The section discusses some important biological and geological events that occurred during each geologic era. The section also informs students about events that result in the sudden appearance or disappearance of species.

 Bellringer

Ask students the following question: "If the history of Earth were the length of 1 calendar year, on what date did modern humans arrive?" (December 31)

Motivate

Discussion —— GENERAL

Geologic Time After students study the photographs in **Figure 1** and **Figure 2,** ask them how rock layers and fossils record Earth's history. Ask students what kinds of changes in Earth's history might be preserved in the rock and fossil records. Have students summarize their answers in a short essay. **LS Logical**

READING WARM-UP

Objectives
- Explain how geologic time is recorded in rock layers.
- Identify important dates on the geologic time scale.
- Explain how environmental changes resulted in the extinction of some species.

Terms to Learn

geologic time scale   period
eon   epoch
era   extinction

READING STRATEGY

Brainstorming The key idea of this section is the geologic time scale. Brainstorm words and phrases related to the geologic time scale.

Figure 1 *Bones of dinosaurs that lived about 150 million years ago are exposed in the quarry wall at Dinosaur National Monument in Utah.*

Time Marches On

How old is the Earth? Well, if the Earth celebrated its birthday every million years, there would be 4,600 candles on its birthday cake! Humans have been around only long enough to light the last candle on the cake.

Try to think of the Earth's history in "fast-forward." If you could watch the Earth change from this perspective, you would see mountains rise up like wrinkles in fabric and quickly wear away. You would see life-forms appear and then go extinct. In this section, you will learn that geologists must "fast-forward" the Earth's history when they write or talk about it. You will also learn about some incredible events in the history of life on Earth.

Geologic Time

Shown in **Figure 1** is the rock wall at the Dinosaur Quarry Visitor Center in Dinosaur National Monument, Utah. Contained within this wall are approximately 1,500 fossil bones that have been excavated by paleontologists. These are the remains of dinosaurs that inhabited the area about 150 million years ago. Granted, 150 million years seems to be an incredibly long period of time. However, in terms of the Earth's history, 150 million years is little more than 3% of the time our planet has existed. It is a little less than 4% of the time represented by the Earth's oldest known rocks.

CHAPTER RESOURCES

Chapter Resource File

- Lesson Plan
- Directed Reading A **BASIC**
- Directed Reading B **SPECIAL NEEDS**

Technology

- Transparencies
  - Bellringer

CONNECTION ACTIVITY
Math —— GENERAL

Calculating Percentage The dinosaur that had the smallest ratio of brain size to body size was the stegosaurus. The 30 ft long, 3,800 lb stegosaurus had a 2.5 oz brain. Have students calculate the percentage of the stegosaurus's total body weight that its brain represents. (The brain represents 0.004% of its total body weight.) **LS Logical**

Figure 2 *Well-preserved plant and animal fossils are common in the Green River formation. Clockwise from the upper right are a fossil leaf, a dragonfly, a fish, and a turtle.*

The Rock Record and Geologic Time

One of the best places in North America to see the Earth's history recorded in rock layers is in Grand Canyon National Park. The Colorado River has cut the canyon nearly 2 km deep in some places. Over the course of 6 million years, the river has eroded countless layers of rock. These layers represent almost half, or nearly 2 billion years, of Earth's history.

✔ Reading Check How much geologic time is represented by the rock layers in the Grand Canyon? (*See the Appendix for answers to Reading Checks.*)

The Fossil Record and Geologic Time

Figure 2 shows sedimentary rocks that belong to the Green River formation. These rocks, which are found in parts of Wyoming, Utah, and Colorado, are thousands of meters thick. These rocks were once part of a system of ancient lakes that existed for a period of millions of years. Fossils of plants and animals are common in these rocks and are very well preserved. Burial in the fine-grained lake-bed sediments preserved even the most delicate structures.

INTERNET ACTIVITY

For another activity related to this chapter, go to **go.hrw.com** and type in the keyword **HZ5FOSW.**

Teach

CONNECTION to Life Science — ADVANCED

Paleobotany The study of Earth's history has given rise to highly specific subdivisions of Earth science. Paleobotany, for example, is the study of the history of the plant kingdom. Have interested students find out how plant and pollen fossils can provide clues about past environments and tell how these environments have changed over time. **LS Verbal**

ACTIVITY — BASIC

Learning About the Eons As you begin to discuss the geologic time scale, write the names of the four eons on the board. Ask students to use what they have learned to help you list the characteristics of each eon. Have students find the dates of each eon, the biological events that define each eon, and other facts. You may wish to continue this activity with the eras and periods. Have students copy the information in their **science journal** for future study and review. **LS Logical** *English Language Learners*

Answer to Reading Check

approximately 2 billion years

Homework — ADVANCED

Research Before the development of the theory of plate tectonics and the invention of radiometric dating, scientists developed many elaborate experiments to determine the age of the Earth. In the mid-1700s, a French scientist estimated that the Earth was 75,000 years old. He based his estimate on the cooling rate of iron cannonballs.

By the 1930s, the estimated age of Earth reached 1 billion years, but it was not until the middle of the 20th century that the current estimate of 4.6 billion years was determined. Have interested students research the different methods that were used in the past to estimate the age of the Earth. **LS Verbal**

Teach, *continued*

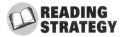

READING STRATEGY — GENERAL

Mnemonics Help students devise mnemonic sentences to learn and remember the eons of geologic history. For example, "**H**appy **A**ardvarks **Pr**ance for **Ph**otographers" could be used to recall the **H**adean, **A**rchean, **Pr**oterozoic, and **Ph**anerozoic eons. LS Auditory

English Language Learners

CONNECTION ACTIVITY
Language Arts — GENERAL

Writing **Geologic Newspapers** As students read about the geologic time scale, encourage them to consider why scientists chose to divide geologic time in this way. Have them think about the important biological, climatological, and geological differences between each era. After students finish reading about each era, have them work independently to write the front-page headlines for an imaginary newspaper printed at the close of each era. The headlines should detail the important events and characteristics of the era. For example, the front page of the *Mesozoic Times* might herald, "Mammals Appear—Warmblooded" and "Hairy Critters—Can We Trust Them?" If students wish to research more about geologic history, they can write creative articles under each headline.
LS Visual

Phanerozoic Eon

(543 million years ago to the present)
The rock and fossil record mainly represents the Phanerozoic eon, which is the eon in which we live.

Proterozoic Eon

(2.5 billion years ago to 543 million years ago)
The first organisms with well-developed cells appeared during this eon.

Archean Eon

(3.8 billion years ago to 2.5 billion years ago)
The earliest known rocks on Earth formed during this eon.

Hadean Eon

(4.6 billion years ago to 3.8 billion years ago)
The only rocks that scientists have found from this eon are meteorites and rocks from the moon.

Geologic Time Scale

Eon	Era	Period	Epoch	Millions of years ago
PHANEROZOIC EON	Cenozoic	Quaternary	Holocene	0.01
			Pleistocene	1.8
		Tertiary	Pliocene	5.3
			Miocene	23.8
			Oligocene	33.7
			Eocene	54.8
			Paleocene	65
	Mesozoic	Cretaceous		144
		Jurassic		206
		Triassic		248
	Paleozoic	Permian		290
		Pennsylvanian		323
		Mississippian		354
		Devonian		417
		Silurian		443
		Ordovician		490
		Cambrian		543
PROTEROZOIC EON				2,500
ARCHEAN EON				3,800
HADEAN EON				4,600

Figure 3 *The geologic time scale accounts for Earth's entire history. It is divided into four major parts called* eons. *Dates given for intervals on the geologic time scale are estimates.*

The Geologic Time Scale

The geologic column represents the billions of years that have passed since the first rocks formed on Earth. Altogether, geologists study 4.6 billion years of Earth's history! To make their job easier, geologists have created the geologic time scale. The **geologic time scale,** which is shown in **Figure 3,** is a scale that divides Earth's 4.6 billion–year history into distinct intervals of time.

Reading Check Define the term *geologic time scale.*

Answer to Reading Check

The geologic time scale is a scale that divides Earth's 4.6 billion–year history into distinct intervals of time.

CHAPTER RESOURCES

Technology

Transparencies
- The Geologic Time Scale

Divisions of Time

Geologists have divided Earth's history into sections of time, as shown on the geologic time scale in **Figure 3.** The largest divisions of geologic time are **eons** (EE AHNZ). There are four eons—the Hadean eon, the Archean eon, the Proterozoic eon, and the Phanerozoic eon. The Phanerozoic eon is divided into three **eras,** which are the second-largest divisions of geologic time. The three eras are further divided into **periods,** which are the third-largest divisions of geologic time. Periods are divided into **epochs** (EP uhks), which are the fourth-largest divisions of geologic time.

The boundaries between geologic time intervals represent shorter intervals in which visible changes took place on Earth. Some changes are marked by the disappearance of index fossil species, while others are recognized only by detailed paleontological studies.

The Appearance and Disappearance of Species

At certain times during Earth's history, the number of species has increased or decreased dramatically. An increase in the number of species often comes as a result of either a relatively sudden increase or decrease in competition among species. *Hallucigenia,* shown in **Figure 4,** appeared during the Cambrian period, when the number of marine species greatly increased. On the other hand, the number of species decreases dramatically over a relatively short period of time during a mass extinction event. **Extinction** is the death of every member of a species. Gradual events, such as global climate change and changes in ocean currents, can cause mass extinctions. A combination of these events can also cause mass extinctions.

geologic time scale the standard method used to divide the Earth's long natural history into manageable parts

eon the largest division of geologic time

era a unit of geologic time that includes two or more periods

period a unit of geologic time into which eras are divided

epoch a subdivision of a geologic period

extinction the death of every member of a species

Figure 4 Hallucigenia, named for its "bizarre and dreamlike quality," was one of numerous marine organisms to make its appearance during the early Cambrian period.

Geologic Time Scale Have students reproduce **Figure 3** in their **science journal.** Students should leave enough space so that they can add details about the history of life on Earth for each eon and era. **LS** Verbal

Quiz — GENERAL

1. What are the largest divisions of time in the geologic time scale? (eons)

2. During which era did plants start to appear on land? (Paleozoic era)

Alternative Assessment — GENERAL

PORTFOLIO **Making a Geologic History Book** Have students work independently to make construction-paper cutouts of fossils that might be found in each era of Earth's history. Encourage students to create both plant and animal fossils. Students should then paste each era's fossils on rock layers made from construction paper. Students should create five layers for each era and attach all of the layers together so that they fold like an accordion. Students can then annotate each layer by describing the time period the rocks and fossils were deposited, and they can paste in small illustrations of what the environment was like during that time period. Students can display their accordion books for the class to enjoy. **LS** Visual

Figure 5 *Jungles were present during the Paleozoic era, but there were no birds singing in the trees and no monkeys swinging from the branches. Birds and mammals didn't evolve until much later.*

The Paleozoic Era—Old Life

The Paleozoic era lasted from about 543 million to 248 million years ago. It is the first era well represented by fossils.

Marine life flourished at the beginning of the Paleozoic era. The oceans became home to a diversity of life. However, there were few land organisms. By the middle of the Paleozoic, all modern groups of land plants had appeared. By the end of the era, amphibians and reptiles lived on the land, and insects were abundant. **Figure 5** shows what the Earth might have looked like late in the Paleozoic era. The Paleozoic era came to an end with the largest mass extinction in Earth's history. Some scientists believe that ocean changes were a likely cause of this extinction, which killed nearly 90% of all species.

The Mesozoic Era—The Age of Reptiles

The Mesozoic era began about 248 million years ago. The Mesozoic is known as the *Age of Reptiles* because reptiles, such as the dinosaurs shown in **Figure 6,** inhabited the land.

During this time, reptiles dominated. Small mammals appeared about the same time as dinosaurs, and birds appeared late in the Mesozoic era. Many scientists think that birds evolved directly from a type of dinosaur. At the end of the Mesozoic era, about 15% to 20% of all species on Earth, including the dinosaurs, became extinct. Global climate change may have been the cause.

Figure 6 *Imagine walking in the desert and bumping into these fierce creatures! It's a good thing humans didn't evolve in the Mesozoic era, which was dominated by dinosaurs.*

✓ **Reading Check** Why is the Mesozoic known as the *Age of Reptiles*?

ACTIVITY — ADVANCED

Prehistoric Illustrations Encourage advanced learners to use the Internet to research illustrations of prehistoric eras. Students can print the pictures and share them with the class, or students can create their own dioramas. As an extension, challenge students to find inaccuracies in the illustrations. **LS** Visual

Answer to Reading Check

The Mesozoic era is known as the Age of Reptiles because reptiles, including the dinosaurs, were the dominant organisms on land.

The Cenozoic Era—The Age of Mammals

The Cenozoic era, as shown in **Figure 7,** began about 65 million years ago and continues to the present. This era is known as the *Age of Mammals.* During the Mesozoic era, mammals had to compete with dinosaurs and other animals for food and habitat. After the mass extinction at the end of the Mesozoic era, mammals flourished. Unique traits, such as regulating body temperature internally and bearing young that develop inside the mother, may have helped mammals survive the environmental changes that probably caused the extinction of the dinosaurs.

Figure 7 *Thousands of species of mammals evolved during the Cenozoic era. This scene shows species from the early Cenozoic era that are now extinct.*

SECTION Review

Summary

- The geologic time scale divides Earth's 4.6 billion–year history into distinct intervals of time. Divisions of geologic time include eons, eras, periods, and epochs.

- The boundaries between geologic time intervals represent visible changes that have taken place on Earth.

- The rock and fossil record represents mainly the Phanerozoic eon, which is the eon in which we live.

- At certain times in Earth's history, the number of life-forms has increased or decreased dramatically.

Using Key Terms

1. Use each of the following terms in the same sentence: *era, period,* and *epoch.*

Understanding Key Ideas

2. The unit of geologic time that began 65 million years ago and continues to the present is the

   a. Holocene epoch.

   b. Cenozoic era.

   c. Phanerozoic eon.

   d. Quaternary period.

3. What are the major time intervals represented by the geologic time scale?

4. Explain how geologic time is recorded in rock layers.

5. What kinds of environmental changes cause mass extinctions?

Critical Thinking

6. **Making Inferences** What future event might mark the end of the Cenozoic era?

7. **Identifying Relationships** How might a decrease in competition between species lead to the sudden appearance of many new species?

Interpreting Graphics

8. Look at the illustration below. On the Earth-history clock shown, 1 h equals 383 million years, and 1 min equals 6.4 million years. In millions of years, how much more time is represented by the Proterozoic eon than by the Phanerozoic eon?

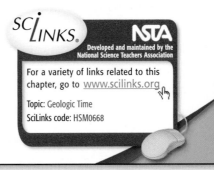

Phanerozoic eon

Hadean eon

Proterozoic eon

Archean eon

For a variety of links related to this chapter, go to www.scilinks.org

Topic: Geologic Time
SciLinks code: HSM0668

Homework —— GENERAL

Prehistoric Animals Ask each student to choose a favorite prehistoric animal. Then, have students find information about that animal and the time period in which it lived. University Web sites are an excellent place to look for this information. Students can present their information as an oral presentation or on a poster. **LS Visual**

CHAPTER RESOURCES

Chapter Resource File

- Section Quiz GENERAL
- Section Review GENERAL
- Vocabulary and Section Summary GENERAL

How Do You Stack Up?

Teacher's Notes

Time Required

Two 45-minute class periods

Lab Ratings

🧪	🧪🧪	🧪🧪🧪	🧪🧪🧪🧪
EASY			HARD

Teacher Prep 🧪
Student Set-Up 🧪🧪
Concept Level 🧪🧪🧪
Clean Up 🧪

MATERIALS

The activity works best if the class is divided into four groups. The materials listed on the student page are enough for each group.

Preparation Notes

Students may need to review the geologic column and the principle of superposition before performing this activity. Also, be certain that your students understand what an index fossil is.

Thicknesses of layers given in the lab are the thicknesses of only the stratigraphic sections. The rock layers represented by the sections would probably be much thicker. However, the relative thicknesses of the layers are represented in the measurements given (i.e., a layer that is 4 cm thick is twice as thick as a layer that is 2 cm thick).

  Model-Making Lab

OBJECTIVES

Make a model of a geologic column.

Interpret the geologic history represented by the geologic column you have made.

MATERIALS

- paper, white
- pencil
- pencils or crayons, assorted colors
- ruler, metric
- scissors
- tape, transparent

SAFETY

How Do You Stack Up?

According to the principle of superposition, in undisturbed sequences of sedimentary rock, the oldest layers are on the bottom. Geologists use this principle to determine the relative age of the rocks in a small area. In this activity, you will model what geologists do by drawing sections of different rock outcrops. Then, you will create a part of the geologic column, showing the geologic history of the area that contains all of the outcrops.

Procedure

1. Use a metric ruler and a pencil to draw four boxes on a blank piece of paper. Each box should be 3 cm wide and at least 6 cm tall. (You can trace the boxes shown on the next page.)

2. With colored pencils, copy the illustrations of the four outcrops on the next page. Copy one illustration in each of the four boxes. Use colors and patterns similar to those shown.

3. Pay close attention to the contact between layers—straight or wavy. Straight lines represent bedding planes, where deposition was continuous. Wavy lines represent unconformities, where rock layers may be missing. The top of each outcrop is incomplete, so it should be a jagged line. (Assume that the bottom of the lowest layer is a bedding plane.)

4. Use a black crayon or pencil to add the symbols representing fossils to the layers in your drawings. Pay attention to the shapes of the fossils and the layers that they are in.

5. Write the outcrop number on the back of each section.

6. Carefully cut the outcrops out of the paper, and lay the individual outcrops next to each other on your desk or table.

7. Find layers that have the same rocks and contain the same fossils. Move each outcrop up or down to line up similar layers next to each other.

8. If unconformities appear in any of the outcrops, there may be rock layers missing. You may need to examine other sections to find out what fits between the layers above and below the unconformities. Leave room for these layers by cutting the outcrops along the unconformities (wavy lines).

Lab Notes

Explain that the geologic column for the entire Earth is constructed from smaller columns that are similar to the hypothetical column in this lab. Stratigraphic sections are pieced together to form short columns, and short columns are pieced together to form longer columns. All columns put together make up the geologic column for the entire Earth.

CHAPTER RESOURCES

Chapter Resource File

 • Datasheet for Chapter Lab
• Lab Notes and Answers

Technology

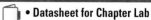 Classroom Videos
• Lab Video

9 Eventually, you should be able to make a geologic column that represents all four of the outcrops. It will show rock types and fossils for all the known layers in the area.

10 Tape the pieces of paper together in a pattern that represents the complete geologic column.

Analyze the Results

1 **Examining Data** How many layers are in the part of the geologic column that you modeled?

2 **Examining Data** Which is the oldest layer in your column? Which rock layer is the youngest? How do you know? Describe these layers in terms of rock type or the fossils they contain.

3 **Classifying** List the fossils in your column from oldest to youngest. Label the youngest and oldest fossils.

4 **Analyzing Data** Look at the unconformity in outcrop 2. Which rock layers are partially or completely missing? How do you know?

Draw Conclusions

5 **Drawing Conclusions** Which (if any) fossils can be used as index fossils for a single layer? Why are these fossils considered index fossils? What method(s) would be required to determine the absolute age of these fossils?

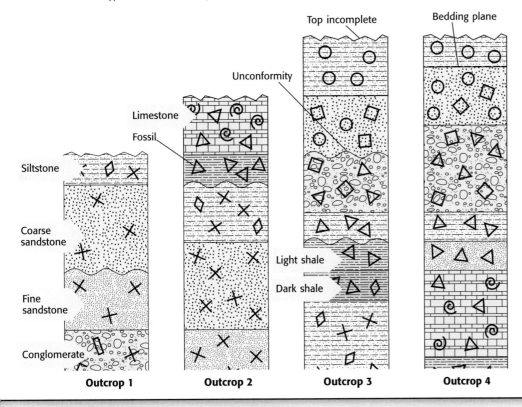

Outcrop 1 • Outcrop 2 • Outcrop 3 • Outcrop 4

Labels: Top incomplete, Bedding plane, Unconformity, Limestone, Fossil, Siltstone, Coarse sandstone, Fine sandstone, Conglomerate, Light shale, Dark shale

Analyze the Results

1. There are 12 layers in this part of the geologic column.

2. The conglomerate that contains rectangles and X fossils is the oldest. The siltstone that contains circle fossils is the youngest.

3. The relative age of the fossils from oldest to youngest is rectangles, X's, diamonds, triangles, spirals, squares, and circles.

4. In Outcrop 2, part of the siltstone and all of the dark shale are missing. This information can be determined by comparing the outcrop with the geologic column.

Draw Conclusions

5. Index fossils include the spirals in the limestone and the rectangles in the conglomerate. These fossils are considered index fossils because they existed for a short range of geologic time. To determine the absolute age of the fossils, you would need to use radiometric dating.

CLASSROOM TESTED & APPROVED

Dwight Patton
Carroll T. Welch Middle School
Horizon City, Texas

Chapter Review

Assignment Guide

SECTION	QUESTIONS
1	2, 5, 14, 17
2	6, 9, 11, 22–25
3	10, 12, 15
4	4, 7, 13, 16, 20, 21
5	8, 19
2 and 3	3, 18
2 and 5	1

ANSWERS

Using Key Terms

1. Sample answer: Super-position is the principle that states that younger rocks lie above older rocks in undis-turbed sequences. The geologic column is an ideal sequence of rock layers that contains all the known fossil and rock layers on Earth, arranged from oldest to youngest. The geologic time scale is a scale that divides Earth's 4.6 billion year history into distinct intervals of time.

2. Sample answer: Uniformi-tarianism is the theory that gradual geologic processes that we observe in the pres-ent were also active in the past. This theory argues that slow gradual change shapes the Earth. Catastrophism is the theory that past episodes of sudden and drastic change are responsible for the major geologic features that change the Earth.

USING KEY TERMS

1 In your own words, write a definition for each of the following terms: *super-position, geologic column,* and *geologic time scale.*

For each pair of terms, explain how the meanings of the terms differ.

2 *uniformitarianism* and *catastrophism*

3 *relative dating* and *absolute dating*

4 *trace fossil* and *index fossil*

UNDERSTANDING KEY IDEAS

Multiple Choice

5 Which of the following does not describe catastrophic change?

  a. widespread
  b. sudden
  c. rare
  d. gradual

6 Scientists assign relative ages by using

  a. absolute dating.
  b. the principle of superposition.
  c. radioactive half-lives.
  d. carbon-14 dating.

7 Which of the following is a trace fossil?

  a. an insect preserved in amber
  b. a mammoth frozen in ice
  c. wood replaced by minerals
  d. a dinosaur trackway

8 The largest divisions of geologic time are called

  a. periods.
  b. eras.
  c. eons.
  d. epochs.

9 Rock layers cut by a fault formed

  a. after the fault.
  b. before the fault.
  c. at the same time as the fault.
  d. There is not enough information to determine the answer.

10 Of the following isotopes, which is stable?

  a. uranium-238
  b. potassium-40
  c. carbon-12
  d. carbon-14

11 A surface that represents a missing part of the geologic column is called a(n)

  a. intrusion.
  b. fault.
  c. unconformity.
  d. fold.

12 Which method of radiometric dating is used mainly to date the remains of organisms that lived within the last 50,000 years?

  a. carbon-14 dating
  b. potassium-argon dating
  c. uranium-lead dating
  d. rubidium-strontium dating

3. Sample answer: Relative dating is a method of comparing rocks or fossils to each other to determine which ones are older. Absolute dating is a method of deter-mining the age of something in years.

4. Sample answer: A trace fossil is any naturally preserved evidence of animal activity. An index fossil is a fossil of an organism that lived during a relatively short, well-defined geologic time span. It is used to establish the age of rock layers.

Understanding Key Ideas

5. d
6. b
7. d
8. c
9. b
10. c
11. c
12. a

Short Answer

13 Describe three processes by which fossils form.

14 Identify the role of uniformitarianism in Earth science.

15 Explain how radioactive decay occurs.

16 Describe two ways in which scientists use fossils to determine environmental change.

17 Explain the role of paleontology in the study of Earth's history.

CRITICAL THINKING

18 **Concept Mapping** Use the following terms to create a concept map: *age, half-life, absolute dating, radioactive decay, radiometric dating, relative dating, superposition, geologic column,* and *isotopes.*

19 **Applying Concepts** Identify how changes in environmental conditions can affect the survival of a species. Give two examples.

20 **Identifying Relationships** Why do paleontologists know more about hard-bodied organisms than about soft-bodied organisms?

21 **Analyzing Processes** Why isn't a 100 million–year-old fossilized tree made of wood?

INTERPRETING GRAPHICS

Use the diagram below to answer the questions that follow.

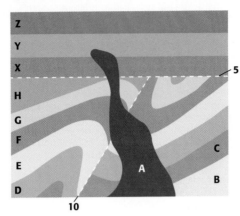

22 Is intrusion **A** younger or older than layer **X**? Explain.

23 What feature is marked by **5**?

24 Is intrusion **A** younger or older than fault **10**? Explain.

25 Other than the intrusion and faulting, what event happened in layers **B, C, D, E, F, G,** and **H**? Number this event, the intrusion, and the faulting in the order that they happened.

15. Radioactive decay occurs as an unstable isotope breaks down into a stable isotope. This change happens as the isotope loses an electron and as a neutron becomes a proton.

16. Paleontologists use fossils to reconstruct past climates and to determine water depth in the oceans.

17. Paleontologists piece together the history of life on Earth by using fossils as their data.

Critical Thinking

18. An answer to this exercise can be found at the end of this book.

19. Changes in environmental conditions can change or eliminate a species' habitat, so a species cannot meet its basic needs. Both global climate change and changes in ocean currents can cause the extinction of species.

20. Hard-bodied organisms are more easily preserved, so more of these organisms have been studied.

21. The tree is not made of wood because the wood tissue in the tree was completely replaced by minerals.

Interpreting Graphics

22. younger

23. an angular unconformity

24. Intrusion A is younger than fault 10 because the intrusion is not disturbed by the fault.

25. folding; Folding occurred, and then the fault occurred. After erosion and deposition of layers X and Y, the intrusion occurred.

13. Sample answer: Fossils are formed by the process of petrifaction, in which minerals replace an organism's tissue. Fossils are formed when organisms become trapped in hardened tree sap, or amber. Fossils are formed when an organism is preserved by sediment that slows decay.

14. Uniformitarianism is the guiding principle in Earth science. The geologic processes shaping the Earth today have been at work throughout Earth's history.

Standardized Test Preparation

Teacher's Note

To provide practice under more realistic testing conditions, give students 20 minutes to answer all of the questions in this Standardized Test Preparation.

MISCONCEPTION ///ALERT

Answers to the standardized test preparation can help you identify student misconceptions and misunderstandings.

READING

Passage 1

1. B
2. G
3. C

✚ TEST DOCTOR

Question 1: Although the word *exceptional* can describe something beautiful (choice A), the passage indicates that the nodules are exceptional because they are out of the ordinary, or extraordinary (choice B).

READING

Read each of the passages below. Then, answer the questions that follow each passage.

Passage 1 Three hundred million years ago, the region that is now Illinois had a different climate than it does today. Swamps and shallow bays covered much of the area. No fewer than 500 species of plants and animals lived in this environment. Today, the remains of these organisms are found beautifully preserved within nodules. Nodules are round or oblong structures usually composed of cemented sediments that sometimes contain the fossilized hard parts of plants and animals. The Illinois nodules are <u>exceptional</u> because the soft parts of organisms are found together with hard parts. For this reason, these nodules are found in fossil collections around the world.

1. In the passage, what is the meaning of the word *exceptional*?
A beautiful
B extraordinary
C average
D large

2. According to the passage, which of the following statements about nodules is correct?
F Nodules are rarely round or oblong.
G Nodules are usually composed of cemented sediment.
H Nodules are not found in present-day Illinois.
I Nodules always contain fossils.

3. Which of the following is a fact in the passage?
A The Illinois nodules are not well known outside of Illinois.
B Illinois has had the same climate throughout Earth's history.
C Both the hard and soft parts of organisms are preserved in the Illinois nodules.
D Fewer than 500 species of plants and animals have been found in Illinois nodules.

Passage 2 In 1995, paleontologist Paul Sereno and his team were working in an unexplored region of Morocco when they made an <u>astounding</u> find—an enormous dinosaur skull! The skull measured approximately 1.6 m in length, which is about the height of a refrigerator. Given the size of the skull, Sereno concluded that the skeleton of the animal it came from must have been about 14 m long—about as big as a school bus. The dinosaur was even larger than *Tyrannosaurus rex*! The newly discovered 90 million–year-old predator most likely chased other dinosaurs by running on large, powerful hind legs, and its bladelike teeth meant certain death for its prey.

1. In the passage, what does the word *astounding* mean?
A important
B new
C incredible
D one of a kind

2. Which of the following is evidence that the dinosaur described in the passage was a predator?
F It had bladelike teeth.
G It had a large skeleton.
H It was found with the bones of a smaller animal nearby.
I It is 90 million years old.

3. What types of information do you think that fossil teeth provide about an organism?
A the color of its skin
B the types of food it ate
C the speed that it ran
D the mating habits it had

Passage 2

1. C
2. F
3. B

✚ TEST DOCTOR

Question 3: Only choice B could be correct. Speed (choice C) could be determined by fossilized footprints. Color of skin (choice A) would require a frozen sample, but this would still be difficult to determine. Mating habits (choice D) would also be difficult to determine.

Use the graph below to answer the questions that follow.

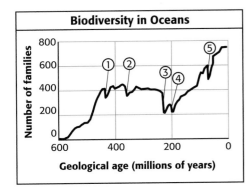

Biodiversity in Oceans

1. At which point in Earth's history did the greatest mass-extinction event take place?
   A at point 1, the Ordovician-Silurian boundary
   B at point 3, the Permian-Triassic boundary
   C at point 4, the Triassic-Jurassic boundary
   D at point 5, the Cretaceous-Tertiary boundary

2. Immediately following the Cretaceous-Tertiary extinction, represented by point 5, approximately how many families of marine organisms remained in the Earth's oceans?
   F 200 marine families
   G 300 marine families
   H 500 marine families
   I 700 marine families

3. Approximately how many million years ago did the Ordovician-Silurian mass-extinction event, represented by point 1, take place?
   A 200 million years ago
   B 250 million years ago
   C 350 million years ago
   D 420 million years ago

MATH

Read each question below, and choose the best answer.

1. Carbon-14 is a radioactive isotope with a half-life of 5,730 years. How much carbon-14 would remain in a sample that is 11,460 years old?
   A 12.5%
   B 25%
   C 50%
   D 100%

2. If a sample contains an isotope with a half-life of 10,000 years, how old would the sample be if 1/8 of the original isotope remained in the sample?
   F 20,000 years
   G 30,000 years
   H 40,000 years
   I 50,000 years

3. If a sample contains an isotope with a half-life of 5,000 years, how old would the sample be if 1/4 of the original isotope remained in the sample?
   A 10,000 years
   B 20,000 years
   C 30,000 years
   D 40,000 years

4. If Earth history spans 4.6 billion years and the Phanerozoic eon was 543 million years, what percentage of Earth history does the Phanerozoic eon represent?
   F about 6%
   G about 12%
   H about 18%
   I about 24%

5. Humans live in the Holocene epoch. If the Holocene epoch has lasted approximately 10,000 years, what percentage of the Quaternary period, which began 1.8 million years ago, is represented by the Holocene?
   A about 0.0055%
   B about 0.055%
   C about 0.55%
   D about 5.5%

Standardized Test Preparation

INTERPRETING GRAPHICS

1. B
2. H
3. D

 **TEST DOCTOR**

Question 2: Choice H is the correct answer. Students may choose choice G or F if they mistakenly look at points 3 or 4. If they look at the point of recovery after the Cretaceous-Tertiary extinction, they may choose choice I.

MATH

1. B
2. G
3. A
4. G
5. C

 **TEST DOCTOR**

Question 1: To determine the correct percentage, students should assume that a new fossil has all of its carbon-14 (100%) and that it loses half of its carbon-14 every 5,730 years. After 11,460 years, half of half of the original carbon-14 would be left. So, $1/2 \times 1/2 = 1/4 = 25\%$ (choice B).

CHAPTER RESOURCES

Chapter Resource File

• Standardized Test Preparation **GENERAL**

State Resources

For specific resources for your state, visit **go.hrw.com** and type in the keyword **HSMSTR**.

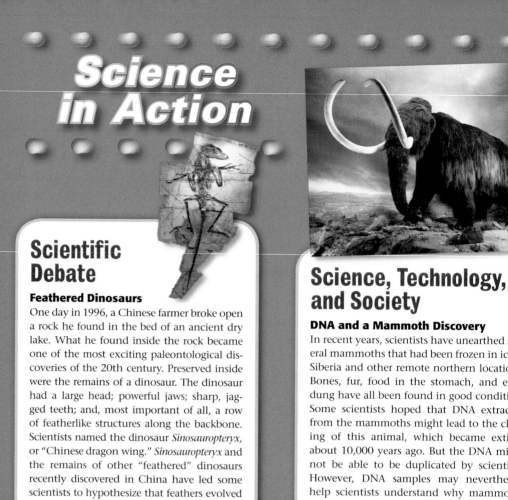

Science in Action

Scientific Debate

Background

Since the 1990s, well-preserved fossils of dinosaurs that have featherlike structures have been found in northern China. For many vertebrate paleontologists, these fossils provide support for the theory that birds are descended from theropods, a group of dinosaurs that include *Tyrannosaurus* and *Velociraptor*. Paleontologists think that the "feathered" dinosaurs were flightless and that the feathers were used for warmth or display.

Science, Technology, and Society

Background

Movies such as *Jurassic Park* may lead some students to believe that DNA extracted from the preserved remains of organisms that have died a long time ago will tell us everything about ancient life. In reality, it is difficult to obtain and study DNA. Large, complex molecules such as DNA are broken down by bacteria and enzymes soon after the death of an organism. The DNA becomes fragmented and cannot be pieced together again. Even the DNA of organisms such as mammoths that have been preserved in ice becomes fragmented.

Scientific Debate

Feathered Dinosaurs

One day in 1996, a Chinese farmer broke open a rock he found in the bed of an ancient dry lake. What he found inside the rock became one of the most exciting paleontological discoveries of the 20th century. Preserved inside were the remains of a dinosaur. The dinosaur had a large head; powerful jaws; sharp, jagged teeth; and, most important of all, a row of featherlike structures along the backbone. Scientists named the dinosaur *Sinosauropteryx*, or "Chinese dragon wing." *Sinosauropteryx* and the remains of other "feathered" dinosaurs recently discovered in China have led some scientists to hypothesize that feathers evolved through theropod (three-toed) dinosaurs. Other paleontologists disagree. They believe the structures along the backbone of these dinosaurs are not feathers but the remains of elongated spines, like those that run down the head and back of an iguana.

Science, Technology, and Society

DNA and a Mammoth Discovery

In recent years, scientists have unearthed several mammoths that had been frozen in ice in Siberia and other remote northern locations. Bones, fur, food in the stomach, and even dung have all been found in good condition. Some scientists hoped that DNA extracted from the mammoths might lead to the cloning of this animal, which became extinct about 10,000 years ago. But the DNA might not be able to be duplicated by scientists. However, DNA samples may nevertheless help scientists understand why mammoths became extinct. One theory about why mammoths became extinct is that they were killed off by disease. Using DNA taken from fossilized mammoth bone, hair, or dung, scientists can check to see if it contains the DNA of a disease-causing pathogen that led to the extinction of the mammoths.

Language Arts ACTIVITY

Paleontologists often give dinosaurs names that describe something unusual about the animal's head, body, feet, or size. These names have Greek or Latin roots. Research the names of some dinosaurs, and find out what the names mean. Create a list of dinosaur names and their meanings.

Math ACTIVITY

The male Siberian mammoth reached a height of about 3 m at the shoulder. Females reached a height of about 2.5 m at the shoulder. What is the ratio of the maximum height of a female Siberian mammoth to the height of a male Siberian mammoth?

Answer to Language Arts Activity
Answers may vary.

Answer to Math Activity
2.5:3.0

Lizzie May

Amateur Paleontologist For Lizzie May, summer vacations have meant trips into the Alaskan wilderness with her stepfather, geologist/paleontologist Kevin May. The purpose of these trips has not been for fun. Instead, Kevin and Lizzie have been exploring the Alaskan wilderness for the remains of ancient life—dinosaurs, in particular.

At age 18, Lizzie May has gained the reputation of being Alaska's most famous teenage paleontologist. It is a reputation that is well deserved. To date, Lizzie has collected hundreds of dinosaur bones and located important sites of dinosaur, bird, and mammal tracks. In her honor and as a result of her hard work in the field, scientists named the skeleton of a dinosaur discovered by the Mays "Lizzie." "Lizzie" is a duckbill dinosaur, or hadrosaur, that lived approximately 90 million years ago. "Lizzie" is the oldest dinosaur ever found in Alaska and one of the earliest known duckbill dinosaurs in North America.

The Mays have made other, equally exciting discoveries. On one summer trip, Kevin and Lizzie located six dinosaur and bird track sites that dated back 97 million to 144 million years. On another trip, the Mays found a fossil marine reptile more than 200 million years old—an ichthyosaur—that had to be removed with the help of a military helicopter. You have to wonder what other exciting adventures are in store for Lizzie and Kevin!

Social Studies

WRITING SKILL Lizzie May is not the only young person to have made a mark in dinosaur paleontology. Using the Internet or another source, research people such as Bucky Derflinger, Johnny Maurice, Brad Riney, and Wendy Sloboda, who as young people made contributions to the field of dinosaur study. Write a short essay summarizing your findings.

go.hrw.com

To learn more about these Science in Action topics, visit **go.hrw.com** and type in the keyword **HZ5FOSF.**

Current Science

Check out Current Science® articles related to this chapter by visiting go.hrw.com. Just type in the keyword **HZ5CS06.**

People in Science

Teaching Strategy GENERAL

Lizzie May shares the following fossil-hunting tips:

- If you are interested in finding bones, figure out in advance what the bones look like. This advice sounds obvious, but it's really helpful to know exactly what you are looking for.

- Bones are usually a different color from the dirt around them. So, you can look for white objects in the middle of the brown and black dirt. Sometimes, the bone will be the same color as the dirt, but as you sift through dirt, the inner portion of bones will stand out because the inner portion will be white.

- To find tracks, you need to be in the right place at the right time. Learn the kind of lighting that is right for finding tracks. Then, go out at that time to look for depressions in the Earth.

- Here's a clue for finding the right place to locate tracks. Tracks are often preserved in sedimentary rock near rivers. Being able to tell where the river channel is and has been is helpful.

- Stay in good shape—you don't want anything to slow you down when you are out in the field. It's hard work but is really fun!

- Volunteer at a museum!

Answer to Social Studies Activity
Answers may vary.

Plate Tectonics
Chapter Planning Guide

Compression guide:
To shorten instruction because of time limitations, omit Section 4.

OBJECTIVES	LABS, DEMONSTRATIONS, AND ACTIVITIES	TECHNOLOGY RESOURCES
PACING • 90 min pp. 94–103 **Chapter Opener**	**SE** Start-up Activity, p. 95 `GENERAL`	**OSP** Parent Letter ■ `GENERAL` **CD** Student Edition on CD-ROM **CD** Guided Reading Audio CD ■ **TR** Chapter Starter Transparency* **VID** Brain Food Video Quiz
Section 1 Inside the Earth • Identify the layers of the Earth by their composition. • Identify the layers of the Earth by their physical properties. • Describe a tectonic plate. • Explain how scientists know about the structure of Earth's interior.	**TE** Activity Earth Models, p. 96 `GENERAL` **TE** Connection Activity Math, p. 97 `GENERAL` **TE** Connection Activity Language Arts, p. 100 `GENERAL` **SE** Quick Lab Tectonic Ice Cubes, p. 101 ◆ `GENERAL` **CRF** Datasheet for Quick Lab* **TE** Group Activity Modeling a Tectonic Plate, p. 101 ◆ `GENERAL` **SE** School-to-Home Activity Build a Seismograph, p. 102 `GENERAL` **LB** Labs You Can Eat Rescue Near the Center of the Earth* ◆ `GENERAL`	**CRF** Lesson Plans* **TR** Bellringer Transparency* **TR** The Composition of the Earth* **TR** The Earth's Lithosphere and Asthenosphere* **TR** The Earth's Mesosphere, Outer Core, and Inner Core* **TR** The Tectonic Plates; Close-Up of a Tectonic Plate* **TR** Discoveries of the Earth's Interior* **CD** Science Tutor
PACING • 45 min pp. 104–107 **Section 2 Restless Continents** • Describe Wegener's hypothesis of continental drift. • Explain how sea-floor spreading provides a way for continents to move. • Describe how new oceanic lithosphere forms at mid-ocean ridges. • Explain how magnetic reversals provide evidence for sea-floor spreading.	**SE** Science in Action Math, Social Studies, and Language Arts Activities, pp. 126–127 `GENERAL` **LB** Labs You Can Eat Cracks in the Hard-Boiled Earth* ◆ `BASIC` **LB** Whiz-Bang Demonstrations Thar She Blows!* ◆ `GENERAL` **LB** Long-Term Projects & Research Ideas Legend Has It* `ADVANCED`	**CRF** Lesson Plans* **TR** Bellringer Transparency* **TR** The Breakup of Pangaea* **TR** *LINK TO LIFE SCIENCE* Evolution of the Galápagos Finches* **TR** Sea-Floor Spreading* **CD** Science Tutor
PACING • 90 min pp. 108–111 **Section 3 The Theory of Plate Tectonics** • Describe the three types of tectonic plate boundaries. • Describe the three forces thought to move tectonic plates. • Explain how scientists measure the rate at which tectonic plates move.	**TE** Group Activity Plate Movements, p. 109 `ADVANCED` **TE** Activity Geologic Features at Tectonic Plate Boundaries p. 109 `GENERAL` **SE** Model-Making Lab Convection Connection, p. 120 ◆ `GENERAL` **CRF** Datasheet for Chapter Lab* **LB** Labs You Can Eat Dough Fault of Your Own* ◆ `ADVANCED`	**CRF** Lesson Plans* **TR** Bellringer Transparency* **TR** Tectonic Plate Boundaries: A **TR** Tectonic Plate Boundaries: B **TR** Possible Causes of Tectonic Plate Motion* **CRF** SciLinks Activity* `GENERAL` **VID** Lab Videos for Earth Science
PACING • 45 min pp. 112–119 **Section 4 Deforming the Earth's Crust** • Describe two types of stress that deform rocks. • Describe three major types of folds. • Explain the differences between the three major types of faults. • Identify the most common types of mountains. • Explain the difference between uplift and subsidence.	**TE** Demonstration Modeling Deformation, p. 112 `GENERAL` **TE** Activity Folds that Trap Natural Gas, p. 113 `ADVANCED` **TE** Activity Hanging Walls Versus Footwalls, p. 114 `BASIC` **SE** Quick Lab Modeling Strike-Slip Faults, p. 115 `GENERAL` **CRF** Datasheet for Quick Lab* **TE** Activity Making Models, p. 115 `GENERAL` **TE** Activity Mountain-Building Gallery, p. 117 `GENERAL` **SE** Model-Making Lab Oh, the Pressure!, p. 186 `GENERAL` **CRF** Datasheet for LabBook*	**CRF** Lesson Plans* **TR** Bellringer Transparency* **SE** Internet Activity, p. 118 `GENERAL` **CD** Science Tutor

PACING • 90 min

CHAPTER REVIEW, ASSESSMENT, AND STANDARDIZED TEST PREPARATION

CRF Vocabulary Activity* `GENERAL`
SE Chapter Review, pp. 122–123 `GENERAL`
CRF Chapter Review* ■ `GENERAL`
CRF Chapter Tests A* ■ `GENERAL`, B* `ADVANCED`, C* `SPECIAL NEEDS`
SE Standardized Test Preparation, pp. 124–125 `GENERAL`
CRF Standardized Test Preparation* `GENERAL`
CRF Performance-Based Assessment* `GENERAL`
OSP Test Generator `GENERAL`
CRF Test Item Listing* `GENERAL`

Online and Technology Resources

Visit **go.hrw.com** for a variety of free resources related to this textbook. Enter the keyword **HZ5TEC**.

Holt Online Learning

Students can access interactive problem-solving help and active visual concept development with the *Holt Science and Technology* Online Edition available at **www.hrw.com**.

 Guided Reading Audio CD
Also in Spanish

A direct reading of each chapter for auditory learners, reluctant readers, and Spanish-speaking students.

 Science Tutor CD-ROM

Excellent for remediation and test practice.

SKILLS DEVELOPMENT RESOURCES	SECTION REVIEW AND ASSESSMENT	CORRELATIONS
SE Pre-Reading Activity, p. 94 `GENERAL` **OSP** Science Puzzlers, Twisters & Teasers `GENERAL`		National Science Education Standards SAI 1, SAI 2; ES 1b, 2a
CRF Directed Reading A* ■ `BASIC`, B* `SPECIAL NEEDS` **CRF** Vocabulary and Section Summary* ■ `GENERAL` **SE** Reading Strategy Reading Organizer, p. 96 `GENERAL` **SE** Math Practice Using Models, p. 98 `GENERAL` **TE** Reading Strategy Prediction Guide, p. 98 `GENERAL` **TE** Inclusion Strategies, p. 99 **TE** Reading Strategy Activity, p. 99 `GENERAL` **CRF** Reinforcement Worksheet The Layered Earth* `BASIC` **CRF** Critical Thinking Planet of Waves* `ADVANCED`	**SE** Reading Checks, pp. 97, 98, 101, 102 `GENERAL` **TE** Reteaching, p. 102 `BASIC` **TE** Quiz, p. 102 `GENERAL` **TE** Alternative Assessment, p. 102 `GENERAL` **SE** Section Review,* p. 103 ■ `GENERAL` **CRF** Section Quiz* ■ `GENERAL`	UCP 2; SAI 1, 2; ST 2; ES 1a
CRF Directed Reading A* ■ `BASIC`, B* `SPECIAL NEEDS` **CRF** Vocabulary and Section Summary* ■ `GENERAL` **SE** Reading Strategy Paired Summarizing, p. 104 `GENERAL`	**SE** Reading Checks, pp. 104, 107 `GENERAL` **TE** Reteaching, p. 106 `BASIC` **TE** Homework, p. 106 `GENERAL` **TE** Quiz, p. 106 `GENERAL` **TE** Alternative Assessment, p. 106 `GENERAL` **SE** Section Review,* p. 107 ■ `GENERAL` **CRF** Section Quiz* ■ `GENERAL`	UCP 2; SAI 1, 2; ST 2; SPSP 5; HNS 1, 2, 3; ES 1b, 2a
CRF Directed Reading A* ■ `BASIC`, B* `SPECIAL NEEDS` **CRF** Vocabulary and Section Summary* ■ `GENERAL` **SE** Reading Strategy Brainstorming, p. 108 `GENERAL` **MS** Math Skills for Science A Shortcut for Multiplying Large Numbers* `GENERAL` **CRF** Reinforcement Worksheet A Moving Jigsaw Puzzle* `BASIC`	**SE** Reading Checks, pp. 109, 110 `GENERAL` **TE** Homework, p. 110 `ADVANCED` **TE** Reteaching, p. 110 `BASIC` **TE** Quiz, p. 110 `GENERAL` **TE** Alternative Assessment, p. 110 `GENERAL` **SE** Section Review,* p. 111 ■ `GENERAL` **CRF** Section Quiz* ■ `GENERAL`	UCP 2; SAI 1, 2; ST 2; SPSP 3–5; HNS 1; ES 1b, 2a
CRF Directed Reading A* ■ `BASIC`, B* `SPECIAL NEEDS` **CRF** Vocabulary and Section Summary* ■ `GENERAL` **SE** Reading Strategy Discussion, p. 112 `GENERAL` **TE** Reading Strategy Sketching Folds and Faults, p. 113 `GENERAL` **SE** Connection to Social Studies The Naming of the Appalachian Mountains, p. 117 `GENERAL` **TE** Inclusion Strategies, p. 118 ◆	**SE** Reading Checks, pp. 112, 114, 116 `GENERAL` **TE** Homework, p. 113 `GENERAL` **TE** Reteaching, p. 118 `BASIC` **TE** Quiz, p. 118 `GENERAL` **TE** Alternative Assessment, p. 118 `GENERAL` **SE** Section Review,* p. 119 ■ `GENERAL` **CRF** Section Quiz* ■ `GENERAL`	UCP 2; SAI 1, 2; ES 1b, 1c, 1d, 2a

One-Stop Planner® CD-ROM

This CD-ROM package includes:
- Lab Materials QuickList Software
- Holt Calendar Planner
- Customizable Lesson Plans
- Printable Worksheets
- ExamView® Test Generator
- Interactive Teacher Edition
- Holt PuzzlePro® Resources
- Holt PowerPoint® Resources

SCILINKS®
NSTA

www.scilinks.org

Maintained by the **National Science Teachers Association.** See Chapter Enrichment pages for a complete list of topics.

Current Science®

Check out **Current Science** articles and activities by visiting the HRW Web site at **go.hrw.com.** Just type in the keyword **HZ5CS07T.**

 Classroom Videos

- **Lab Videos** demonstrate the chapter lab.
- **Brain Food Video Quizzes** help students review the chapter material.
- **CNN Videos** bring science into your students' daily life.

Chapter Resources

Visual Resources

CHAPTER STARTER TRANSPARENCY

This Really Happened!

BELLRINGER TRANSPARENCIES

Section: Inside the Earth
If you journeyed to the center of the Earth, what do you think you would see along the way?

Draw an illustration of the journey in your **science journal.**

Section: Restless Continents
Judge what is meant by the following statement: "The United States is moving westward." From what you know about geology and plate tectonics explain if you believe this statement to be true or false.

Record your answer in your **science journal.**

TEACHING TRANSPARENCIES

The Composition of the Earth

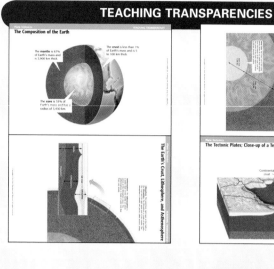

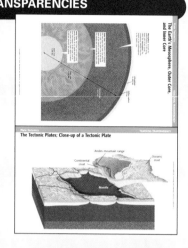

The Tectonic Plates; Close-up of a Tectonic Plate

TEACHING TRANSPARENCIES

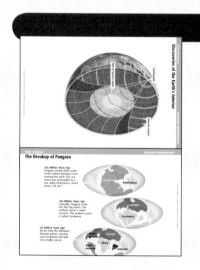

Discoveries of the Earth's Interior

The Breakup of Pangaea

Sea-Floor Spreading

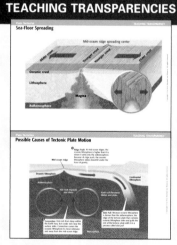

Possible Causes of Tectonic Plate Motion

Evolution of the Galapagos Finches

LINK TO LIFE SCIENCE

Chapter: The Evolution of Living Things

CONCEPT MAPPING TRANSPARENCY

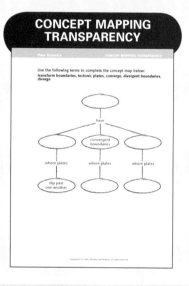

Use the following terms to complete the concept map below:
transform boundaries, tectonic plates, converge, divergent boundaries, diverge

Planning Resources

LESSON PLANS

Lesson Plan   SAMPLE

Section: Waves

PARENT LETTER

SAMPLE

Dear Parent,

ALSO IN SPANISH

TEST ITEM LISTING

TEST ITEM LISTING
The World of Earth Science   SAMPLE

MULTIPLE CHOICE

One-Stop Planner® CD-ROM

This CD-ROM includes all of the resources shown here and the following time-saving tools:

- *Lab Materials QuickList Software*
- *Customizable lesson plans*
- *Holt Calendar Planner*
- *The powerful ExamView® Test Generator*

Meeting Individual Needs

DIRECTED READING A

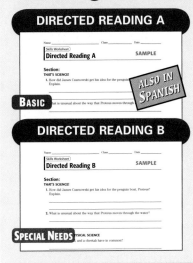

Directed Reading A — SAMPLE

Section: THAT'S SCIENCE!

1. How did James Czarnowski get his idea for the penguin... Explain.

BASIC

ALSO IN SPANISH

DIRECTED READING B

Directed Reading B — SAMPLE

Section: THAT'S SCIENCE!

1. How did James Czarnowski get his idea for the penguin boat, Proteus? Explain.

2. What is unusual about the way that Proteus moves through the water?

SPECIAL NEEDS

VOCABULARY ACTIVITY

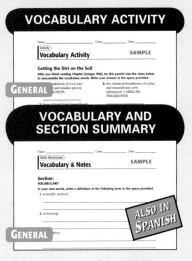

Vocabulary Activity — SAMPLE

Getting the Dirt on the Soil

After you finish reading Chapter: [Unique Title], try this puzzle! Use the clues below to unscramble the vocabulary words. Write your answer in the space provided.

GNETH

substances: CAMILCHE THEARIGWEN

GENERAL

VOCABULARY AND SECTION SUMMARY

Vocabulary & Notes — SAMPLE

Section: VOCABULARY

In your own words, write a definition of the following term in the space provided.

1. scientific method

2. technology

GENERAL

ALSO IN SPANISH

REINFORCEMENT

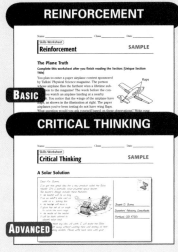

Reinforcement — SAMPLE

The Plane Truth

Complete this worksheet after you finish reading the Section: [Unique Section Title]

You plan to enter a paper airplane contest sponsored by Talkin' Physical Science magazine...

BASIC

CRITICAL THINKING

Critical Thinking — SAMPLE

A Solar Solution

ADVANCED

SCILINKS ACTIVITY

SciLinks Activity — SAMPLE

MARINE ECOSYSTEMS

Go to www.scilinks.com. To find links related to marine ecosystems, type in the keyword...

GENERAL

SCIENCE PUZZLERS, TWISTERS & TEASERS

CHAPTER 7 SCIENCE PUZZLERS, TWISTERS & TEASERS

Plate Tectonics

Tectonic Rhyme Time

1. Professor Bankston, an inventor/architect, has made some creations. Some sound more useful than others. Each of the clues below indicates a two-word rhyming answer that describes one of professor Bankston's creations. Write the words in the blank.

a. the amount of force put on a given material, and a machine for applying that force

b. the outermost layer of earth, and oxidation particles that cover the iron portion of it

GENERAL

Labs and Activities

LONG-TERM PROJECTS & RESEARCH IDEAS

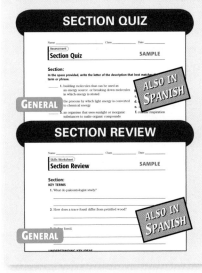

PROJECT 35 STUDENT WORKSHEET — DESIGN YOUR OWN

Legend Has It . . .

According to Irish legend, two giants—Finn McCool of Ireland and Finn Gall of Scotland—were feuding. In order to sneak up on his foe, Finn McCool built a bridge out of huge stone columns, which spanned the great distance between his friend Finn Gall's. Tired from the effort, McCool went home to rest before the great battle. Finn Gall, having discovered the bridge, arrived at his enemy's home demanding to see McCool. McCool's clever wife pretended to her husband and said that only she and her sleeping baby were home. Finn Gall thought to himself, "If this huge thing is the baby, the father must be gargantuan!" Not wishing to fight such an enormous rival, Finn Gall raced home over the bridge, destroying it as he went. All that is left of the bridge are its two ends: the Giant's Causeway, in Northern Ireland, and Fingal's Cave, in Scotland.

INTERNET KEYWORDS: columnar jointing, basalt column

The Science Behind the Myth

1. The Giant's Causeway and Fingal's Cave are two locations where dramatic basalt columns have formed...

Research Ideas

ADVANCED

WHIZ-BANG DEMONSTRATIONS

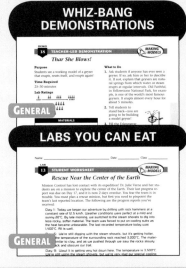

DEMO 18 TEACHER-LED DEMONSTRATION — MAKING MODELS

Thar She Blows!

Purpose
Students see a working model of a geyser that erupts, resets itself, and erupts again!

Time Required
25–30 minutes

Lab Ratings

MATERIALS

What to Do

1. Ask students if anyone has ever seen a geyser. If so, ask him or her to describe it. If not, explain that geysers are natural springs from which water or steam erupts at regular intervals...

GENERAL

LABS YOU CAN EAT

LAB 13 STUDENT WORKSHEET — MAKING MODELS

Rescue Near the Center of the Earth

Mission Control has lost contact with its expedition! Dr. Julie Verne and her students are on a mission to explore the center of the Earth...

Day 1: Today we began our adventure by drilling with rock hammers at a constant rate of 12.5 km/h...

GENERAL

LABS YOU CAN EAT

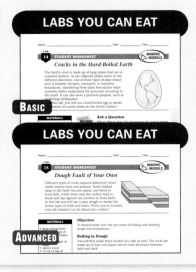

LAB 14 STUDENT WORKSHEET — MAKING MODELS

Cracks in the Hard-Boiled Earth

The Earth's crust is made up of large plates that are in constant motion. As two adjacent plates move in two different directions, one of three types of plate boundaries is formed: divergent, convergent, or transform boundaries...

MATERIALS

Ask a Question

BASIC

LABS YOU CAN EAT

LAB 15 STUDENT WORKSHEET — MAKING MODELS

Dough Fault of Your Own

Different types of rocks respond differently when under intense heat and pressure. Rocks heated deep in the Earth become plastic and tend to form folds...

MATERIALS

Objective
To demonstrate how the processes of folding and faulting shape rock formations

Rolling in Dough

ADVANCED

DATASHEETS FOR QUICK LABS

TEACHER RESOURCE PAGE

Quick Lab — DATASHEET FOR QUICK LAB

Reaction to Stress — SAMPLE

Background
The graph below illustrates changes that occur in the membrane potential of a neuron during an action potential. Use the graph to answer the following questions. Refer to Figure 3 as needed.

DATASHEETS FOR CHAPTER LABS

TEACHER RESOURCE PAGE

Skills Practice Lab — DATASHEET FOR CHAPTER LAB

Using Scientific Methods — SAMPLE

Teacher's Notes
TIME REQUIRED
One 45-minute class period.

DATASHEETS FOR LABBOOK

TEACHER RESOURCE PAGE

Skills Practice Lab — DATASHEET FOR LABBOOK LAB

Does It All Add Up? — SAMPLE

Teacher's Notes
TIME REQUIRED
One 45-minute class period.

Review and Assessments

SECTION QUIZ

Assessment

Section Quiz — SAMPLE

Section:

In the space provided, write the letter of the description that best matches the term or phrase.

_____ 1. building molecules that can be used as an energy source or breaking down molecules in which energy is stored
_____ 2. the process by which light energy is converted to chemical energy
_____ 3. an organism that uses sunlight or inorganic substances to make organic compounds

a.
b.
c.
d.
e.
f. cellular respiration

GENERAL

ALSO IN SPANISH

SECTION REVIEW

Skills Worksheet

Section Review — SAMPLE

Section:
KEY TERMS

1. What do paleontologist study?

2. How does a trace fossil differ from petrified wood?

GENERAL

ALSO IN SPANISH

CHAPTER REVIEW

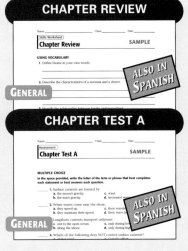

Skills Worksheet

Chapter Review — SAMPLE

USING VOCABULARY

1. Define biome in your own words.

2. Describe the characteristics of a savanna and a desert.

GENERAL

ALSO IN SPANISH

CHAPTER TEST A

Assessment

Chapter Test A — SAMPLE

MULTIPLE CHOICE

In the space provided, write the letter of the term or phrase that best completes each statement or best answers each question.

_____ 1. Surface currents are formed by
a. the moon's gravity.
b. the sun's gravity.
c. wind.
d. increased water density.

_____ 2. When waves come near the shore,
a. they speed up.
b. they maintain their speed.
c. their wavelength increases.
d. their wave height increases.

GENERAL

ALSO IN SPANISH

CHAPTER TEST B

Assessment

Chapter Test B — SAMPLE

MULTIPLE CHOICE

In the space provided, write the letter of the term or phrase that best completes each statement or answers each question.

_____ 1. Surface currents are formed by
a. the moon's gravity.
b. the sun's gravity.
c. wind.
d. increased water density.

_____ 2. When waves come near the shore,
a. they speed up.
b. they maintain their speed.
c. their wavelength increases.
d. their wave height increases.

ADVANCED

CHAPTER TEST C

Assessment

Chapter Test C — SAMPLE

MULTIPLE CHOICE

In the space provided, write the letter of the term or phrase that best completes each statement or best answers each question.

_____ 1. Surface currents are formed by
a. the moon's gravity.
b. the sun's gravity.
c. wind.
d. increased water density.

_____ 2. When waves come near the shore,
a. they speed up.
b. they maintain their speed.
c. their wavelength increases.
d. their wave height increases.

SPECIAL NEEDS

STANDARDIZED TEST PREPARATION

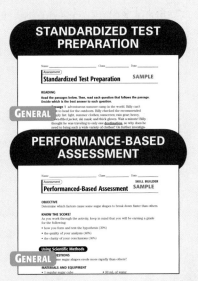

Assessment

Standardized Test Preparation — SAMPLE

READING
Read the passages below. Then, read each question that follows the passage. Decide which is the best answer to each question.

Passage 1 adventure summer camp in the world. Billy can't wait to head for the outdoors. Billy checked the recommended supply list: light, summer clothes, sunscreen, rain gear, heavy, down-filled jacket, ski mask, and thick gloves. Wait a minute! Billy thought he was traveling to only one destination, so why does he need to bring such a wide variety of clothes? On further investiga-

GENERAL

PERFORMANCE-BASED ASSESSMENT

Assessment

Performance-Based Assessment — SKILL BUILDER SAMPLE

OBJECTIVE
Determine which factors cause water sugar shapes to break down faster than others.

KNOW THE SCORE!
As you work through the activity, keep in mind that you will be earning a grade for the following:
• how you form and test the hypothesis (30%)
• the quality of your analysis (40%)
• the clarity of your conclusions (30%)

Using Scientific Methods
QUESTIONS
Do some sugar shapes erode rapidly than others?

MATERIALS AND EQUIPMENT
• 1 regular sugar cube   • 90 mL of water

GENERAL

This Chapter Enrichment provides relevant and interesting information to expand and enhance your presentation of the chapter material.

Section 1

Inside the Earth

Continents and the Earth's Crust

- Continents are large, continuous landmasses composed of crust that is generally much older than the surrounding oceanic crust. The core or central, older, stabler part of a continent, called a *craton,* is generally composed of ancient, crystalline igneous and metamorphic rock. Cratons range from 3.9 billion to 200 million years old. Rocks of the North American craton are exposed more or less without interruption in the eastern two-thirds of Canada, along the U.S. margins of Lake Superior, and in most of Greenland.

Heat Within the Earth

- The Earth's internal heat contributes to the process of differentiation—the division of the Earth into layers that have distinct characteristics. This heat has three main sources: the decay of radioactive elements, which is a continuous process; the collapse of iron into the Earth's core during the process of differentiation 4.5 billion years ago; and leftover energy from the accretion and compression of particles that coalesced to form Earth 4.6 billion years ago.

Is That a Fact!

◆ Earth's magnetic poles have reversed more than 177 times in the last 85 million years. The most recent reversal occurred within the last 600,000 years. By using complex computer models, scientists are beginning to understand how this process happens, but they are unable to predict when the poles will reverse again or how life on Earth will be affected by this reversal.

Earth's Inner Core

- Research conducted in 1996 suggests that the solid inner core of the Earth spins faster than the rest of the planet. This 2,456 km wide sphere of hot iron moves at a speed that would allow it to lap Earth's surface once every 400 years. This information may give scientists clues about how the Earth formed.

- The Earth's outer core is a hot, electrically conducting liquid that is thought to be continuously moved by convection. This layer's conductivity combines with the differential spin of the Earth's inner core to create powerful electric currents that, in turn, generate the Earth's magnetic field.

Section 2

Restless Continents

Continental Drift: An Old Idea

- The idea that the continents were once joined together was not a new idea in Alfred Wegener's time. In 1620, Francis Bacon noted that the continents seemed to fit together like a jigsaw puzzle, but no one could understand how they moved. In 1858, a French scientist named Antonio Snider-Pellegrini cited fossil evidence that suggested the continents had been joined. In 1910, an American geologist named Frank Taylor pointed out geologic similarities between South America and Africa. Wegener's studies in 1915 were the first exhaustive research on the topic and combined evidence from many disciplines. Neither Wegener nor Taylor could explain how the continents had separated, and their observations were dismissed. It was not until the discovery of sea-floor spreading that the continental drift hypothesis was accepted.

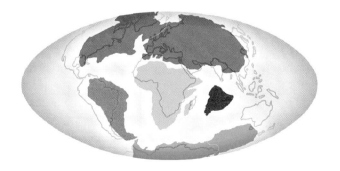

Testing the Continental Drift Hypothesis

- After sea-floor spreading was discovered in the 1960s, research groups tested Wegener's hypothesis using as many methods as possible:
  - The edges of continental slopes were mapped with sonar and have been shown to fit together even better than the coastlines do.
  - New radiometric dating methods showed that rocks in corresponding parts of Africa and South America formed at the same time.

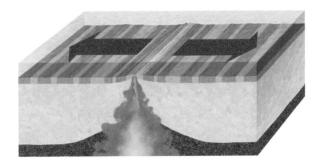

  - The dating of igneous rocks around mid-ocean ridges showed a symmetrical pattern, in which older rocks were located farther away from the rifts. Few rocks older than 180 million years were discovered on the ocean floor. This discovery indicates that the oceanic lithosphere is continuously recycled.
  - Scientists found that zones of magnetic reversals also followed a symmetrical pattern on either side of mid-ocean ridges. The pattern of reversals matched the pattern revealed by the ages of the rocks.
  - The horizontal magnetic reversals recorded in the ocean floor matched those recorded in vertical sequences of lava flows on continents.

Section 3

The Theory of Plate Tectonics

Trenches

- Where an oceanic plate subducts under another tectonic plate, a long, steep-sided trench forms on the sea floor. On average, subduction trenches are 2,000 to 4,000 m deeper than the rest of the ocean floor. Nevertheless, some animals, including species of sea cucumbers, sea anemones, and marine worms, are capable of living in the cold, pressurized depths of ocean trenches.

Is That a Fact!

- ◆ The Mariana Trench, which is 2,500 km long and 11,033 m below sea level at its deepest point, is the deepest known place on Earth.

Section 4

Deforming the Earth's Crust

Fault Versus Fold

- Tectonic activity exerts a tremendous amount of pressure on crustal rocks. Whether they bend or break depends on several factors:
  - **Type of Stress** If stress is applied gradually, rocks often fold; if stress is applied suddenly, rocks tend to fault.
  - **Composition of Rock** Brittle rocks, such as sandstone, tend to break; ductile rocks, such as shale, tend to fold.
  - **Temperature** As the temperature at the point of stress increases, rocks are more likely to fold rather than fault.

SciLinks is maintained by the National Science Teachers Association to provide you and your students with interesting, up-to-date links that will enrich your classroom presentation of the chapter.

Visit www.scilinks.org and enter the SciLinks code for more information about the topic listed.

Topic: Composition of the Earth
SciLinks code: HSM0329

Topic: Plate Tectonics
SciLinks code: HSM1171

Topic: Structure of the Earth
SciLinks code: HSM1468

Topic: Faults
SciLinks code: HSM0566

Topic: Tectonic Plates
SciLinks code: HSM1497

Topic: Mountain Building
SciLinks code: HSM0999

Overview

Tell students that this chapter will help them learn about the structure of the Earth and the forces that continually reshape the crust of our planet.

Assessing Prior Knowledge

Students should be familiar with the following topics:

• the principle of uniformitarianism

• the geologic time scale

Identifying Misconceptions

Students may think that the theory of plate tectonics was developed a long time ago. Stress that this key concept in geology was accepted in the mainstream of geologic thought less than 50 years ago. Parents and teachers may remember learning alternative theories in Earth science classes. Even today, scientists have still not fully identified the mechanisms of tectonic plate movement. Although the theory of plate tectonics was accepted in relatively recent times, it is still the best explanation for many different lines of geologic evidence and observations.

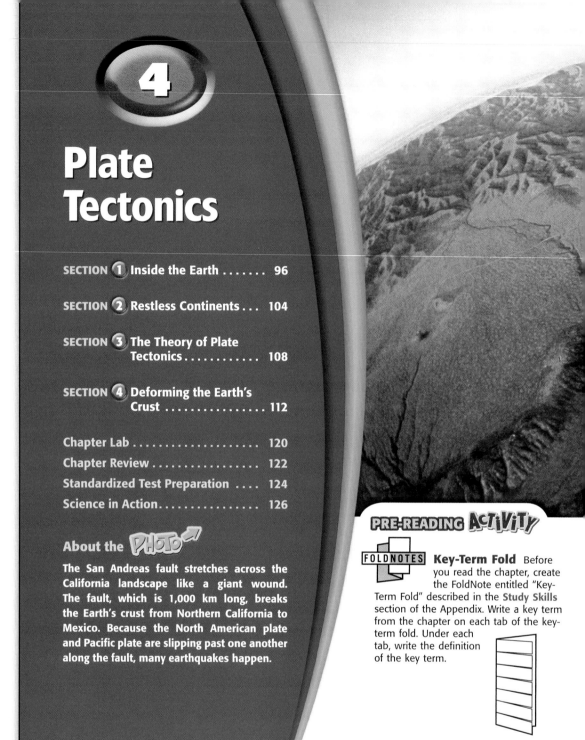

4

Plate Tectonics

About the PHOTO

The San Andreas fault stretches across the California landscape like a giant wound. The fault, which is 1,000 km long, breaks the Earth's crust from Northern California to Mexico. Because the North American plate and Pacific plate are slipping past one another along the fault, many earthquakes happen.

PRE-READING ACTIVITY

FOLDNOTES **Key-Term Fold** Before you read the chapter, create the FoldNote entitled "Key-Term Fold" described in the **Study Skills** section of the Appendix. Write a key term from the chapter on each tab of the key-term fold. Under each tab, write the definition of the key term.

Standards Correlations

National Science Education Standards

The following codes indicate the National Science Education Standards that correlate to this chapter. The full text of the standards is at the front of the book.

Chapter Opener
SAI 1, 2; ES 1a, 2a

Section 1 Inside the Earth
UCP 2; SAI 1, 2; ST 2; ES 1a

Section 2 Restless Continents
UCP 2; HNS 1, 2, 3; ES 1b, 2a; SPSP 5; ST 2; SAI 1, 2

Section 3 The Theory of Plate Tectonics
UCP 2; HNS 2; ES 1b, 2a; SPSP 3, 4, 5; *LabBook:* SAI 1, 2

Section 4 Deforming the Earth's Crust
UCP 2; SAI 1; ES 1b, 2a; SAI 1, 2

Chapter Lab
SAI 1, 2

Chapter Review
UCP 2; SAI 1, 2; HNS 2; ES 1a, 1b, 2a; ST 2

Science in Action
UCP 2; ES 1b, 2a; HNS 1, 2, 3; ST 2; SAI 1, 2

Answers

1. Sample answer: The stacks of paper buckle and fold over. Some of the paper in one stack slid under the paper in the other stack.

2. Sample answer: No, some pieces of paper slid under the opposite stack. Other pieces of paper slid into the other stack.

3. Sample answer: Continental collisions form high mountain ranges, such as the Himalayas.

START-UP ACTIVITY

Continental Collisions

As you can see, continents not only move but can also crash into each other. In this activity, you will model the collision of two continents.

Procedure

1. Obtain **two stacks of paper** that are each about 1 cm thick.

2. Place the two stacks of paper on a **flat surface,** such as a desk.

3. Very slowly, push the stacks of paper together so that they collide. Continue to push the stacks until the paper in one of the stacks folds over.

Analysis

1. What happens to the stacks of paper when they collide with each other?

2. Are all of the pieces of paper pushed upward? If not, what happens to the pieces that are not pushed upward?

3. What type of landform will most likely result from this continental collision?

Plate Tectonics   CHAPTER STARTER

This Really Happened!

It was a grueling climb to the top of Mount Everest. The temperature was well below freezing, and the blinding snow made it difficult to see. These harsh conditions and the extreme altitude are what make Mount Everest one of the most difficult mountains to climb. But these conditions did not stop a professional mountain climber by the name of Wally Berg. He was on a mission—a scientific mission that had been years in the planning.

Once at the top of the world's highest mountain, some 8,848 m high, Wally began drilling a hole in the rock. At this altitude the air is so thin that even easy tasks are difficult to accomplish. Wally brought bottles of oxygen with him to make his breathing easier.

Why did Wally drill a hole in Mount Everest? He needed the hole in order to secure a special device that receives and records signals from a network of satellites called the Global Positioning System (GPS).

GPS can pinpoint the exact location of these special receivers over long periods of time. In analyzing GPS data, scientists found out that Mount Everest not only is moving but also is growing taller every year. Over a year's time, the mountain moves northeast about 27 mm and grows from 3 to 5 mm taller!

Why is Mount Everest moving and growing? The answer is *plate tectonics.* Plate tectonics is also the reason why California has so many earthquakes and why volcanoes are found all around the rim of the Pacific Ocean. Get ready to learn much more about plate tectonics in this chapter.

Chapter Starter Transparency
Use this transparency to help students begin thinking about how tectonic forces have created tall mountains.

CHAPTER RESOURCES

Technology

📠 **Transparencies**
- Chapter Starter Transparency

READING SKILLS

💿 **Student Edition on CD-ROM**

💿 **Guided Reading Audio CD**
- English or Spanish

📹 **Classroom Videos**
- Brain Food Video Quiz

Workbooks

📓 **Science Puzzlers, Twisters & Teasers**
- Plate Tectonics **GENERAL**

Chapter 4 • Plate Tectonics **95**

SECTION
1

Focus

Overview

This section describes the classification of the Earth according to composition (crust, mantle, and core) and according to physical structure (lithosphere, asthenosphere, mesosphere, outer core, and inner core). This section also describes tectonic plates. The section concludes with a discussion of how scientists study seismic waves to map the Earth's interior.

🔊 Bellringer

Ask students, "If you journeyed to the center of the Earth, what do you think you would observe along the way?" Have students draw an illustration of their journey in their **science journal.**

Motivate

ACTIVITY ———— GENERAL

Earth Models Have groups of students use materials of their choice to build a cutaway scale model of the Earth based on the dimensions shown in **Figure 3.** Encourage students to be creative. For example, they could use a chain of paperclips 64 clips long (34 clips for the core, 29 clips for the mantle, and 1 clip for the crust). **LS Kinesthetic/ Visual**

READING WARM-UP

Objectives

● Identify the layers of the Earth by their composition.

● Identify the layers of the Earth by their physical properties.

● Describe a tectonic plate.

● Explain how scientists know about the structure of Earth's interior.

Terms to Learn

crust   asthenosphere
mantle   mesosphere
core   tectonic plate
lithosphere

READING STRATEGY

Reading Organizer As you read this section, create an outline of the section. Use the headings from the section in your outline.

Inside the Earth

If you tried to dig to the center of the Earth, what do you think you would find? Would the Earth be solid or hollow? Would it be made of the same material throughout?

Actually, the Earth is made of several layers. Each layer is made of different materials that have different properties. Scientists think about physical layers in two ways—by their composition and by their physical properties.

The Composition of the Earth

The Earth is divided into three layers—the crust, the mantle, and the core—based on the compounds that make up each layer. A *compound* is a substance composed of two or more elements. The less dense compounds make up the crust and mantle, and the densest compounds make up the core. The layers form because heavier elements are pulled toward the center of the Earth by gravity, and elements of lesser mass are found farther from the center.

The Crust

The outermost layer of the Earth is the **crust.** The crust is 5 to 100 km thick. It is the thinnest layer of the Earth.

As **Figure 1** shows, there are two types of crust—continental and oceanic. Both continental crust and oceanic crust are made mainly of the elements oxygen, silicon, and aluminum. However, the denser oceanic crust has almost twice as much iron, calcium, and magnesium, which form minerals that are denser than those in the continental crust.

Figure 1 *Oceanic crust is thinner and denser than continental crust.*

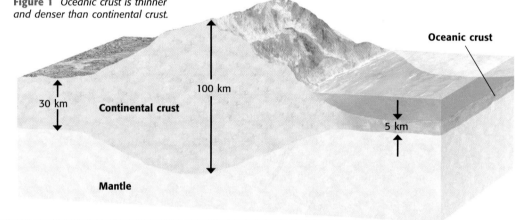

Oceanic crust

100 km

30 km   **Continental crust**

5 km

Mantle

Is That a Fact!

Two lines of evidence indicate that Earth's core is a mixture of iron and nickel. The core's density, which is similar to a mixture of iron and nickel, was determined by studying the way seismic waves travel through it. The Earth's magnetic field also suggests this composition.

The Mantle

The layer of the Earth between the crust and the core is the **mantle.** The mantle is much thicker than the crust and contains most of the Earth's mass.

No one has ever visited the mantle. The crust is too thick to drill through to reach the mantle. Scientists must draw conclusions about the composition and other physical properties of the mantle from observations made on the Earth's surface. In some places, mantle rock pushes to the surface, which allows scientists to study the rock directly.

As you can see in **Figure 2,** another place scientists look for clues about the mantle is the ocean floor. Magma from the mantle flows out of active volcanoes on the ocean floor. These underwater volcanoes have given scientists many clues about the composition of the mantle. Because the mantle has more magnesium and less aluminum and silicon than the crust does, the mantle is denser than the crust.

The Core

The layer of the Earth that extends from below the mantle to the center of the Earth is the **core.** Scientists think that the Earth's core is made mostly of iron and contains smaller amounts of nickel but almost no oxygen, silicon, aluminum, or magnesium. As shown in **Figure 3,** the core makes up roughly one-third of the Earth's mass.

✓ Reading Check Briefly describe the layers that make up the Earth. (*See the Appendix for answers to Reading Checks.*)

Figure 2 *Volcanic vents on the ocean floor, such as this vent off the coast of Hawaii, allow magma to rise up through the crust from the mantle.*

crust the thin and solid outermost layer of the Earth above the mantle

mantle the layer of rock between the Earth's crust and core

core the central part of the Earth below the mantle

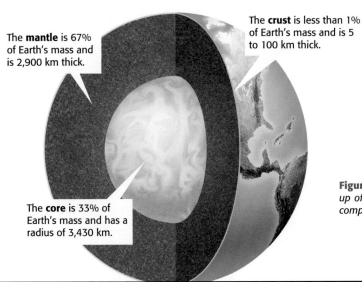

The **mantle** is 67% of Earth's mass and is 2,900 km thick.

The **crust** is less than 1% of Earth's mass and is 5 to 100 km thick.

The **core** is 33% of Earth's mass and has a radius of 3,430 km.

Figure 3 *The Earth is made up of three layers based on the composition of each layer.*

Answer to Reading Check

The crust is the thin, outermost layer of the Earth. It is 5 km to 100 km thick and is mainly made up of the elements oxygen, silicon, and aluminum. The mantle is the layer between the crust and core. It is 2,900 km thick, is denser than the crust, and contains most of the Earth's mass. The core is the Earth's innermost layer. The core has a radius of 3,430 km and is made mostly of iron.

Answers to Math Practice

150 km ÷ 6,380 km = 0.0235 = 2.35%

2.35% × 1.00 m = 0.0235 m, or 2.35 cm

READING STRATEGY — GENERAL

Prediction Guide Before students read this page, ask them the following question: "If you could burrow to the center of the Earth, what would you expect to happen to the pressure, the temperature, and the physical state of matter?" (Each successive layer will become hotter and have higher pressure. The solidity of layers will depend on temperature, pressure, and chemical composition.) **LS** Logical

Discussion — BASIC

The Plastic Asthenosphere Students may be confused by the use of the word *plastic* in the description of the asthenosphere. Remind students that plastic has two meanings. In this case, *plastic* means "malleable." English Language **LS** Verbal Learners

Answer to Reading Check

The five physical layers of the Earth are the lithosphere, asthenosphere, mesosphere, outer core, and inner core.

MATH PRACTICE

Using Models
Imagine that you are building a model of the Earth that will have a radius of 1 m. You find out that the average radius of the Earth is 6,380 km and that the thickness of the lithosphere is about 150 km. What percentage of the Earth's radius is the lithosphere? How thick (in centimeters) would you make the lithosphere in your model?

The Physical Structure of the Earth

Another way to look at the Earth is to examine the physical properties of its layers. The Earth is divided into five physical layers—the lithosphere, asthenosphere, mesosphere, outer core, and inner core. As shown in the figure below, each layer has its own set of physical properties.

✓ Reading Check What are the five physical layers of the Earth?

Lithosphere The outermost, rigid layer of the Earth is the **lithosphere.** The lithosphere is made of two parts—the crust and the rigid upper part of the mantle. The lithosphere is divided into pieces called *tectonic plates.*

Asthenosphere The **asthenosphere** is a plastic layer of the mantle on which pieces of the lithosphere move. The asthenosphere is made of solid rock that flows very slowly.

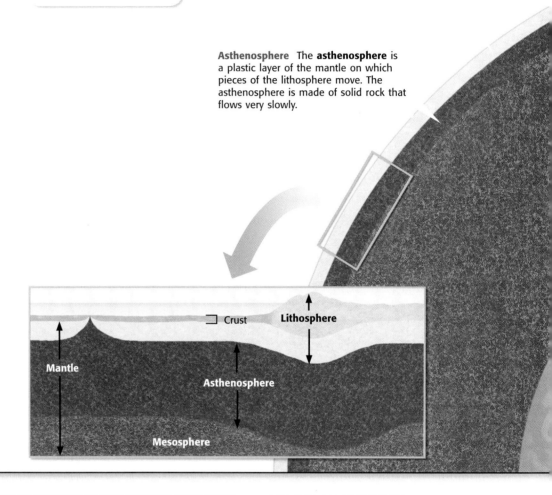

CHAPTER RESOURCES
Technology

Transparencies
• The Earth's Lithosphere and Asthenosphere
• The Earth's Mesosphere, Outer Core, and Inner Core

MISCONCEPTION ///ALERT\\\

Chemical and Physical Properties
Some students may not understand that the two systems of naming Earth's layers describe different properties. *Crust, mantle,* and *core* describe differences in chemical composition; *lithosphere, asthenosphere, mesosphere, outer core,* and *inner core* describe differences in the response of the material to stress caused by differences in temperature and pressure.

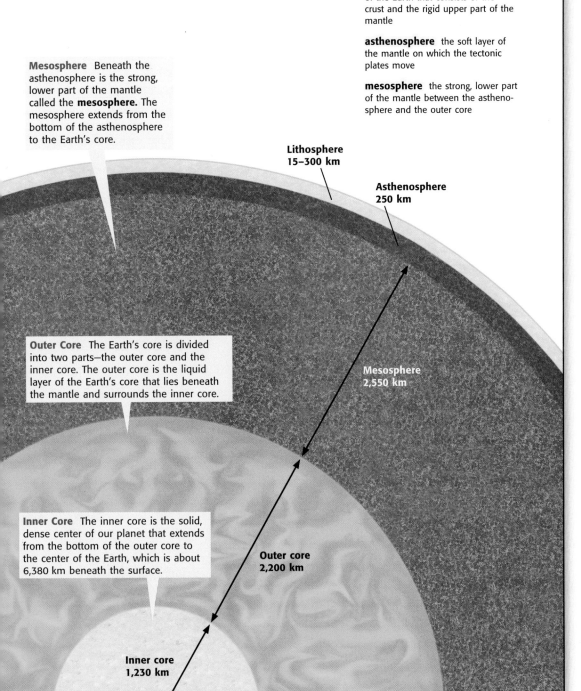

Mesosphere Beneath the asthenosphere is the strong, lower part of the mantle called the **mesosphere.** The mesosphere extends from the bottom of the asthenosphere to the Earth's core.

lithosphere the solid, outer layer of the Earth that consists of the crust and the rigid upper part of the mantle

asthenosphere the soft layer of the mantle on which the tectonic plates move

mesosphere the strong, lower part of the mantle between the asthenosphere and the outer core

Lithosphere 15–300 km

Asthenosphere 250 km

Mesosphere 2,550 km

Outer Core The Earth's core is divided into two parts—the outer core and the inner core. The outer core is the liquid layer of the Earth's core that lies beneath the mantle and surrounds the inner core.

Inner Core The inner core is the solid, dense center of our planet that extends from the bottom of the outer core to the center of the Earth, which is about 6,380 km beneath the surface.

Outer core 2,200 km

Inner core 1,230 km

READING STRATEGY — GENERAL

Activity Encourage students to look up and learn the meanings of the following prefixes and terms: *litho-* and *lithosphere*; *astheno-* and *asthenosphere*; and *meso-* and *mesosphere*. (The prefix *litho-* means "rock." The lithosphere is the Earth's outermost rigid layer. The prefix *astheno-* means "weak." The asthenosphere is a layer of slowly flowing rock beneath the lithosphere. The prefix *meso-* means "middle." The mesosphere lies between the asthenosphere and the core.) If students know the meaning of the prefix, they may find it easier to remember the physical characteristics and locations of the Earth's layers. **LS** Verbal   English Language Learners

Using the Figure — GENERAL
Physical Structure of the Earth Define the term *viscous*, and have students read about each layer in the illustration on these two pages. Ask students to sketch a simple model of the Earth's physical layers in their **science journals** and label each layer "Solid," "Liquid," or "Viscous." Ask students what pattern they notice as they work from the outside of the model to the inside. (The lithosphere is solid. The asthenosphere is viscous. The mesosphere is viscous. The outer core is liquid. The inner core is solid.) Ask students to explain why the inner core is not liquid. (Although the inner core is very hot, it is solid because of the pressure exerted on it.) **LS** Visual/Logical

INCLUSION Strategies

- *Learning Disabled*
- *Attention Deficit Disorder*
- *Visually Impaired*

Organize students into groups. Give each group modeling clay in three colors, a piece of cardboard, and self-stick notes. Ask each group to use the clay to create a model of the Earth's layers. After groups create their model, ask each group to label each layer with a self-stick note. Next, ask each group to write two facts about each layer on individual self-stick notes and apply them to the appropriate place on the model. Have each group share their model and facts with the class. English Language Learners **LS** Kinesthetic/Logical

Writing **Tectonic Essay** *Tectonic* comes from the Greek word *tektonikos*, which means "of a builder." Ask students to consider how this meaning is appropriate for tectonic plates. Ask students, "In what ways are tectonic plates responsible for building features on the Earth's surface?" Have students write a short essay that describes how the movement of tectonic plates slowly shapes the landscape around us. **LS Verbal**

BRAIN FOOD

The Deepest Hole The deepest hole ever drilled into the continental crust was in the Kola Peninsula, in Russia, in 1984. It was 12,226 m deep! Because the temperature of the crust increases with depth, it is impossible to drill much deeper into crust. Hot rock flows around the drill bit and fills the hole faster than the hole can be drilled. Ask students, "How deep is the hole compared to the height of Mount Everest? Did it extend to the mantle?" (12,226 m − 8,850 m = 3,376 m; no)

tectonic plate a block of lithosphere that consists of the crust and the rigid, outermost part of the mantle

Tectonic Plates

Pieces of the lithosphere that move around on top of the asthenosphere are called **tectonic plates**. But what exactly does a tectonic plate look like? How big are tectonic plates? How and why do they move around? To answer these questions, begin by thinking of the lithosphere as a giant jigsaw puzzle.

A Giant Jigsaw Puzzle

All of the tectonic plates have names, some of which you may already know. Some of the major tectonic plates are named on the map in **Figure 4.** Notice that each tectonic plate fits together with the tectonic plates that surround it. The lithosphere is like a jigsaw puzzle, and the tectonic plates are like the pieces of a jigsaw puzzle.

Notice that not all tectonic plates are the same. For example, compare the size of the South American plate with that of the Cocos plate. Tectonic plates differ in other ways, too. For example, the South American plate has an entire continent on it and has oceanic crust, but the Cocos plate has only oceanic crust. Some tectonic plates, such as the South American plate, include both continental and oceanic crust.

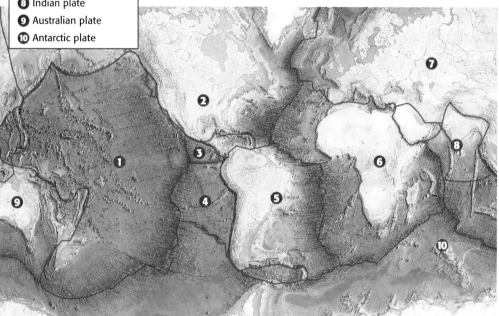

Major Tectonic Plates
1. Pacific plate
2. North American plate
3. Cocos plate
4. Nazca plate
5. South American plate
6. African plate
7. Eurasian plate
8. Indian plate
9. Australian plate
10. Antarctic plate

Figure 4 *Tectonic plates fit together like the pieces of a giant jigsaw puzzle.*

MISCONCEPTION ALERT

Tectonic Plates Students may think that tectonic plates are always neatly divided along continental lines, but the lines are not so neat. For example, the North American plate includes the North American continent, Greenland, half of Iceland, and part of Eurasia. All six of the Earth's large continental plates contain a continent and a large section of oceanic crust. Some of the 10 other small tectonic plates contain only oceanic crust.

Figure 5 The South American Plate

This image shows what you might see if you could lift the South American plate out of its position between other tectonic plates.

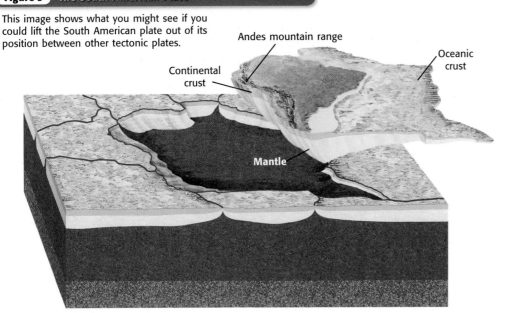

Andes mountain range

Continental crust

Oceanic crust

Mantle

A Tectonic Plate Close-Up

What would a tectonic plate look like if you could lift it out of its place? **Figure 5** shows what the South American plate might look like if you could. Notice that this tectonic plate not only consists of the upper part of the mantle but also consists of both oceanic crust and continental crust. The thickest part of the South American plate is the continental crust. The thinnest part of this plate is in the mid-Atlantic Ocean.

Like Ice Cubes in a Bowl of Punch

Think about ice cubes floating in a bowl of punch. If there are enough cubes, they will cover the surface of the punch and bump into one another. Parts of the ice cubes are below the surface of the punch and displace the punch. Large pieces of ice displace more punch than small pieces of ice. Tectonic plates "float" on the asthenosphere in a similar way. The plates cover the surface of the asthenosphere, and they touch one another and move around. The lithosphere displaces the asthenosphere. Thick tectonic plates, such as those made of continental crust, displace more asthenosphere than do thin plates, such as those made of oceanic lithosphere.

 Reading Check Why do tectonic plates made of continental lithosphere displace more asthenosphere than tectonic plates made of oceanic lithosphere do?

Quick Lab

Tectonic Ice Cubes

1. Take the bottom half of a clear, **2 L soda bottle** that has been cut in half. Make sure that the label has been removed.

2. Fill the bottle with **water** to about 1 cm below the top edge of the bottle.

3. Get **three pieces of irregularly shaped ice** that are small, medium, and large.

4. Float the ice in the water, and note how much of each piece is below the surface of the water.

5. Do all pieces of ice float mostly below the surface? Which piece is mostly below the surface? Why?

Reteaching — **BASIC**

Putting the Layers in Order
List Earth's physical layers on the board in random order. Have students arrange the list in the correct order. Then, have students help you write the compositional layers beside the physical layers (using brackets to indicate overlaps). Then, have students help you describe the characteristics of each layer.
 Logical

Quiz — **GENERAL**

Ask students whether each of the statements below is true or false. Have students correct false statements.

1. The inner core of the Earth is solid and made primarily of iron. (true)

2. The asthenosphere is the thinnest physical layer. (false, the lithosphere is the thinnest layer)

Alternative Assessment — **GENERAL**

Journey to the Center of the Earth Have students write a story describing their "journey to the center of the Earth," or have them write a travel guide that describes the experience of traveling through Earth's different layers. Have them draw and color-code a model of Earth to include with their project. Emphasize that this model must show layers defined by chemical composition and by physical properties. **Visual**

Build a Seismograph
Seismographs are instruments that seismologists, scientists who study earthquakes, use to detect seismic waves. Research seismograph designs with your parent. For example, a simple seismograph can be built by using a weight suspended by a spring next to a ruler. With your parent, attempt to construct a home seismograph based on a design you have selected. Outline each of the steps used to build your seismograph, and present the written outline to your teacher.

 ACTIVITY

Mapping the Earth's Interior

How do scientists know things about the deepest parts of the Earth, where no one has ever been? Scientists have never even drilled through the crust, which is only a thin skin on the surface of the Earth. So, how do we know so much about the mantle and the core?

Would you be surprised to know that some of the answers come from earthquakes? When an earthquake happens, vibrations called *seismic waves* are produced. Seismic waves travel at different speeds through the Earth. Their speed depends on the density and composition of material that they pass through. For example, a seismic wave traveling through a solid will go faster than a seismic wave traveling through a liquid.

When an earthquake happens, machines called *seismographs* measure the times at which seismic waves arrive at different distances from an earthquake. Seismologists can then use these distances and travel times to calculate the density and thickness of each physical layer of the Earth. **Figure 6** shows how seismic waves travel through the Earth.

✓ **Reading Check** What are some properties of seismic waves?

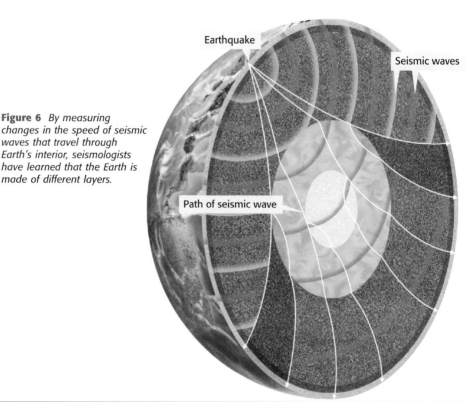

Figure 6 *By measuring changes in the speed of seismic waves that travel through Earth's interior, seismologists have learned that the Earth is made of different layers.*

Earthquake

Seismic waves

Path of seismic wave

CHAPTER RESOURCES

Technology

Transparencies
• Discoveries of the Earth's Interior

Answer to Reading Check

Answers may vary. A seismic wave traveling through a solid will go faster than a seismic wave traveling through a liquid.

Summary

- The Earth is made up of three layers—the crust, the mantle, and the core—based on chemical composition. Less dense compounds make up the crust and mantle. Denser compounds make up the core.

- The Earth is made up of five main physical layers: the lithosphere, the asthenosphere, the mesosphere, the outer core, and the inner core.

- Tectonic plates are large pieces of the lithosphere that move around on the Earth's surface.

- The crust in some tectonic plates is mainly continental. Other plates have only oceanic crust. Still other plates include both continental and oceanic crust.

- Thick tectonic plates, such as those in which the crust is mainly continental, displace more asthenosphere than do thin plates, such as those in which the crust is mainly oceanic.

- Knowledge about the layers of the Earth comes from the study of seismic waves caused by earthquakes.

Using Key Terms

For each pair of terms, explain how the meanings of the terms differ.

1. *crust* and *mantle*

2. *lithosphere* and *asthenosphere*

Understanding Key Ideas

3. The part of the Earth that is molten is the
   a. crust.
   b. mantle.
   c. outer core.
   d. inner core.

4. The part of the Earth on which the tectonic plates move is the
   a. lithosphere.
   b. asthenosphere.
   c. mesosphere.
   d. crust.

5. Identify the layers of the Earth by their chemical composition.

6. Identify the layers of the Earth by their physical properties.

7. Describe a tectonic plate.

8. Explain how scientists know about the structure of the Earth's interior.

Interpreting Graphics

9. According to the wave speeds shown in the table below, which two physical layers of the Earth are densest?

Speed of Seismic Waves in Earth's Interior

Physical layer	Wave speed
Lithosphere	7 to 8 km/s
Asthenosphere	7 to 11 km/s
Mesosphere	11 to 13 km/s
Outer core	8 to 10 km/s
Inner core	11 to 12 km/s

Critical Thinking

10. **Making Comparisons** Explain the difference between the crust and the lithosphere.

11. **Analyzing Ideas** Why does a seismic wave travel faster through solid rock than through water?

SCI**LINKS**

NSTA
Developed and maintained by the
National Science Teachers Association

For a variety of links related to this chapter, go to www.scilinks.org
Topic: Composition of the Earth; Structure of the Earth
SciLinks code: HSM0329; HSM1468

Answers to Section Review

1. Sample answer: The crust is the thin, outermost layer of the Earth. It is made mainly of less dense compounds and is less than 1% of the Earth's mass. The mantle is a thick layer beneath the crust. The mantle is made of dense compounds and is 67% of the Earth's mass.

2. Sample answer: The lithosphere is rigid and is divided into tectonic plates. The asthenosphere is a layer of soft mantle material that flows very slowly.

3. c

4. b

CHAPTER RESOURCES

Chapter Resource File

- Section Quiz GENERAL
- Section Review GENERAL
- Vocabulary and Section Summary GENERAL
- Reinforcement Worksheet BASIC
- Critical Thinking ADVANCED
- Datasheet for Quick Lab

5. The crust is made mainly of the elements oxygen, silicon, and aluminum. The mantle has more magnesium and less aluminum and silicon than the crust has. The core is made mostly of iron.

6. The lithosphere is the outermost, rigid layer of the Earth. Beneath the lithosphere is the asthenosphere, a plastic layer of the mantle on which the lithosphere moves. The mesosphere is the strong, lower part of the mantle. The outer core is the liquid layer of the Earth's core that lies between the mantle and the inner core. The solid, dense center of our planet is the inner core.

7. A tectonic plate is a large piece of the Earth's lithosphere that moves slowly on top of the asthenosphere. Tectonic plates are composed of continental crust, oceanic crust, and both continental and oceanic crust.

8. Scientists can measure the speeds at which seismic waves travel through different parts of the Earth. This measurement helps them calculate the density and thickness of each layer the waves pass through.

9. According to the wave speeds in the table, the mesosphere and the inner core are the two densest physical layers. (In reality, the outer core and inner core are the two densest layers. Because the outer core is liquid, wave speed through the outer core is slower than it is in the mesosphere.)

10. The crust is the thin, outermost layer of the Earth that is compositionally different than the mantle. The lithosphere is a thick layer containing both the crust and upper mantle but which is rigid compared to the underlying asthenosphere.

11. Seismic waves travel through solid rock faster than they do through water because solid rock is denser than water.

SECTION

2

Focus

Overview

This section explains the continental drift hypothesis and how the continents have moved to their present locations. Students will learn that support for this hypothesis came when mid-ocean ridges were discovered. They will also learn that sea-floor spreading was supported by the record of reversals of the Earth's magnetic field present in oceanic crust.

🎧 Bellringer

Ask students to explain why the following statement is true or false: "The North American continent is moving westward." (true; The plate that North America sits on is moving to the west.)

Motivate

ACTIVITY ———— GENERAL

Reconstructing Pangaea Have students work in small groups to create a model of Pangaea. Provide each group with two world maps. Have the groups cut the continents out of one map and treat them as puzzle pieces by seeing how they best fit together. Refer to both the complete and the altered maps, and help students explain and demonstrate how each continent moved from its original position. **English Language Learners**
LS Visual

READING WARM-UP

Objectives

- Describe Wegener's hypothesis of continental drift.
- Explain how sea-floor spreading provides a way for continents to move.
- Describe how new oceanic lithosphere forms at mid-ocean ridges.
- Explain how magnetic reversals provide evidence for sea-floor spreading.

Terms to Learn

continental drift
sea-floor spreading

READING STRATEGY

Paired Summarizing Read this section silently. In pairs, take turns summarizing the material. Stop to discuss ideas that seem confusing.

Restless Continents

Have you ever looked at a map of the world and noticed how the coastlines of continents on opposite sides of the oceans appear to fit together like the pieces of a puzzle? Is it just coincidence that the coastlines fit together well? Is it possible that the continents were actually together sometime in the past?

Wegener's Continental Drift Hypothesis

One scientist who looked at the pieces of this puzzle was Alfred Wegener (VAY guh nuhr). In the early 1900s, he wrote about his hypothesis of *continental drift*. **Continental drift** is the hypothesis that states that the continents once formed a single landmass, broke up, and drifted to their present locations. This hypothesis seemed to explain a lot of puzzling observations, including the observation of how well continents fit together.

Continental drift also explained why fossils of the same plant and animal species are found on continents that are on different sides of the Atlantic Ocean. Many of these ancient species could not have crossed the Atlantic Ocean. As you can see in **Figure 1,** without continental drift, this pattern of fossils would be hard to explain. In addition to fossils, similar types of rock and evidence of the same ancient climatic conditions were found on several continents.

✓ **Reading Check** How did fossils provide evidence for Wegener's hypothesis of continental drift? (*See the Appendix for answers to Reading Checks.*)

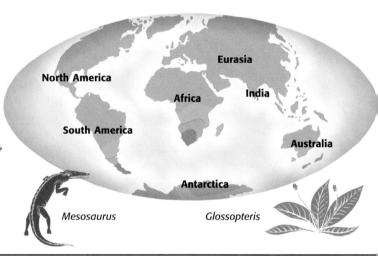

Figure 1 *Fossils of* Mesosaurus, *a small, aquatic reptile, and* Glossopteris, *an ancient plant species, have been found on several continents.*

 Mesosaurus   *Glossopteris*

CHAPTER RESOURCES

Chapter Resource File

- **Lesson Plan**
- **Directed Reading A** BASIC
- **Directed Reading B** SPECIAL NEEDS

Technology

- **Transparencies**
- Bellringer
- The Breakup of Pangaea
- ***LINK TO LIFE SCIENCE*** The Evolution of the Galápagos Finches

Answer to Reading Check

Similar fossils were found on landmasses that are very far apart. The best explanation for this phenomenon is that the landmasses were once joined.

Figure 2 The Drifting Continents

245 Million Years Ago
Pangaea existed when some of the earliest dinosaurs were roaming the Earth. The continent was surrounded by a sea called *Panthalassa*, which means "all sea."

180 Million Years Ago
Gradually, Pangaea broke into two big pieces. The northern piece is called *Laurasia*. The southern piece is called *Gondwana*.

65 Million Years Ago
By the time the dinosaurs became extinct, Laurasia and Gondwana had split into smaller pieces.

The Breakup of Pangaea

Wegener made many observations before proposing his hypothesis of continental drift. He thought that all of the present continents were once joined in a single, huge continent. Wegener called this continent *Pangaea* (pan JEE uh), which is Greek for "all earth." We now know from the hypothesis of plate tectonics that Pangaea existed about 245 million years ago. We also know that Pangaea further split into two huge continents—Laurasia and Gondwana—about 180 million years ago. As shown in **Figure 2,** these two continents split again and formed the continents we know today.

Sea-Floor Spreading

When Wegener put forth his hypothesis of continental drift, many scientists would not accept his hypothesis. From the calculated strength of the rocks, it did not seem possible for the crust to move in this way. During Wegener's life, no one knew the answer. It wasn't until many years later that evidence provided some clues to the forces that moved the continents.

continental drift the hypothesis that states that the continents once formed a single landmass, broke up, and drifted to their present locations

Evidence for Continental Drift
Organize the class into groups of three. Ask each group to choose one of the following lines of evidence that support the continental drift hypothesis: fossil similarities, landform similarities, and sea-floor spreading. Have each group work for 20 min to gather evidence for the continental drift hypothesis, and then ask groups to share their findings with the class.
LS Logical Co-op Learning

Quiz ——— GENERAL

1. What material creates new lithosphere at a mid-ocean ridge? (solidified magma)

2. What was Pangaea? (the large landmass that later broke up to form two supercontinents and then fragmented further to form the six continents that exist today)

Alternative Assessment ——— GENERAL

Writing **Sea-Floor Spreading**
Have students write a paragraph explaining how sea-floor spreading causes continents to move apart. Students should also include a diagram of this process. **LS** Logical/Visual

---

Figure 3 Sea-Floor Spreading

Sea-floor spreading creates new oceanic lithosphere at mid-ocean ridges.

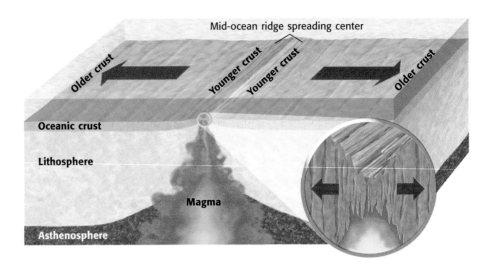

sea-floor spreading the process by which new oceanic lithosphere forms as magma rises toward the surface and solidifies

Figure 4 *The polarity of Earth's magnetic field changes over time.*

Mid-Ocean Ridges and Sea-Floor Spreading

A chain of submerged mountains runs through the center of the Atlantic Ocean. The chain is part of a worldwide system of mid-ocean ridges. Mid-ocean ridges are underwater mountain chains that run through Earth's ocean basins.

Mid-ocean ridges are places where sea-floor spreading takes place. **Sea-floor spreading** is the process by which new oceanic lithosphere forms as magma rises toward the surface and solidifies. As the tectonic plates move away from each other, the sea floor spreads apart and magma fills in the gap. As this new crust forms, the older crust gets pushed away from the mid-ocean ridge. As **Figure 3** shows, the older crust is farther away from the mid-ocean ridge than the younger crust is.

Evidence for Sea-Floor Spreading: Magnetic Reversals

Some of the most important evidence of sea-floor spreading comes from magnetic reversals recorded in the ocean floor. Throughout Earth's history, the north and south magnetic poles have changed places many times. When the poles change places, the polarity of Earth's magnetic poles changes, as shown in **Figure 4.** When Earth's magnetic poles change places, this change is called a *magnetic reversal.*

CONNECTION to Physical Science — GENERAL

Sonar Researchers used sonar to discover that the ocean floor is not flat. In the 1950s, scientists broadcast sound waves toward the sea floor and measured how long it took the waves to return. The echoes revealed valleys and mountains. Scientists were amazed to find a chain of undersea mountains snaking thousands of kilometers around the globe—the mid-ocean ridges.

Homework ——— GENERAL

Mid-Ocean Ridges Have students research and answer the following questions about **Figure 3:**

• Why does molten rock from the mantle come to the surface at the ridges?

• Why does the ocean floor spread apart at the ridges?

• Why is rock formed at the ridges called *new rock*?

Emphasize that mid-ocean ridges are not always in the middle of an ocean. **LS** Verbal

_____ 19. Magnetic stripes near mid-oceanic ridges supported the theory of sea-floor spreading because:

    a. the patterns were different on each side of the ridge   c. the patterns were the same on each side of the ridge

    b. they showed no change over time   d. the pattern disappeared

_____ 20. As the temperature of magma increases, it rises because

    a. its mass decreases   c. its density decreases

    b. its density increases   d. its volume decreases

Short Answer (4 points each)

Use the diagram to answer each question.

Plate Boundaries

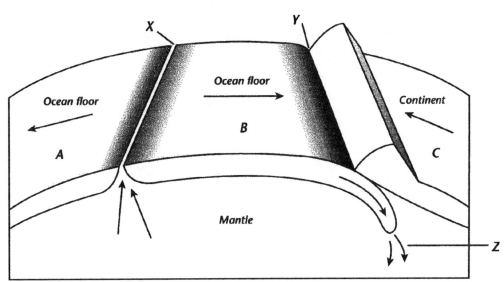

21. Which type of plate boundary occurs at X (convergent, divergent, or transform)?

22. Name the feature that forms at Y.

23. Name the process shown at Z?

24. Which type of plate boundary occurs at Y (convergent, divergent, or transform)?

25. Name the feature that forms at X.

Magnetic Reversals and Sea-Floor Spreading

The molten rock at the mid-ocean ridges contains tiny grains of magnetic minerals. These mineral grains contain iron and are like compasses. They align with the magnetic field of the Earth. When the molten rock cools, the record of these tiny compasses remains in the rock. This record is then carried slowly away from the spreading center of the ridge as sea-floor spreading occurs.

As you can see in **Figure 5,** when the Earth's magnetic field reverses, the magnetic mineral grains align in the opposite direction. The new rock records the direction of the Earth's magnetic field. As the sea floor spreads away from a mid-ocean ridge, it carries with it a record of magnetic reversals. This record of magnetic reversals was the final proof that sea-floor spreading does occur.

✔ **Reading Check** How is a record of magnetic reversals recorded in molten rock at mid-ocean ridges?

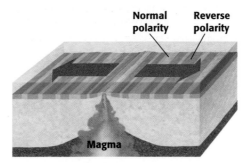

Normal polarity   Reverse polarity

Magma

Figure 5 *Magnetic reversals in oceanic crust are shown as bands of light blue and dark blue oceanic crust. Light blue bands indicate normal polarity, and dark blue bands indicate reverse polarity.*

SECTION Review

Summary

- Wegener hypothesized that continents drift apart from one another and have done so in the past.
- The process by which new oceanic lithosphere forms at mid-ocean ridges is called sea-floor spreading.
- As tectonic plates separate, the sea floor spreads apart and magma fills in the gap.
- Magnetic reversals are recorded over time in oceanic crust.

Using Key Terms

1. In your own words, write a definition for each of the following terms: *continental drift* and *sea-floor spreading.*

Understanding Key Ideas

2. At mid-ocean ridges,
   a. the crust is older.
   b. sea-floor spreading occurs.
   c. oceanic lithosphere is destroyed.
   d. tectonic plates are colliding.

3. Explain how oceanic lithosphere forms at mid-ocean ridges.

4. What is magnetic reversal?

Math Skills

5. If a piece of sea floor has moved 50 km in 5 million years, what is the yearly rate of sea-floor motion?

Critical Thinking

6. **Identifying Relationships** Explain how magnetic reversals provide evidence for sea-floor spreading.

7. **Applying Concepts** Why do bands indicating magnetic reversals appear to be of similar width on both sides of a mid-ocean ridge?

8. **Applying Concepts** Why do you think that old rocks are rare on the ocean floor?

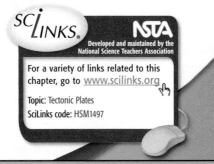

SC*LINKS.* **NSTA**
Developed and maintained by the National Science Teachers Association

For a variety of links related to this chapter, go to www.scilinks.org

Topic: Tectonic Plates
SciLinks code: HSM1497

Answer to Reading Check

The molten rock at mid-ocean ridges contains tiny grains of magnetic minerals. The minerals align with the Earth's magnetic field before the rock cools and hardens. When the Earth' magnetic field reverses, the orientation of the mineral grains in the rocks will also change.

CHAPTER RESOURCES

Chapter Resource File

- **Section Quiz** GENERAL
- **Section Review** GENERAL
- **Vocabulary and Section Summary** GENERAL

Technology

Transparencies
- Sea-Floor Spreading

Overview

This section discusses the theory of plate tectonics. Students will learn about possible causes of some plate movements. Students will also learn about types of plate boundaries.

Bellringer

Have students calculate the number of years that New York and the northwest coast of Africa took to reach their current locations, 6,760 km apart, if the sea floor is spreading at an average of 4 cm per year. 6,760 km = 676,000,000 cm ÷ 4 cm = 169,000,000 y. Point out that this number is fairly close to the estimate of when the breakup of Pangaea began 180 million years ago.)

Discussion —— GENERAL

A Preposterous Theory Write the word "preposterous" on the board. Then, discuss its meaning. Students may not realize how controversial and revolutionary the theory of plate tectonics was. Discuss why the idea that the enormous landmasses could "slide" across the asthenosphere seemed preposterous to most people. **LS** Verbal

SECTION 3

The Theory of Plate Tectonics

It takes an incredible amount of force to move a tectonic plate! But where does this force come from?

As scientists' understanding of mid-ocean ridges and magnetic reversals grew, scientists formed a theory to explain how tectonic plates move. **Plate tectonics** is the theory that the Earth's lithosphere is divided into tectonic plates that move around on top of the asthenosphere. In this section, you will learn what causes tectonic plates to move. But first you will learn about the different types of tectonic plate boundaries.

Tectonic Plate Boundaries

A boundary is a place where tectonic plates touch. All tectonic plates share boundaries with other tectonic plates. These boundaries are divided into three types: convergent, divergent, and transform. The type of boundary depends on how the tectonic plates move relative to one another. Tectonic plates can collide, separate, or slide past each other. Earthquakes can occur at all three types of plate boundaries. The figure below shows examples of tectonic plate boundaries.

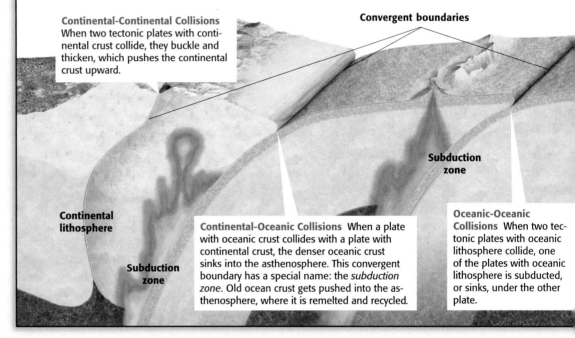

Continental-Continental Collisions When two tectonic plates with continental crust collide, they buckle and thicken, which pushes the continental crust upward.

Convergent boundaries

Continental lithosphere

Subduction zone

Continental-Oceanic Collisions When a plate with oceanic crust collides with a plate with continental crust, the denser oceanic crust sinks into the asthenosphere. This convergent boundary has a special name: the *subduction zone*. Old ocean crust gets pushed into the asthenosphere, where it is remelted and recycled.

Subduction zone

Oceanic-Oceanic Collisions When two tectonic plates with oceanic lithosphere collide, one of the plates with oceanic lithosphere is subducted, or sinks, under the other plate.

CONNECTION to Physical Science — GENERAL

Temperature and Density Point out how the movement of tectonic plates is driven by differences in temperature and density. In slab pull and ridge push, gravity pulls the oceanic plate downward because the oceanic plate is denser than the continental lithosphere. In convection, hot material rises because it is less dense than cooler material, which sinks.

Convergent Boundaries

When two tectonic plates collide, the boundary between them is a **convergent boundary.** What happens at a convergent boundary depends on the kind of crust at the leading edge of each tectonic plate. The three types of convergent boundaries are continental-continental boundaries, continental-oceanic boundaries, and oceanic-oceanic boundaries.

Divergent Boundaries

When two tectonic plates separate, the boundary between them is called a **divergent boundary.** New sea floor forms at divergent boundaries. Mid-ocean ridges are the most common type of divergent boundary.

Transform Boundaries

When two tectonic plates slide past each other horizontally, the boundary between them is a **transform boundary.** The San Andreas Fault in California is a good example of a transform boundary. This fault marks the place where the Pacific and North American plates are sliding past each other.

Reading Check Define the term *transform boundary*. (*See the Appendix for answers to Reading Checks.*)

plate tectonics the theory that explains how large pieces of the Earth's outermost layer, called *tectonic plates,* move and change shape

convergent boundary the boundary formed by the collision of two lithospheric plates

divergent boundary the boundary between two tectonic plates that are moving away from each other

transform boundary the boundary between tectonic plates that are sliding past each other horizontally

Sliding Past At a transform boundary, two tectonic plates slide past one another. Because tectonic plates have irregular edges, they grind and jerk as they slide, which produces earthquakes.

Divergent boundary

Oceanic lithosphere

Transform boundary

Moving Apart At a divergent boundary, two tectonic plates separate from each other. As they move apart, magma rises to fill the gap. At a mid-ocean ridge, the rising magma cools to form new sea floor.

Asthenosphere

Group ACTIVITY — ADVANCED

Plate Movements Ask groups of students to explain why continental-oceanic convergent boundaries and oceanic-oceanic convergent boundaries result in subduction, whereas continental-continental convergent boundaries do not. Then, have students do the following: create an illustrated chart showing the five types of boundary movements, and write captions explaining both how the boundaries move and what forces are responsible for their movement.

LS Logical/Visual

Answer to Reading Check

A transform boundary forms when two tectonic plates slide past each other horizontally.

Teach

ACTIVITY ———— GENERAL

Geologic Features at Tectonic Plate Boundaries Ask students to form hypotheses about what kinds of geologic features exist at different types of plate boundaries. Then, have them compare a topographic world map with a world map of tectonic plates. Help students conduct library and Internet research to find out if their hypotheses were correct.
LS Logical/Visual

MISCONCEPTION ALERT

Laws and Theories Students may think that if a theory is accepted by enough people for a long enough period of time, the theory will become a scientific law. Emphasize that scientific laws and theories are both correct and useful but that they serve different functions. A scientific law is a concise statement of fact that is accepted as true and universal. Theories are statements that are products of many scientific observations and may encompass numerous hypotheses or laws. Like a scientific law, a theory is accepted as true, but theories are much more complex than laws. A scientific law can be compared to an observation of a rubber ball. When dropped under constant conditions, the ball will always bounce as predicted. Bouncing is the only action the ball performs. On the other hand, a theory can be compared to a car. A car has many components that perform different tasks and work in unison. A part of the car may be improved, but the general function of the car is unchanged. **LS** Logical

Possible Causes of Tectonic Plate Motion

You have learned that plate tectonics is the theory that the lithosphere is divided into tectonic plates that move around on top of the asthenosphere. What causes the motion of tectonic plates? Remember that the solid rock of the asthenosphere flows very slowly. This movement occurs because of changes in density within the asthenosphere. These density changes are caused by the outward flow of thermal energy from deep within the Earth. When rock is heated, it expands, becomes less dense, and tends to rise to the surface of the Earth. As the rock gets near the surface, the rock cools, becomes more dense, and tends to sink. **Figure 1** shows three possible causes of tectonic plate motion.

Reading Check What causes changes in density in the asthenosphere?

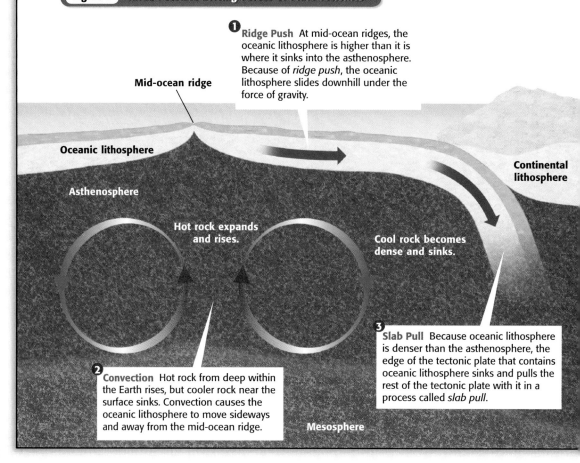

Figure 1 Three Possible Driving Forces of Plate Tectonics

❶ Ridge Push At mid-ocean ridges, the oceanic lithosphere is higher than it is where it sinks into the asthenosphere. Because of *ridge push*, the oceanic lithosphere slides downhill under the force of gravity.

Mid-ocean ridge

Oceanic lithosphere

Asthenosphere

Continental lithosphere

Hot rock expands and rises.

Cool rock becomes dense and sinks.

❸ Slab Pull Because oceanic lithosphere is denser than the asthenosphere, the edge of the tectonic plate that contains oceanic lithosphere sinks and pulls the rest of the tectonic plate with it in a process called *slab pull*.

❷ Convection Hot rock from deep within the Earth rises, but cooler rock near the surface sinks. Convection causes the oceanic lithosphere to move sideways and away from the mid-ocean ridge.

Mesosphere

Tracking Tectonic Plate Motion

How fast do tectonic plates move? The answer to this question depends on many factors, such as the type and shape of the tectonic plate and the way that the tectonic plate interacts with the tectonic plates that surround it. Tectonic plate movements are so slow and gradual that you can't see or feel them—the movement is measured in centimeters per year.

The Global Positioning System

Scientists use a system of satellites called the *global positioning system* (GPS), shown in **Figure 2,** to measure the rate of tectonic plate movement. Radio signals are continuously beamed from satellites to GPS ground stations, which record the exact distance between the satellites and the ground station. Over time, these distances change slightly. By recording the time it takes for the GPS ground stations to move a given distance, scientists can measure the speed at which each tectonic plate moves.

GPS satellite

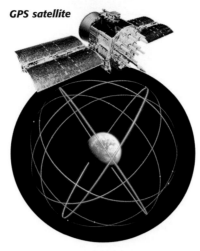

Figure 2 *The image above shows the orbits of the GPS satellites.*

SECTION Review

Summary

- Boundaries between tectonic plates are classified as convergent, divergent, or transform.
- Ridge push, convection, and slab pull are three possible driving forces of plate tectonics.
- Scientists use data from a system of satellites called the global positioning system to measure the rate of motion of tectonic plates.

Using Key Terms

1. In your own words, write a definition for the term *plate tectonics.*

Understanding Key Ideas

2. The speed a tectonic plate moves per year is best measured in
   a. kilometers per year.
   b. centimeters per year.
   c. meters per year.
   d. millimeters per year.

3. Briefly describe three possible driving forces of tectonic plate movement.

4. Explain how scientists use GPS to measure the rate of tectonic plate movement.

Math Skills

5. If an orbiting satellite has a diameter of 60 cm, what is the total surface area of the satellite? (Hint: *surface area* = $4\pi r^2$)

Critical Thinking

6. **Identifying Relationships** When convection takes place in the mantle, why does cool rock material sink and warm rock material rise?

7. **Analyzing Processes** Why does oceanic crust sink beneath continental crust at convergent boundaries?

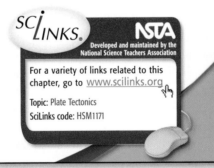

SCiLINKS

Developed and maintained by the National Science Teachers Association

For a variety of links related to this chapter, go to www.scilinks.org

Topic: Plate Tectonics
SciLinks code: HSM1171

Answers to Section Review

1. Sample answer: Plate tectonics is the theory that the lithosphere is divided into tectonic plates that move slowly across the asthenosphere.

2. b

3. Three possible driving forces of tectonic plate movement are ridge push, slab pull, and convection. Ridge push occurs when an oceanic plate slides down the boundary between the lithosphere and asthenosphere because of gravity. Slab pull occurs when the sinking edge of an oceanic plate pulls the rest of the plate down with it into the subduction zone. Convection occurs when hot mantle material in the asthenosphere convects and causes the tectonic plate to move sideways.

4. In the GPS process, radio signals are beamed from satellites to ground stations. The distance between the satellites and a ground station is recorded. Over time, these distances change slightly. Scientists can measure the rate at which tectonic plates move by recording the time it takes for ground stations to move a given distance.

5. $(4 \times 3.1416 \times 30\ cm^2) = 11,310\ cm^2$

6. During the convection process in the mantle, cooler material sinks because it is denser than warmer material.

7. Oceanic crust sinks beneath continental crust at convergent boundaries because oceanic crust is denser than continental crust.

CHAPTER RESOURCES

Chapter Resource File

- Section Quiz **GENERAL**
- Section Review **GENERAL**
- Vocabulary and Section Summary **GENERAL**
- Reinforcement Worksheet **BASIC**
- SciLinks Activity **GENERAL**

Technology

Transparencies
- Possible Causes of Tectonic Plate Motion

Focus

Overview

This section explores effects of tectonic forces on the Earth's crust. Students will learn how stress on rock causes it to fold or fault in various ways. The section also discusses how different types of mountains form from the action of tectonic forces and volcanic activity.

Bellringer

Display photographs of each type of mountain discussed in this section. Have students write a description of each example and suggest how each might have formed.

Motivate

Demonstration —— GENERAL

Modeling Deformation Display two thin strips of modeling clay, one frozen and one at room temperature. Have a volunteer demonstrate what happens when the warm clay is bent. (It folds.)

Ask students to predict what will happen to the frozen clay when a force is applied to it. Provide protective gloves, and have a second volunteer attempt to bend the frozen clay. (It should break.) **LS Kinesthetic/Visual**

Deforming the Earth's Crust

Have you ever tried to bend something, only to have it break? Take long, uncooked pieces of spaghetti, and bend them very slowly but only a little. Now, bend them again, but this time, bend them much farther and faster. What happened?

How can a material bend at one time and break at another time? The answer is that the stress you put on the material was different each time. *Stress* is the amount of force per unit area on a given material. The same principle applies to the rocks in the Earth's crust. Different things happen to rock when different types of stress are applied.

Deformation

The process by which the shape of a rock changes because of stress is called *deformation*. In the example above, the spaghetti deformed in two different ways—by bending and by breaking. **Figure 1** illustrates this concept. The same thing happens in rock layers. Rock layers bend when stress is placed on them. But when enough stress is placed on rocks, they can reach their elastic limit and break.

Compression and Tension

The type of stress that occurs when an object is squeezed, such as when two tectonic plates collide, is called **compression.** When compression occurs at a convergent boundary, large mountain ranges can form.

Another form of stress is *tension*. **Tension** is stress that occurs when forces act to stretch an object. As you might guess, tension occurs at divergent plate boundaries, such as mid-ocean ridges, when two tectonic plates pull away from each other.

Reading Check How do the forces of plate tectonics cause rock to deform? (*See the Appendix for answers to Reading Checks.*)

Figure 1 *When a small amount of stress is placed on uncooked spaghetti, the spaghetti bends. Additional stress causes the spaghetti to break.*

CHAPTER RESOURCES

Chapter Resource File

- Lesson Plan
- Directed Reading A BASIC
- Directed Reading B SPECIAL NEEDS

Technology

Transparencies
- Bellringer

Answer to Reading Check

Compression can cause rocks to be pushed into mountain ranges as tectonic plates collide at convergent boundaries. Tension can pull rocks apart as tectonic plates separate at divergent boundaries.

Figure 2 Folding: When Rock Layers Bend Because of Stress

Unstressed
Undeformed Rock Layers

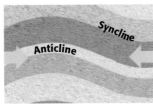
Horizontal stress
Syncline
Anticline

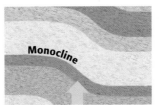
Vertical stress
Monocline

Folding

The bending of rock layers because of stress in the Earth's crust is called **folding.** Scientists assume that all rock layers started as horizontal layers. So, when scientists see a fold, they know that deformation has taken place.

Types of Folds

Depending on how the rock layers deform, different types of folds are made. **Figure 2** shows the two most common types of folds—*anticlines,* or upward-arching folds, and *synclines,* downward, troughlike folds. Another type of fold is a *monocline.* In a monocline, rock layers are folded so that both ends of the fold are horizontal. Imagine taking a stack of paper and laying it on a table. Think of the sheets of paper as different rock layers. Now put a book under one end of the stack. You can see that both ends of the sheets are horizontal, but all of the sheets are bent in the middle.

Folds can be large or small. The largest folds are measured in kilometers. Other folds are also obvious but are much smaller. These small folds can be measured in centimeters. **Figure 3** shows examples of large and small folds.

compression stress that occurs when forces act to squeeze an object

tension stress that occurs when forces act to stretch an object

folding the bending of rock layers due to stress

Figure 3 *The large photo shows mountain-sized folds in the Rocky Mountains. The small photo shows a rock that has folds smaller than a penknife.*

ACTIVITY — **BASIC**

Hanging Walls Versus Footwalls

Have students refer to **Figure 4** while you give the following explanation of hanging walls and footwalls: "When a fault occurs at an angle, the hanging wall is the block above the fault surface and the footwall is the block beneath the fault surface." Have students identify the hanging walls and footwalls in **Figure 5.** Have students do hand motions as they explain so that they can feel compression and tension. **LS Visual/Kinesthetic**

Discussion — **GENERAL**

Forces that Cause Faults Have students look at **Figure 5,** and point out that in a normal fault the hanging wall moves downward. Ask students to describe the tectonic force that causes this type of fault movement. (tension or stretching from plate movements pulling rocks apart) Have a student volunteer to use **Figure 5** to discuss the forces that cause reverse faults. (When plate movements squeeze rocks, compression forces the hanging wall up and the footwall down.) **English Language Learners**
LS Visual/Logical

Fault

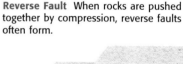

Footwall   Hanging wall

Figure 4 *The position of a fault block determines whether it is a hanging wall or a footwall.*

fault a break in a body of rock along which one block slides relative to another

Faulting

Some rock layers break when stress is applied to them. The surface along which rocks break and slide past each other is called a **fault.** The blocks of crust on each side of the fault are called *fault blocks*.

When a fault is not vertical, understanding the difference between its two sides—the *hanging wall* and the *footwall*—is useful. **Figure 4** shows the difference between a hanging wall and a footwall. Two main types of faults can form. The type of fault that forms depends on how the hanging wall and footwall move in relationship to each other.

Normal Faults

A *normal fault* is shown in **Figure 5.** When a normal fault moves, it causes the hanging wall to move down relative to the footwall. Normal faults usually occur when tectonic forces cause tension that pulls rocks apart.

Reverse Faults

A *reverse fault* is shown in **Figure 5.** When a reverse fault moves, it causes the hanging wall to move up relative to the footwall. This movement is the reverse of a normal fault. Reverse faults usually happen when tectonic forces cause compression that pushes rocks together.

✓ Reading Check How does the hanging wall in a normal fault move in relation to a reverse fault?

Figure 5 **Normal and Reverse Faults**

Normal Fault When rocks are pulled apart because of tension, normal faults often form.

Reverse Fault When rocks are pushed together by compression, reverse faults often form.

Answer to Reading Check
In a normal fault, the hanging wall moves down. In a reverse fault, the hanging wall moves up.

Is That a Fact!

Thrust faults are large-scale, low-angle, reverse faults caused by the collision of tectonic plates. They are an example of what can happen when stress (compression) is applied to the crust. An important example of thrust faulting in the United States is the Idaho-Wyoming thrust belt. Large-scale folding can also result from compression.

Telling the Difference Between Faults

It's easy to tell the difference between a normal fault and a reverse fault in drawings with arrows. But what types of faults are shown in **Figure 6**? You can certainly see the faults, but which one is a normal fault, and which one is a reverse fault? In the top left photo in **Figure 6,** one side has obviously moved relative to the other side. You can tell this fault is a normal fault by looking at the order of sedimentary rock layers. If you compare the two dark layers near the surface, you can see that the hanging wall has moved down relative to the footwall.

Strike-Slip Faults

A third major type of fault is called a *strike-slip fault.* An illustration of a strike-slip fault is shown in **Figure 7.** *Strike-slip faults* form when opposing forces cause rock to break and move horizontally. If you were standing on one side of a strike-slip fault looking across the fault when it moved, the ground on the other side would appear to move to your left or right. The San Andreas Fault in California is a spectacular example of a strike-slip fault.

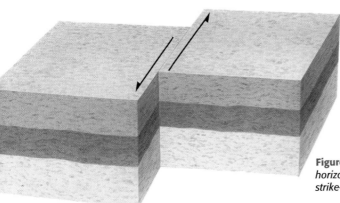

Figure 7 *When rocks are moved horizontally by opposing forces, strike-slip faults often form.*

Teach, continued

BRAIN FOOD

The "Solid" Earth
Ask students to write a one-page paper explaining their thoughts about the following quote from *Planet Earth* by Jonathan Weiner: "What we have been pleased to call 'solid Earth' is not as solid as we thought. It is energetic, dynamic, and fundamentally restless."
LS Logical

CONNECTION to Astronomy ———— GENERAL

Extraterrestrial Mountains and Mountain Ranges Earth is not the only place with mountains. Astronomers give extraterrestrial mountains the name *mons,* and extraterrestrial mountain ranges are called either *montes* or *highlands.* Encourage students to find out more about the formation of mountains on Mercury, Venus, Mars, Earth's moon, or on one of the moons of Jupiter or Saturn. Have students compare the mountains they study with mountains on Earth.
LS Logical

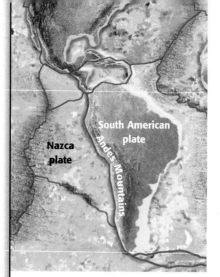

Figure 8 *The Andes Mountains formed on the edge of the South American plate where it converges with the Nazca plate.*

Figure 9 *The Appalachian Mountains were once as tall as the Himalaya Mountains but have been worn down by hundreds of millions of years of weathering and erosion.*

Plate Tectonics and Mountain Building

You have just learned about several ways the Earth's crust changes because of the forces of plate tectonics. When tectonic plates collide, land features that start as folds and faults can eventually become large mountain ranges. Mountains exist because tectonic plates are continually moving around and colliding with one another. As shown in **Figure 8,** the Andes Mountains formed above the subduction zone where two tectonic plates converge.

When tectonic plates undergo compression or tension, they can form mountains in several ways. Take a look at three of the most common types of mountains—folded mountains, fault-block mountains, and volcanic mountains.

Folded Mountains

The highest mountain ranges in the world are made up of folded mountains. These ranges form at convergent boundaries where continents have collided. *Folded mountains* form when rock layers are squeezed together and pushed upward. If you place a pile of paper on a table and push on opposite edges of the pile, you will see how folded mountains form.

An example of a folded mountain range that formed at a convergent boundary is shown in **Figure 9.** About 390 million years ago, the Appalachian Mountains formed when the landmasses that are now North America and Africa collided. Other examples of mountain ranges that consist of very large and complex folds are the Alps in central Europe, the Ural Mountains in Russia, and the Himalayas in Asia.

✓ **Reading Check** Explain how folded mountains form.

Answer to Reading Check
Folded mountains form when rock layers are squeezed together and pushed upward.

Is That a Fact!

The Sierra Nevada mountain range, in California, and the Teton Range, in Wyoming, are examples of fault-block mountains. The Appalachian Mountains, in eastern North America, are an example of folded mountains.

Figure 10 When the crust is subjected to tension, the rock can break along a series of normal faults, which creates fault-block mountains.

Fault-Block Mountains

When tectonic forces put enough tension on the Earth's crust, a large number of normal faults can result. *Fault-block mountains* form when this tension causes large blocks of the Earth's crust to drop down relative to other blocks. **Figure 10** shows one way that fault-block mountains form.

When sedimentary rock layers are tilted up by faulting, they can produce mountains that have sharp, jagged peaks. As shown in **Figure 11,** the Tetons in western Wyoming are a spectacular example of fault-block mountains.

Volcanic Mountains

Most of the world's major volcanic mountains are located at convergent boundaries where oceanic crust sinks into the asthenosphere at subduction zones. The rock that is melted in subduction zones forms magma, which rises to the Earth's surface and erupts to form *volcanic mountains*. Volcanic mountains can also form under the sea. Sometimes these mountains can rise above the ocean surface to become islands. The majority of tectonically active volcanic mountains on the Earth have formed around the tectonically active rim of the Pacific Ocean. The rim has become known as the *Ring of Fire*.

Figure 11 The Tetons formed as a result of tectonic forces that stretched the Earth's crust and caused it to break in a series of normal faults.

Reteaching ———— BASIC

Review of Mountain Building

After students have read this section, invite volunteers to sketch examples of each type of mountain on the board. Ask other students to explain how each mountain type forms by referring to the diagram and by adding labels and arrows to show the direction of forces at work. **LS Visual** English Language Learners

Quiz ———————— GENERAL

1. What three features form when rock layers bend? (anticlines, synclines, and monoclines)

2. Why are the Appalachian Mountains no longer located at the edge of the North American plate? (The Appalachians formed when North America and Africa collided. In time, the plates separated and so much new crust was created that the mountains were no longer at the plate boundary.)

Alternative Assessment ——— GENERAL

Identifying the Forces That Create Mountains

Have students choose a mountain range to research. Then, ask students to identify in writing the relationship between the mountain range and the forces that created it. **LS Logical**

For another activity related to this chapter, go to **go.hrw.com** and type in the keyword **HZ5TECW**.

uplift the rising of regions of the Earth's crust to higher elevations

subsidence the sinking of regions of the Earth's crust to lower elevations

Uplift and Subsidence

Vertical movements in the crust are divided into two types—uplift and subsidence. The rising of regions of Earth's crust to higher elevations is called **uplift**. Rocks that are uplifted may or may not be highly deformed. The sinking of regions of Earth's crust to lower elevations is known as **subsidence** (suhb SIED'ns). Unlike some uplifted rocks, rocks that subside do not undergo much deformation.

Uplifting of Depressed Rocks

The formation of mountains is one type of uplift. Uplift can also occur when large areas of land rise without deforming. One way areas rise without deforming is a process known as *rebound*. When the crust rebounds, it slowly springs back to its previous elevation. Uplift often happens when a weight is removed from the crust.

Subsidence of Cooler Rocks

Rocks that are hot take up more space than cooler rocks. For example, the lithosphere is relatively hot at mid-ocean ridges. The farther the lithosphere is from the ridge, the cooler and denser the lithosphere becomes. Because the oceanic lithosphere now takes up less volume, the ocean floor subsides.

Tectonic Letdown

Subsidence can also occur when the lithosphere becomes stretched in rift zones. A *rift zone* is a set of deep cracks that forms between two tectonic plates that are pulling away from each other. As tectonic plates pull apart, stress between the plates causes a series of faults to form along the rift zone. As shown in **Figure 12,** the blocks of crust in the center of the rift zone subside.

Figure 12 *The East African Rift, from Ethiopia to Kenya, is part of a divergent boundary, but you can see how the crust has subsided relative to the blocks at the edge of the rift zone.*

INCLUSION Strategies

• *Learning Disabled*
• *Behavior Control Issues*

Organize students into groups of four. Hand out a deck of cards that contain terms and concepts from this section. A different-colored set of cards should contain the definitions for the terms and concepts. Ask each group to match the terms to the correct definition. Have the groups work as a team when reviewing definitions. Students can use their text-books as a resource if necessary. Next, ask groups to separate terms and definitions into two decks. A team of two students should choose from the term deck and attempt to give the definition without looking at the card. The other two members can give clues if requested. Ask students to write down terms they have difficulty remembering in their **science journal. LS Logical**

SECTION
Review

Summary

- Compression and tension are two forces of plate tectonics that can cause rock to deform.
- Folding occurs when rock layers bend because of stress.
- Faulting occurs when rock layers break because of stress and then move on either side of the break.
- Mountains are classified as either folded, fault-block, or volcanic depending on how they form.

- Mountain building is caused by the movement of tectonic plates. Folded mountains and volcanic mountains form at convergent boundaries. Fault-block mountains form at divergent boundaries.
- Uplift and subsidence are the two types of vertical movement in the Earth's crust. Uplift occurs when regions of the crust rise to higher elevations. Subsidence occurs when regions of the crust sink to lower elevations.

Using Key Terms

For each pair of key terms, explain how the meanings of the terms differ.

1. *compression* and *tension*
2. *uplift* and *subsidence*

Understanding Key Ideas

3. The type of fault in which the hanging wall moves up relative to the footwall is called a
   a. strike-slip fault.
   b. fault-block fault.
   c. normal fault.
   d. reverse fault.

4. Describe three types of folds.
5. Describe three types of faults.
6. Identify the most common types of mountains.
7. What is rebound?
8. What are rift zones, and how do they form?

Critical Thinking

9. **Predicting Consequences** If a fault occurs in an area where rock layers have been folded, which type of fault is it likely to be? Why?

10. **Identifying Relationships** Would you expect to see a folded mountain range at a mid-ocean ridge? Explain your answer.

Interpreting Graphics

Use the diagram below to answer the questions that follow.

11. What type of fault is shown in the diagram?
12. At what kind of tectonic boundary would you most likely find this fault?

SCI LINKS.

NSTA
Developed and maintained by the
National Science Teachers Association

For a variety of links related to this chapter, go to www.scilinks.org

Topic: Faults; Mountain Building
SciLinks code: HSM0566; HSM0999

4. The three types of folds include anticlines, which are upward-arching folds; synclines, which are downward-arching folds; and monoclines, in which rock layers are folded so that both ends of the fold are horizontal.

5. The three types of faults include normal faults, in which the hanging wall moves down relative to the footwall; reverse faults, in which the hanging wall moves up relative to the footwall; and strike-slip faults, in which opposing forces cause rock to break and move horizontally.

6. The most common types of mountains are folded mountains, fault-block mountains, and volcanic mountains.

7. Rebound is a process in which Earth's crust slowly springs back to its previous elevation.

8. Rift zones are a set of deep cracks in the Earth's crust that form when two tectonic plates are pulling away from each other. As tectonic plates pull apart, stress builds up between the plates. This stress causes strain in the Earth's crust, and a series of faults forms along the rift zone.

9. A reverse fault is likely to form because both reverse faults and folding occur in areas where compression takes place.

10. No, you would be more likely to see volcanic mountains where magma is rising along the mid-ocean ridge spreading center.

11. a reverse fault

12. a convergent boundary

Answers to Section Review

1. Sample answer: Compression is stress that occurs when forces act to squeeze an object. Tension is stress that occurs when forces act to stretch an object.

2. Sample answer: Uplift is the rising of Earth's crust to higher elevations. Subsidence is the sinking of Earth's crust to lower elevations.

3. d

CHAPTER RESOURCES

Chapter Resource File

- Section Quiz GENERAL
- Section Review GENERAL
- Vocabulary and Section Summary GENERAL
- Datasheet for Quick Lab

Convection Connection

Teacher's Notes

Time Required
One 45-minute class period

Lab Ratings

EASY ——————————→ HARD

Teacher Prep 🝪
Student Set-Up 🝪🝪🝪
Concept Level 🝪🝪
Clean Up 🝪🝪

MATERIALS
The materials listed on the student page are enough for a group of 2 or 3 students.

Safety Caution
Remind students to review all safety cautions and icons before beginning this lab activity.

Preparation Notes
Because of the volume of water being used, you may wish to set up the blocks and hot plates ahead of time. Also, breezes and drafts may move the craft sticks, so eliminate or reduce as many of these variables as possible.

Convection Connection

Some scientists think that convection currents within the Earth's mantle cause tectonic plates to move. Because these convection currents cannot be observed directly, scientists use models to simulate the process. In this activity, you will make your own model to simulate tectonic plate movement.

Ask a Question

1 How can I make a model of convection currents in the Earth's mantle?

Form a Hypothesis

2 Turn the question above into a statement in which you give your best guess about what factors will have the greatest effect on your convection model.

Test the Hypothesis

3 Place two hot plates side by side in the center of your lab table. Be sure that they are away from the edge of the table.

4 Place the pan on top of the hot plates. Slide the wooden blocks under the pan to support the ends. Make sure that the pan is level and secure.

5 Fill the pan with cold water. The water should be at least 4 cm deep. Turn on the hot plates, and put on your gloves.

6 After a minute or two, tiny bubbles will begin to rise in the water above the hot plates. Gently place two craft sticks on the water's surface.

7 Use the pencil to align the sticks parallel to the short ends of the pan. The sticks should be about 3 cm apart and near the center of the pan.

8 As soon as the sticks begin to move, place a drop of food coloring in the center of the pan. Observe what happens to the food coloring.

OBJECTIVES

Model convection currents to simulate plate tectonic movement.

Draw conclusions about the role of convection in plate tectonics.

MATERIALS
- craft sticks (2)
- food coloring
- gloves, heat-resistant
- hot plates, small (2)
- pan, aluminum, rectangular
- pencil
- ruler, metric
- thermometers (3)
- water, cold
- wooden blocks

SAFETY

Terry J. Rakes
Elmwood Jr. High
Rogers, Arkansas

CHAPTER RESOURCES

Chapter Resource File
- Datasheet for Chapter Lab
- Lab Notes and Answers

Technology

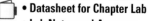 Classroom Videos
- Lab Video

LabBook
- Oh, the Pressure!

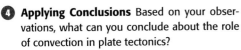

9. With the help of a partner, hold one thermometer bulb just under the water at the center of the pan. Hold the other two thermometers just under the water near the ends of the pan. Record the temperatures.

10. When you are finished, turn off the hot plates. After the water has cooled, carefully empty the water into a sink.

Analyze the Results

1. **Explaining Events** Based on your observations of the motion of the food coloring, how does the temperature of the water affect the direction in which the craft sticks move?

Draw Conclusions

2. **Drawing Conclusions** How does the motion of the craft sticks relate to the motion of the water?

3. **Applying Conclusions** How does this model relate to plate tectonics and the movement of the continents?

4. **Applying Conclusions** Based on your observations, what can you conclude about the role of convection in plate tectonics?

Applying Your Data

Suggest a substance other than water that might be used to model convection in the mantle. Consider using a substance that flows more slowly than water.

Analyze the Results

1. Based on the motion of the food coloring, the warmer water rises and the cooler water sinks. Therefore, as the water warms, the craft sticks should move in a direction away from the center of the pan.

Draw Conclusions

2. The hot water flowed outward from the center of the pan. This movement pushed the sticks away from each other and toward the edges of the pan. (In some cases, the sticks may move together.)

3. Convection currents within the Earth's mantle may move tectonic plates in the same way that the convecting water moved the craft sticks. The convection currents in this model were created by the hot plates warming the water. In the mantle, convection currents are caused by thermal energy from deep within the Earth.

4. Answers will vary but should include a description of how convection may be at least partially responsible for the movement of tectonic plates.

Applying Your Data

Suggestions for improving the model will vary. Students may suggest increasing the size of the model or using model tectonic plates that have differing sizes and densities. Students may also suggest incorporating the processes of ridge push or slab pull into the model.

Assignment Guide

SECTION	QUESTIONS
1	1, 3, 6, 11, 12, 21–24
2	2, 13, 14
3	7, 16, 18, 19
4	4, 5, 8–10, 15, 20
1, 2, and 3	17

ANSWERS

Using Key Terms

1. Sample answer: Scientists divide the Earth into the crust, mantle, and core based on the chemical elements that make up each of these layers.

2. continental drift

3. asthenosphere

4. Tension

5. uplift

Understanding Key Ideas

6. b

7. c

8. b

9. d

10. a

11. c

12. Scientists can measure the differences in the speeds of seismic waves that travel through the Earth's interior to calculate the density and thickness of each of the Earth's physical layers.

13. As oceanic crust spreads away from a mid-ocean ridge, the crust carries bands that contain minerals that were aligned with Earth's magnetic field when the crust was formed. The similar sequence of bands on both sides of a mid-ocean ridge, even at a large distance from the ridge, indicates that the sea floor is spreading away from a center.

USING KEY TERMS

1 Use the following terms in the same sentence: *crust, mantle,* and *core*.

Complete each of the following sentences by choosing the correct term from the word bank.

> asthenosphere uplift
> tension continental drift

2 The hypothesis that continents can drift apart and have done so in the past is known as ___.

3 The ___ is the soft layer of the mantle on which the tectonic plates move.

4 ___ is stress that occurs when forces act to stretch an object.

5 The rising of regions of the Earth's crust to higher elevations is called ___.

UNDERSTANDING KEY IDEAS

Multiple Choice

6 The strong, lower part of the mantle is a physical layer called the
  a. lithosphere.
  b. mesosphere.
  c. asthenosphere.
  d. outer core.

7 The type of tectonic plate boundary that forms from a collision between two tectonic plates is a
  a. divergent plate boundary.
  b. transform plate boundary.
  c. convergent plate boundary.
  d. normal plate boundary.

8 The bending of rock layers due to stress in the Earth's crust is known as
  a. uplift.
  b. folding.
  c. faulting.
  d. subsidence.

9 The type of fault in which the hanging wall moves up relative to the footwall is called a
  a. strike-slip fault.
  b. fault-block fault.
  c. normal fault.
  d. reverse fault.

10 The type of mountain that forms when rock layers are squeezed together and pushed upward is the
  a. folded mountain.
  b. fault-block mountain.
  c. volcanic mountain.
  d. strike-slip mountain.

11 Scientists' knowledge of the Earth's interior has come primarily from
  a. studying magnetic reversals in oceanic crust.
  b. using a system of satellites called the *global positioning system*.
  c. studying seismic waves generated by earthquakes.
  d. studying the pattern of fossils on different continents.

Short Answer

12 Explain how scientists use seismic waves to map the Earth's interior.

13 How do magnetic reversals provide evidence of sea-floor spreading?

14 Explain how sea-floor spreading provides a way for continents to move.

15 Describe two types of stress that deform rock.

16 What is the global positioning system (GPS), and how does GPS allow scientists to measure the rate of motion of tectonic plates?

CRITICAL THINKING

17 Concept Mapping Use the following terms to create a concept map: *sea-floor spreading, convergent boundary, divergent boundary, subduction zone, transform boundary,* and *tectonic plates.*

18 Applying Concepts Why does oceanic lithosphere sink at subduction zones but not at mid-ocean ridges?

19 Identifying Relationships New tectonic material continually forms at divergent boundaries. Tectonic plate material is also continually destroyed in subduction zones at convergent boundaries. Do you think that the total amount of lithosphere formed on the Earth is about equal to the amount destroyed? Why?

20 Applying Concepts Folded mountains usually form at the edge of a tectonic plate. How can you explain folded mountain ranges located in the middle of a tectonic plate?

INTERPRETING GRAPHICS

Imagine that you could travel to the center of the Earth. Use the diagram below to answer the questions that follow.

Composition	Structure
Crust (50 km)	Lithosphere (150 km)
Mantle (2,900 km)	Asthenosphere (250 km)
	Mesosphere (2,550 km)
Core (3,430 km)	Outer core (2,200 km)
	Inner core (1,228 km)

21 How far beneath the Earth's surface would you have to go before you were no longer passing through rock that had the composition of granite?

22 How far beneath the Earth's surface would you have to go to find liquid material in the Earth's core?

23 At what depth would you find mantle material but still be within the lithosphere?

24 How far beneath the Earth's surface would you have to go to find solid iron and nickel in the Earth's core?

16. The global positioning system is a system of satellites that orbit the Earth. Radio signals are continuously beamed from these satellites to ground stations. The distance between satellites and ground stations is recorded. By recording the time it takes for ground stations to move a given distance, scientists can measure the rate at which tectonic plates move.

Critical Thinking

17. 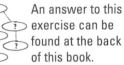 An answer to this exercise can be found at the back of this book.

18. Answers may vary. At a subduction zone, the lithosphere is denser than it is at a mid-ocean ridge. Convection causes oceanic lithosphere to move away from the mid-ocean ridge. Oceanic lithosphere is also higher at a mid-ocean ridge, so oceanic lithosphere moves down toward the subduction zone because of gravity.

19. Answers may vary. The amount of crust formed is roughly equal to the amount of crust destroyed. If this were not true, the Earth would either be expanding or shrinking.

20. At the time they formed, the folded mountains must have been on the edge of a tectonic plate. New material was later added to the tectonic plate, causing the folded mountains to be located closer to the center of the continent.

Interpreting Graphics

21. 50 km

22. 150 km + 250 km + 2,550 km = 2,950 km

23. between 50 km and 150 km

24. 150 km + 250 km + 2,550 km + 2,200 km = 5,150 km

14. As new crust forms at mid-ocean ridges, plates on either side of the ridge move away from the ridge. Therefore, continents on those plates also move.

15. Compression and tension are two types of stress that deform rock. Compression squeezes rock at convergent plate boundaries; tension stretches rock at divergent plate boundaries.

CHAPTER RESOURCES

Chapter Resource File

- Chapter Review `GENERAL`
- Chapter Test A `GENERAL`
- Chapter Test B `ADVANCED`
- Chapter Test C `SPECIAL NEEDS`
- Vocabulary Activity `GENERAL`

Workbooks

Study Guide
- Assessment resources are also available in Spanish.

Standardized Test Preparation

Standardized Test
Preparation

Teacher's Note

To provide practice under more realistic testing conditions, give students 20 minutes to answer all of the questions in this Standardized Test Preparation.

MISCONCEPTION
/// **ALERT** \\\

Answers to the standardized test preparation can help you identify student misconceptions and misunderstandings.

READING

Passage 1

1. C

2. H

3. B

✚ **TEST DOCTOR**

Question 3: Answer B is correct. The *Glomar Challenger* drilled into the ocean floor to obtain cores that contained fossils that would enable scientists on board the vessel to determine the relative age of the sea floor at various distances from mid-ocean ridges.

READING

Read each of the passages below. Then, answer the questions that follow each passage.

Passage 1 The Deep Sea Drilling Project was a program to retrieve and research rocks below the ocean to test the hypothesis of sea-floor spreading. For 15 years, scientists studying sea-floor spreading <u>conducted</u> research aboard the ship *Glomar Challenger*. Holes were drilled in the sea floor from the ship. Long, cylindrical lengths of rock, called *cores,* were obtained from the drill holes. By examining fossils in the cores, scientists discovered that rock closest to mid-ocean ridges was the youngest. The farther from the ridge the holes were drilled, the older the rock in the cores was. This evidence supported the idea that sea-floor spreading creates new lithosphere at mid-ocean ridges.

1. In the passage, what does *conducted* mean?

  A directed

  B led

  C carried on

  D guided

2. Why were cores drilled in the sea floor from the *Glomar Challenger*?

  F to determine the depth of the crust

  G to find minerals in the sea-floor rock

  H to examine fossils in the sea-floor rock

  I to find oil and gas in the sea-floor rock

3. Which of the following statements is a fact according to the passage?

  A Rock closest to mid-ocean ridges is older than rock at a distance from mid-ocean ridges.

  B One purpose of scientific research on the *Glomar Challenger* was to gather evidence for sea-floor spreading.

  C Fossils examined by scientists came directly from the sea floor.

  D Evidence gathered by scientists did not support sea-floor spreading.

Passage 2 The Himalayas are a range of mountains that is 2,400 km long and that <u>arcs</u> across Pakistan, India, Tibet, Nepal, Sikkim, and Bhutan. The Himalayas are the highest mountains on Earth. Nine mountains, including Mount Everest, the highest mountain on Earth, are more than 8,000 m tall. The formation of the Himalaya Mountains began about 80 million years ago. A tectonic plate carrying the Indian subcontinent collided with the Eurasian plate. The Indian plate was driven beneath the Eurasian plate. This collision caused the uplift of the Eurasian plate and the formation of the Himalayas. This process is continuing today.

1. In the passage, what does the word *arcs* mean?

  A forms a circle

  B forms a plane

  C forms a curve

  D forms a straight line

2. According to the passage, which geologic process formed the Himalaya Mountains?

  F divergence

  G subsidence

  H strike-slip faulting

  I convergence

3. Which of the following statements is a fact according to the passage?

  A The nine tallest mountains on Earth are located in the Himalaya Mountains.

  B The Himalaya Mountains are located within six countries.

  C The Himalaya Mountains are the longest mountain range on Earth.

  D The Himalaya Mountains formed more than 80 million years ago.

Passage 2

1. C

2. I

3. B

✚ **TEST DOCTOR**

Question 2: Convergence is the logical answer to this question. The Himalayas are the product of the continent-continent collision of the tectonic plate carrying the Indian subcontinent and the Eurasian plate.

The illustration below shows the relative velocities (in centimeters per year) and directions in which tectonic plates are separating and colliding. Arrows that point away from one another indicate plate separation. Arrows that point toward one another indicate plate collision. Use the illustration below to answer the questions that follow.

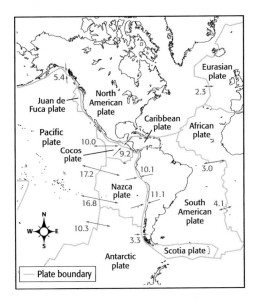

1. Between which two tectonic plates does spreading appear to be the fastest?
   A the Australian plate and the Pacific plate
   B the Antarctic plate and the Pacific plate
   C the Nazca plate and the Pacific plate
   D the Cocos plate and the Pacific plate

2. Where do you think mountain building is taking place?
   F between the African plate and the South American plate
   G between the Nazca plate and the South American plate
   H between the North American plate and the Eurasian plate
   I between the African plate and the North American plate

MATH

Read each question below, and choose the best answer.

1. The mesosphere is 2,550 km thick, and the asthenosphere is 250 km thick. If you assume that the lithosphere is 150 km thick and that the crust is 50 km thick, how thick is the mantle?
   A 2,950 km
   B 2,900 km
   C 2,800 km
   D 2,550 km

2. If a seismic wave travels through the mantle at an average velocity of 8 km/s, how many seconds will the wave take to travel through the mantle?
   F 318.75 s
   G 350.0 s
   H 362.5 s
   I 368.75 s

3. If the crust in a certain area is subsiding at the rate of 2 cm per year and has an elevation of 1,000 m, what elevation will the crust have in 10,000 years?
   A 500 m
   B 800 m
   C 1,200 m
   D 2,000 m

4. Assume that a very small oceanic plate is located between a mid-ocean ridge and a subduction zone. At the ridge, the plate is growing at a rate of 5 km every 1 million years. At the subduction zone, the plate is being destroyed at a rate of 10 km every 1 million years. If the oceanic plate is 100 km across, how long will it take the plate to disappear?
   F 100 million years
   G 50 million years
   H 20 million years
   I 5 million years

INTERPRETING GRAPHICS

1. C
2. G

TEST DOCTOR

Question 2: G is the only logical answer. Mountain building takes place at convergent boundaries. The Nazca plate and the South American plate are the only two plates that are converging.

MATH

1. B
2. H
3. B
4. H

TEST DOCTOR

Question 1: B is the correct answer. Obtaining the correct answer requires adding the thicknesses of the mesosphere, the asthenosphere, and the lithosphere and subtracting the thickness of the crust as follows: 2,550 km + 250 km + (150 km − 50 km) = 2,900 km.

Question 2: H is the correct answer. (2,900 km ÷ 8 km/s = 362.5 s, or a little more than 6 min)

Question 3: B is the correct answer. If the crust is subsiding at the rate of 2 cm/y, it will subside 200 m in 10,000 y (.02 m × 10,000 y = 200 m). If the current elevation is 1,000 m, the elevation will be 800 m (1,000 m − 200 m = 800 m) in 10,000 y.

Question 4: H is the correct answer. There is a net loss of 5 km of crust every 1 million years. If the plate is 100 km across, it will take 20 million years (100 km ÷ 5 km x 1,000,000 y) for the plate to disappear.

Standardized Test Preparation

CHAPTER RESOURCES

Chapter Resource File

• Standardized Test Preparation **GENERAL**

State Resources

For specific resources for your state, visit **go.hrw.com** and type in the keyword **HSMSTR**.

Science, Technology, and Society

Background

In addition to GPS satellites, satellite laser ranging (SLR) satellites are used to track the motion of tectonic plates. The *LAGEOS II SLR* satellite (pictured at right) is 60 cm in diameter and weighs approximately 405 kg. Imbedded in the surface of the satellite are 426 three-dimensional prisms. These prisms reflect laser beams directly back to their source.

Scientific Discoveries

Background

Megaplumes are giant, rotating disks of hot water that drift horizontally through the ocean. Megaplumes form at mid-ocean ridges during underwater volcanic eruptions. During an eruption, a column of boiling seawater rises upward from the volcano and expands until it forms a disk. The disks of megaplumes can drift through the oceans for hundreds of kilometers over a period of months. The first megaplume was discovered in 1986 along the Juan de Fuca Ridge, which is located approximately 300 miles off the northwest coast of the United States. Since 1986, at least seven more megaplumes have been recorded along the ridge.

Science in Action

Science, Technology, and Society

Using Satellites to Track Plate Motion

When you think of laser beams firing, you may think of science fiction movies. However, scientists use laser beams to determine the rate and direction of motion of tectonic plates. From ground stations on Earth, laser beams are fired at several small satellites orbiting 5,900 km above Earth. From the satellites, the laser beams are reflected back to ground stations. Differences in the time it takes signals to be reflected from targets are measured over a period of time. From these differences, scientists can determine the rate and direction of plate motion.

Social Studies ACTIVITY

WRITING SKILL Research a society that lives at an active plate boundary. Find out how the people live with dangers such as volcanoes and earthquakes. Include your findings in a short report.

This scientist is using a laser to test one of the satellites that will be used to track plate motion.

Scientific Discoveries

Megaplumes

Eruptions of boiling water from the sea floor form giant, spiral disks that twist through the oceans. Do you think it's impossible? Oceanographers have discovered these disks at eight locations at mid-ocean ridges over the past 20 years. These disks, which may be tens of kilometers across, are called *megaplumes*. Megaplumes are like blenders. They mix hot water with cold water in the oceans. Megaplumes can rise hundreds of meters from the ocean floor to the upper layers of the ocean. They carry gases and minerals and provide extra energy and food to animals in the upper layers of the ocean.

Language Arts ACTIVITY

WRITING SKILL Did you ever wonder about the origin of the name *Himalaya*? Research the origin of the name *Himalaya*, and write a short report about what you find.

Answers to Social Studies Activity

Have students give a short report on the society they researched. Before each report, have students find the geographical location of that society on a tectonic map of the world.

Answers to Language Arts Activity

Students should include in their report that the name *Himalaya* comes from the Sanskrit word *hima*, which means "snow," and *alaya*, which means "abode." Therefore, the word *Himalaya* means "the abode of snow."

People in Science

Alfred Wegener

Continental Drift Alfred Wegener's greatest contribution to science was the hypothesis of continental drift. This hypothesis states that continents drift apart from one another and have done so in the past. To support his hypothesis, Wegener used geologic, fossil, and glacial evidence gathered on both sides of the Atlantic Ocean. For example, Wegener recognized similarities between rock layers in North America and Europe and between rock layers in South America and Africa. He believed that these similarities could be explained only if these geologic features were once part of the same continent.

Although continental drift explained many of his observations, Wegener could not find scientific evidence to develop a complete explanation of how continents move. Most scientists were skeptical of Wegener's hypothesis and dismissed it as foolishness. It was not until the 1950s and 1960s that the discoveries of magnetic reversals and sea-floor spreading provided evidence of continental drift.

Math ACTiViTY

The distance between South America and Africa is 7,200 km. As new crust is created at the mid-ocean ridge, South America and Africa are moving away from each other at a rate of about 3.5 cm per year. How many millions of years ago were South America and Africa joined?

To learn more about these Science in Action topics, visit go.hrw.com and type in the keyword **HZ5TECF**.

Current Science

Check out Current Science® articles related to this chapter by visiting go.hrw.com. Just type in the keyword **HZ5CS07**.

People in Science

Teaching Strategy GENERAL

Many geologists ridiculed Wegener's hypothesis because they had been taught that continents and ocean basins were in fixed positions. These scientists knew of no force that could move an entire continent, and they discounted the evidence that continental drift had occurred.

The formation of a new hypothesis is an essential part of scientific inquiry. Yet, scientists are often met with opposition when they challenge conventional theories. Encourage students to investigate other scientists whose hypotheses were rejected during their lifetime but later were accepted. Students may want to explore the controversial hypotheses of Copernicus, Mendel, or Darwin or explore some modern controversies in the scientific community.

CONNECTION ACTiViTY
Math — BASIC

Breaking Up Is Hard to Do
The distance between New York and Paris increases every year. Currently, the two cities are moving apart by about 2 cm per year. Have students calculate the increase in distance in 1 million years. (20 km) Ask students how much the distance will increase in 100 million years. (2,000 km)
LS Logical

Compression guide:
To shorten instruction because of time limitations, omit the Chapter Lab.

OBJECTIVES	LABS, DEMONSTRATIONS, AND ACTIVITIES	TECHNOLOGY RESOURCES
PACING • 90 min pp. 128–135 **Chapter Opener**	SE **Start-up Activity**, p. 129 ◆ GENERAL	OSP **Parent Letter** ■ GENERAL CD **Student Edition on CD-ROM** CD **Guided Reading Audio CD** ■ TR **Chapter Starter Transparency*** VID **Brain Food Video Quiz**
Section 1 What Are Earthquakes? • Explain where earthquakes take place. • Explain what causes earthquakes. • Identify three different types of faults that occur at plate boundaries. • Describe how energy from earthquakes travels through the Earth.	TE **Demonstration** Faults and Earthquakes, p. 131 ◆ BASIC SE **Quick Lab** Modeling Seismic Waves, p. 134 GENERAL CRF **Datasheet for Quick Lab*** SE **Science in Action** Math, Social Studies, and Language Arts Activities, pp. 152–153 GENERAL	CRF **Lesson Plans*** TR **Bellringer Transparency*** TR **Elastic Rebound*** TR *LINK TO PHYSICAL SCIENCE* Comparing Transverse and Longitudinal Waves* TR **Primary Waves; Secondary Waves; Surface Waves*** CRF **SciLinks Activity*** GENERAL
PACING • 45 min pp. 136–139 **Section 2 Earthquake Measurement** • Explain how earthquakes are detected. • Describe how to locate an earthquake's epicenter. • Explain how the strength of an earthquake is measured. • Explain how the intensity of an earthquake is measured.	TE **Activity** Exploring a Seismic Network, p. 136 GENERAL SE **Skills Practice Lab** Earthquake Waves, p. 187 GENERAL CRF **Datasheet for LabBook*** LB **Long-Term Projects & Research Ideas** A Whole Lotta Shakin'* ADVANCED	CRF **Lesson Plans*** TR **Bellringer Transparency*** TR **Finding an Earthquake's Epicenter*** CD **Science Tutor**
PACING • 90 min pp. 140–145 **Section 3 Earthquakes and Society** • Explain how earthquake-hazard level is determined. • Compare methods of earthquake forecasting. • Describe five ways to safeguard buildings against earthquakes. • Outline earthquake safety procedures.	TE **Connection Activity** Art, p. 140 GENERAL TE **Connection Activity** Math, p. 141 GENERAL TE **Activity** Tools of the Trade, p. 142 ADVANCED TE **Demonstration** Flexible Buildings, p. 143 BASIC TE **Connection Activity** Real Life, p. 143 ◆ GENERAL SE **Connection to Physics** Earthquake Proof Buildings, p. 144 GENERAL SE **School-to-Home Activity** Disaster Planning, p. 145 GENERAL SE **Inquiry Lab** Quake Challenge, p. 146 ◆ GENERAL CRF **Datasheet for Chapter Lab*** LB **Whiz-Bang Demonstrations** When Buildings Boogie* ◆ GENERAL	CRF **Lesson Plans*** TR **Bellringer Transparency*** SE **Internet Activity**, p. 141 GENERAL VID **Lab Videos for Earth Science** CD **Science Tutor**

PACING • 90 min

CHAPTER REVIEW, ASSESSMENT, AND STANDARDIZED TEST PREPARATION

CRF **Vocabulary Activity*** GENERAL
SE **Chapter Review**, pp. 148–149 GENERAL
CRF **Chapter Review*** ■ GENERAL
CRF **Chapter Tests A*** ■ GENERAL, **B*** ADVANCED, **C*** SPECIAL NEEDS
SE **Standardized Test Preparation**, pp. 150–151 GENERAL
CRF **Standardized Test Preparation*** GENERAL
CRF **Performance-Based Assessment*** GENERAL
OSP **Test Generator** GENERAL
CRF **Test Item Listing*** GENERAL

Online and Technology Resources

Visit **go.hrw.com** for a variety of free resources related to this textbook. Enter the keyword **HZ5EQK**.

Holt Online Learning

Students can access interactive problem-solving help and active visual concept development with the *Holt Science and Technology* Online Edition available at **www.hrw.com.**

 Guided Reading Audio CD
Also in Spanish

A direct reading of each chapter for auditory learners, reluctant readers, and Spanish-speaking students.

 Science Tutor
CD-ROM

Excellent for remediation and test practice.

SKILLS DEVELOPMENT RESOURCES	SECTION REVIEW AND ASSESSMENT	CORRELATIONS
SE Pre-Reading Activity, p. 128 GENERAL **OSP** Science Puzzlers, Twisters & Teasers GENERAL		National Science Education Standards SAI 1, 2
CRF Directed Reading A* ■ BASIC, B* SPECIAL NEEDS **CRF** Vocabulary and Section Summary* ■ GENERAL **SE** Reading Strategy Paired Summarizing, p. 130 GENERAL **TE** Inclusion Strategies, p. 134	**SE** Reading Checks, pp. 131, 133, 135 GENERAL **TE** Homework, p. 131 ADVANCED **TE** Homework, p. 132 GENERAL **TE** Reteaching, p. 134 BASIC **TE** Quiz, p. 134 GENERAL **TE** Alternative Assessment, p.134 GENERAL **SE** Section Review,* p. 135 ■ GENERAL **CRF** Section Quiz* ■ GENERAL	UCP 2; SAI 1, 2; SPSP 3, 4; ES 1b
CRF Directed Reading A* ■ BASIC, B* SPECIAL NEEDS **CRF** Vocabulary and Section Summary* ■ GENERAL **SE** Reading Strategy Reading Organizer, p. 136 GENERAL **SE** Connection to Social Studies New Madrid Earthquakes, p. 138 GENERAL **CRF** Reinforcement Worksheet Complete a Seismic Story* BASIC **MS** Math Skills for Science Earthquake Power!* GENERAL **CRF** Critical Thinking Nearthlings Unite!* ADVANCED	**SE** Reading Checks, pp. 136, 138 GENERAL **TE** Reteaching, p. 138 BASIC **TE** Quiz, p. 138 GENERAL **TE** Alternative Assessment, p. 138 GENERAL **SE** Section Review,* p. 139 ■ GENERAL **CRF** Section Quiz* ■ GENERAL	UCP 3; SAI 1, 2; ST 2; ES 1b; *LabBook:* UCP 3; SAI 2; SPSP 3, 4; HNS 1, 3
CRF Directed Reading A* ■ BASIC, B* SPECIAL NEEDS **CRF** Vocabulary and Section Summary* ■ GENERAL **TE** Reading Strategy Discussion, p. 140 GENERAL **TE** Reading Strategy Prediction Guide, p. 141 GENERAL **TE** Inclusion Strategies, p. 144 ◆ **MS** Math Skills for Science Dividing Whole Numbers with Long Division* GENERAL	**SE** Reading Checks, pp. 141, 142, 144 GENERAL **TE** Homework, p. 142 GENERAL **TE** Reteaching, p. 144 BASIC **TE** Quiz, p. 144 GENERAL **TE** Alternative Assessment, p. 144 GENERAL **SE** Section Review,* p. 145 ■ GENERAL **CRF** Section Quiz* ■ GENERAL	UCP 2, 3; SAI 1; ST 2; SPSP 1, 3, 4, 5; ES 1b; *Chapter Lab:* UCP 2, 5; SAI 1; ST 1; SPSP 5

Visual Resources

CHAPTER STARTER TRANSPARENCY

Brace Yourself!

Imagine visiting Kobe, Japan. The date is January 17, 1995. It's early in the morning—5:46 A.M. to be exact—and you're in a taxi on the Hanshin Expressway. The expressway is elevated, supported by a long row of large columns. All of a sudden, the superhighway starts twisting like a giant snake. The truck in front of you disappears as the taxi driver slams on the brakes.

The shaking lasts for less than a minute. For nearly half a kilometer in front of you, the expressway has collapsed. It looks as if something jerked the ground right out from under it, snapping the support column like twigs. You now know why the truck disappeared, and you feel very lucky the taxi stopped in time.

The event you just imagined witnessing was the Great Hanshin earthquake. It killed 5,500 people and left 300,000 others homeless. Nearly 200,000 buildings were destroyed.

While the earthquake tremor lasted less than a minute, terrible disasters continued afterward. Natural gas lines that ruptured started huge fires. Pipes carrying the water that would have been used to put out the fires were broken, so the fires burned for days. Kobe was devastated.

In this chapter, you will learn what causes earthquakes and how earthquakes work. You will also learn how they affect our lives.

BELLRINGER TRANSPARENCIES

Section: What Are Earthquakes?
What do you think an earthquake is? Do you think the way earthquakes are portrayed on television and in movies is accurate? Why or why not?

Write your answer in your **science journal.**

Section: Earthquake Measurement
Create a qualitative scale for gauging earthquake intensity. Describe the effects of very minor earthquakes and extreme earthquakes. What kind of damage would be done to buildings, water and power supplies, animals, and people?

Record your response in your **science journal.**

TEACHING TRANSPARENCIES

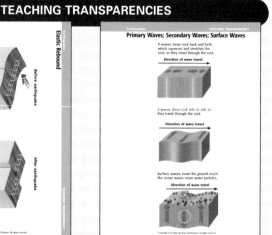

Elastic Rebound

Primary Waves; Secondary Waves; Surface Waves

TEACHING TRANSPARENCIES

Finding an Earthquake's Epicenter

Comparing Longitudinal and Transverse Waves

LINK TO PHYSICAL SCIENCE

Chapter: The Energy of Waves

CONCEPT MAPPING TRANSPARENCY

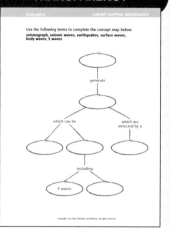

Use the following terms to complete the concept map below:
seismograph, seismic waves, earthquakes, surface waves, body waves, S waves

Planning Resources

LESSON PLANS

Lesson Plan	SAMPLE

Section: Waves

Pacing

Regular Schedule: with lab(s)2 days   without lab(s)2 days
Block Schedule: with lab(s) 1 1/2 days   without lab(s)1 day

Objectives
1. Relate the seven properties of life to a living organism.
2. Describe seven themes that can help you to organize what you learn about biology.
3. Identify the tiny structures that make up all living organisms.
4. Differentiate between reproduction and heredity and between metabolism and homeostasis.

National Science Education Standards Covered
LSInter1:Cells have particular structures that underlie their functions.
LSMat1: Most cell functions involve chemical reactions.
LSBeh1:Cells store and use information to guide their functions.
UCP1:Cell functions are regulated.
SI1: Cells can differentiate and form complete multicellular organisms.
PS1: Species evolve over time.
ESS1: The great diversity of organisms is the result of more than 3.5 billion years of evolution.
ESS2: Natural selection and its evolutionary consequences provide a scientific explanation for the fossil record of ancient life forms as well as for the striking molecular similarities observed among the diverse species of living organisms.
ST1: The millions of different species of plants, animals, and microorganisms that live on Earth today are related by descent from common ancestors.
ST2: The energy for life primarily comes from the sun.
SPSP1: The complexity and organization of organisms accommodates the need for obtaining, transforming, transporting, releasing, and eliminating the matter and energy used to sustain the organism.
SPSP6: As matter and energy flow through different levels of organization of living systems—cells, organs, communities—and between living systems and the physical environment, chemical elements are recombined in different ways.
HNS1: Organisms have behavioral responses to internal changes and to external stimuli.

PARENT LETTER

SAMPLE

Dear Parent,

Your son's or daughter's science class will soon begin exploring the chapter entitled "The World of Physical Science." In this chapter, students will learn about how the scientific method applies to the world of physical science and the role of physical science in the world. By the end of the chapter, students should demonstrate a clear understanding of the chapter's main ideas and be able to discuss the following topics:

1. physical science is the study of energy and matter (Section 1)
2. the role of physical science in the world around them (Section 1)
3. careers that rely on physical science (Section 1)
4. the steps used in the scientific method (Section 2)
5. examples of technology (Section 2)
6. how the scientific method is used to answer questions and solve problems (Section 2)
7. how our knowledge of science changes over time (Section 2)
8. how models represent real objects or systems (Section 3)
9. examples of different ways models are used in science (Section 3)
10. the importance of the International System of Units (Section 4)
11. the appropriate units to use for particular measurements (Section 4)
12. how area and density are derived quantities (Section 4)

Questions to Ask Along the Way

You can help your son or daughter learn about these topics by asking interesting questions such as the following:

• What are some surprising careers that use physical science?
• What is a characteristic of a good hypothesis?
• When is it a good idea to use a model?
• Why do Americans measure things in terms of inches and yards and meters?

ALSO IN SPANISH

TEST ITEM LISTING

TEST ITEM LISTING
The World of Earth Science   SAMPLE

MULTIPLE CHOICE

1. A limitation of models is that
  a. they are large enough to see
  b. they do not act exactly like the things that they model
  c. they are smaller than the things that they model
  d. they model unfamiliar things
  Answer: B   Difficulty: 1   Section: 3   Objective: 2

2. The length 10 m is equal to
  a. 100 cm.   c. 10,000 mm.
  b. 1,000 cm.   d. Both (b) and (c)
  Answer: B   Difficulty: 1   Section: 3   Objective: 2

3. To be valid, a hypothesis must be
  a. testable.   c. made into a law.
  b. supported by evidence.   d. Both (a) and (b)
  Answer: B   Difficulty: 1   Section: 3   Objective: 2

4. The statement "Sheila has a stain on her shirt" is an example of a(n)
  a. law.   c. observation.
  b. hypothesis.   d. prediction.
  Answer: B   Difficulty: 1   Section: 3   Objective: 2

5. A hypothesis is often developed out of
  a. observations.   c. laws.
  b. experiments.   d. Both (a) and (b)
  Answer: B   Difficulty: 1   Section: 3   Objective: 2

6. How many milliliters are in 3.5 kL?
  a. 3,500 mL   c. 3,500,000 mL
  b. 0.0035 mL   d. 35,000 mL
  Answer: B   Difficulty: 1   Section: 3   Objective: 2

7. A gram of textile is an example of a
  a. law.   c. model.
  b. theory.   d. unit.
  Answer: B   Difficulty: 1   Section: 3   Objective: 2

8. A lab has the safety icons shown below. These icons mean that you should wear
  a. only safety goggles   c. safety goggles and a lab apron
  b. only a lab apron   d. safety goggles, a lab apron, and gloves
  Answer: B   Difficulty: 1   Section: 3   Objective: 2

9. The law of conservation of mass says the lot of mass before a chemical change is
  a. more than the total mass after the change.
  b. less than the total mass after the change.
  c. the same as the total mass after the change.
  d. not the same as the total mass after the change.
  Answer: B   Difficulty: 1   Section: 3   Objective: 2

10. In which of the following areas might you find a geochemist at work?
  a. studying the chemistry of rocks   c. studying fishes
  b. studying forests   d. studying the atmosphere
  Answer: B   Difficulty: 1   Section: 3   Objective: 2

One-Stop Planner® CD-ROM

This CD-ROM includes all of the resources shown here and the following time-saving tools:

• *Lab Materials QuickList Software*
• *Customizable lesson plans*
• *Holt Calendar Planner*
• *The powerful ExamView® Test Generator*

Meeting Individual Needs

DIRECTED READING A

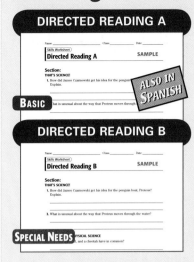

Name _____ Class _____ Date _____

Skills Worksheet
Directed Reading A — SAMPLE

Section:
THAT'S SCIENCE!
1. How did James Czarnowski get his idea for the penguin boat, Proteus? Explain.

BASIC — *ALSO IN SPANISH*

DIRECTED READING B

Name _____ Class _____ Date _____

Skills Worksheet
Directed Reading B — SAMPLE

Section:
THAT'S SCIENCE!
1. How did James Czarnowski get his idea for the penguin boat, Proteus? Explain.

2. What is unusual about the way that Proteus moves through the water?

SPECIAL NEEDS PHYSICAL SCIENCE

VOCABULARY ACTIVITY

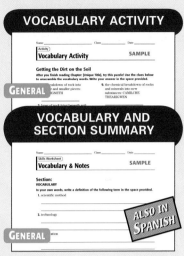

Name _____ Class _____ Date _____

Activity
Vocabulary Activity — SAMPLE

Getting the Dirt on the Soil
After you finish reading Chapter [Unique Title], try this puzzle! Use the clues below to unscramble the vocabulary words. Write your answer in the space provided.

GENERAL

VOCABULARY AND SECTION SUMMARY

Name _____ Class _____ Date _____

Skills Worksheet
Vocabulary & Notes — SAMPLE

Section:
VOCABULARY
In your own words, write a definition of the following term in the space provided.
1. scientific method

2. technology

GENERAL — *ALSO IN SPANISH*

REINFORCEMENT

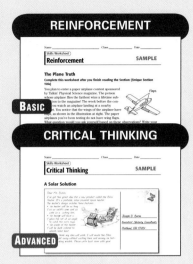

Name _____ Class _____ Date _____

Skills Worksheet
Reinforcement — SAMPLE

The Plane Truth

BASIC

CRITICAL THINKING

Name _____ Class _____ Date _____

Skills Worksheet
Critical Thinking — SAMPLE

A Solar Solution

ADVANCED

SCILINKS ACTIVITY

Name _____ Class _____ Date _____

Activity
SciLinks Activity — SAMPLE

MARINE ECOSYSTEMS
Go to www.scilinks.com. To find links related to marine ecosystems, type in the keyword HL5400. Then, use the links to answer the questions about marine ecosys-

GENERAL

SCIENCE PUZZLERS, TWISTERS & TEASERS

CHAPTER
8 SCIENCE PUZZLERS, TWISTERS & TEASERS
Earthquakes

Wordquake
1. Professor Punjabi's office has just been shaken by a mighty earthquake. Ironically, he had just finished assembling his six favorite words from the chapter on earthquakes. Now his words are broken in to pieces. Can you put them back together? The letters in each cluster cannot be rearranged or broken into pieces.

DIV SE VI ENT HO MOLO IS
HAN U GIST AKE SHIN MO
ERG MO KING

GENERAL

Labs and Activities

LONG-TERM PROJECTS & RESEARCH IDEAS

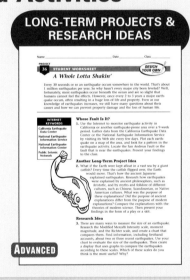

Name _____ Date _____ Class _____

PROJECT
36 STUDENT WORKSHEET — DESIGN YOUR OWN
A Whole Lotta Shakin'

Every 30 seconds or so an earthquake occurs somewhere in the world. That's about 1 million earthquakes per year. So why hasn't every major city been leveled? Well, fortunately, most earthquakes occur beneath the ocean and are so slight than humans cannot feel the effects. However, once every 2 to 3 years a major earthquake occurs, often resulting in a huge loss of life and property. Even as our knowledge of earthquakes increases, we still have many questions about their causes and how we can prevent property damage and the loss of human life.

Whose Fault Is It?
1. Use the Internet to monitor earthquake activity in California or another earthquake-prone area over a 4-week period. Gather data from the California Earthquake Data Center or the National Earthquake Information Service by visiting its Web site every few days. Plot each earthquake on a map of the area, and look for a pattern in the earthquake activity. Locate the San Andreas Fault or the fault that is near the earthquakes. Present your findings to the class.

Another Long-Term Project Idea
2. What if the Earth were kept afloat in a vast sea by a giant catfish? Every time the catfish flipped over, the Earth would move. That's how the ancient Japanese explained earthquakes. Research how earthquakes were explained by ancient philosophers, such as Aristotle, and by myths and folklore of different cultures, such as Chinese, Scandinavian, or Native American cultures. What was the purpose of these explanations? Did the purpose of ancient explanations differ from the purpose of modern explanations? Compare the explanations with the theories of modern science. Then present your findings in the form of a play or a skit.

Research Idea
3. There are many ways to measure the size of an earthquake. Research the Modified Mercalli Intensity scale, moment magnitude, and the Richter scale, and create a chart that compares them. Find information, including firsthand accounts, about two or three recent earthquakes. Use your chart to evaluate the size of the earthquakes. Then create a display that uses graphs to compare the earthquakes according to these scales. Which of these scales do you think is the most useful? Why?

ADVANCED

WHIZ-BANG DEMONSTRATIONS

Name _____ Date _____ Class _____

DEMO
19 TEACHER-LED DEMONSTRATION — MAKING MODELS
When Buildings Boogie

Purpose
Students learn how different structures vibrate at different frequencies and learn why earthquakes affect neighboring buildings differently.

Time Required
10–15 minutes

Lab Ratings
EASY ▲ ▲ ▲ ▲ HARD
TEACHER PREP ▲ ▲
CONCEPT LEVEL ▲ ▲ ▲
CLEAN UP ▲

MATERIALS
• construction paper, about 20 × 50 cm
• metric ruler
• scissors
• masking tape or transparent tape
• piece of cardboard, 30 × 8 cm
• ball bearing or BB
• plastic drinking straw

Advance Preparation
• Cut the construction paper into five strips 3 cm wide. The longest strip should be about 50 cm long, and each successive strip should be about 8 cm shorter than the previous one.
• Create rings by taping the ends of each strip together. Then tape the rings to the cardboard, arranging them in a row from largest to smallest, as shown in the diagram.

• Put the ball bearing or BB in the straw, and close both ends with a small piece of the construction paper. Secure the paper with tape; you want the ball bearing to move freely in the straw and not become stuck to the tape.)
The purpose of the straw is to hear the frequency.
• Attach the straw apparatus to the cardboard base with tape so that the straw is parallel to the rings. Move the cardboard back and forth a few times to be certain that you can hear the ball bearing tapping the ends of the straw. If you cannot, readjust the straw's position.

What to Do
1. Tell students that you are going to simulate an earthquake to see how different objects respond to the vibrations.
2. Begin to shake the cardboard base back and forth. Start very slowly, and continue to increase the frequency with which you move the cardboard back and forth. Explain to students that they can hear the frequency of the movement by listening to the ball bearing.

continued...

GENERAL

DATASHEETS FOR QUICK LABS

TEACHER RESOURCE PAGE

Quick Lab — DATASHEET FOR QUICK LAB
Reaction to Stress — SAMPLE

Background
The graph below illustrates changes that occur in the membrane potential of a neuron during an action potential. Use the graph to answer the following questions. Refer to Figure 3 as needed.

DATASHEETS FOR CHAPTER LABS

TEACHER RESOURCE PAGE

Skills Practice Lab — DATASHEET FOR CHAPTER LAB
Using Scientific Methods — SAMPLE

Teacher's Notes
TIME REQUIRED
One 45-minute class period.

DATASHEETS FOR LABBOOK

TEACHER RESOURCE PAGE

Skills Practice Lab — DATASHEET FOR LABBOOK LAB
Does It All Add Up? — SAMPLE

Teacher's Notes
TIME REQUIRED
One 45-minute class period.

Review and Assessments

SECTION QUIZ

Name _____ Class _____ Date _____

Assessment
Section Quiz — SAMPLE

Section:
In the space provided, write the letter of the description that best matches the term or phrase.
_____ 1. building substances that can be used as an energy source, or breaking down molecules in which energy is stored
_____ 2. the process by which light energy is converted to chemical energy
_____ 3. an organism that uses sunlight or inorganic substances to make organic compounds

a.
b.
c.
d.
e.
f. cellular respiration

GENERAL — *ALSO IN SPANISH*

SECTION REVIEW

Name _____ Class _____ Date _____

Skills Worksheet
Section Review — SAMPLE

Section:
KEY TERMS
1. What do paleontologist study?

2. How does a trace fossil differ from petrified wood?

3. fossil.

GENERAL — *ALSO IN SPANISH*

UNDERSTANDING KEY IDEAS

CHAPTER REVIEW

Name _____ Class _____ Date _____

Skills Worksheet
Chapter Review — SAMPLE

USING VOCABULARY
1. Define biome in your own words.

2. Describe the characteristics of a savanna and a desert.

3. Identify the relationship between tundra and permafrost.

GENERAL — *ALSO IN SPANISH*

CHAPTER TEST A

Name _____ Class _____ Date _____

Assessment
Chapter Test A — SAMPLE

MULTIPLE CHOICE
In the space provided, write the letter of the term or phrase that best completes each statement or best answers each question.
_____ 1. Surface currents are formed by
a. the moon's gravity.   c. wind.
b. the sun's gravity.   d. increased water
_____ 2. When waves come near the shore,
a. they speed up.   c. their wave
b. they maintain their speed. d. their wave b
_____ Longshore currents transport sediment
a. out to the open ocean.   c. only during low
b. along the shore.   d. only during high
_____ Which of the following does NOT control surface currents?

GENERAL — *ALSO IN SPANISH*

CHAPTER TEST B

Name _____ Class _____ Date _____

Assessment
Chapter Test B — SAMPLE

MULTIPLE CHOICE
In the space provided, write the letter of the term or phrase that best completes each statement or best answers each question.
_____ 1. Surface currents are formed by
a. the moon's gravity.   c. wind.
b. the sun's gravity.   d. increased water density.
_____ When waves come near the shore,
a. they speed up.   c. their wavelength increases.
b. they maintain their speed. d. their wave height increases.

ADVANCED

CHAPTER TEST C

Name _____ Class _____ Date _____

Assessment
Chapter Test C — SAMPLE

MULTIPLE CHOICE
In the space provided, write the letter of the term or phrase that best completes each statement or best answers each question.
_____ 1. Surface currents formed by
a. the moon's gravity.   c. wind.
b. the sun's gravity.   d. increased water density.
_____ When waves come near the shore,
a. they speed up.   c. their wavelength increases.
b. they maintain their speed. d. their wave height increases.
_____ currents transport sediment
a. the open ocean.   c. only during low tide.
b. along the shore.   d. only during high tide.
_____ Which of the following does NOT control surface currents?

SPECIAL NEEDS

STANDARDIZED TEST PREPARATION

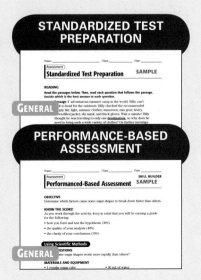

Name _____ Class _____ Date _____

Assessment
Standardized Test Preparation — SAMPLE

READING
Read the passages below. Then, read each question that follows the passage. Decide which is the best answer to each question.

GENERAL

PERFORMANCE-BASED ASSESSMENT

Name _____ Class _____ Date _____

Assessment — SKILL BUILDER
Performanced-Based Assessment — SAMPLE

OBJECTIVE
Determine which factors cause some sugar cubes to break down faster than others.

KNOW THE SCORE!
As you work through the activity, keep in mind that you will be earning a grade for the following:
• how you form and test the hypothesis (30%)
• the quality of your analysis (40%)
• the clarity of your conclusions (30%)

Using Scientific Methods
QUESTIONS

MATERIALS AND EQUIPMENT
• 1 regular sugar cube   • 90 mL of water

GENERAL

This Chapter Enrichment provides relevant and interesting information to expand and enhance your presentation of the chapter material.

Section 1

What Are Earthquakes?

Earthquake Origins

- Earthquakes originate at different depths. Shallow earthquakes are those that originate within about 60 km of Earth's surface. Intermediate-depth earthquakes originate between depths of about 60 km and 300 km. Deep earthquakes originate below 300 km.

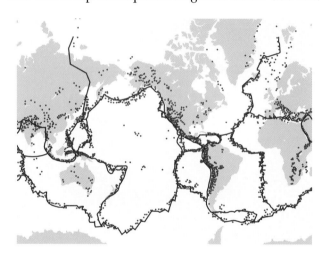

- Tectonic activity is not the only source of earthquakes. Earthquakes can also be caused by volcanic eruptions and by the impacts of cosmic bodies. These earthquakes, however, are less common than those occurring along faults.

The New Madrid Earthquakes

- Eyewitnesses to the 1811–1812 earthquakes in New Madrid, Missouri, reported seeing bright flashes of light and a dull glow in the sky over a wide area. Reeking sulfurous odors also accompanied the quakes. Many survivors were convinced that the quakes were a heavenly sign meant to frighten the local citizens back to church. As a result, church attendance in the area rose between 1811 and 1812!

The Punishment of Loki

- In Scandinavian mythology, earthquakes are believed to be caused by the clever prankster Loki. The gods decided to punish Loki when they discovered that he had killed Balder, the god of light and joy. Loki was chained in a deep cave, and a huge, poisonous snake was hung above him. As the poison from the snake's fangs dripped down, Loki's sister tried to protect him by catching the poison in a cup. Sometimes, however, a drop of poison would splash Loki, causing him unbearable pain. At those times, he would pull so violently on his chains that the ground above would tremble.

Is That a Fact!

- ◆ In 1755, in Lisbon, Portugal, an earthquake occurred that killed an estimated 60,000 people. Because it happened near midday on a religious holiday, many fatalities occurred when churches collapsed on churchgoers. This tragedy resulted in an analytic and systematic approach to studying earthquakes, the basis of seismology.

Section 2

Earthquake Measurement

Chinese Earthquake Measurement

- A Chinese man named Chang Heng designed the first known "earthquake detector" around 132 CE. Heng's earthquake detector was a bronze urn decorated with six dragons' heads. Each head held a bronze ball in its mouth. A pendulum was suspended inside the urn. During a tremor, the pendulum would strike the urn, causing one of the balls to drop into the mouth of a bronze toad below. The ball would make a loud noise, signaling the occurrence of an earthquake. By noting which ball fell, people could supposedly determine the direction of the earthquake's epicenter.

Magnitude Versus Intensity

- Earthquakes can be measured by magnitude or intensity. An earthquake's magnitude is a quantitative measurement of its strength. The Richter scale, and other, more modern scales, are used to measure magnitude. Intensity is a qualitative measurement of an earthquake's effect in a particular area. The Modified Mercalli Intensity Scale is used to assess shaking. This scale incorporates observations of the earthquake's effects at a particular location. Although an earthquake may have different intensities at different locations, it has only one magnitude.

Is That a Fact!

- ◆ The strongest earthquake recorded since the invention of seismographs occurred in Chile in 1960. It measured 9.5 on the Richter scale. This magnitude is equivalent to detonating more than 1 billion tons of TNT!

Section 3

Earthquakes and Society

Magnetometers

- Magnetometers are devices that measure changes in the Earth's magnetic field. Some theories suggest that changes in the Earth's magnetic field might be indicative of an upcoming earthquake, although such theories are controversial.

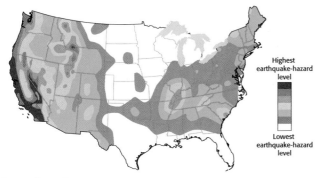

Highest
earthquake-hazard
level

Lowest
earthquake-hazard
level

Aftershocks

- Aftershocks occur in sequences that take place within a particular time frame. They are most numerous after an earthquake and decrease with time. The largest aftershocks often occur within hours of an earthquake. These aftershocks can be the same size or smaller than the earthquake they follow. However, seismologists have found that the number of

aftershocks decreases, but their magnitude does not necessarily decrease. Therefore, large aftershocks can occur months after an earthquake. Aftershocks may also produce their own subsequences, with an aftershock generating other aftershocks.

Survival of Structures

- The ability of a structure to withstand a quake depends on a variety of factors, including the composition of the ground on which the structure stands. Structures built on waterlogged or unconsolidated sediment, such as sand, are more likely to suffer intense damage than structures built on bedrock.

Is That a Fact!

- ◆ Sand boils are common during earthquakes that occur in areas with unconsolidated sediments. Loose, sandy sediments behave as fluids do as the ground moves. This condition can create a miniature "geyser" that spews buried debris from beneath the Earth's surface.

- ◆ One of the best structures for resisting damage from earthquakes is a wood-framed building. Wood-framed buildings are not very rigid and can therefore flex quite a bit without collapsing.

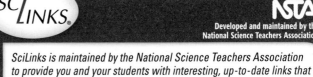

SCi**LINKS**.

NSTA
Developed and maintained by the
National Science Teachers Association

SciLinks is maintained by the National Science Teachers Association to provide you and your students with interesting, up-to-date links that will enrich your classroom presentation of the chapter.

Visit www.scilinks.org and enter the SciLinks code for more information about the topic listed.

Topic: What Is an Earthquake?
SciLinks code: HSM1658

Topic: Earthquakes and Society
SciLinks code: HSM0455

Topic: Earthquake Measurement
SciLinks code: HSM0452

Overview

Tell students that this chapter will help them learn about earthquakes. The chapter is an introduction to the geophysical concepts that seismologists use in the study of earthquakes.

Assessing Prior Knowledge

Students should be familiar with the following topics:

- plate tectonics
- faults

Identifying Misconceptions

Students often assume that earthquakes are relatively rare phenomena. Point out that thousands of small earthquakes happen every day. Also, students may assume that earthquakes occur only near plate boundaries, in areas such as southern California. Point out that earthquakes can happen far from plate boundaries, for example, in places such as Charleston, South Carolina. Finally, students may think that the loss of life that occurs during an earthquake is a direct result of Earth movement. Point out that the majority of deaths are caused by the collapse of buildings and the disease and famine that may result from the disruption of infrastructure.

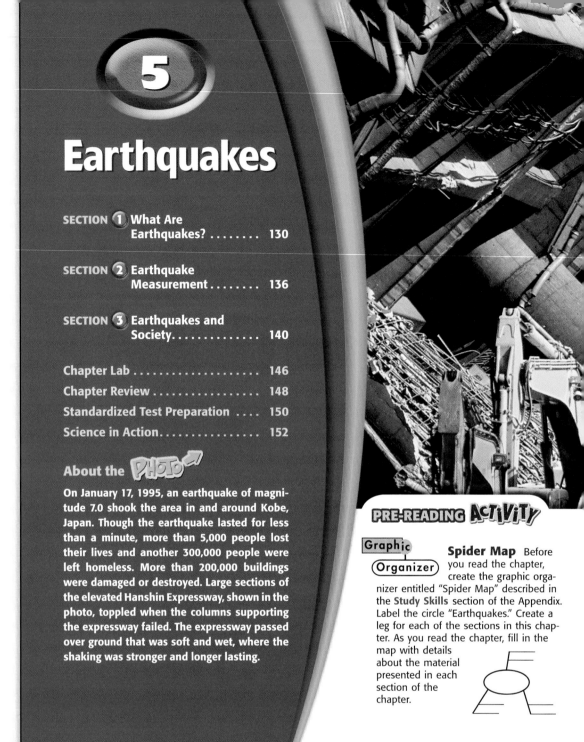

5

Earthquakes

About the PHOTO

On January 17, 1995, an earthquake of magnitude 7.0 shook the area in and around Kobe, Japan. Though the earthquake lasted for less than a minute, more than 5,000 people lost their lives and another 300,000 people were left homeless. More than 200,000 buildings were damaged or destroyed. Large sections of the elevated Hanshin Expressway, shown in the photo, toppled when the columns supporting the expressway failed. The expressway passed over ground that was soft and wet, where the shaking was stronger and longer lasting.

PRE-READING ACTIVITY

Graphic Organizer

Spider Map Before you read the chapter, create the graphic organizer entitled "Spider Map" described in the **Study Skills** section of the Appendix. Label the circle "Earthquakes." Create a leg for each of the sections in this chapter. As you read the chapter, fill in the map with details about the material presented in each section of the chapter.

Standards Correlations

National Science Education Standards

The following codes indicate the National Science Education Standards that correlate to this chapter. The full text of the standards is at the front of the book.

Chapter Opener
SAI 1, 2

Section 1 What Are Earthquakes?
UCP 2; SAI 1, 2; SPSP 3, 4; ES 1b

Section 2 Earthquake Measurement
UCP 3; HNS 1, 3; SPSP 3,4; ST 2; SAI 1, 2; *LabBook*: SAI 1, SAI 2

Section 3 Earthquakes and Society
UCP 2, 3; SAI 1; ST 2; SPSP 1, 3, 4, 5; ES 1b; HNS 2

Chapter Lab
SAI 1, 2

Chapter Review
UCP 2, 3; ES 1b; ST 2; SPSP 1, 3, 4; HNS 2; SAI 1, 2

Science in Action
UCP 2; ES 1b; ST 2; SPSP 3, 5; HNS 1, 2, 3; SAI 1, 2

FOR EACH GROUP
- clothes hanger, plastic
- clothes hanger, wire
- goggles, safety
- paper (1 per student)
- protractor (1 per student)
- stick, wooden, small

Safety Caution: Remind students to review all safety cautions and icons before beginning this lab activity.

Teacher's Note: Assist students who have difficulty using the protractors. You may want to provide them with paper on which the angles have already been drawn.

Answers

1. Answers may vary depending on the materials used and on the strength of the materials. The wooden stick would most likely break at greater angles, the wire hanger would bend, and the plastic hanger would bend but return to its original shape.

2. Answers may vary. Desirable building materials would behave in the same way as the materials that did not break or bend permanently.

START-UP ACTIVITY

Bend, Break, or Shake

In this activity, you will test different materials in a model earthquake setting.

Procedure

1. Gather a **small wooden stick,** a **wire clothes hanger,** and a **plastic clothes hanger.**

2. Draw a straight line on a **sheet of paper.** Use a **protractor** to measure and draw the following angles from the line: 20°, 45°, and 90°.

3. Put on your **safety goggles.** Using the angles that you drew as a guide, try bending each item 20° and then releasing it. What happens? Does it break? If it bends, does it return to its original shape?

4. Repeat step 3, but bend each item 45°. Repeat the test again, but bend each item 90°.

Analysis

1. How do the different materials' responses to bending compare?

2. Where earthquakes happen, engineers use building materials that are flexible but that do not break or stay bent. Which materials from this experiment would you want building materials to behave like? Explain your answer.

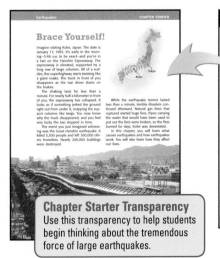

Chapter Starter Transparency
Use this transparency to help students begin thinking about the tremendous force of large earthquakes.

CHAPTER RESOURCES

Technology

 Transparencies
- Chapter Starter Transparency

READING SKILLS

 Student Edition on CD-ROM

Guided Reading Audio CD
- English or Spanish

Classroom Videos
- Brain Food Video Quiz

Workbooks

Science Puzzlers, Twisters & Teasers
- Earthquakes **GENERAL**

Focus

Overview

This section discusses the seismic events known as earthquakes. Students learn where earthquakes most commonly occur and what causes them. The section also covers different kinds of faults and discusses how earthquakes travel as waves of energy through the Earth.

Bellringer

Ask students to write a few sentences describing what they think an earthquake is. Ask students to review what they wrote after completing this section.

Motivate

Discussion ——— GENERAL

Seismic Definitions Explain to students that *seismos* is a Greek word that means "to shake." Have students make a list of all the words that contain the root *seis-*. (These include *seismology, seismologist, seismic, seismograph, Seismosaurus,* and *seismogram.*) Have students copy the words onto a sheet of paper and consult a dictionary to divide each word into its proper parts. Then, have students define each word part and write a definition of each complete term using the meanings of its parts. **LS Logical**   English Language Learners

READING WARM-UP

Objectives

- Explain where earthquakes take place.
- Explain what causes earthquakes.
- Identify three different types of faults that occur at plate boundaries.
- Describe how energy from earthquakes travels through the Earth.

Terms to Learn

seismology   P waves
deformation   S waves
elastic rebound
seismic waves

READING STRATEGY

Paired Summarizing Read this section silently. In pairs, take turns summarizing the material. Stop to discuss ideas that seem confusing.

What Are Earthquakes?

Have you ever felt the earth move under your feet? Many people have. Every day, somewhere within this planet, an earthquake is happening.

The word *earthquake* defines itself fairly well. But there is more to earthquakes than just the shaking of the ground. An entire branch of Earth science, called **seismology** (siez MAHL uh jee), is devoted to studying earthquakes. Earthquakes are complex, and they present many questions for *seismologists,* the scientists who study earthquakes.

Where Do Earthquakes Occur?

Most earthquakes take place near the edges of tectonic plates. *Tectonic plates* are giant pieces of Earth's thin, outermost layer. Tectonic plates move around on top of a layer of plastic rock. **Figure 1** shows the Earth's tectonic plates and the locations of recent major earthquakes.

Tectonic plates move in different directions and at different speeds. Two plates can push toward or pull away from each other. They can also slip slowly past each other. As a result of these movements, numerous features called faults exist in the Earth's crust. A *fault* is a break in the Earth's crust along which blocks of the crust slide relative to one another. Earthquakes occur along faults because of this sliding.

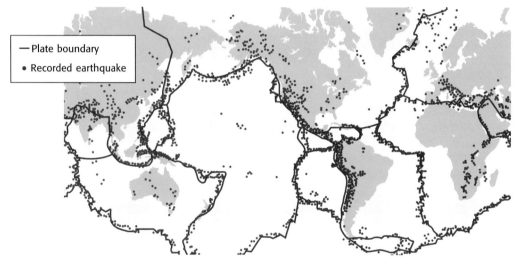

— Plate boundary
• Recorded earthquake

Figure 1 *The largest and most active earthquake zone lies along the plate boundaries surrounding the Pacific Ocean.*

CHAPTER RESOURCES

Chapter Resource File

- Lesson Plan
- Directed Reading A **BASIC**
- Directed Reading B **SPECIAL NEEDS**

Technology

- Transparencies
  - Bellringer
  - Elastic Rebound

MISCONCEPTION //// ALERT \\\\

Earthquake Frequency Earthquakes are not a rare phenomenon. In fact, more than 3 million earthquakes with Richter magnitudes of 1 or more happen each year—about one every 10 seconds! Most earthquakes are too weak to be felt by humans. The Ring of Fire, a volcanic zone that lies along the plate boundaries surrounding the Pacific Ocean, is the world's largest and most active earthquake zone.

What Causes Earthquakes?

As tectonic plates push, pull, or slip past each other, stress increases along faults near the plates' edges. In response to this stress, rock in the plates deforms. **Deformation** is the change in the shape of rock in response to stress. Rock along a fault deforms in mainly two ways. It deforms in a plastic manner, like a piece of molded clay, or in an elastic manner, like a rubber band. *Plastic deformation,* which is shown in **Figure 2,** does not lead to earthquakes.

Elastic deformation, however, does lead to earthquakes. Rock can stretch farther without breaking than steel can, but rock will break at some point. Think of elastically deformed rock as a stretched rubber band. You can stretch a rubber band only so far before it breaks. When the rubber band breaks, it releases energy. Then, the broken pieces return to their unstretched shape.

Elastic Rebound

The sudden return of elastically deformed rock to its original shape is called **elastic rebound.** Elastic rebound is like the return of the broken rubber-band pieces to their unstretched shape. Elastic rebound occurs when more stress is applied to rock than the rock can withstand. During elastic rebound, energy is released. Some of this energy travels as seismic waves. These seismic waves cause an earthquake, as shown in **Figure 3.**

✓ **Reading Check** How does elastic rebound relate to earthquakes? (*See the Appendix for answers to Reading Checks.*)

Figure 2 *This road cut is adjacent to the San Andreas Fault in southern California. The rocks in the cut have undergone deformation because of the continuous motion of the fault.*

seismology the study of earthquakes

deformation the bending, tilting, and breaking of the Earth's crust; the change in the shape of rock in response to stress

elastic rebound the sudden return of elastically deformed rock to its undeformed shape

Figure 3   Elastic Rebound and Earthquakes

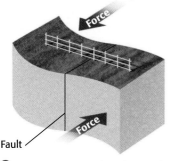

Before earthquake

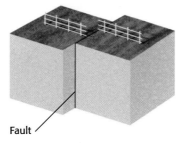

After earthquake

Fault

Fault

❶ Tectonic forces push rock on either side of the fault in opposite directions, but the rock is locked together and does not move. The rock deforms in an elastic manner.

❷ When enough stress is applied, the rock slips along the fault and releases energy.

Answer to Reading Check

During elastic rebound, rock releases energy. Some of this energy travels as seismic waves that cause earthquakes.

Using the Figure – GENERAL

Faults and Tectonics Each circle in the figure is a magnified view of a fault at the edge of a tectonic plate. In fact, large systems of multiple faults define the boundaries between plates. The sliding of crust along these faults and the overall movement of crust along plate boundaries are similar. For example, the block of crust to the right of the reverse fault moves down relative to the block to the left of the fault. Similarly, the plate to the right of the convergent plate boundary moves down relative to the plate to the left of the boundary. **LS** Visual/Logical

Homework ——— GENERAL

Illustrating Faults
Ask students to draw the three types of faults illustrated on these pages. Students should label each fault and state the type of plate motion that creates each fault. Encourage students to locate an example of each type of tectonic plate boundary on a map. (An example of a transform plate boundary is the San Andreas Fault in California; an example of a convergent plate boundary is off the west coast of South America; an example of a divergent plate boundary is the Mid-Atlantic Ridge, on the bottom of the Atlantic Ocean.) **LS** Visual   English Language Learners

Faults at Tectonic Plate Boundaries

A specific type of plate motion takes place at different tectonic plate boundaries. Each type of motion creates a particular kind of fault that can produce earthquakes. Examine **Table 1** and the diagram below to learn more about plate motion.

Table 1 **Plate Motion and Fault Types**

Plate motion	Major fault type
Transform	strike-slip fault
Convergent	reverse fault
Divergent	normal fault

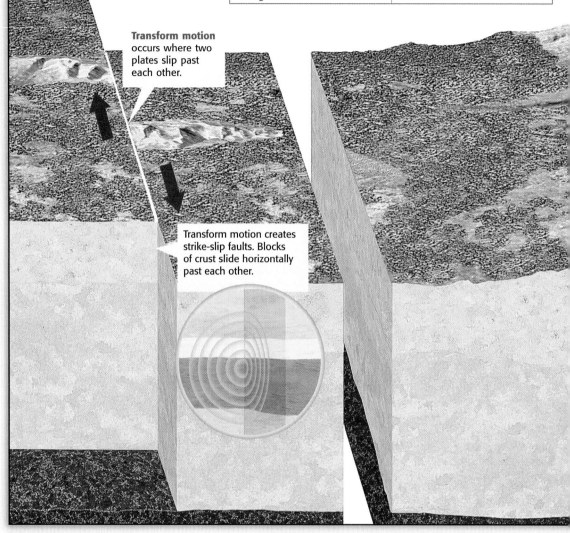

Transform motion occurs where two plates slip past each other.

Transform motion creates strike-slip faults. Blocks of crust slide horizontally past each other.

MISCONCEPTION ALERT

Aftershocks A general misconception is that aftershocks do not present the same level of danger as the earthquake, or mainshock, that they follow. Seismological evidence has proven that the opposite can be true. Aftershocks can be powerful earthquakes. An aftershock of magnitude 6.5 followed 3 hours after the 1992 magnitude 7.3 Landers earthquake! Aftershocks can be as damaging as, or even more damaging than, a mainshock. The reasons are that building damage is cumulative and aftershocks vary in location and in the pattern of radiation from the mainshock.

Earthquake Zones

Earthquakes can happen both near Earth's surface or far below it. Most earthquakes happen in the earthquake zones along tectonic plate boundaries. Earthquake zones are places where a large number of faults are located. The San Andreas Fault Zone in California is an example of an earthquake zone. But not all faults are located at tectonic plate boundaries. Sometimes, earthquakes happen along faults in the middle of tectonic plates.

✓ **Reading Check** Where are earthquake zones located?

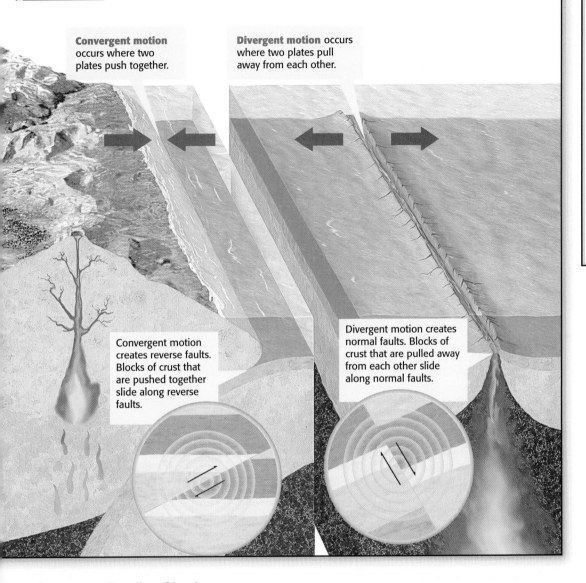

Convergent motion occurs where two plates push together.

Divergent motion occurs where two plates pull away from each other.

Convergent motion creates reverse faults. Blocks of crust that are pushed together slide along reverse faults.

Divergent motion creates normal faults. Blocks of crust that are pulled away from each other slide along normal faults.

Answer to Reading Check

Earthquake zones are usually located along tectonic plate boundaries.

Answers to Quick Lab

4. P waves are represented in step 2; S waves are represented in step 3.

Reteaching ———— BASIC

P and S Waves Tell students that the *P* in P waves and the *S* in S waves each stand for two descriptive words. The letters describe how each type of wave affects rock—P stands for *pressure,* and S stands for *shear.* P also stands for *primary,* and S stands for *secondary.* This scheme describes the arrival times of each type of wave— P waves always arrive first, and S waves always arrive second. **LS Logical**

Quiz ———— GENERAL

1. What is a fault? (A fault is a break in the Earth's crust along which blocks of the crust slide relative to one another.)

2. How does rock that is along a fault deform in response to a decrease in stress? (Rock deforms in an elastic manner, as a rubber band does, by snapping back to its original shape.)

Alternative Assessment ———— GENERAL

Concept Mapping Have students create a concept map explaining the relationship between tectonic plate motion and fault types. **LS Visual**

Modeling Seismic Waves

1. Stretch a **spring toy** lengthwise on a **table.**

2. Hold one end of the spring while a partner holds the other end. Push your end toward your partner's end, and observe what happens.

3. Repeat step 2, but this time shake the spring from side to side.

4. Which type of seismic wave is represented in step 2? in step 3?

seismic wave a wave of energy that travels through the Earth, away from an earthquake in all directions

P wave a seismic wave that causes particles of rock to move in a back-and-forth direction

S wave a seismic wave that causes particles of rock to move in a side-to-side direction

How Do Earthquake Waves Travel?

Waves of energy that travel through the Earth are called **seismic waves.** Seismic waves that travel through the Earth's interior are called *body waves.* There are two types of body waves: P waves and S waves. Seismic waves that travel along the Earth's surface are called *surface waves.* Each type of seismic wave travels through Earth's layers in a different way and at a different speed. Also, the speed of a seismic wave depends on the kind of material the wave travels through.

P Waves

Waves that travel through solids, liquids, and gases are called **P waves** (pressure waves). They are the fastest seismic waves, so P waves always travel ahead of other seismic waves. P waves are also called *primary waves,* because they are always the first waves of an earthquake to be detected. To understand how P waves affect rock, imagine a cube of gelatin sitting on a plate. Like most solids, gelatin is an elastic material. It wiggles if you tap it. Tapping the cube of gelatin changes the pressure inside the cube, which momentarily deforms the cube. The gelatin then reacts by springing back to its original shape. This process is how P waves affect rock, as shown in **Figure 4.**

S Waves

Rock can also be deformed from side to side. After being deformed from side to side, the rock springs back to its original position and S waves are created. **S waves,** or shear waves, are the second-fastest seismic waves. S waves shear rock side to side, as shown in **Figure 4,** which means they stretch the rock sideways. Unlike P waves, S waves cannot travel through parts of the Earth that are completely liquid. Also, S waves are slower than P waves and always arrive later. Thus, another name for S waves is *secondary waves.*

Figure 4 **Body Waves**

P waves move rock back and forth, which squeezes and stretches the rock, as they travel through the rock.

Direction of wave travel

S waves shear rock side to side as they travel through the rock.

Direction of wave travel

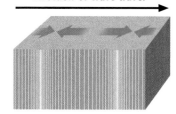

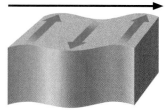

Surface Waves

Surface waves move along the Earth's surface and produce motion mostly in the upper few kilometers of Earth's crust. There are two types of surface waves. One type of surface wave produces motion up, down, and around, as shown in **Figure 5**. The other type produces back-and-forth motion like the motion produced by S waves. Surface waves are different from body waves in that surface waves travel more slowly and are more destructive.

Reading Check Explain the differences between surface waves and body waves.

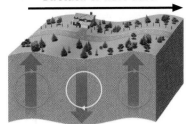

Figure 5 **Surface Waves**

Surface waves move the ground much like ocean waves move water particles.

Direction of wave travel

SECTION Review

Summary

- Earthquakes occur mainly near the edges of tectonic plates.

- Elastic rebound is the direct cause of earthquakes.

- Three major types of faults occur at tectonic plate boundaries: normal faults, reverse faults, and strike-slip faults.

- Earthquake energy travels as body waves through the Earth's interior or as surface waves along the surface of the Earth.

Using Key Terms

Complete each of the following sentences by choosing the correct term from the word bank.

Deformation	P waves
Elastic rebound	S waves

1. _____ is the change in shape of rock due to stress.

2. _____ always travel ahead of other waves.

Understanding Key Ideas

3. Seismic waves that shear rock side to side are called
   a. surface waves.
   b. S waves.
   c. P waves.
   d. Both (b) and (c)

4. Where do earthquakes occur?

5. What is the direct cause of earthquakes?

6. Describe the three types of plate motion and the faults that are characteristic of each type of motion.

7. What is an earthquake zone?

Math Skills

8. A seismic wave is traveling through the Earth at an average rate of speed of 8 km/s. How long will it take the wave to travel 480 km?

Critical Thinking

9. **Applying Concepts** Given what you know about elastic rebound, why do you think some earthquakes are stronger than others?

10. **Identifying Relationships** Why are surface waves more destructive to buildings than P waves or S waves are?

11. **Identifying Relationships** Why do you think the majority of earthquake zones are located at tectonic plate boundaries?

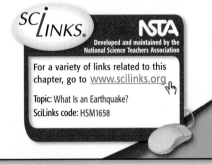

SCiLINKS **NSTA**
Developed and maintained by the National Science Teachers Association

For a variety of links related to this chapter, go to www.scilinks.org

Topic: What Is an Earthquake?
SciLinks code: HSM1658

CONNECTION to
Physical Science—ADVANCED

Seismic Waves Use the teaching transparency "Comparing Transverse and Longitudinal Waves" to discuss the differences between P waves (longitudinal) and S waves (transverse). P waves travel faster than S waves. P waves travel through solids, liquids, and gases; S waves cannot travel through materials that are completely liquid. P waves move rock back and forth between a squeezed and stretched position, and S waves shear rock back and forth.

Focus

Overview

In this section, students learn how seismographs are used to detect and locate earthquakes. This section explains the difference between an earthquake's focus and epicenter. Students will also learn how the Richter scale is used to measure the magnitude of earthquakes.

 Bellringer

Ask students to create a qualitative scale for gauging earthquake intensity. Students should use brief phrases to describe the effects of very minor to extreme earthquakes. Discuss the advantages and disadvantages of their finished scale.

Motivate

ACTIVITY ——————— GENERAL

Exploring a Seismic Network

Have students locate a map on the Internet that shows worldwide seismic stations. Students should select an earthquake of magnitude 5.5 or greater that has been recorded at one of these stations during the past month. Have students find press releases that relate to the earthquake they have selected and then write a short report on the quake. **LS Visual/Logical**

READING WARM-UP

Objectives
- Explain how earthquakes are detected.
- Describe how to locate an earthquake's epicenter.
- Explain how the strength of an earthquake is measured.
- Explain how the intensity of an earthquake is measured.

Terms to Learn

seismograph epicenter
seismogram focus

READING STRATEGY

Reading Organizer As you read this section, create an outline of the section. Use the headings from the section in your outline.

seismograph an instrument that records vibrations in the ground and determines the location and strength of an earthquake

seismogram a tracing of earthquake motion that is created by a seismograph

epicenter the point on Earth's surface directly above an earthquake's starting point, or focus

focus the point along a fault at which the first motion of an earthquake occurs

---

Earthquake Measurement

Imagine walls shaking, windows rattling, and glassware and dishes clinking and clanking. After only seconds, the vibrating stops and the sounds die away.

Within minutes, news reports give information about the strength, the time, and the location of the earthquake. You are amazed at how scientists could have learned this information so quickly.

Locating Earthquakes

How do seismologists know when and where earthquakes begin? They depend on earthquake-sensing instruments called seismographs. **Seismographs** are instruments located at or near the surface of the Earth that record seismic waves. When the waves reach a seismograph, the seismograph creates a seismogram. A **seismogram** is a tracing of earthquake motion and is created by a seismograph.

Determining Time and Location of Earthquakes

Seismologists use seismograms to calculate when an earthquake began. Seismologists find an earthquake's start time by comparing seismograms and noting the differences in arrival times of P waves and S waves. Seismologists also use seismograms to find an earthquake's epicenter. An **epicenter** is the point on the Earth's surface directly above an earthquake's starting point. A **focus** is the point inside the Earth where an earthquake begins. **Figure 1** shows the location of an earthquake's epicenter and its focus.

Reading Check How do seismologists determine an earthquake's start time? (*See the Appendix for answers to Reading Checks.*)

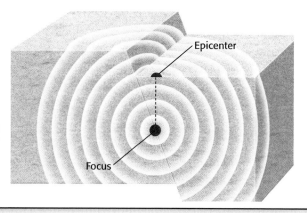

Figure 1 *An earthquake's epicenter is on the Earth's surface directly above the earthquake's focus.*

Epicenter

Focus

CHAPTER RESOURCES

Chapter Resource File

- Lesson Plan
- Directed Reading A **BASIC**
- Directed Reading B **SPECIAL NEEDS**

Technology

Transparencies
- Bellringer
- Finding an Earthquake's Epicenter

Answer to Reading Check

Seismologists determine an earthquake's start time by comparing seismograms and noting differences in arrival times of P waves and S waves.

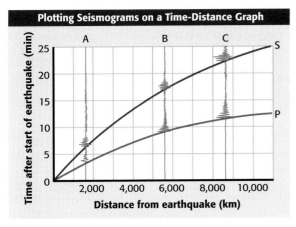

Plotting Seismograms on a Time-Distance Graph

Figure 2 After identifying P and S waves, seismologists can use the time difference to determine an earthquake's start time and the distance from the epicenter to each station. The vertical axis tells how much time passed between the start of the earthquake and the arrival of seismic waves at a station. The horizontal axis tells the distance between a station and the earthquake's epicenter.

The S-P Time Method

Perhaps the simplest method by which seismologists find an earthquake's epicenter is the *S-P time method*. The first step in this method is to collect several seismograms of the same earthquake from different locations. Then, the seismograms are placed on a time-distance graph. The seismogram tracing of the first P wave is lined up with the P-wave time-distance curve, and the tracing of the first S wave is lined up with the S-wave curve, as shown in **Figure 2**. The distance of each station from the earthquake can be found by reading the horizontal axis. After finding out the distances, a seismologist can locate an earthquake's epicenter, as shown in **Figure 3**.

Figure 3 **Finding an Earthquake's Epicenter**

❶ A circle is drawn around a seismograph station. The radius of the circle equals the distance from the seismograph to the epicenter. (This distance is taken from the time-distance graph.)

❷ When a second circle is drawn around another seismograph station, the circle overlaps the first circle in two spots. One of these spots is the earthquake's epicenter.

❸ When a circle is drawn around a third seismograph station, all three circles intersect in one spot—the earthquake's epicenter. In this case, the epicenter was in San Francisco.

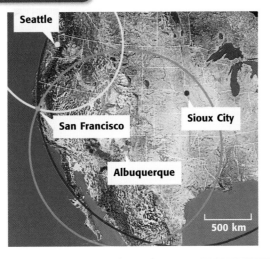

CONNECTION to
History — GENERAL

The Richter Magnitude Scale   In the 1920s, when Charles Richter was a graduate student, he was working on a catalog of earthquakes in southern California. He wanted to find an objective way to compare earthquakes. Up to that point, geologists used the Mercalli scale to classify earthquakes. The Mercalli scale was based on the observations of people who witnessed an earthquake and on the damage it caused. Richter wanted to devise a more quantitative measure of earthquake strength. This desire led him to develop what is now called the Richter scale in 1935, which is based on measurements of ground motion.

Reteaching — BASIC

Defining Terms Have students help you come up with definitions for the following terms: *seismograph, seismogram, epicenter, focus, S-P time method, Richter magnitude scale,* and *Modified Mercalli Intensity Scale.*

LS Logical   English Language Learners

Quiz — GENERAL

1. How is an earthquake's epicenter related to its focus? (The epicenter is the point on the Earth's surface directly above the focus, which is where the earthquake originates.)

2. As seismic waves travel farther, what happens to the difference in arrival times of P waves and S waves? (It increases.)

Alternative Assessment — GENERAL

Recent Earthquakes

PORTFOLIO Have students identify 10 recent earthquakes with a magnitude greater than 5.0 on the Richter scale. Students can compile their findings in a table that includes the epicenter and the magnitude of the quake, the damage it caused, and any other interesting information about the quake. Challenge students to find trends in the data.

LS Logical

During the winter of 1811–1812, three of the most powerful earthquakes in U.S. history were centered near New Madrid, Missouri, thousands of miles from the nearest tectonic plate boundary. Research the New Madrid earthquakes, and summarize your findings in a one-page essay.

Measuring Earthquake Strength and Intensity

"How strong was the earthquake?" is a common question asked of seismologists. This question is not easy to answer. But it is an important question for anyone living near an earthquake zone. Fortunately, seismograms can be used not only to determine an earthquake's epicenter and its start time but also to find out an earthquake's strength.

The Richter Magnitude Scale

Throughout much of the 20th century, seismologists used the *Richter magnitude scale*, commonly called the Richter scale, to measure the strength of earthquakes. Seismologist Charles Richter created the scale in the 1930s. Richter wanted to compare earthquakes by measuring ground motion recorded by seismograms at seismograph stations.

Earthquake Ground Motion

A measure of the strength of an earthquake is called *magnitude*. The Richter scale measures the ground motion from an earthquake and adjusts for distance to find its strength. Each time the magnitude increases by one unit, the measured ground motion becomes 10 times larger. For example, an earthquake with a magnitude of 5.0 on the Richter scale will produce 10 times as much ground motion as an earthquake with a magnitude of 4.0. Furthermore, an earthquake with a magnitude of 6.0 will produce 100 times as much ground motion (10 × 10) as an earthquake with a magnitude of 4.0. **Table 1** shows the differences in the estimated effects of earthquakes with each increase of one unit of magnitude.

✓ **Reading Check** How are magnitude and ground motion related in the Richter scale?

Table 1 Effects of Different-Sized Earthquakes	
Magnitude	**Estimated effects**
2.0	can be detected only by seismograph
3.0	can be felt at epicenter
4.0	can be felt by most people in the area
5.0	causes damage at epicenter
6.0	can cause widespread damage
7.0	can cause great, widespread damage

Answer to Reading Check

Each time the magnitude increases by 1 unit, the amount of ground motion increases by 10 times.

Answer to Social Studies Activity

Have students present their one-page summary to the class. Encourage students to use visual aids, such as maps of the earthquake area, in their presentations. A variety of books have been written on the New Madrid earthquakes, and accounts are also available on the Internet.

Modified Mercalli Intensity Scale

A measure of the degree to which an earthquake is felt by people and the amount of damage caused by the earthquake, if any, is called *intensity*. Currently, seismologists in the United States use the Modified Mercalli Intensity Scale to measure earthquake intensity. This scale is a numerical scale that uses Roman numerals from I to XII to describe increasing earthquake intensity levels. An intensity level of I describes an earthquake that is not felt by most people. An intensity level of XII indicates total damage of an area. **Figure 4** shows the type of damage caused by an earthquake that has a Modified Mercalli intensity level of XI.

Because the effects of an earthquake vary from place to place, any earthquake will have more than one intensity value. Intensity values are usually higher near an earthquake's epicenter.

Figure 4 *Intensity values for the 1906 San Francisco earthquake varied from place to place. The maximum intensity level was XI.*

SECTION Review

Summary

- Seismologists detect seismic waves and record them as seismograms.
- The S-P time method is the simplest method to use to find an earthquake's epicenter.
- Seismologists use the Richter scale to measure an earthquake's strength.
- Seismologists use the Modified Mercalli Intensity Scale to measure an earthquake's intensity.

Using Key Terms

1. In your own words, write a definition for each of the following terms: *epicenter* and *focus*.

Understanding Key Ideas

2. What is the difference between a seismograph and a seismogram?

3. Explain how earthquakes are detected.

4. Briefly explain the steps of the S-P time method for locating an earthquake's epicenter.

5. Why might an earthquake have more than one intensity value?

Math Skills

6. How much more ground motion is produced by an earthquake of magnitude 7.0 than by an earthquake of magnitude 4.0?

Critical Thinking

7. **Making Inferences** Why is a 6.0 magnitude earthquake so much more destructive than a 5.0 magnitude earthquake?

8. **Identifying Bias** Which do you think is the more important measure of earthquakes, strength or intensity? Explain.

9. **Making Inferences** Do you think an earthquake of moderate magnitude can produce high Modified Mercalli intensity values?

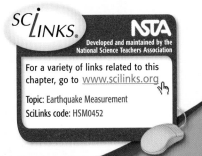

SCILINKS

Developed and maintained by the National Science Teachers Association

For a variety of links related to this chapter, go to www.scilinks.org

Topic: Earthquake Measurement
SciLinks code: HSM0452

Answers to Section Review

1. Sample answer: An epicenter is the point on Earth's surface above the focus. A focus is the point along a fault where an earthquake starts.

2. A seismograph is the instrument used to record seismic waves. A seismogram is the tracing of earthquake motion created by a seismograph.

3. Earthquakes are detected by seismographs located at or near the Earth's surface.

4. Seismologists collect seismograms of an earthquake from at least three seismograph stations and place them on a time-distance graph. The distance of each station from the epicenter can then be found. These distances are used to draw circles around seismograph stations. The radius of each circle is the distance of the seismograph from the earthquake's epicenter. The point of intersection of these circles is the earthquake's epicenter.

5. Because the effects of an earthquake can vary from place to place, an earthquake can have more than one intensity value. Higher intensity values are more likely to be seen near the epicenter of an earthquake.

6. An earthquake of magnitude 7.0 will produce 1,000 times (10 × 10 × 10) more ground motion than an earthquake of magnitude 4.0.

7. An earthquake of magnitude 6.0 is much more destructive than an earthquake of 5.0 because an earthquake of magnitude 6.0 produces 10 times more ground motion.

8. Answers may vary. Sample answer: Intensity is a more important measure of earthquakes because the damage caused by an earthquake is something people can see.

9. Sample answer: A moderate earthquake might produce high intensity values near the epicenter of the earthquake.

Focus

Overview

In this section, students learn how earthquake hazard is determined. The section explores the methods seismologists use to make forecasts about earthquakes. Students learn about the technologies used to reinforce buildings against earthquakes. The section concludes with a discussion of earthquake safety procedures.

Bellringer

If any of your students have experienced an earthquake, have them write a short paragraph describing how they felt and what they did to protect themselves during the earthquake. Have students who have not experienced an earthquake write a paragraph describing what they think they would do during a moderate earthquake.

Motivate

Discussion ——— GENERAL

Hazard Levels Have students examine **Figure 1.** Challenge them to explain why the West Coast has such high levels of earthquake hazard. If they need a hint, have them look again at **Figure 1** in Section 1. (There is a tectonic plate boundary along the western coast of the United States.) **LS Logical/Visual**

Earthquakes and Society

Imagine that you are in class and the ground begins to shake beneath your feet. What do you do?

Seismologists are not able to predict the exact time when and place where an earthquake will occur. They can, at best, make forecasts based on the frequency with which earthquakes take place. Therefore, seismologists are always looking for better ways to forecast when and where earthquakes will happen. In the meantime, it is important for people in earthquake zones to be prepared before an earthquake strikes.

Earthquake Hazard

Earthquake hazard is a measurement of how likely an area is to have damaging earthquakes in the future. An area's earthquake-hazard level is determined by past and present seismic activity. The map in **Figure 1** shows that some areas of the United States have a higher earthquake-hazard level than others do. This variation is caused by differences in seismic activity. The greater the seismic activity, the higher the earthquake-hazard level. The West Coast, for example, has a very high earthquake-hazard level because it has a lot of seismic activity.

Look at the map. What earthquake-hazard level or levels are shown in the area in which you live? How do the hazard levels of nearby areas compare with your area's hazard level?

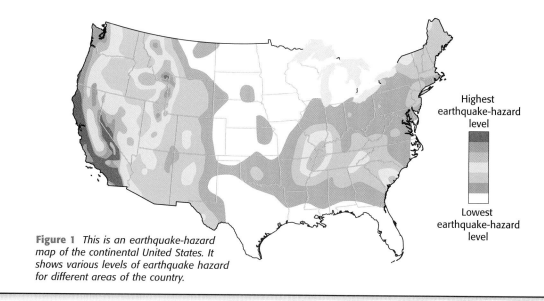

Highest earthquake-hazard level

Lowest earthquake-hazard level

Figure 1 *This is an earthquake-hazard map of the continental United States. It shows various levels of earthquake hazard for different areas of the country.*

CONNECTION ACTIVITY
Art ——————— GENERAL

The Protection of Art Treasures Have students find out what has been done to protect sculptures from earthquake damage at the J. Paul Getty Museum in Pacific Palisades, California, or at another museum in an earthquake-prone area. **LS Logical**

Table 1 Worldwide Earthquake Frequency
(Based on Observations Since 1900)

Descriptor	Magnitude	Average number annually
Great	8.0 and higher	1
Major	7.0–7.9	18
Strong	6.0–6.9	120
Moderate	5.0–5.9	800
Light	4.0–4.9	about 6,200
Minor	3.0–3.9	about 49,000
Very minor	2.0–2.9	about 365,000

Earthquake Forecasting

Forecasting when and where earthquakes will occur and their strength is difficult. By looking carefully at areas of seismic activity, seismologists have discovered some patterns in earthquakes that allow them to make some general predictions.

Strength and Frequency

Earthquakes vary in strength. And you can probably guess that earthquakes don't occur on a set schedule. But what you may not know is that the strength of earthquakes is related to how often they occur. **Table 1** provides more detail about this relationship worldwide.

The relationship between earthquake strength and frequency is also at work on a local scale. For example, each year approximately 1.6 earthquakes with a magnitude of 4.0 on the Richter scale occur in the Puget Sound area of Washington State. Over this same time period, approximately 10 times as many earthquakes with a magnitude of 3.0 occur in this area. Scientists use these statistics to make forecasts about the strength, location, and frequency of future earthquakes.

✔ Reading Check What is the relationship between the strength of earthquakes and earthquake frequency? (*See the Appendix for answers to Reading Checks.*)

The Gap Hypothesis

Another method of forecasting an earthquake's strength, location, and frequency is based on the gap hypothesis. The **gap hypothesis** is a hypothesis that states that sections of active faults that have had relatively few earthquakes are likely to be the sites of strong earthquakes in the future. The areas along a fault where relatively few earthquakes have occurred are called **seismic gaps.**

INTERNET ACTIVITY

For another activity related to this chapter, go to **go.hrw.com** and type in the keyword **HZ5EQKW.**

gap hypothesis a hypothesis that is based on the idea that a major earthquake is more likely to occur along the part of an active fault where no earthquakes have occurred for a certain period of time

seismic gap an area along a fault where relatively few earthquakes have occurred recently but where strong earthquakes have occurred in the past

Is That a Fact!

On March 27, 1964, an earthquake with a magnitude of 9.2 occurred in southern Alaska. The earthquake, which is the strongest recorded earthquake in North America, lasted for about 4 minutes. The port on Montague Island was raised 10 m, which stranded ships that had been docked in the port. After the earthquake, a devastating tsunami swept along the Pacific Northwest coastline.

Tools of the Trade Have interested students research the various types of instruments used to detect seismic activity, including tiltmeters, gravimeters, strainmeters, magnetometers, and laser range finders. Students' findings should include illustrations and detailed descriptions of how the instruments work. **LS** Logical/Visual

Debate — GENERAL

Nuclear Waste Disposal?
Scientists must consider the geologic stability of potential sites for nuclear waste facilities. Have students research and debate the issue of nuclear waste disposal. Have them consider that there are few viable options for the disposal of the world's nuclear waste. Remind them that no one can be sure that an area will be stable over the thousands of years it takes for nuclear waste to decay. **LS** Interpersonal

Homework — GENERAL

Presentation Have students create a poster to promote earthquake safety. Posters should focus on one of the following: how to prepare for an earthquake, what to do during an earthquake, or what to do after an earthquake. Students can create a display to educate the school about earthquake safety. **LS** Visual

---

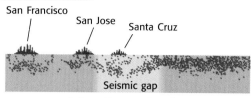

Figure 2   A Seismic Gap on the San Andreas Fault

This diagram shows a cross section of the San Andreas Fault. Note how the seismic gap was filled by the 1989 Loma Prieta earthquake and its aftershocks. *Aftershocks* are weaker earthquakes that follow a stronger earthquake.

- Earthquakes prior to 1989 earthquake

- 1989 earthquake and aftershocks

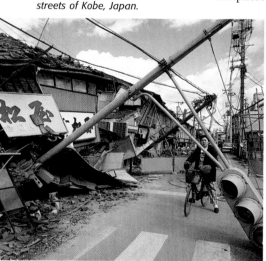

Figure 3 *During the January 17, 1995, earthquake, the fronts of entire buildings collapsed into the streets of Kobe, Japan.*

Using the Gap Hypothesis

Not all seismologists believe the gap hypothesis is an accurate method of forecasting earthquakes. But some seismologists think the gap hypothesis helped forecast the approximate location and strength of the 1989 Loma Prieta earthquake in the San Francisco Bay area. The seismic gap that they identified is illustrated in **Figure 2.** In 1988, these seismologists predicted that over the next 30 years there was a 30% chance that an earthquake with a magnitude of at least 6.5 would fill this seismic gap. Were they correct? The Loma Prieta earthquake, which filled in the seismic gap in 1989, measured 6.9 on the Richter scale. Their prediction was very close, considering how complicated the forecasting of earthquakes is.

Earthquakes and Buildings

Figure 3 shows what can happen to buildings during an earthquake. These buildings were not designed or constructed to withstand the forces of an earthquake.

Today, older structures in seismically active places, such as California, are being made more earthquake resistant. The process of making older structures more earthquake resistant is called *retrofitting*. A common way to retrofit an older home is to securely fasten it to its foundation. Steel can be used to strengthen structures made of brick.

Reading Check Explain the meaning of the term *retrofitting*.

Answer to Reading Check
Retrofitting is the process of making older structures more earthquake resistant.

WEiRD SCIENCE

Engineers have devised giant shock absorbers for buildings. The shock absorbers contain a ferrofluid solution that becomes rigid in a magnetic field. When an earthquake occurs, a computer controls electromagnets in the shock absorbers to damp the vibrations!

Earthquake-Resistant Buildings

A lot has been learned from building failure during earthquakes. Armed with this knowledge, architects and engineers use the newest technology to design and construct buildings and bridges to better withstand earthquakes. Carefully study **Figure 4** to learn more about this modern technology.

Figure 4 Earthquake-Resistant Building Technology

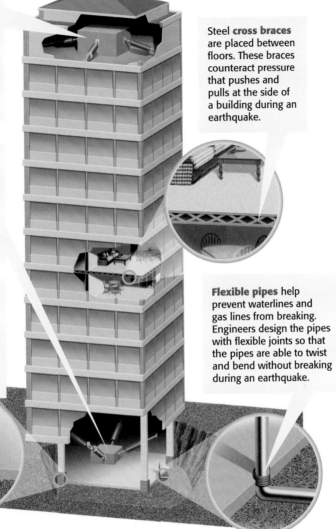

The **mass damper** is a weight placed in the roof of a building. Motion sensors detect building movement during an earthquake and send messages to a computer. The computer then signals controls in the roof to shift the mass damper to counteract the building's movement.

The **active tendon system** works much like the mass damper system in the roof. Sensors notify a computer that the building is moving. Then, the computer activates devices to shift a large weight to counteract the movement.

Base isolators act as shock absorbers during an earthquake. They are made of layers of rubber and steel wrapped around a lead core. Base isolators absorb seismic waves, preventing them from traveling through the building.

Steel **cross braces** are placed between floors. These braces counteract pressure that pushes and pulls at the side of a building during an earthquake.

Flexible pipes help prevent waterlines and gas lines from breaking. Engineers design the pipes with flexible joints so that the pipes are able to twist and bend without breaking during an earthquake.

CONNECTION TO Physics

WRITING SKILL **Earthquake Proof Buildings** During earthquakes, buildings often sway from side to side when the ground beneath them moves. This swaying can cause structural damage to buildings. Scientists and engineers are developing computer-controlled systems that counteract the swaying of buildings during earthquakes. Research a computer-controlled system that uses mass dampers or active tendons to reduce damage to buildings. Summarize your research in a short essay.

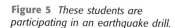

Figure 5 *These students are participating in an earthquake drill.*

Are You Prepared for an Earthquake?

If you live in an area where earthquakes are common, there are many things you can do to protect yourself and your property from earthquakes. Plan ahead so that you will know what to do before, during, and after an earthquake. Stick to your plan as closely as possible.

Before the Shaking Starts

The first thing you should do is safeguard your home against earthquakes. You can do so by putting heavier objects on lower shelves so that they do not fall during the earthquake. You can also talk to a parent about having your home strengthened. Next, you should find safe places within each room of your home and outside of your home. Then, make a plan with others (your family, neighbors, or friends) to meet in a safe place after the earthquake is over. This plan ensures that you will all know who is safe. During the earthquake, waterlines, power lines, and roadways may be damaged. So, you should store water, nonperishable food, a fire extinguisher, a flashlight with batteries, a portable radio, medicines, and a first-aid kit in a place you can access after the earthquake.

When the Shaking Starts

The best thing to do if you are indoors when an earthquake begins is to crouch or lie face down under a table or desk in the center of a room, as shown in **Figure 5.** If you are outside, lie face down away from buildings, power lines, and trees and cover your head with your hands. If you are in a car on an open road, you should stop the car and remain inside.

✓ *Reading Check* **Explain what you would do if you were in class and an earthquake began to shake the ground.**

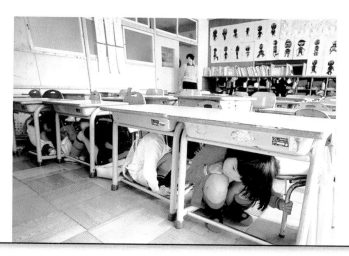

After the Shaking Stops

Being in an earthquake is a startling and often frightening experience for most people. After being in an earthquake, you should not be surprised to find yourself and others puzzled about what took place. You should try to calm down and get your bearings as quickly as possible. Then, remove yourself from immediate danger, such as downed power lines, broken glass, and fire hazards. Always stay out of damaged buildings, and return home only when you are told that it is safe to do so by someone in authority. Be aware that there may be aftershocks, which may cause more damage to structures. Recall your earthquake plan, and follow it.

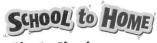

SCHOOL to HOME

Disaster Planning

With your parent, create a plan that will protect your family in the event of a natural disaster, such as an earthquake. The plan should include steps to take before, during, and after a disaster. Present your disaster plan in the form of an oral report to your class.

ACTIVITY

SECTION Review

Summary

- Earthquake hazard is a measure of how likely an area is to have earthquakes in the future.
- Seismologists use their knowledge of the relationship between earthquake strength and frequency and of the gap hypothesis to forecast earthquakes.
- Homes and buildings and bridges can be strengthened to decrease earthquake damage.
- People who live in earthquake zones should safeguard their home against earthquakes.

Using Key Terms

1. In your own words, write a definition for each of the following terms: *gap hypothesis* and *seismic gap*.

Understanding Key Ideas

2. A weight that is placed on a building to make the building earthquake resistant is called a(n)
   a. active tendon system.
   b. cross brace.
   c. mass damper.
   d. base isolator.

3. How is an area's earthquake-hazard level determined?

4. Compare the strength and frequency method with the gap hypothesis method for predicting earthquakes.

5. What is a common way of making homes more earthquake resistant?

6. Describe four pieces of technology that are designed to make buildings earthquake resistant.

7. Name five items that you should store in case of an earthquake.

Math Skills

8. Of the approximately 420,000 earthquakes recorded each year, about 140 have a magnitude greater than 6.0. What percentage of total earthquakes have a magnitude greater than 6.0?

Critical Thinking

9. **Evaluating Hypotheses** Seismologists predict that there is a 20% chance that an earthquake of magnitude 7.0 or greater will fill a seismic gap during the next 50 years. Is the hypothesis incorrect if the earthquake does not happen? Explain your answer.

10. **Applying Concepts** Why is a large earthquake often followed by numerous aftershocks?

SCLINKS.

NSTA
Developed and maintained by the National Science Teachers Association

For a variety of links related to this chapter, go to www.scilinks.org

Topic: Earthquakes and Society
SciLinks code: HSM0455

---

4. Sample answer: According to the strength and frequency method, earthquake strength is related to how often earthquakes occur. The gap hypothesis predicts an earthquake's strength and location by finding out the parts of an active fault where no earthquakes have recently occurred.

5. Sample answer: A common way of making a home more earthquake resistant is to securely fasten it to its foundation.

6. Answers may vary. Sample answer: Flexible pipes that are able to twist and bend during earthquakes prevent water and gas lines from breaking. A base isolator made of rubber and steel wrapped around lead absorbs seismic waves. A mass damper placed in the roof of a building counteracts the movement of the building during an earthquake. Cross braces placed between floors in a building counteract pressure that pushes and pulls at the side of a building.

7. Answers may vary. Sample answer: nonperishable food, a flashlight, a portable radio, a fire extinguisher, and a first-aid kit

8. $140 \div 420,000 \times 100 = .03\%$

9. The hypothesis is not incorrect because there was only a 20% probability an earthquake would fill the seismic gap.

10. Aftershocks follow a large earthquake because the earthquake causes elastically deformed rock along other nearby faults to break.

Answers to Section Review

1. Sample answer: According to the gap hypothesis, strong earthquakes are likely to occur along sections of active faults that have had relatively few earthquakes. A seismic gap is an area along an active fault where relatively few earthquakes have occurred.

2. c

3. The earthquake hazard level of a particular area is determined by the amount of past and present seismic activity that has occurred in the area.

CHAPTER RESOURCES

Chapter Resource File

- Section Quiz **GENERAL**
- Section Review **GENERAL**
- Vocabulary and Section Summary **GENERAL**
- Critical Thinking **ADVANCED**

Quake Challenge

Teacher's Notes

Time Required

One 45-minute class period

Lab Ratings

EASY —————→ HARD

Teacher Prep 🧪🧪
Student Set-Up 🧪
Concept Level 🧪🧪
Clean Up 🧪🧪

MATERIALS

The materials listed on the student page are enough for 2 students.

Safety Caution

Remind students to review all safety cautions and icons before beginning this lab activity.

Preparation Notes

Make the gelatin 24 hours in advance. When making the gelatin, experiment with the ratio of water to gelatin. The more water you use, the more "wiggly" your gelatin will be. Cut the gelatin squares ahead of time, and place each square on a piece of wax paper. For steps 8 and 9, you will need to create a gelatin square large enough to place all the student structures on. This allows each group's structure to be evaluated on its own merit.

Using Scientific Methods

Inquiry Lab

Quake Challenge

In many parts of the world, people must have earthquakes in mind when they construct buildings. Each building must be designed so that the structure is protected during an earthquake. Architects have greatly improved the design of buildings since 1906, when an earthquake and the fires it caused destroyed much of San Francisco. In this activity, you will use marshmallows and toothpicks to build a structure that can withstand a simulated earthquake. In the process, you will discover some of the ways a building can be built to withstand an earthquake.

Ask a Question

1 What features help a building withstand an earthquake? How can I use this information to build my structure?

Form a Hypothesis

2 Brainstorm with a classmate to design a structure that will resist the simulated earthquake. Write two or three sentences to describe your design. Explain why you think your design will be able to withstand a simulated earthquake.

OBJECTIVES

Build a model of a structure that can withstand a simulated earthquake.

Evaluate ways in which you can strengthen your model.

MATERIALS

- gelatin, square, approximately 8 × 8 cm
- marshmallows (10)
- paper plate
- toothpicks (10)

SAFETY

Test the Hypothesis

3 Follow your design to build a structure using the toothpicks and marshmallows.

4 Set your structure on a square of gelatin, and place the gelatin on a paper plate.

5 Shake the square of gelatin to test whether your building will remain standing during a quake. Do not pick up the gelatin.

6 If your first design does not work well, change it until you find a design that does. Try to determine why your building is falling so that you can improve your design each time.

7 Sketch your final design.

Helen Schiller
Northwood Middle School
Taylors, South Carolina

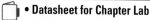

CHAPTER RESOURCES

Chapter Resource File

- **Datasheet for Chapter Lab**
- **Lab Notes and Answers**

Technology

 Classroom Videos
  - Lab Video

LabBook

- Earthquake Waves

⑧ After you have tested your final design, place your structure on the gelatin square on your teacher's desk.

⑨ When every group has added a structure to the teacher's gelatin, your teacher will simulate an earthquake by shaking the gelatin. Watch to see which buildings withstand the most severe quake.

Analyze the Results

① **Explaining Events** Which buildings were still standing after the final earthquake? What features made them more stable?

② **Analyzing Results** How would you change your design in order to make your structure more stable?

Draw Conclusions

③ **Evaluating Models** This was a simple model of a real-life problem for architects. Based on this activity, what advice would you give to architects who design buildings in earthquake zones?

④ **Evaluating Models** What are some limitations of your earthquake model?

⑤ **Making Predictions** How could your research have an impact on society?

Analyze the Results

1. Answers may vary. Sample answer: Structures that had a wide base generally withstood the earthquake. Structures that used triangles in the design also were successful.

2. Answers may vary. Sample answer: By experimenting with different design shapes, such as cubes or triangles, we could find the most stable structure.

Draw Conclusions

3. Buildings designed in earthquake zones should have wide and flexible foundations. The buildings should also be reinforced to prevent collapse.

4. Answers may vary. Accept all reasonable answers. Sample answer: Rocks and gelatin have very different physical properties, such as hardness and density. Seismic waves may have different effects on rock than shaking does on gelatin.

5. Answers may vary. Accept all reasonable answers. Sample answer: By changing the design of our marshmallow-and-toothpick building, we can come up with better designs for buildings.

CHAPTER RESOURCES

Workbooks

 Whiz-Bang Demonstrations
• When Buildings Boogie **GENERAL**

 Long-Term Projects & Research Ideas
• A Whole Lotta Shakin' **ADVANCED**

Chapter Review

Assignment Guide

SECTION	QUESTIONS
1	1, 5–7, 14, 18, 20
2	2, 3, 11, 12, 21–23
3	4, 8–10, 13, 15, 17, 19
1 and 2	16

ANSWERS

Using Key Terms

1. Sample answer: A seismic wave is released when elastically deformed rock along a fault slips. A P wave is the fastest seismic wave and can move through all parts of the Earth. An S wave moves rock from side to side as the wave travels through the Earth.

2. Sample answer: A seismograph is an instrument that is used to record seismic waves. A seismogram is the tracing of earthquake motion created by a seismograph.

3. Sample answer: A focus is the point along a fault where an earthquake starts. An epicenter is the point on Earth's surface above the focus.

4. Sample answer: The gap hypothesis states that strong earthquakes are likely to occur along sections of active faults that have had relatively few earthquakes. Seismic gaps are areas along active faults where relatively few earthquakes have occurred.

USING KEY TERMS

1 Use each of the following terms in a separate sentence: *seismic wave*, *P wave*, and *S wave*.

For each pair of terms, explain how the meanings of the terms differ.

2 *seismograph* and *seismogram*

3 *epicenter* and *focus*

4 *gap hypothesis* and *seismic gap*

UNDERSTANDING KEY IDEAS

Multiple Choice

5 When rock is ___, energy builds up in it. Seismic waves occur as this energy is ___.

 a. plastically deformed, increased
 b. elastically deformed, released
 c. plastically deformed, released
 d. elastically deformed, increased

6 Reverse faults are created

 a. by divergent plate motion.
 b. by convergent plate motion.
 c. by transform plate motion.
 d. All of the above

7 The last seismic waves to arrive are

 a. P waves.
 b. body waves.
 c. S waves.
 d. surface waves.

8 If an earthquake begins while you are in a building, the safest thing for you to do is

 a. to run out into an open space.
 b. to get under the strongest table, chair, or other piece of furniture.
 c. to call home.
 d. to crouch near a wall.

9 How many major earthquakes (magnitude 7.0 to 7.9) happen on average in the world each year?

 a. 1
 b. 18
 c. 120
 d. 800

10 ___ counteract pressure that pushes and pulls at the side of a building during an earthquake.

 a. Base isolators
 b. Mass dampers
 c. Active tendon systems
 d. Cross braces

Short Answer

11 Can the S-P time method be used with one seismograph station to locate the epicenter of an earthquake? Explain your answer.

12 Explain how the Richter scale and the Modified Mercalli Intensity Scale are different.

13 What is the relationship between the strength of earthquakes and earthquake frequency?

Understanding Key Ideas

 5. b
 6. b
 7. d
 8. b
 9. b
10. d

11. No, a minimum of three seismograph stations are needed to find an earthquake's epicenter using the S-P time method.

12. The Richter magnitude scale measures the ground motion from an earthquake and adjusts for distance to find earthquake strength. The Modified Mercalli Intensity Scale measures the degree to which an earthquake is felt by people and the amount of damage caused by an earthquake.

13. With each step down in earthquake strength or magnitude, the number of earthquakes per year is greater.

14 Explain the way that different seismic waves affect rock as they travel through it.

15 Describe some steps you can take to protect yourself and your property from earthquakes.

CRITICAL THINKING

16 **Concept Mapping** Use the following terms to create a concept map: *focus, epicenter, earthquake start time, seismic waves, P waves,* and *S waves.*

17 **Identifying Relationships** Would a strong or light earthquake be more likely to happen along a major fault where there have not been many recent earthquakes? Explain. (Hint: Think about the average number of earthquakes of different magnitudes that occur annually.)

18 **Applying Concepts** Japan is located near a point where three tectonic plates converge. What would you imagine the earthquake-hazard level in Japan to be? Explain why.

19 **Applying Concepts** You learned that if you are in a car during an earthquake and are out in the open, it is best to stay in the car. Can you think of any situation in which you might want to leave a car during an earthquake?

20 **Identifying Relationships** You use gelatin to simulate rock in an experiment in which you are investigating the way different seismic waves affect rock. In what ways is your gelatin model limited?

INTERPRETING GRAPHICS

The graph below illustrates the relationship between earthquake magnitude and the height of tracings on a seismogram. Charles Richter initially formed his magnitude scale by comparing the heights of seismogram readings for different earthquakes. Use the graph below to answer the questions that follow.

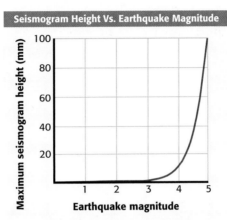

Seismogram Height Vs. Earthquake Magnitude

21 According to the graph, what would the magnitude of an earthquake be if its maximum seismogram height is 10 mm?

22 According to the graph, what is the difference in maximum seismogram height (in mm) between an earthquake of magnitude 4.0 and an earthquake of magnitude 5.0?

23 Look at the shape of the curve on the graph. What does this tell you about the relationship between seismogram heights and earthquake magnitudes? Explain.

14. P waves move rock back and forth, squeezing and stretching the rock. S waves stretch rock sideways as well as back and forth. Surface waves move rock up, down, and around, or in a back-and-forth motion.

15. Answers may vary. Sample answer: You should protect yourself and your property against earthquakes by creating an earthquake kit of items you may need after a strong, damaging earthquake. You should put heavy items closer to the floor so that they do not fall during earthquakes. You should find safe places within each room of your home or outdoors in the event there is an earthquake.

Critical Thinking

16. An answer to this exercise can be found at the end of this book.

17. Answers may vary. Sample answer: Based on the average number of earthquakes of different magnitudes that happen annually, a light earthquake would be more likely to happen along a major fault where there have not been many major earthquakes.

18. Because most earthquakes occur at tectonic plate boundaries, the earthquake-hazard level in Japan would be high.

19. Answers may vary. Sample answer: You might want to leave your car if it was stranded on or beneath a highway overpass.

20. A gelatin model is limited because it does not have the same properties as rock, such as density and hardness.

Interpreting Graphics

21. 4

22. 100 mm − 10 mm = 90 mm

23. Students should recognize that seismogram heights increase at a greater rate with each increase in earthquake magnitude. The relationship is logarithmic, not linear.

CHAPTER RESOURCES

Chapter Resource File

 • Chapter Review **GENERAL**
• Chapter Test A **GENERAL**
• Chapter Test B **ADVANCED**
• Chapter Test C **SPECIAL NEEDS**
• Vocabulary Activity **GENERAL**

Workbooks

Study Guide
• Assessment resources are also available in Spanish.

Teacher's Note

To provide practice under more realistic testing conditions, give students 20 minutes to answer all of the questions in this Standardized Test Preparation.

MISCONCEPTION /// ALERT \\\

Answers to the standardized test preparation can help you identify student misconceptions and misunderstandings.

READING

Passage 1

1. B
2. H
3. D

✚ **TEST DOCTOR**

Question 2: The correct answer is H. In the passage, it is stated that the earthquake lasted 20 s. Students may think answer H is true because the passage describes changes that happened between 5:04 P.M. and 5:05 P.M.

Question 3: The correct answer is D. In the passage, it is stated that the earthquake happened during the 1989 World Series. Students are incorrect if they think that answer C is correct, because the earthquake, at magnitude 6.9, was a strong earthquake, not light to moderate.

Standardized Test Preparation

READING

Read each of the passages below. Then, answer the questions that follow each passage.

Passage 1 At 5:04 P.M. on October 14, 1989, life in California's San Francisco Bay area seemed normal. While 62,000 fans filled Candlestick Park to watch the third game of the World Series, other people were rushing home from a day's work. By 5:05 P.M., the area had changed drastically. The area was rocked by the 6.9 magnitude Loma Prieta earthquake, which lasted 20 s and caused 68 deaths, 3,757 injuries, and the destruction of more than 1,000 homes. Considering that the earthquake was of such a high magnitude and that the earthquake happened during rush hour, it is amazing that more people did not die.

1. In the passage, what does the word *drastically* mean?
   A continuously
   B severely
   C gradually
   D not at all

2. Which of the following statements about the Loma Prieta earthquake is false?
   F The earthquake happened during rush hour.
   G The earthquake destroyed more than 1,000 homes.
   H The earthquake lasted for 1 min.
   I The earthquake had a magnitude of 6.9.

3. Which of the following statements is a fact in the passage?
   A Thousands of people were killed in the Loma Prieta earthquake.
   B The Loma Prieta earthquake happened during the morning rush hour.
   C The Loma Prieta earthquake was a light to moderate earthquake.
   D The Loma Prieta earthquake occurred during the 1989 World Series.

Passage 2 In the United States, seismologists use the Modified Mercalli Intensity Scale to measure the intensity of earthquakes. Japanese seismologists, however, use the Shindo scale to measure earthquake intensity. Earthquakes are <u>assigned</u> a number between 1 and 7 on the scale. Shindo 1 indicates a slight earthquake. Such an earthquake is felt by few people, usually people who are sitting. Shindo 7 indicates a severe earthquake. An earthquake that causes great destruction, such as the earthquake that struck Kobe, Japan, in January 1995, would be classified as Shindo 7.

1. In the passage, what does the word *assigned* mean?
   A named
   B voted
   C given
   D chosen

2. Which of the following statements about the Shindo scale is true?
   F The Shindo scale is used to measure earthquake strength.
   G The Shindo scale, which ranges from 1 to 7, is used to rank earthquake intensity.
   H The Shindo scale is the same as the Modified Mercalli Intensity Scale.
   I Seismologists all over the world use the Shindo scale.

3. Which of the following is a fact in the passage?
   A American seismologists use the Richter scale instead of the Shindo scale.
   B Japanese seismologists measure the intensity of large earthquakes only.
   C The Kobe earthquake was too destructive to be given a Shindo number.
   D Shindo 1 indicates a slight earthquake.

Passage 2

1. C
2. G
3. D

✚ **TEST DOCTOR**

Question 2: The correct answer is G. The passage explicitly states that Japanese seismologists use the Shindo scale to rate earthquake intensity on a scale of 1 to 7. Students may think answer F is correct if they confuse the concepts of strength and intensity.

Question 3: The correct answer is D. In the passage, it is stated that Japanese seismologists use Shindo 1 to indicate a slight earthquake. Students may think A is the correct answer if they confuse the Richter magnitude scale with the Shindo scale of earthquake intensity.

Use the graph below to answer the questions that follow.

Plotting Seismograms on a Time-Distance Graph

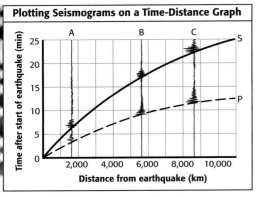

1. According to the seismogram, which waves travel the **fastest**?
   A P waves travel the fastest.
   B S waves travel the fastest.
   C P waves and S waves travel at the same speed.
   D The graph does not show how fast P waves and S waves travel.

2. What is the approximate difference in minutes between the time the first P waves arrived at station B and the time the first S waves arrived at station B?
   F 22 1/2 min
   G 10 1/2 min
   H 8 min
   I 3 min

3. Station A is approximately how much closer to the epicenter than station B is?
   A 1,800 km
   B 4,000 km
   C 5,800 km
   D 8,600 km

Read each question below, and choose the best answer.

1. If a seismic wave travels at a rate of 12 km/s, how far will it travel away from the earthquake in 1 min?
   A 7,200 km
   B 720 km
   C 72 km
   D 7.2 km

2. If a P wave travels a distance of 70 km in 10 s, what is its speed?
   F 700 km/s
   G 70 km/s
   H 7 km/s
   I 0.7 km/s

3. Each time the magnitude of an earthquake increases by 1 unit, the amount of energy released is 31.7 times greater. How much greater is the energy for a magnitude 7.0 earthquake than a magnitude 5.0 earthquake?
   A 31,855 times as strong
   B 63.4 times as strong
   C 634 times as strong
   D 1,005 times as strong

4. An approximate relationship between earthquake magnitude and frequency is that when magnitude increases by 1.0, 10 times fewer earthquakes occur. Thus, if 150 earthquakes of magnitude 2.0 happen in your area this year, about how many 4.0 magnitude earthquakes will happen in your area this year?
   F 50
   G 10
   H 2
   I 0

5. If an average of 421,140 earthquakes occur annually, what percentage of these earthquakes are minor earthquakes if 49,000 minor earthquakes occur annually?
   A approximately .01%
   B approximately .12%
   C approximately 12%
   D approximately 86%

1. A
2. H
3. B

TEST DOCTOR

Question 2: The correct answer is H. Students may think answer I is correct if they use station A to obtain the answer instead of station B. They may think answer G is correct if they use station C to obtain the answer instead of station B.

Question 3: The correct answer is B. The graph indicates that recording station A is approximately 4,000 km closer to the epicenter than recording station B.

MATH

1. B
2. H
3. D
4. H
5. C

TEST DOCTOR

Question 3: The correct answer is D. An earthquake of magnitude 7.0 is approximately 1,005 times (31.7^2) as strong as an earthquake of magnitude 5.0. Students may obtain an incorrect answer if they multiply 31.7 times 2 or by 20, or cube 31.7 instead of squaring it.

Question 4: The correct answer is H. With each increase of 1.0 unit of magnitude, there is a decrease in earthquake frequency of 10 times. Because $150 \div 10^2 = 1.5$, 2 is the only logical answer. Students may think answer F is correct if they divide 150 by 2. Students may think answer G is correct if they divide 150 by 20.

Standardized Test Preparation

CHAPTER RESOURCES

Chapter Resource File

• Standardized Test Preparation GENERAL

State Resources

For specific resources for your state, visit **go.hrw.com** and type in the keyword **HSMSTR**.

Weird Science

Background

There have been many studies on the different types of animal responses to the geophysical environment. Most of these studies indicate that the behavior of living organisms is affected by electromagnetic fields. Studies have been performed on how migrating birds find their way and how fish navigate. Fish such as catfish and sharks use electroreceptors to detect objects around them and to communicate. Even earthworms respond to changes in Earth's magnetic field.

Science, Technology, and Society

Background

During the summer of 2002, a pilot hole 2 km in depth was drilled at the SAFOD site. When drilling concluded, seismometers were placed in the drill hole to locate the microearthquakes that will be targeted with SAFOD.

Science in Action

SAFOD PILOT HOLE
Source: Martyn Unsworth

Weird Science

Can Animals Predict Earthquakes?

Is it possible that animals close to the epicenter of an earthquake are able to sense changes in their environment? And should we be paying attention to such animal behavior? As long ago as the 1700s, unusual animal activity prior to earthquakes has been recorded. Examples include domestic cattle seeking higher ground and zoo animals refusing to enter their shelters at night. Other animals, such as lizards, snakes, and small mammals, evacuate their underground burrows, and wild birds leave their usual habitats. These events occur days, hours, or even minutes before an earthquake.

Language Arts ACTIVITY

WRITING SKILL Create an illustrated field guide of animal activity to show how animal activity can predict earthquakes. Each illustration must have a paragraph that describes the activity of a specific animal.

Science, Technology, and Society

San Andreas Fault Observatory at Depth (SAFOD)

Seismologists are creating an underground observatory in Parkfield, California, to study earthquakes along the San Andreas Fault. The observatory will be named the San Andreas Fault Observatory at Depth (SAFOD). A deep hole will be drilled directly into the fault zone near a point where earthquakes of magnitude 6.0 have been recorded. Instruments will be placed at the bottom of the hole, 3 to 4 km beneath Earth's surface. These instruments will make seismological measurements of earthquakes and measure the deformation of rock.

Social Studies ACTIVITY

Research the great San Francisco earthquake of 1906. Find images of the earthquake on the Internet and download them, or cut them out of old magazines. Create a photo collage of the earthquake that shows San Francisco before and after the earthquake.

Answer to Language Arts Activity

Have students bring their field guides to class. In the classroom, have students play the role of scientists who are discussing how animal behavior might be used to forecast earthquakes. Students should use facts taken from their field guides to discuss animal behavior that might be useful in earthquake forecasting.

Answer to Social Studies Activity

Have students bring their montages to class. Create a classroom exhibit using the student montages. Use the exhibit to stimulate a discussion about the type of damage that can be caused by a major earthquake, such as the earthquake that struck San Francisco in 1906.

Hiroo Kanamori

Seismologist Hiroo Kanamori is a seismologist at the California Institute of Technology in Pasadena, California. Dr. Kanamori studies how earthquakes occur and tries to reduce their impact on our society. He also analyzes what the effects of earthquakes on oceans are and how earthquakes create giant ocean waves called *tsunamis* (tsoo NAH meez). Tsunamis are very destructive to life and property when they reach land. Kanamori has discovered that even some weak earthquakes can cause powerful tsunamis. He calls these events *tsunami earthquakes,* and he has learned to predict when tsunamis will form. In short, when tectonic plates grind together slowly, special waves called *long-period seismic waves* are created. When Kanamori sees a long-period wave recorded on a seismogram, he knows a tsunami will form. Because long-period waves travel faster than tsunamis, they arrive at recording stations earlier. When an earthquake station records an earthquake, information about that earthquake is provided to a tsunami warning center. The center determines if the earthquake may cause a tsunami and, if so, issues a tsunami warning to areas that may be affected.

Math

An undersea earthquake causes a tsunami to form. The tsunami travels across the open ocean at 800 km/h. How long will the tsunami take to travel from the point where it formed to a coastline 3,600 km away?

To learn more about these Science in Action topics, visit **go.hrw.com** and type in the keyword **HZ5EQKF.**

Current Science

Check out Current Science® articles related to this chapter by visiting go.hrw.com. **Just type in the keyword HZ5CS08.**

Careers

Background

In 1996, Dr. Kanamori received the Bucher Medal for his outstanding achievements in seismology. He and his colleague Tom Hanks bridged the gap between seismology and physics by developing an earthquake scale called the "moment magnitude scale." It rates earthquakes by the minimum energy released and is consistent with the Richter scale.

Answer to Math Activity

The speed of the tsunami in the open ocean is 800 km/h. It will take the tsunami 4.5 h to travel the 3,600 km distance to the coastline (3,600 km ÷ 800 km/h = 4.5 h).

Volcanoes
Chapter Planning Guide

Compression guide:
To shorten instruction because of time limitations, omit the Chapter Lab.

OBJECTIVES	LABS, DEMONSTRATIONS, AND ACTIVITIES	TECHNOLOGY RESOURCES
PACING • 45 min pp. 154–161 **Chapter Opener**	SE **Start-up Activity,** p. 155 ◆ GENERAL	OSP **Parent Letter** ■ GENERAL CD **Student Edition on CD-ROM** CD **Guided Reading Audio CD** ▥ TR **Chapter Starter Transparency*** VID **Brain Food Video Quiz**
Section 1 Volcanic Eruptions • Distinguish between nonexplosive and explosive volcanic eruptions. • Identify the features of a volcano. • Explain how the composition of magma affects the type of volcanic eruption that will occur. • Describe four types of lava and four types of pyroclastic material.	TE **Activity** Volcano Pen Pals, p. 156 GENERAL TE **Group Activity** Volcanic Radio Show, p. 157 GENERAL SE **Connection to Social Studies** Fertile Farmlands, p. 159 GENERAL TE **Group Activity** Describing Viscosity, p. 159 GENERAL SE **Quick Lab** Modeling an Explosive Eruption, p. 160 GENERAL CRF **Datasheet for Quick Lab***	CRF **Lesson Plans*** TR **Bellringer Transparency*** TR ***LINK TO PHYSICAL SCIENCE*** Models of a Solid, a Liquid, and a Gas* TR **Four Types of Lava*** CD **Science Tutor**
PACING • 45 min pp. 162–165 **Section 2 Effects of Volcanic Eruptions** • Explain how volcanic eruptions can affect climate. • Compare the three types of volcanoes. • Compare craters, calderas, and lava plateaus.	TE **Connection Activity** History, p. 163 GENERAL TE **Activity** Classifying Volcanoes, p. 163 BASIC TE **Activity** Book Report, p. 163 ADVANCED TE **Connection Activity** Astronomy, p. 164 ADVANCED SE **Skills Practice Lab** Some Go "Pop," Some Do Not, p. 191 GENERAL CRF **Datasheet for LabBook*** LB **Whiz-Bang Demonstrations** How's Your Lava Life?* ◆ GENERAL CD **Interactive Explorations CD-Rom,** What's the Matter? ADVANCED	CRF **Lesson Plans*** TR **Bellringer Transparency*** TR **Three Types of Volcanoes*** TR **The Formation of a Caldera*** CD **Science Tutor**
PACING • 90 min pp. 166–171 **Section 3 Causes of Volcanic Eruptions** • Describe the formation and movement of magma. • Explain the relationship between volcanoes and plate tectonics. • Summarize the methods scientists use to predict volcanic eruptions.	SE **Quick Lab** Reaction to Stress, p. 167 ◆ GENERAL CRF **Datasheet for Quick Lab*** TE **Connection Activity** Math, p. 168 GENERAL SE **School-to-Home Activity** Tectonic Models, p. 169 GENERAL TE **Group Activity** Preparing for an Eruption, p. 169 ADVANCED SE **Skills Practice Lab** Volcano Verdict, p. 172 ◆ GENERAL CRF **Datasheet for Chapter Lab*** LB **Labs You Can Eat** Hot Spots* ◆ GENERAL LB **Whiz-Bang Demonstrations** What Makes a Vent Event?* ◆ GENERAL LB **Long-Term Projects & Research Ideas** A City Lost and Found* ADVANCED SE **Science In Action** Math, Social Studies, and Language Arts Activities, pp. 178–179 GENERAL	CRF **Lesson Plans*** TR **Bellringer Transparency*** TR **The Location of Major Volcanoes*** TR **How Magma Forms at a Divergent Boundary*** TR **How Magma Forms at a Convergent Boundary*** SE **Internet Activity,** p. 171 GENERAL CRF **SciLinks Activity*** GENERAL VID **Lab Videos for Earth Science** CD **Science Tutor**

PACING • 90 min

CHAPTER REVIEW, ASSESSMENT, AND STANDARDIZED TEST PREPARATION

CRF **Vocabulary Activity*** GENERAL
SE **Chapter Review,** pp. 174–175 GENERAL
CRF **Chapter Review*** ■ GENERAL
CRF **Chapter Tests A*** ■ GENERAL, **B*** ADVANCED, **C*** SPECIAL NEEDS
SE **Standardized Test Preparation,** pp. 176–177 GENERAL
CRF **Standardized Test Preparation*** GENERAL
CRF **Performance-Based Assessment*** GENERAL
OSP **Test Generator** GENERAL
CRF **Test Item Listing*** GENERAL

Online and Technology Resources

Visit **go.hrw.com** for a variety of free resources related to this textbook. Enter the keyword **HZ5VOL.**

Holt Online Learning

Students can access interactive problem-solving help and active visual concept development with the *Holt Science and Technology* Online Edition available at **www.hrw.com.**

 Guided Reading Audio CD Also in Spanish

A direct reading of each chapter for auditory learners, reluctant readers, and Spanish-speaking students.

 Science Tutor CD-ROM

Excellent for remediation and test practice.

SKILLS DEVELOPMENT RESOURCES	SECTION REVIEW AND ASSESSMENT	CORRELATIONS
SE **Pre-Reading Activity**, p. 154 `GENERAL` OSP **Science Puzzlers, Twisters & Teasers** `GENERAL`		National Science Education Standards SAI 1; ST 1; SPSP 3
CRF **Directed Reading A*** ■ `BASIC`, **B*** `SPECIAL NEEDS` CRF **Vocabulary and Section Summary*** ■ `GENERAL` SE **Reading Strategy** Reading Organizer, p. 156 `GENERAL` TE **Inclusion Strategies**, p. 159 CRF **Critical Thinking** Eruption Disruption* `BASIC`	SE **Reading Checks**, pp. 157, 158, 160 `GENERAL` TE **Reteaching**, p. 160 `BASIC` TE **Quiz**, p. 160 `GENERAL` TE **Alternative Assessment**, p. 160 `BASIC` SE **Section Review,*** p. 161 ■ `GENERAL` TE **Homework**, p. 161 `GENERAL` CRF **Section Quiz*** `GENERAL`	SAI 1; HNS 2; ES 1c
CRF **Directed Reading A*** ■ `BASIC`, **B*** `SPECIAL NEEDS` CRF **Vocabulary and Section Summary*** ■ `GENERAL` SE **Reading Strategy** Paired Summarizing, p. 162 `GENERAL` CRF **Reinforcement Worksheet** A Variety of Volcanoes* `BASIC`	SE **Reading Checks**, pp. 162, 164 `GENERAL` TE **Reteaching**, p. 164 `BASIC` TE **Quiz**, p. 164 `GENERAL` TE **Alternative Assessment**, p. 164 `GENERAL` SE **Section Review,*** p. 165 `GENERAL` CRF **Section Quiz*** `GENERAL`	ST 2; SPSP 3, 4; ES 1c; *LabBook:* SAI 1
CRF **Directed Reading A*** ■ `BASIC`, **B*** `SPECIAL NEEDS` CRF **Vocabulary and Section Summary*** ■ `GENERAL` SE **Reading Strategy** Reading Organizer, p. 166 `GENERAL` SE **Math Practice** How Hot is Hot?, p. 168 `GENERAL` TE **Inclusion Strategies**, p. 169 MS **Math Skills for Science** Using Temperature Scales* `GENERAL` CRF **Reinforcement Worksheet** Tectonic Plate Movement* `BASIC`	SE **Reading Checks**, pp. 167, 169, 170 `GENERAL` TE **Reteaching**, p. 170 `BASIC` TE **Quiz**, p. 170 `GENERAL` TE **Alternative Assessment**, p. 170 `ADVANCED` TE **Homework**, p. 170 `GENERAL` SE **Section Review,*** p. 171 ■ `GENERAL` CRF **Section Quiz*** ■ `GENERAL`	UCP 3; SAI 1; ST 2; ES 1b, 1c; *Chapter Lab:* SAI 1

One-Stop Planner® CD-ROM

This CD-ROM package includes:
- Lab Materials QuickList Software
- Holt Calendar Planner
- Customizable Lesson Plans
- Printable Worksheets
- ExamView® Test Generator
- Interactive Teacher Edition
- Holt PuzzlePro® Resources
- Holt PowerPoint® Resources

SCLINKS.
NSTA

www.scilinks.org

Maintained by the **National Science Teachers Association.** See Chapter Enrichment pages for a complete list of topics.

Current Science®

Check out **Current Science** articles and activities by visiting the HRW Web site at **go.hrw.com**. Just type in the keyword **HZ5CS09T**.

Classroom Videos

- **Lab Videos** demonstrate the chapter lab.
- **Brain Food Video Quizzes** help students review the chapter material.
- **CNN Videos** bring science into your students' daily life.

Visual Resources

CHAPTER STARTER TRANSPARENCY

This Really Happened!

Auguste Ciparis was a condemned man. He was sentenced to be executed for murder in the town of St. Pierre, on Martinique, a small volcanic island in the Caribbean Sea. On the morning of May 8, 1902, Ciparis sat in jail waiting for his breakfast. As he waited, disaster struck the town—a disaster that killed thousands of people.

That morning, one of the island's volcanoes, Mount Pelée, erupted in a series of explosions. The eruption sent a fiery cloud of volcanic debris, super-heated steam, and toxic gases through the town. Everyone in St. Pierre, nearly 30,000 people, died. Everyone, that is, except Auguste.

Auguste had survived the deadliest volcanic eruption of the century. Underground in his dungeon, Auguste had been sheltered from the worst of the fiery fallout. Auguste cried out for help for four

days before rescuers found him. He was exhausted and badly burned, but alive. Spared from execution, Auguste joined the Barnum & Bailey circus. Known as Ludger Sylbaris, the Prisoner of St. Pierre, Auguste was hired to tell his tale and show off his burns in a replica of the dungeon that had saved his life.

BELLRINGER TRANSPARENCIES

Section: Volcanic Eruptions
Make a labeled drawing illustrating what happens when a volcano erupts. Then sketch a design for a model that simulates a volcanic eruption.

Illustrate your response in your **science journal**.

Section: Effects of Volcanic Eruptions
Look through this section, and write a definition for the following terms: *shield volcano, cinder cone volcano, composite volcano, volcanic crater,* and *caldera*.

Record your definitions in your **science journal**.

TEACHING TRANSPARENCIES

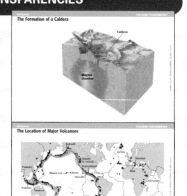

Four Types of Lava

The Formation of a Caldera

Three Types of Volcanoes

The Location of Major Volcanoes

TEACHING TRANSPARENCIES

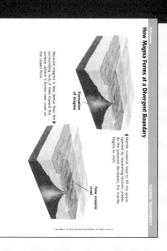

How Magma Forms at a Divergent Boundary

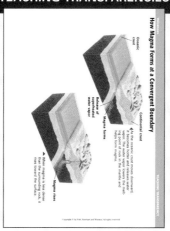

How Magma Forms at a Convergent Boundary

Models of a Solid, a Liquid, and a Gas

LINK TO PHYSICAL SCIENCE

Chapter: States of Matter

CONCEPT MAPPING TRANSPARENCY

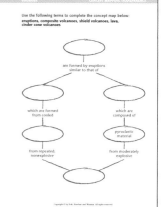

Use the following terms to complete the concept map below: eruptions, composite volcanoes, shield volcanoes, lava, cinder cone volcanoes

Planning Resources

LESSON PLANS

Lesson Plan SAMPLE

Section: Waves

Pacing
Regular Schedule: with lab(s):2 days without labs:2 days
Block Schedule: with lab(s):1 1/2 days without labs:1 day

Objectives
1. Relate the seven properties of life to a living organism.
2. Describe seven themes that can help you to organize what you learn about biology.
3. Identify the tiny structures that make up all living organisms.
4. Differentiate between reproduction and heredity and between metabolism and homeostasis.

National Science Education Standards Covered
LSInter4:Cells have particular structures that underlie their functions.
LSMat1: Most cell functions involve chemical reactions.
LSBeh1: Cells store and use information to guide their functions.
UCP1: Cell functions are regulated.
SI1: Cells can differentiate and form complete multicellular organisms.
PS1: Species evolve over time.
ESS1: The great diversity of organisms is the result of more than 3.5 billion years of evolution.
ESS2: Natural selection and its evolutionary consequences provide a scientific explanation for the fossil record of ancient life forms as well as for the striking molecular similarities observed among the diverse species of living organisms.
ST1: The millions of different species of plants, animals, and microorganisms that live on Earth today are related by descent from common ancestors.
ST2: The energy for life primarily comes from the sun.
SPSP1: The complexity and organization of organisms accommodates the need for obtaining, transforming, transporting, releasing, and eliminating the matter and energy used to sustain the organism.
SPSP6: As matter and energy flows through different levels of organization of living systems—cells, organs, communities—and between living systems and the physical environment, chemical elements are recombined in different ways.
HNS1: Organisms have behavioral responses to internal changes and to external stimuli.

PARENT LETTER

SAMPLE

Dear Parent,

Your son's or daughter's science class will soon begin exploring the chapter entitled "The World of Physical Science." In this chapter, students will learn about how the scientific method applies to the world of physical science and the role of physical science in the world. By the end of the chapter, students should demonstrate a clear understanding of the chapter's main ideas and be able to discuss the following topics:

1. physical science as the study of energy and matter (Section 1)
2. the role of physical science in the world around them (Section 1)
3. careers that rely on physical science (Section 1)
4. the steps used in the scientific method (Section 2)
5. examples of technology (Section 2)
6. how the scientific method is used to answer questions and solve problems (Section 2)
7. how our knowledge of science changes over time (Section 2)
8. how models represent real objects or systems (Section 3)
9. examples of different ways models are used in science (Section 3)
10. the importance of the International System of Units (Section 4)
11. the appropriate units to use for particular measurements (Section 4)
12. how area and density are derived quantities (Section 4)

Questions to Ask Along the Way

You can help your son or daughter learn about these topics by asking interesting questions such as the following:

- What are some surprising careers that use physical science?
- What is a characteristic of a good hypothesis?
- When is it a good idea to use a model?
- Why do Americans measure things in terms of inches and yards and meters?

ALSO IN SPANISH

TEST ITEM LISTING

TEST ITEM LISTING
The World of Earth Science SAMPLE

MULTIPLE CHOICE

1. A limitation of models is that
   a. they are large enough to see
   b. they do not act exactly like the things that they model
   c. they are smaller than the things that they model
   d. they model unfamiliar things.
   Answer: B   Difficulty: 1   Section: 3   Objective: 2

2. The length 10 m is equal to
   a. 100 cm.   c. 10,000 mm.
   b. 1,000 cm.   d. Both (b) and (c).
   Answer: B   Difficulty: 1   Section: 3   Objective: 2

3. To be valid, a hypothesis must be
   a. testable.   c. made into a law.
   b. supported by evidence.   d. Both (a) and (b)
   Answer: B   Difficulty: 1   Section: 2   Objective: 2

4. The statement "Sheila has a stain on her shirt" is an example of a(n)
   a. law.   c. observation.
   b. hypothesis.   d. prediction.
   Answer: C   Difficulty: 1   Section: 2   Objective: 2

5. A hypothesis is often developed out of
   a. observations.   c. laws.
   b. experiments.   d. Both (a) and (b)
   Answer: B   Difficulty: 1   Section: 2   Objective: 2

6. How many milliliters are in 3.5 kL?
   a. 3,500 mL.   c. 3,500,000 mL.
   b. 0.0035 mL.   d. 35,000 mL.
   Answer: B   Difficulty: 1   Section: 3   Objective: 2

7. A map of Seattle is an example of a
   a. law.   c. model.
   b. theory.   d. unit.
   Answer: B   Difficulty: 1   Section: 3   Objective: 2

8. A lab has the safety icons shown below. These icons mean that you should wear
   a. only safety goggles   c. safety goggles and a lab apron
   b. only a lab apron   d. safety goggles, a lab apron, and gloves
   Answer: B   Difficulty: 1   Section: 1   Objective: 3

9. The law of conservation of mass says the total all mass before a chemical change is
   a. more than the total mass after the change.
   b. less than the total mass after the change.
   c. the same as the total mass after the change.
   d. not the same as the total mass after the change.
   Answer: B   Difficulty: 1   Section: 3   Objective: 2

10. In which of the following areas might you lead a geochemist at work?
    a. studying the chemistry of rocks   c. studying geometry
    b. studying history   d. studying the atmosphere
    Answer: B   Difficulty: 1   Section: 3   Objective: 2

One-Stop Planner® CD-ROM

This CD-ROM includes all of the resources shown here and the following time-saving tools:

- *Lab Materials QuickList Software*
- *Customizable lesson plans*
- *Holt Calendar Planner*
- *The powerful ExamView® Test Generator*

Meeting Individual Needs

DIRECTED READING A

BASIC · **ALSO IN SPANISH**

DIRECTED READING B
SPECIAL NEEDS

VOCABULARY ACTIVITY
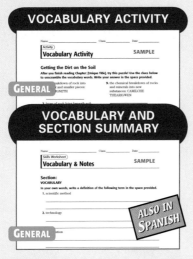
GENERAL

VOCABULARY AND SECTION SUMMARY
GENERAL · **ALSO IN SPANISH**

REINFORCEMENT
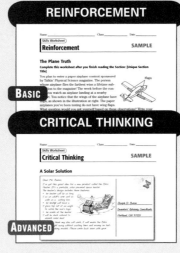
BASIC

CRITICAL THINKING
ADVANCED

SCILINKS ACTIVITY
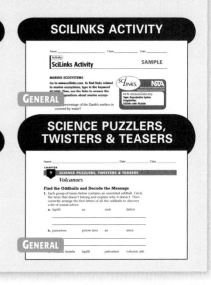
GENERAL

SCIENCE PUZZLERS, TWISTERS & TEASERS
GENERAL

Labs and Activities

LONG-TERM PROJECTS & RESEARCH IDEAS

ADVANCED

WHIZ-BANG DEMONSTRATIONS

GENERAL

WHIZ-BANG DEMONSTRATIONS
GENERAL

LABS YOU CAN EAT

GENERAL

DATASHEETS FOR QUICK LABS

DATASHEETS FOR CHAPTER LABS

DATASHEETS FOR LABBOOK

Review and Assessments

SECTION QUIZ

GENERAL · **ALSO IN SPANISH**

SECTION REVIEW
GENERAL · **ALSO IN SPANISH**

CHAPTER REVIEW
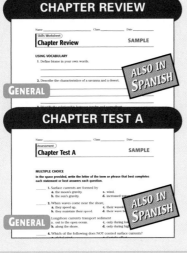
GENERAL · **ALSO IN SPANISH**

CHAPTER TEST A
GENERAL · **ALSO IN SPANISH**

CHAPTER TEST B
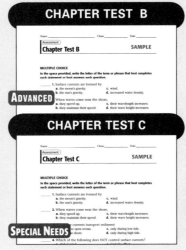
ADVANCED

CHAPTER TEST C
SPECIAL NEEDS

STANDARDIZED TEST PREPARATION
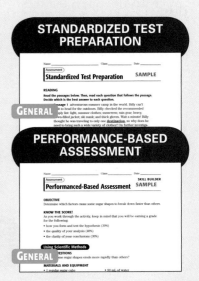
GENERAL

PERFORMANCE-BASED ASSESSMENT
GENERAL

This Chapter Enrichment provides relevant and interesting information to expand and enhance your presentation of the chapter material.

Section 1

Volcanic Eruptions

Mineral Formation in Subduction Zones

- The formation of commercially valuable minerals is common in areas where subduction creates volcanoes. As magma that is formed from subducted crust rises, the magma heats the surrounding rocks, which causes the fluids the rocks contain to circulate around and above the magma body. The hot fluids react with the magma and surrounding rocks and dissolve some metals (including iron, lead, silver, and gold). As the water-rich fluid rises through Earth's crust, mineral precipitation occurs at points where the fluid cools. This process can form rich mineral veins.

The Origin of Volcanic Terms

- Many terms for nonexplosive eruptions are Hawaiian. For example, lava that blows into fine, spiky strands are called *Pele's hair,* for the Hawaiian goddess of fire. *Limu o Pele,* which means "Pele's seaweed," is the term for delicate, translucent sheets of spatter filled with tiny glass bubbles.

- The terms for explosive eruptions, however, are generally not Hawaiian. For example, *nuée ardente,* a French term that means "burning cloud," is a hot mass of volcanic gases, ash, and debris that is expelled explosively and then travels at tremendous speeds down a mountainside.

Is That a Fact!

- The Tambora eruption in Indonesia was the largest in the last 200 years. The eruption and the resulting tsunamis killed more than 10,000 people. Ash covered so much land that farmland was devastated; disease and famine killed 80,000 more people.

- During the Tambora eruption, so much ash was thrown into the atmosphere that weather patterns were affected worldwide. Scholars believe the eruption caused the "Year Without a Summer" in 1816, when snow fell in New England in July.

Section 2

Effects of Volcanic Eruptions

Islands of Survival

- Nonexplosive volcanoes, such as Kilauea, on the island of Hawaii, may produce many different lava flows during an eruption. If these flows surround an area of forest, they create an island in a sea of lava. Hawaiians call such areas *kipukas,* which means "islands of survival." Over the last 20 years, biologists have studied populations of animals isolated in kipukas and have found interesting evidence to support evolution. Picture-wing drosophila flies have exhibited changes that ultimately could produce new species.

Is That a Fact!

- In the Caribbean, a submarine volcano named Kick'em Jenny is gaining a very bad reputation. As one sailboat captain said, "Kick'em Jenny . . . has a reputation of kicking up a nasty sea." Between 1986 and 1996, the volcano grew more than 50 m; its top is now only 200 m below sea level. It's close enough to the surface that eruptions can cause waves and turbulence in the sea. Volcanologists are concerned that a large eruption could cause devastating tsunamis throughout the Caribbean.

- When lava flows in a defined channel, a crust eventually forms on the surface of the lava. If the crust remains stationary while the lava below is still flowing, a lava tube or a lava cave several kilometers long may form.

Section 3

Causes of Volcanic Eruptions

Merapi, "Mountain of Fire"

● There are more active volcanoes in Indonesia than anywhere on Earth—130! One of the most dangerous volcanoes is called Merapi, or "Mountain of Fire," on the island of Java. Since 1548, Merapi has erupted violently 68 times. In 1998, it became active again, and people began to evacuate the area. Scientists are worried about the city of Yogyakarta, which is 70 km north of the volcano and is home to about 500,000 people. A large eruption could destroy the city.

Predicting the Mount Pinatubo Eruptions

● Perhaps the most successful prediction of a volcanic eruption was on Mount Pinatubo, in the Philippines. When Pinatubo became active in March and April 1991, scientists rushed to the area and quickly established monitoring systems. Scientists from the Philippines and the United States distributed a five-level alert system to civil defense and local officials. Evacuations began when an eruption appeared imminent (level 4 alert); more than 250,000 people evacuated the area. The eruption caused enormous losses of land, housing, and crops, but because of the preparations and warnings, only 300 people died during the eruption. Lahars killed an additional 500 people.

● Most volcanic eruptions are not as predictable as those of Mount Pinatubo. For example, the monitoring methods used at Pinatubo have been much less successful on Montserrat, in the Caribbean.

Predicting the Eruption of Mount St. Helens

● Earthquake tremors are often a sign that a volcano is about to erupt. In the months before the eruption of Mount St. Helens, small earthquakes, which grew in number and intensity, shook the area.

On March 27, 1980, the volcano began venting steam and ash. Geologists had set up seismometers to record the frequency, location, and magnitude of the quakes. Electronic surveying equipment employed laser beams to measure ground swelling as the lava dome rose. Tiltmeters measured changes in the mountain's slope. Stream gauges recorded water temperatures, pH levels, and amounts of dissolved minerals in the waters around the volcano. Gas sensors on the ground and in aircraft monitored hydrogen, carbon dioxide, and sulfur dioxide levels that might signal the movement of magma toward the surface.

Is That a Fact!

◆ The youngest Hawaiian "island," Loihi, is 3,500 m above the ocean floor. But it must grow almost 1 km before coming out of the ocean, which, scientists say, could take more than 20,000 years. However, it is difficult to predict when the volcano will become an island. For example, during a 1997 eruption the summit of Loihi sank by 50 to 100 m!

SciLinks is maintained by the National Science Teachers Association to provide you and your students with interesting, up-to-date links that will enrich your classroom presentation of the chapter.

Visit www.scilinks.org and enter the SciLinks code for more information about the topic listed.

Topic: Volcanic Eruptions
SciLinks code: HSM1616

Topic: What Causes Volcanoes?
SciLinks code: HSM1654

Topic: Volcanic Effects
SciLinks code: HSM1615

Overview

This chapter discusses volcanoes, the effects of eruptions, and how eruptions are predicted. About 500 million people live near active volcanoes. Volcanoes are carefully studied so that eruptions may be predicted.

Assessing Prior Knowledge

Students should be familiar with the following topics:

• the rock cycle
• plate tectonics
• changes of state

Identifying Misconceptions

Students may think that all volcanic eruptions are explosive and destructive. Point out that the majority of volcanic activity is nonexplosive. Also, reinforce the idea that volcanic activity plays a major role in forming the Earth's crust and in creating fertile land. Students may also think that volcanoes are uncommon and that volcanic activity is rare. Point out that the Earth has more than 1,300 active volcanoes and that at any moment, between 1 and 20 volcanoes are erupting on land. Many more volcanoes are erupting on the ocean floor. Volcano World is a Website that has updates on volcanoes that are currently erupting.

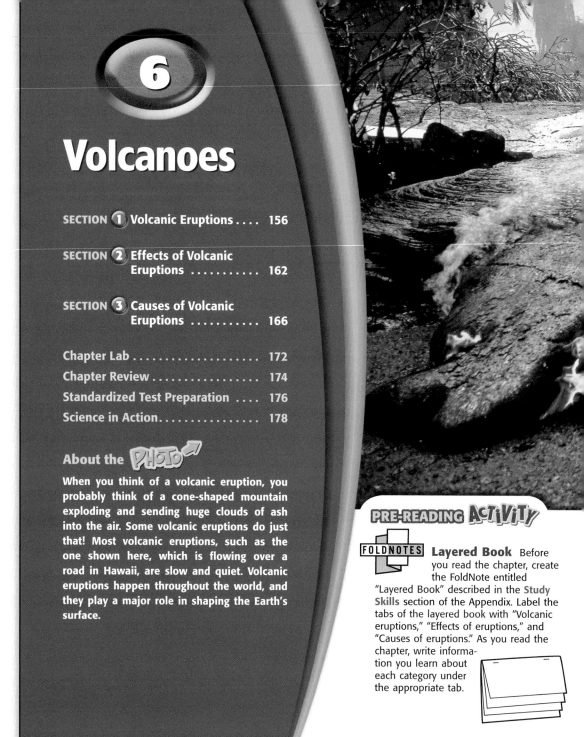

6

Volcanoes

About the PHOTO

When you think of a volcanic eruption, you probably think of a cone-shaped mountain exploding and sending huge clouds of ash into the air. Some volcanic eruptions do just that! Most volcanic eruptions, such as the one shown here, which is flowing over a road in Hawaii, are slow and quiet. Volcanic eruptions happen throughout the world, and they play a major role in shaping the Earth's surface.

PRE-READING ACTIVITY

FOLDNOTES **Layered Book** Before you read the chapter, create the FoldNote entitled "Layered Book" described in the **Study Skills** section of the Appendix. Label the tabs of the layered book with "Volcanic eruptions," "Effects of eruptions," and "Causes of eruptions." As you read the chapter, write information you learn about each category under the appropriate tab.

Standards Correlations

National Science Education Standards

The following codes indicate the National Science Education Standards that correlate to this chapter. The full text of the standards is at the front of the book.

Chapter Opener
SAI 1; ST 1; SPSP 3, 4

Section 1 Volcanic Eruptions
SAI 1; HNS 2; ES 1c

Section 2 Effects of Volcanic Eruptions
ST 2; SPSP 3, 4; ES 1c; *LabBook:* SAI 1

Section 3 Causes of Volcanic Eruptions
UCP 3; SAI 1; ST 2; ES 1b, 1c

Chapter Lab
SAI 1; ST 2

Chapter Review
ES 1b, 1c

Science In Action
SPSP 3, SPSP 5; HNS 1, 2

START-UP ACTIVITY

Anticipation

In this activity, you will build a simple model of a volcano and you will try to predict an eruption.

Procedure

1. Place **10 mL of baking soda** on a sheet of tissue. Fold the corners of the tissue over the baking soda, and place the tissue packet in a **large pan.**

2. Put **modeling clay** around the top edge of a **funnel.** Press that end of the funnel over the tissue packet to make a tight seal.

3. After you put on **safety goggles,** add **50 mL of vinegar** and **several drops of liquid dish soap** to a **200 mL beaker** and stir.

4. Predict how long it will take the volcano to erupt after the liquid is poured into the funnel. Then, carefully pour the liquid into the funnel, and use a **stopwatch** to measure how long the volcano takes to begin erupting.

Analysis

1. Based on your observations, explain what happened to cause the eruption.

2. How accurate was your prediction? By how many seconds did the class predictions vary?

3. How do the size of the funnel opening and the amount of baking soda and vinegar affect the amount of time that the volcano takes to erupt?

Focus

Overview

In this section, students will learn how the composition of magma affects volcanic eruptions. Students will also learn to identify the internal structure of a volcano and the types of lava and pyroclastic material released during an eruption.

Bellringer

Have students create in their **science journal** a labeled drawing that illustrates what happens when a volcano erupts. Then, have students describe the photographs shown on this page and the next. Ask them to think about why the characteristics of volcanic eruptions vary.

Motivate

ACTiViTY ——— GENERAL

Writing

Volcano Pen Pals Have students write a letter to a friend from a fictional survivor of a volcanic eruption. Have students describe the volcano hours before the eruption, during the eruption, and after the eruption. Students can then exchange letters and read the letters to the class. **LS Verbal**

Volcanic Eruptions

Think about the force released when the first atomic bomb exploded during World War II. Now imagine an explosion 10,000 times stronger, and you will get an idea of how powerful a volcanic eruption can be.

The explosive pressure of a volcanic eruption can turn an entire mountain into a billowing cloud of ash and rock in a matter of seconds. But eruptions are also creative forces—they help form fertile farmland. They also create some of the largest mountains on Earth. During an eruption, molten rock, or *magma,* is forced to the Earth's surface. Magma that flows onto the Earth's surface is called *lava.* **Volcanoes** are areas of Earth's surface through which magma and volcanic gases pass.

Nonexplosive Eruptions

At this moment, volcanic eruptions are occurring around the world—on the ocean floor and on land. Nonexplosive eruptions are the most common type of eruption. These eruptions produce relatively calm flows of lava, such as those shown in **Figure 1.** Nonexplosive eruptions can release huge amounts of lava. Vast areas of the Earth's surface, including much of the sea floor and the Northwest region of the United States, are covered with lava from nonexplosive eruptions.

READING WARM-UP

Objectives

● Distinguish between nonexplosive and explosive volcanic eruptions.

● Identify the features of a volcano.

● Explain how the composition of magma affects the type of volcanic eruption that will occur.

● Describe four types of lava and four types of pyroclastic material.

Terms to Learn

volcano   vent
magma chamber

READING STRATEGY

Reading Organizer As you read this section, make a table comparing types of lava and pyroclastic material.

volcano a vent or fissure in the Earth's surface through which magma and gases are expelled

Figure 1   **Examples of Nonexplosive Eruptions**

Sometimes, nonexplosive eruptions can spray lava into the air. Lava fountains, such as this one, pulse with the pressure of escaping gases.

▲ The speed of a lava flow can range from a slow creep to as fast as 60 km/h.

CHAPTER RESOURCES

Chapter Resource File

• Lesson Plan
• Directed Reading A **BASIC**
• Directed Reading B **SPECIAL NEEDS**

Technology

Transparencies
• Bellringer

MISCONCEPTION
///ALERT\\\

Nonexplosive Eruptions Although explosive volcanoes get the most attention, nonexplosive eruptions play a much more significant role in shaping our world. For instance, much of the ocean floor is basaltic pillow lava, and nonexplosive volcanoes formed many of the islands in the Pacific Ocean.

Explosive Eruptions

Explosive eruptions, such as the one shown in **Figure 2,** are much rarer than nonexplosive eruptions. However, the effects of explosive eruptions can be incredibly destructive. During an explosive eruption, clouds of hot debris, ash, and gas rapidly shoot out from a volcano. Instead of producing lava flows, explosive eruptions cause molten rock to be blown into tiny particles that harden in the air. The dust-sized particles, called *ash,* can reach the upper atmosphere and can circle the Earth for years. Larger pieces of debris fall closer to the volcano. An explosive eruption can also blast millions of tons of lava and rock from a volcano. In a matter of seconds, an explosive eruption can demolish an entire mountainside, as shown in **Figure 3.**

✔ **Reading Check** List two differences between explosive and nonexplosive eruptions. (*See the Appendix for answers to Reading Checks.*)

Figure 2 *In what resembles a nuclear explosion, volcanic ash rockets skyward during the 1990 eruption of Mount Redoubt in Alaska.*

Figure 3 *Within seconds, the 1980 eruption of Mount St. Helens in Washington State caused the side of the mountain to collapse. The blast scorched and flattened 600 km² of forest.*

Section 1 • Volcanic Eruptions **157**

CONNECTION to
Physical Science—**ADVANCED**

States of Matter Use the teaching transparency entitled "Models of a Solid, a Liquid, and a Gas" to discuss changes of state in magma. When water or carbon dioxide is a part of the crystal structure of minerals in a rock, these compounds are in the solid state. When rock melts to form magma, the water or carbon dioxide is released into the molten liquid. In other words, the water or carbon dioxide is dissolved in the magma. When temperature and pressure conditions are right, water and carbon dioxide in the magma solution *exsolve,* or vaporize, changing from liquid to gas. The exsolution of gases forms bubbles that greatly increase the volume of the magma. When the magma erupts on the surface, it cools and solidifies, changing from a liquid to a solid. The gases escape into the air, but they leave distinctive round holes called *vesicles.* **LS** Visual

Answer to Reading Check

Because silica-rich magma has a high viscosity, it tends to trap gases and plug volcanic vents. This causes pressure to build up and can result in an explosive eruption.

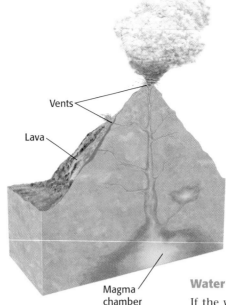

Figure 4 *Volcanoes form when lava is released from vents.*

Vents
Lava
Magma chamber

magma chamber the body of molten rock that feeds a volcano

vent an opening at the surface of the Earth through which volcanic material passes

What Is Inside a Volcano?

If you could look inside an erupting volcano, you would see the features shown in **Figure 4.** A **magma chamber** is a body of molten rock deep underground that feeds a volcano. Magma rises from the magma chamber through cracks in the Earth's crust to openings called **vents.** Magma is released from the vents during an eruption.

What Makes Up Magma?

By comparing the composition of magma from different eruptions, scientists have made an important discovery. The composition of the magma affects how explosive a volcanic eruption is. The key to whether an eruption will be explosive lies in the silica, water, and gas content of the magma.

Water and Magma Are an Explosive Combination

If the water content of magma is high, an explosive eruption is more likely. Because magma is underground, it is under intense pressure and water stays dissolved in the magma. If the magma quickly moves to the surface, the pressure suddenly decreases and the water and other compounds, such as carbon dioxide, become gases. As the gases expand rapidly, an explosion can result. This process is similar to what happens when you shake a can of soda and open it. When a can of soda is shaken, the CO_2 dissolved in the soda is released and pressure builds up. When the can is opened, the soda shoots out, just as lava shoots out of a volcano during an explosive eruption. In fact, some lava is so frothy with gas when it reaches the surface that its solid form, called *pumice,* can float in water!

Silica-Rich Magma Traps Explosive Gases

Magma that has a high silica content also tends to cause explosive eruptions. Silica-rich magma has a stiff consistency. It flows slowly and tends to harden in a volcano's vents. As a result, it plugs the vent. As more magma pushes up from below, pressure increases. If enough pressure builds up, an explosive eruption takes place. Stiff magma also prevents water vapor and other gases from easily escaping. Gas bubbles trapped in magma can expand until they explode. When they explode, the magma shatters and ash and pumice are blasted from the vent. Magma that contains less silica has a more fluid, runnier consistency. Because gases escape this type of magma more easily, explosive eruptions are less likely to occur.

✓ **Reading Check** How do silica levels affect an eruption?

CHAPTER RESOURCES

Technology

Transparencies
- *LINK TO PHYSICAL SCIENCE* Models of a Solid, a Liquid, and a Gas
- Four Types of Lava

Lava cools very slowly not only because it is very hot to start with but also because it is a good insulator. When a lava flow in Mexico in 1952 stopped, the flow was 10 m thick. Four years later, in 1956, the lava still steamed when it rained.

What Erupts from a Volcano?

Magma erupts as either lava or pyroclastic (PIE roh KLAS tik) material. *Lava* is liquid magma that flows from a volcanic vent. *Pyroclastic material* forms when magma is blasted into the air and hardens. Nonexplosive eruptions produce mostly lava. Explosive eruptions produce mostly pyroclastic material. Over many years—or even during the same eruption—a volcano's eruptions may alternate between lava and pyroclastic eruptions.

Types of Lava

The viscosity of lava, or how lava flows, varies greatly. To understand viscosity, remember that a milkshake has high viscosity and a glass of milk has low viscosity. Lava that has high viscosity is stiff. Lava that has low viscosity is more fluid. The viscosity of lava affects the surface of a lava flow in different ways, as shown in **Figure 5.** *Blocky lava* and *pahoehoe* (puh HOY HOY) have a high viscosity and flow slowly. Other types of lava flows, such as *aa* (AH AH) and *pillow lava,* have lower viscosities and flow more quickly.

CONNECTION TO
Social Studies

Fertile Farmlands Volcanic ash helps create some of the most fertile farmland in the world. Use a world map and reference materials to find the location of volcanoes that have helped create farmland in Italy, Africa, South America, and the United States. Make an illustrated map on a piece of poster board to share your findings.

ACTIVITY

Figure 5 Four Types of Lava

◄ **Aa** is so named because of the painful experience of walking barefoot across its jagged surface. This lava pours out quickly and forms a brittle crust. The crust is torn into jagged pieces as molten lava continues to flow underneath.

Pahoehoe lava flows slowly, ► like wax dripping from a candle. Its glassy surface has rounded wrinkles.

◄ **Pillow lava** forms when lava erupts underwater. As you can see here, this lava forms rounded lumps that are the shape of pillows.

Blocky lava is cool, stiff lava ► that does not travel far from the erupting vent. Blocky lava usually oozes from a volcano and forms jumbled heaps of sharp-edged chunks.

Group ACTIVITY — GENERAL

Describing Viscosity Introduce the concept of viscosity by having students describe the observable differences in flow rate as you pour molasses or honey, vegetable oil, and water down a gently sloping cookie sheet. (They should observe that the molasses or honey flows slowest, oil flows somewhat faster, and water flows very fast.) Explain that viscosity is a liquid's resistance to flow. Honey has a high viscosity, so it flows very slowly. Water has a low viscosity, so it flows quickly. Ask the students how magma's composition affects its viscosity. (The more silica that is present in magma, the greater the viscosity of the magma.) **LS Logical**

INCLUSION Strategies

- *Visually Impaired*
- *Learning Disabled*
- *Behavior Control Issues*

Organize students into small groups. Give each group colored modeling clay, a piece of cardboard, and self-stick notes. Have each group create a cross-section of a volcano on the cardboard using the modeling clay. Next, students should label the parts of their model using the self-stick notes. After the volcano is labeled, students should add notes with three facts they have learned about volcanoes and attach the notes to the base of their model. **LS Kinesthetic**

MISCONCEPTION ALERT

The Force of Water Students may think that it seems illogical that water makes magma more likely to explode. Explain that magma contains water and that the water is dissolved in the magma. When the water changes from a liquid to a gas, the volume of the magma increases dramatically. This change causes a pressure increase that can generate a large explosive force. Discuss with students what would happen if water is boiled in a pot with a tight lid. Then, have students think of other examples in which water can have an explosive force, such as in a car's radiator or in popcorn.

Reteaching — BASIC

Volcano Field Guide Have students make an illustrated field guide to volcanic eruptions and types of lava. Students can add to the field guides as they read other sections in this chapter.
LS Visual

Quiz — GENERAL

1. Describe the lava flow from a nonexplosive eruption. (a calm stream of magma that flows out of a vent onto Earth's surface)

2. Describe an explosive eruption. (Ash, hot debris, gases, and chunks of rock spew from a volcano.)

3. Define *blocky lava, pahoehoe,* and *aa.* (Blocky lava is cool, stiff lava that doesn't travel far from the erupting vent. Pahoehoe is lava that flows slowly and forms a wrinkled surface. Aa is lava that flows more quickly than pahoehoe and that forms a brittle, jagged crust.)

Alternative Assessment — BASIC

Making Lava Provide students with cornstarch, salt, and water to make a paste. Then, have students experiment with the ingredients to create representations of the types of lava discussed in this section. Have students work independently to describe the eruptions that would produce each lava type.
LS Kinesthetic

Figure 6 Four Types of Pyroclastic Material

 **Volcanic bombs** are large blobs of magma that harden in the air. The shape of this bomb was caused by the magma spinning through the air as it cooled.

 **Lapilli,** which means "little stones" in Italian, are pebblelike bits of magma that hardened before they hit the ground.

 **Volcanic ash** forms when the gases in stiff magma expand rapidly and the walls of the gas bubbles explode into tiny, glasslike slivers. Ash makes up most of the pyroclastic material in an eruption.

 **Volcanic blocks,** the largest pieces of pyroclastic material, are pieces of solid rock erupted from a volcano.

Types of Pyroclastic Material

Pyroclastic material forms when magma explodes from a volcano and solidifies in the air. This material also forms when powerful eruptions shatter existing rock. The size of pyroclastic material ranges from boulders that are the size of houses to tiny particles that can remain suspended in the atmosphere for years. **Figure 6** shows four types of pyroclastic material: volcanic bombs, volcanic blocks, lapilli (lah PIL IE), and volcanic ash.

✓ **Reading Check** Describe four types of pyroclastic material.

Quick Lab

Modeling an Explosive Eruption

1. Inflate a **large balloon,** and place it in a **cardboard box.**
2. Spread a **sheet** on the floor. Place the box in the middle of the sheet. Mound a thin layer of **sand** over the balloon to make a volcano that is taller than the edges of the box.
3. Lightly mist the volcano with **water.** Sprinkle **tempera paint** on the volcano until the volcano is completely covered.
4. Place **small objects** such as **raisins** randomly on the volcano. Draw a sketch of the volcano.
5. Put on your **safety goggles.** Pop the balloon with a **pin.**
6. Use a **metric ruler** to calculate the average distance that 10 grains of sand and 10 raisins traveled.
7. How did the relative weight of each type of material affect the average distance that the material traveled?
8. Draw a sketch of the exploded volcano.

Answers to Quick Lab

7. Sample answer: Lighter materials such as sand traveled farther than heavier materials such as raisins.

8. Sketches may vary.

Teacher's Notes: This activity will work best if students use a very large balloon and if they cover the top of the balloon with a minimal amount of sand. Placing a few tablespoons of talcum powder inside the balloon will create a more dramatic effect when the balloon is popped. This activity models caldera formation as well. Students who have asthma or allergies to airborne particles should wear a filter mask for this activity.

Answer to Reading Check

Volcanic bombs are large blobs of magma that harden in the air. Lapilli are small pieces of magma that harden in the air. Volcanic blocks are pieces of solid rock erupted from a volcano. Ash forms when gases in stiff magma expand rapidly and the walls of the gas bubbles shatter into tiny glasslike slivers.

Pyroclastic Flows

One particularly dangerous type of volcanic flow is called a *pyroclastic flow*. Pyroclastic flows are produced when enormous amounts of hot ash, dust, and gases are ejected from a volcano. This glowing cloud of pyroclastic material can race downhill at speeds of more than 200 km/h—faster than most hurricane-force winds! The temperature at the center of a pyroclastic flow can exceed 700°C. A pyroclastic flow from the eruption of Mount Pinatubo is shown in **Figure 7**. Fortunately, scientists were able to predict the eruption and a quarter of a million people were evacuated before the eruption.

Figure 7 *The 1991 eruption of Mount Pinatubo in the Philippines released terrifying pyroclastic flows.*

SECTION Review

Summary

- Volcanoes erupt both explosively and nonexplosively.
- Magma that has a high level of water, CO_2, or silica tends to erupt explosively.
- Lava can be classified by its viscosity and by the surface texture of lava flows.
- Pyroclastic material, such as ash and volcanic bombs, forms when magma solidifies as it travels through the air.

Using Key Terms

1. In your own words, write a definition for each of the following terms: *volcano, magma chamber,* and *vent.*

Understanding Key Ideas

2. Which of the following factors influences whether a volcano erupts explosively?
   a. the concentration of volcanic bombs in the magma
   b. the concentration of phosphorus in the magma
   c. the concentration of aa in the magma
   d. the concentration of water in the magma

3. How are lava and pyroclastic material classified? Describe four types of lava.

4. Which produces more pyroclastic material: an explosive eruption or a nonexplosive eruption?

5. Explain how the presence of silica and water in magma increases the chances of an explosive eruption.

6. What is a pyroclastic flow?

Math Skills

7. A sample of magma is 64% silica. Express this percentage as a simplified fraction.

Critical Thinking

8. **Analyzing Ideas** How is an explosive eruption similar to opening a can of soda that has been shaken? Be sure to describe the role of carbon dioxide.

9. **Making Inferences** Predict the silica content of aa, pillow lava, and blocky lava.

10. **Making Inferences** Explain why the names of many types of lava are Hawaiian but the names of many types of pyroclastic material are Italian and Indonesian.

SciLINKS®

Developed and maintained by the National Science Teachers Association

For a variety of links related to this chapter, go to www.scilinks.org

Topic: Volcanic Eruptions
SciLinks code: HSM1616

Homework ——— GENERAL

Writing **Deadly Mudflows** *Lahar* is an Indonesian term for a particularly deadly kind of volcanic mudflow. A lahar is a flow of water-saturated volcanic debris that races down the slope of a volcano with the consistency of wet cement. Volcanic debris can be saturated by the melting of ice or snow during an eruption, or by rain afterwards. When Nevado del Ruiz erupted in Colombia, its lahar killed more than 25,000 people. Have students research lahars from two eruptions. **LS Intrapersonal**

CHAPTER RESOURCES

Chapter Resource File

- **Section Quiz** GENERAL
- **Section Review** GENERAL
- **Vocabulary and Section Summary** GENERAL
- **Datasheet for Quick Lab**

Answers to Section Review

1. Sample answer: A volcano is a landform created by repeated eruptions of lava. A magma chamber is an underground body of magma that feeds a volcano. A vent is an opening through which lava or pyroclastic material passes.

2. d

3. Lava is classified by its surface texture. The way that lava flows may also be used to help classify it. Pyroclastic material is classified by size and how it forms. Four types of lava are aa, pahoehoe, blocky lava, and pillow lava. Aa flows quickly and has a jagged crust. Pahoehoe flows slowly and has a wrinkled surface. Pillow lava erupts underwater and forms rounded lumps. Blocky lava is cool, stiff lava that does not travel far from the erupting vent.

4. an explosive eruption

5. The presence of water increases the chance of an explosive eruption because as the magma body moves toward the surface, the water changes to a gas and expands rapidly. This rapid expansion causes an explosion. Silica-rich magma tends to trap volcanic gases and plug vents. The resulting pressure increase can cause an explosive eruption.

6. A pyroclastic flow is a cloud of very hot ash, dust, and gases that flows from a volcano.

7. $64/100 = 32/50 = 16/25$

8. Magma and soda have carbon dioxide dissolved in them. When the pressure on the magma and the soda is reduced, the carbon dioxide becomes a gas and expands rapidly.

9. Aa and pillow lava have a low viscosity, so they have a low silica content. Blocky lava has a high viscosity, so it has a high silica content.

10. Students should conclude that Indonesian and Italian volcanoes are more likely to erupt explosively than Hawaiian volcanoes.

Focus

Overview

This section explores the effects of volcanic eruptions on Earth. Students will learn to identify different types of volcanoes and physical features created by volcanic activity, such as craters and calderas.

 Bellringer

Write the following terms on the board:

composite volcano, shield volcano, cinder cone volcano, volcanic crater, caldera

Group students in teams of three, and have the groups look through the section to come up with a definition for each of the terms. Have them record their definitions and revise the definitions after they read the section.

Motivate

Discussion ——— GENERAL

Student Impressions of Eruptions Have students discuss the most exciting images they've seen in movies and television programs featuring volcanoes. Have them describe what they think about volcanic eruptions in their **science journal** so that they can revisit these impressions after reading this section. **LS Verbal**

SECTION
2

Effects of Volcanic Eruptions

In 1816, Chauncey Jerome, a resident of Connecticut, wrote that the clothes his wife had laid out to dry the day before had frozen during the night. This event would not have been unusual except that the date was June 10!

At that time, residents of New England did not know that the explosion of a volcanic island on the other side of the world had severely changed the global climate and was causing "The Year Without a Summer."

Volcanic Eruptions and Climate Change

The explosion of Mount Tambora in 1815 blanketed most of Indonesia in darkness for three days. It is estimated that 12,000 people died directly from the explosion and 80,000 people died from the resulting hunger and disease. The global effects of the eruption were not felt until the next year, however. During large-scale eruptions, enormous amounts of volcanic ash and gases are ejected into the upper atmosphere.

As volcanic ash and gases spread throughout the atmosphere, they can block enough sunlight to cause global temperatures to drop. The Tambora eruption affected the global climate enough to cause food shortages in North America and Europe. More recently, the eruption of Mount Pinatubo, shown in **Figure 1,** caused average global temperatures to drop by as much as 0.5°C. Although this may seem insignificant, such a shift can disrupt climates all over the world.

✓ Reading Check How does a volcanic eruption affect climate? *(See the Appendix for answers to Reading Checks.)*

Figure 1 *Ash from the eruption of Mount Pinatubo blocked out the sun in the Philippines for several days. The eruption also affected global climate.*

READING WARM-UP

Objectives

● Explain how volcanic eruptions can affect climate.
● Compare the three types of volcanoes.
● Compare craters, calderas, and lava plateaus.

Terms to Learn

crater
caldera
lava plateau

READING STRATEGY

Paired Summarizing Read this section silently. In pairs, take turns summarizing the material. Stop to discuss ideas that seem confusing.

CHAPTER RESOURCES

Chapter Resource File

 • Lesson Plan
 • Directed Reading A BASIC
 • Directed Reading B SPECIAL NEEDS

Technology

 Transparencies
 • Bellringer
 • Three Types of Volcanoes

Answer to Reading Check

Eruptions release large quantities of ash and gases, which can block sunlight and cause global temperatures to drop.

Different Types of Volcanoes

Volcanic eruptions can cause profound changes in climate. But the changes to Earth's surface caused by eruptions are probably more familiar. Perhaps the best known of all volcanic landforms are the volcanoes themselves. The three basic types of volcanoes are illustrated in **Figure 2.**

Shield Volcanoes

Shield volcanoes are built of layers of lava released from repeated nonexplosive eruptions. Because the lava is very runny, it spreads out over a wide area. Over time, the layers of lava create a volcano that has gently sloping sides. Although their sides are not very steep, shield volcanoes can be enormous. Hawaii's Mauna Kea, the shield volcano shown here, is the tallest mountain on Earth. Measured from its base on the sea floor, Mauna Kea is taller than Mount Everest.

Cinder Cone Volcanoes

Cinder cone volcanoes are made of pyroclastic material usually produced from moderately explosive eruptions. The pyroclastic material forms steep slopes, as shown in this photo of the Mexican volcano Paricutín. Cinder cones are small and usually erupt for only a short time. Paricutín appeared in a cornfield in 1943 and erupted for only nine years before stopping at a height of 400 m. Cinder cones often occur in clusters, commonly on the sides of other volcanoes. They usually erode quickly because the pyroclastic material is not cemented together.

Composite Volcanoes

Composite volcanoes, sometimes called *stratovolcanoes,* are one of the most common types of volcanoes. They form from explosive eruptions of pyroclastic material followed by quieter flows of lava. The combination of both types of eruptions forms alternating layers of pyroclastic material and lava. Composite volcanoes, such as Japan's Mount Fuji (shown here), have broad bases and sides that get steeper toward the top. Composite volcanoes in the western region of the United States include Mount Hood, Mount Rainier, Mount Shasta, and Mount St. Helens.

Figure 2 Three Types of Volcanoes

Shield volcano

Cinder cone volcano

Composite volcano

Reteaching ——— BASIC

Section Quizzes Have students write five quiz questions based on the section. Students should exchange questions and then grade each other's work. Collect the quizzes, and use the best questions in an open-book quiz.

Quiz ——— GENERAL

1. Describe the shapes of shield, cinder cone, and composite volcanoes. (shield volcano: broad with gentle, shallow slopes; cinder cone volcano: generally smaller and steeper with more angled sides; composite volcano: high, covers less area than shield volcanoes, and has sides that are steeper near the peak)

2. What is a lava plateau? (It is a wide, flat landform that is formed from repeated nonexplosive eruptions of lava that spread over a large area.)

Alternative Assessment ——— GENERAL

Volcano Poster Have students draw a poster of each type of volcano. Students must label and write a caption for all of the volcano's parts. Students should also create a cartoon-panel illustration of how craters and calderas form. **LS Visual**

Answer to Reading Check

Calderas form when a magma chamber partially empties and the roof overlying the chamber collapses.

Figure 3 A crater, such as this one in Kamchatka, Russia, forms around the central vent of a volcano.

crater a funnel-shaped pit near the top of the central vent of a volcano

caldera a large, semicircular depression that forms when the magma chamber below a volcano partially empties and causes the ground above to sink

Other Types of Volcanic Landforms

In addition to volcanoes, other landforms are produced by volcanic activity. These landforms include craters, calderas, and lava plateaus. Read on to learn more about these landforms.

Craters

Around the central vent at the top of many volcanoes is a funnel-shaped pit called a **crater.** An example of a crater is shown in **Figure 3.** During less explosive eruptions, lava flows and pyroclastic material can pile up around the vent creating a cone with a central crater. As the eruption stops, the lava that is left in the crater often drains back underground. The vent may then collapse to form a larger crater. If the lava hardens in the crater, the next eruption may blast it away. In this way, a crater becomes larger and deeper.

Calderas

Calderas can appear similar to craters, but they are many times larger. A **caldera** is a large, semicircular depression that forms when the chamber that supplies magma to a volcano partially empties and the chamber's roof collapses. As a result, the ground above the magma chamber sinks, as shown in **Figure 4.** Much of Yellowstone Park is made up of three large calderas that formed when volcanoes collapsed between 1.9 million and 0.6 million years ago. Today, hot springs, such as Old Faithful, are heated by the thermal energy left over from those events.

✓ **Reading Check** How do calderas form?

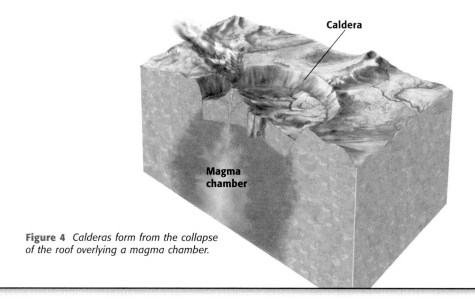

Figure 4 Calderas form from the collapse of the roof overlying a magma chamber.

Labels: Caldera, Magma chamber

CONNECTION ACTIVITY
Astronomy ——— ADVANCED

Lunar Maria Early astronomers thought that the dark patches on the moon were lunar seas. Thus, the areas were called *maria,* which is Latin for "seas." Today, we know that the dark patches are basins filled with basaltic lava that erupted after the moon's formation. Most of the lunar maria are on the side of the moon that faces Earth. Scientists think that after the moon's formation, the tidal attraction of Earth caused volcanic eruptions on the side of the moon that faces Earth. Like the jelly that comes out of a donut when it is squeezed, lava was pushed out of the moon by the Earth's gravitational force deforming the moon's suface more on the side closer to Earth. Have students research volcanism on another planet or moon in our solar system and report their findings to the class. **LS Logical**

Lava Plateaus

The most massive outpourings of lava do not come from individual volcanoes. Most of the lava on Earth's surface erupted from long cracks, or *rifts,* in the crust. In this type of eruption, runny lava can pour out for millions of years and spread over huge areas. A landform that results from repeated eruptions of lava spread over a large area is called a **lava plateau.** The Columbia River Plateau, part of which is shown in **Figure 5,** is a lava plateau that formed between 17 million and 14 million years ago in the northwestern region of the United States. In some places, the Columbia River Plateau is 3 km thick.

Figure 5 *The Columbia River Plateau formed from a massive outpouring of lava that began 17 million years ago.*

lava plateau a wide, flat landform that results from repeated nonexplosive eruptions of lava that spread over a large area

SECTION Review

Summary

- The large volumes of gas and ash released from volcanic eruptions can affect climate.
- Shield volcanoes result from many eruptions of relatively runny lava.
- Cinder cone volcanoes result from mildly explosive eruptions of pyroclastic material.
- Composite volcanoes result from alternating explosive and nonexplosive eruptions.
- Craters, calderas, and lava plateaus are volcanic landforms.

Using Key Terms

Complete each of the following sentences by choosing the correct term from the word bank.

> caldera   crater

1. A ___ is a funnel-shaped hole around the central vent.

2. A ___ results when a magma chamber partially empties.

Understanding Key Ideas

3. Which type of volcano results from alternating explosive and nonexplosive eruptions?
   a. composite volcano
   b. cinder cone volcano
   c. rift-zone volcano
   d. shield volcano

4. Why do cinder cone volcanoes have narrower bases and steeper sides than shield volcanoes do?

5. Why does a volcano's crater tend to get larger over time?

Math Skills

6. The fastest lava flow recorded was 60 km/h. A horse can gallop as fast as 48 mi/h. Could a galloping horse outrun the fastest lava flow? (Hint: 1 km = 0.621 mi)

Critical Thinking

7. **Making Inferences** Why did it take a year for the effects of the Tambora eruption to be experienced in New England?

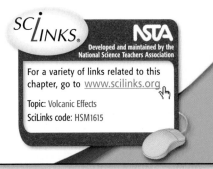

For a variety of links related to this chapter, go to www.scilinks.org

Topic: Volcanic Effects
SciLinks code: HSM1615

SCIENTISTS AT ODDS

Did Volcanism Play a Role in Dinosaur Extinctions? Most scientists think that the dinosaurs became extinct 65 million years ago when a large asteroid struck Earth. However, some scientists think that climatic changes caused by a period of catastrophic volcanism that occurred before and after the impact may have been a factor in the extinctions. Encourage students to find out more about these scientific hypotheses.

SECTION

3

Focus

Overview

In this section, students will learn how magma forms and how pressure affects the temperature at which rocks melt. The section draws a connection between volcanic activity and tectonic movement and concludes with a discussion of the challenges involved in predicting eruptions.

 Bellringer

Ask students to imagine that they live on a volcanic island. Have them list in their **science journal** the signals that would tell them the volcano was about to erupt.

Motivate

Discussion ——— GENERAL

Volcano Safety   Have students brainstorm measures a community could take to protect citizens from a volcanic eruption and then write their ideas in their **science journal.** Have them compare their suggestions with the information they learn in the chapter. **LS Logical**

READING WARM-UP

Objectives

● Describe the formation and movement of magma.

● Explain the relationship between volcanoes and plate tectonics.

● Summarize the methods scientists use to predict volcanic eruptions.

Terms to Learn

rift zone
hot spot

READING STRATEGY

Reading Organizer   As you read this section, make a flowchart of the steps of magma formation in different tectonic environments.

Causes of Volcanic Eruptions

More than 2,000 years ago, Pompeii was a busy Roman city near the sleeping volcano Mount Vesuvius. People did not see Vesuvius as much of a threat. Everything changed when Vesuvius suddenly erupted and buried the city in a deadly blanket of ash that was almost 20 ft thick!

Today, even more people are living on and near active volcanoes. Scientists closely monitor volcanoes to avoid this type of disaster. They study the gases coming from active volcanoes and look for slight changes in the volcano's shape that could indicate that an eruption is near. Scientists know much more about the causes of eruptions than the ancient Pompeiians did, but there is much more to be discovered.

The Formation of Magma

Understanding how magma forms helps explain why volcanoes erupt. Magma forms in the deeper regions of the Earth's crust and in the uppermost layers of the mantle where the temperature and pressure are very high. Changes in pressure and temperature cause magma to form.

Pressure and Temperature

Part of the upper mantle is made of very hot, puttylike rock that flows slowly. The rock of the mantle is hot enough to melt at Earth's surface, but it remains a puttylike solid because of pressure. This pressure is caused by the weight of the rock above the mantle. In other words, the rock above the mantle presses the atoms of the mantle so close together that the rock cannot melt. As **Figure 1** shows, rock melts when its temperature increases or when the pressure on the rock decreases.

Figure 1 *The curved line indicates the melting point of a rock. As pressure decreases and temperature increases, the rock begins to melt.*

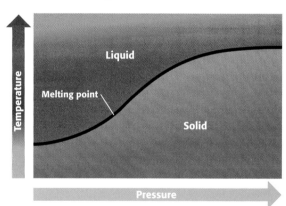

CHAPTER RESOURCES

Chapter Resource File

- Lesson Plan
- Directed Reading A BASIC
- Directed Reading B SPECIAL NEEDS

Technology

Transparencies
- Bellringer
- The Location of Major Volcanoes

Magma Formation in the Mantle

Because the temperature of the mantle is fairly constant, a decrease in pressure is the most common cause of magma formation. Magma often forms at the boundary between separating tectonic plates, where pressure is decreased. Once formed, the magma is less dense than the surrounding rock, so the magma slowly rises toward the surface like an air bubble in a jar of honey.

Where Volcanoes Form

The locations of volcanoes give clues about how volcanoes form. The map in **Figure 2** shows the location of some of the world's major active volcanoes. The map also shows the boundaries between tectonic plates. A large number of volcanoes lie directly on tectonic plate boundaries. In fact, the plate boundaries surrounding the Pacific Ocean have so many volcanoes that the area is called the *Ring of Fire*.

Tectonic plate boundaries are areas where tectonic plates either collide, separate, or slide past one another. At these boundaries, it is possible for magma to form and travel to the surface. About 80% of active volcanoes on land form where plates collide, and about 15% form where plates separate. The remaining few occur far from tectonic plate boundaries.

Reading Check Why are most volcanoes on plate boundaries? *(See the Appendix for answers to Reading Checks.)*

Reaction to Stress

1. Make a pliable "rock" by pouring **60 mL of water** into a **plastic cup** and adding **150 mL of cornstarch**, 15 mL at a time. Stir well each time.

2. Pour half of the cornstarch mixture into a **clear bowl.** Carefully observe how the "rock" flows. Be patient—this process is slow!

3. Scrape the rest of the "rock" out of the cup with a **spoon.** Observe the behavior of the "rock" as you scrape.

4. What happened to the "rock" when you let it flow by itself? What happened when you put stress on the "rock"?

5. How is this pliable "rock" similar to the rock of the upper part of the mantle?

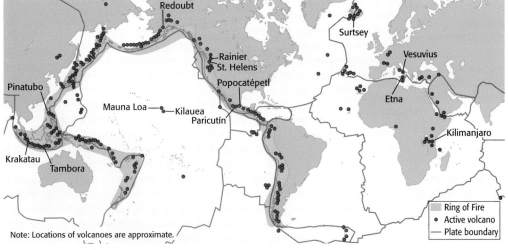

Figure 2 *Tectonic plate boundaries are likely places for volcanoes to form. The Ring of Fire contains nearly 75% of the world's active volcanoes on land.*

Note: Locations of volcanoes are approximate.

Map labels: Redoubt, Surtsey, Rainier, St. Helens, Vesuvius, Popocatépetl, Pinatubo, Mauna Loa, Kilauea, Paricutín, Etna, Krakatau, Tambora, Kilimanjaro

Legend:
- Ring of Fire
- Active volcano
- Plate boundary

Teach

Quick Lab

MATERIALS

FOR EACH GROUP
- bowl, clear
- cornstarch, 150 mL
- cup, plastic
- spoon
- water, 60 mL

Answers

4. When left alone, the "rock" flowed like a liquid does, but flowed very slowly. When stress was applied by the spoon, the "rock" broke like a solid does.

5. Sample answer: The artificial rock is like the mantle because the artificial rock is a puttylike solid that flows very slowly.

Answer to Reading Check

Volcanic activity is common at tectonic plate boundaries because magma tends to form at plate boundaries.

BRAIN FOOD

Rates of Cooling Affect Crystal Size

Igneous rocks form when magma cools and solidifies either at or beneath Earth's surface. Magma that solidifies deep underground usually cools much more slowly than magma that solidifies closer to the surface. The difference in the rate of cooling affects the texture of the igneous rock that forms. Rocks that form from magma that cools slowly contain larger crystals than rocks that form from magma that cools quickly. Ask students how scientists could use information about crystal size to study an igneous outcrop. (By studying mineral type and crystal size, scientists can determine the origin of igneous rock.)

Answer to Math Practice

9/5 × 1,400°C + 32 = 2,552°F

Using the Figure—GENERAL

Plate Tectonics Have students study **Figure 4,** in which a continental plate and an oceanic plate converge.

- Ask students which plate is more dense. (oceanic)

- Explain that when an oceanic plate sinks, or *subducts,* beneath another tectonic plate, the scraping, pushing, and jostling may cause earthquakes and tsunamis.

- Ask students what kind of tectonic plate contains more water. (oceanic)

- Have students explain how water content in mantle rock affects magma formation. (The more water that is present in mantle rock, the more likely the rock is to melt.)

- Have students explain how magma forms when these two tectonic plates converge. (The subducted oceanic plate moves downward, and the high water content and increased temperature cause the rock to melt and form magma.)

- Ask students if they think that explosive eruptions tend to occur near convergent or divergent boundaries. (They tend to occur near convergent boundaries because the water and silica content of the magma is higher near convergent boundaries.)

LS Logical/Visual

How Hot Is Hot?

Inside the Earth, magma can reach a burning-hot 1,400°C! You may be more familiar with Fahrenheit temperatures, so convert 1,400°C to degrees Fahrenheit by using the formula below.

°F = (°C ÷ 5 × 9) + 32

What is the temperature in degrees Fahrenheit?

rift zone an area of deep cracks that forms between two tectonic plates that are pulling away from each other

When Tectonic Plates Separate

At a *divergent boundary,* tectonic plates move away from each other. As tectonic plates separate, a set of deep cracks called a **rift zone** forms between the plates. Mantle rock then rises to fill in the gap. When mantle rock gets closer to the surface, the pressure decreases. The pressure decrease causes the mantle rock to melt and form magma. Because magma is less dense than the surrounding rock, it rises through the rifts. When the magma reaches the surface, it spills out and hardens, creating new crust, as shown in **Figure 3.**

Mid-Ocean Ridges Form at Divergent Boundaries

Lava that flows from undersea rift zones produces volcanoes and mountain chains called *mid-ocean ridges.* Just as a baseball has stitches, the Earth is circled with mid-ocean ridges. At these ridges, lava flows out and creates new crust. Most volcanic activity on Earth occurs at mid-ocean ridges. While most mid-ocean ridges are underwater, Iceland, with its volcanoes and hot springs, was created by lava from the Mid-Atlantic Ridge. In 1963, enough lava poured out of the Mid-Atlantic Ridge near Iceland to form a new island called *Surtsey.* Scientists watched this new island being born!

Figure 3 How Magma Forms at a Divergent Boundary

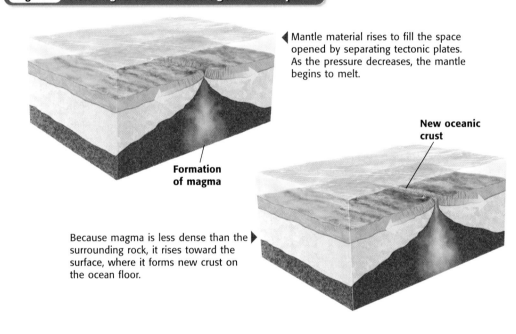

Mantle material rises to fill the space opened by separating tectonic plates. As the pressure decreases, the mantle begins to melt.

New oceanic crust

Formation of magma

Because magma is less dense than the surrounding rock, it rises toward the surface, where it forms new crust on the ocean floor.

CONNECTION ACTIVITY
Math ——————— GENERAL

Kilauea Kilauea, in Hawaii, is one of the most studied volcanoes in the world. It has been erupting regularly since 1983. Every day, enough lava to pave a two-lane road 32 km long pours from the volcano. Have students calculate how long this lava "road" would be if the volcano erupted at that rate for 40 years.

(365 days/y × 32 km/day = 11,680 km/y; 11,680 km/y × 40 y = 467,200 km, more than 10 times the Earth's circumference) **LS** Logical

CHAPTER RESOURCES
Technology
Transparencies
• How Magma Forms at a Divergent Boundary
• How Magma Forms at a Convergent Boundary

Figure 4 **How Magma Forms at a Convergent Boundary**

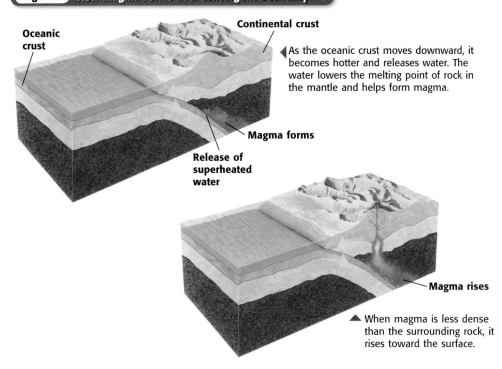

Oceanic crust

Continental crust

As the oceanic crust moves downward, it becomes hotter and releases water. The water lowers the melting point of rock in the mantle and helps form magma.

Magma forms

Release of superheated water

Magma rises

▲ When magma is less dense than the surrounding rock, it rises toward the surface.

When Tectonic Plates Collide

If you slide two pieces of notebook paper into one another on a flat desktop, the papers will either buckle upward or one piece of paper will move under the other. This is similar to what happens at a convergent boundary. A *convergent boundary* is a place where tectonic plates collide. When an oceanic plate collides with a continental plate, the oceanic plate usually slides underneath the continental plate. The process of *subduction,* the movement of one tectonic plate underneath another, is shown in **Figure 4.** Oceanic crust is subducted because it is denser and thinner than continental crust.

Subduction Produces Magma

As the descending oceanic crust scrapes past the continental crust, the temperature and pressure increase. The combination of increased heat and pressure causes the water contained in the oceanic crust to be released. The water then mixes with the mantle rock, which lowers the rock's melting point, causing it to melt. This body of magma can rise to form a volcano.

✓ **Reading Check** How does subduction produce magma?

SCHOOL to HOME

Tectonic Models

Create models of convergent and divergent boundaries by using materials of your choice. Have your teacher approve your list before you start building your model at home with a parent. In class, use your model to explain how each type of boundary leads to the formation of magma.

ACTIVITY

Answer to Reading Check

When a tectonic plate subducts, it becomes hotter and releases water. The water lowers the melting point of the rock above the plate, causing magma to form.

Reteaching —— BASIC

Mantle Plumes Compare a mantle plume to a candle flame and a tectonic plate to a piece of paper passing over the flame. The point on Earth's surface above the mantle plume is called a hot spot. **LS Visual**

English Language Learners

Quiz —— GENERAL

1. What conditions make magma rise? (when magma is less dense than the surrounding rock and when magma has a pathway to the surface)

2. Define a rift zone. (an area of deep cracks that forms at a divergent boundary)

Alternative Assessment —— ADVANCED

Tectonics and Volcanoes Post on the bulletin board a map of the world that shows the location of tectonic plates. Have volunteers use pins and string to outline the plates on the map. Have other students use flagged pins to mark the location of the volcanoes they learned about in this chapter. Then, pair students. Have partners explain how tectonic plate boundaries and volcanoes are related. Each partner should evaluate the other partner's understanding by assessing his or her descriptions of rifts, converging tectonic plates, diverging tectonic plates, subduction, hot spots, and magma formation. **LS Visual** Co-op Learning

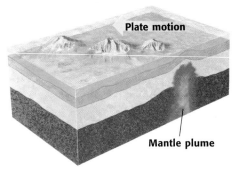

Figure 5 *According to one theory, a string of volcanic islands forms as a tectonic plate passes over a mantle plume.*

hot spot a volcanically active area of Earth's surface far from a tectonic plate boundary

Figure 6 *As if being this close to an active volcano is not dangerous enough, the gases being collected are extremely poisonous.*

Hot Spots

Not all magma develops along tectonic plate boundaries. For example, the Hawaiian Islands, some of the most well-known volcanoes on Earth, are nowhere near a plate boundary. The volcanoes of Hawaii and several other places on Earth are known as *hot spots*. **Hot spots** are volcanically active places on the Earth's surface that are far from plate boundaries. Some scientists think that hot spots are directly above columns of rising magma, called *mantle plumes*. Other scientists think that hot spots are the result of cracks in the Earth's crust.

A hot spot often produces a long chain of volcanoes. One theory is that the mantle plume stays in the same spot while the tectonic plate moves over it, as shown in **Figure 5.** Another theory argues that hot-spot volcanoes occur in long chains because they form along the cracks in the Earth's crust. Both theories may be correct.

✓ **Reading Check** Describe two theories that explain the existence of hot spots.

Predicting Volcanic Eruptions

You now understand some of the processes that produce volcanoes, but how do scientists predict when a volcano is going to erupt? Volcanoes are classified in three categories. *Extinct volcanoes* have not erupted in recorded history and probably never will erupt again. *Dormant volcanoes* are currently not erupting, but the record of past eruptions suggests that they may erupt again. *Active volcanoes* are currently erupting or show signs of erupting in the near future. Scientists study active and dormant volcanoes for signs of a future eruption.

Measuring Small Quakes and Volcanic Gases

Most active volcanoes produce small earthquakes as the magma within them moves upward and causes the surrounding rock to shift. Just before an eruption, the number and intensity of the earthquakes increase and the occurrence of quakes may be continuous. Monitoring these quakes is one of the best ways to predict an eruption.

As **Figure 6** shows, scientists also study the volume and composition of volcanic gases. The ratio of certain gases, especially that of sulfur dioxide, SO_2, to carbon dioxide, CO_2, may be important in predicting eruptions. Changes in this ratio may indicate changes in the magma chamber below.

Answer to Reading Check

According to one theory, a rising body of magma, called a mantle plume, causes a chain of volcanoes to form on a moving tectonic plate. According to another theory, a chain of volcanoes forms along cracks in the Earth's crust.

Homework —— GENERAL

PORTFOLIO

Hot Spots There are volcanic hot spots in Yellowstone Park, Easter Island, Hawaii, the Marquesas, the Canary Islands, Cameroon, Iceland, the Galápagos Islands, and the Samoan Islands. Have each student prepare a report on a hot spot, using maps, models, and details of the hot spot's history. **LS Visual**

Measuring Slope and Temperature

As magma moves upward prior to an eruption, it can cause the Earth's surface to swell. The side of a volcano may even bulge as the magma moves upward. An instrument called a *tiltmeter* helps scientists detect small changes in the angle of a volcano's slope. Scientists also use satellite technology such as the Global Positioning System (GPS) to detect the changes in a volcano's slope that may signal an eruption.

One of the newest methods for predicting volcanic eruptions includes using satellite images. Infrared satellite images record changes in the surface temperature and gas emissions of a volcano over time. If the site is getting hotter, the magma below is probably rising!

INTERNET ACTIVITY

For another activity related to this chapter, go to **go.hrw.com** and type in the keyword **HZ5VOLW.**

SECTION Review

Summary

- Temperature and pressure influence magma formation.

- Most volcanoes form at tectonic boundaries.

- As tectonic plates separate, magma rises to fill the cracks, or rifts, that develop.

- As oceanic and continental plates collide, the oceanic plate tends to subduct and cause the formation of magma.

- To predict eruptions, scientists study the frequency and type of earthquakes associated with the volcano as well as changes in slope, changes in the gases released, and changes in the volcano's surface temperature.

Using Key Terms

1. Use each of the following terms in a separate sentence: *hot spot* and *rift zone.*

Understanding Key Ideas

2. If the temperature of a rock remains constant but the pressure on the rock decreases, what tends to happen?
   a. The temperature increases.
   b. The rock becomes liquid.
   c. The rock becomes solid.
   d. The rock subducts.

3. Which of the following words is a synonym for *dormant*?
   a. predictable
   b. active
   c. dead
   d. sleeping

4. What is the Ring of Fire?

5. Explain how convergent and divergent plate boundaries cause magma formation.

6. Describe four methods that scientists use to predict volcanic eruptions.

7. Why does a oceanic plate tend to subduct when it collides with a continental plate?

Math Skills

8. If a tectonic plate moves at a rate of 2 km every 1 million years, how long would it take a hot spot to form a chain of volcanoes 100 km long?

Critical Thinking

9. **Making Inferences** New crust is constantly being created at mid-ocean ridges. So, why is the oldest oceanic crust only about 150 million years old?

10. **Identifying Relationships** If you are studying a volcanic deposit, would the youngest layers be more likely to be found on the top or on the bottom? Explain your answer.

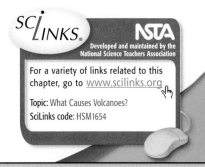

SCILINKS

NSTA

Developed and maintained by the National Science Teachers Association

For a variety of links related to this chapter, go to www.scilinks.org

Topic: What Causes Volcanoes?
SciLinks code: HSM1654

CHAPTER RESOURCES

Chapter Resource File

- **Section Quiz** GENERAL
- **Section Review** GENERAL
- **Vocabulary Section Summary** GENERAL
- **Reinforcement Worksheet** BASIC
- **Scilinks Activity** GENERAL
- **Datasheet for Quick Lab**

Technology

- **Interactive Explorations CD-ROM**
  - **What's the Matter?** GENERAL

Volcano Verdict

Teacher's Notes

Time Required

One 45-minute class period

Lab Ratings

EASY ——————————→ HARD

Teacher Prep 🧪🧪
Student Set-Up 🧪🧪🧪
Concept Level 🧪🧪
Clean Up 🧪🧪

MATERIALS

The materials listed on the student page are sufficient for a pair of students.

Safety Caution

Remind students to review all safety cautions and icons before beginning this activity.

Preparation Notes

You may want to combine this activity with an activity involving a tiltmeter. Emphasize to students that a gas-emissions tester is just one tool used by volcanologists. These scientists must compare the data gathered through many tests before drawing any conclusions.

In this experiment, 10 mL of bromothymol blue may be substituted for limewater. Bromothymol blue changes from blue to yellow-green when carbon dioxide is present.

Gordon Zibelman
Drexel Hill Middle School
Drexel Hill, Pennsylvania

OBJECTIVES

Build a working apparatus to test carbon dioxide levels.

Test the levels of carbon dioxide emitted from a model volcano.

MATERIALS

- baking soda, 15 mL
- bottle, drinking, 16 oz
- box or stand for plastic cup
- clay, modeling
- coin
- cup, clear plastic, 9 oz
- graduated cylinder
- limewater, 1 L
- straw, drinking, flexible
- tissue, bathroom (2 sheets)
- vinegar, white, 140 mL
- water, 100 mL

SAFETY

Volcano Verdict

You will need to pair up with a partner for this exploration. You and your partner will act as geologists who work in a city located near a volcano. City officials are counting on you to predict when the volcano will erupt next. You and your partner have decided to use limewater as a gas-emissions tester. You will use this tester to measure the levels of carbon dioxide emitted from a simulated volcano. The more active the volcano is, the more carbon dioxide it releases.

Procedure

1. Put on your safety goggles, and carefully pour limewater into the plastic cup until the cup is three-fourths full. You have just made your gas-emissions tester.

2. Now, build a model volcano. Begin by pouring 50 mL of water and 70 mL of vinegar into the drink bottle.

3. Form a plug of clay around the short end of the straw, as shown at left. The clay plug must be large enough to cover the opening of the bottle. Be careful not to get the clay wet.

4. Sprinkle 5 mL of baking soda along the center of a single section of bathroom tissue. Then, roll the tissue, and twist the ends so that the baking soda can't fall out.

CHAPTER RESOURCES

Chapter Resource File

📁 • Datasheet for Chapter Lab
 • Lab Notes and Answers

Technology

💻 Classroom Videos
 • Lab Video

LabBook

• Some Go "Pop," Some Do Not

⑤ Drop the tissue into the drink bottle, and immediately put the short end of the straw inside the bottle to make a seal with the clay.

⑥ Put the other end of the straw into the lime-water, as shown at right.

⑦ You have just taken your first measurement of gas levels from the volcano. Record your observations.

⑧ Imagine that it is several days later and you need to test the volcano again to collect more data. Before you continue, toss a coin. If it lands heads up, go to step 9. If it lands tails up, go to step 10. Write down the step that you follow.

⑨ Repeat steps 1–7. This time, add 2 mL of baking soda to the vinegar and water. (Note: You must use fresh water, vinegar, and limewater.) Write down your observations. Go to step 11.

⑩ Repeat steps 1–7. This time, add 8 mL of baking soda to the vinegar and water. (Note: You must use fresh water, vinegar, and limewater.) Write down your observations. Go to step 11.

⑪ Return to step 8 once. Then, answer the questions below.

Analyze the Results

❶ **Explaining Events** How do you explain the difference in the appearance of the limewater from one trial to the next?

❷ **Recognizing Patterns** What does the data that you collected indicate about the activity in the volcano?

Draw Conclusions

❸ **Evaluating Results** Based on your results, do you think it would be necessary to evacuate the city?

❹ **Applying Conclusions** How would a geologist use a gas-emissions tester to predict volcanic eruptions?

Analyze the Results

1. Students should realize that carbon dioxide made the lime-water cloudy. If more carbon dioxide is released, the lime-water becomes cloudier.

2. The answer to this question depends on which steps students followed. If students performed step 9 twice, they should conclude that the volcano is not likely to erupt in the immediate future. (The volcano released less gas in the second and third trials). If students performed step 10 twice, they should conclude that the volcano is likely to erupt. (More gas was released in the second and third trials; and therefore the pressure must be building.) If students performed step 9 and then step 10, an eruption would be likely. If students performed step 10 and then step 9 an eruption would not be likely.

Draw Conclusions

3. Answers may vary. If an eruption appears imminent, the city should be evacuated.

4. A geologist would use a gas-emissions tester in conjunction with other tests to determine if pressure is building within a volcano. As the pressure builds, the volcano is more likely to erupt.

MISCONCEPTION //// ALERT \\\\

Predicting Volcanic Eruptions
Scientists base their predictions of eruptions on several different kinds of evidence. If many types of evidence indicate that an eruption is imminent, they will recommend evacuation. They are much less likely to recommend evacuation if only one kind of evidence suggests that an eruption is imminent.

Assignment Guide

Section	Questions
1	2, 3, 6, 7, 13, 17, 18,
2	1, 5, 10, 15, 16
3	8, 9, 11, 12, 14, 19, 20
1 and 3	4

ANSWERS

Using Key Terms

1. Sample answer: A caldera forms when the roof of a magma chamber collapses. A crater forms when the material above the main vent of a volcano is blasted out.

2. Sample answer: Magma is hot, liquid rock material beneath Earth's surface. Lava is magma that flows onto Earth's surface.

3. Sample answer: Lava is liquid magma that flows out of a volcanic vent onto the ground. Pyroclastic material is mostly ash and solid rock that is blasted into the air during an explosive volcanic eruption.

4. Sample answer: A vent is a spot in Earth's surface through which lava or pyroclastic material passes. A rift is a long crack in Earth's crust.

5. Sample answer: A cinder cone volcano forms when pyroclastic material erupts and piles up around a volcanic vent. A shield volcano forms when lava spreads out over large areas.

USING KEY TERMS

For each pair of terms, explain how the meanings of the terms differ.

1 *caldera* and *crater*

2 *lava* and *magma*

3 *lava* and *pyroclastic material*

4 *vent* and *rift*

5 *cinder cone volcano* and *shield volcano*

UNDERSTANDING KEY IDEAS

Multiple Choice

6 The type of magma that tends to cause explosive eruptions has a

a. high silica content and high viscosity.

b. high silica content and low viscosity.

c. low silica content and low viscosity.

d. low silica content and high viscosity.

7 Lava that flows slowly to form a glassy surface with rounded wrinkles is called

a. aa lava.

b. pahoehoe lava.

c. pillow lava.

d. blocky lava.

8 Magma forms within the mantle most often as a result of

a. high temperature and high pressure.

b. high temperature and low pressure.

c. low temperature and high pressure.

d. low temperature and low pressure.

9 What causes an increase in the number and intensity of small earthquakes before an eruption?

a. the movement of magma

b. the formation of pyroclastic material

c. the hardening of magma

d. the movement of tectonic plates

10 If volcanic dust and ash remain in the atmosphere for months or years, what do you predict will happen?

a. Solar reflection will decrease, and temperatures will increase.

b. Solar reflection will increase, and temperatures will increase.

c. Solar reflection will decrease, and temperatures will decrease.

d. Solar reflection will increase, and temperatures will decrease.

11 At divergent plate boundaries,

a. heat from Earth's core causes mantle plumes.

b. oceanic plates sink, which causes magma to form.

c. tectonic plates move apart.

d. hot spots cause volcanoes.

12 A theory that helps explain the causes of both earthquakes and volcanoes is the theory of

a. pyroclastics.

b. plate tectonics.

c. climatic fluctuation.

d. mantle plumes.

Understanding Key Ideas

6. a

7. b

8. b

9. a

10. d

11. c

12. b

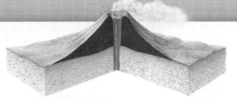

Short Answer

13 How does the presence of water in magma affect a volcanic eruption?

14 Describe four clues that scientists use to predict eruptions.

15 Identify the characteristics of the three types of volcanoes.

16 Describe the positive effects of volcanic eruptions.

CRITICAL THINKING

17 **Concept Mapping** Use the following terms to create a concept map: *volcanic bombs, aa, pyroclastic material, pahoehoe, lapilli, lava,* and *volcano.*

18 **Identifying Relationships** You are exploring a volcano that has been dormant for some time. You begin to keep notes on the types of volcanic debris that you see as you walk. Your first notes describe volcanic ash. Later, your notes describe lapilli. In what direction are you most likely traveling—toward the crater or away from the crater? Explain your answer.

19 **Making Inferences** Loihi is a submarine Hawaiian volcano that might grow to form a new island. The Hawaiian Islands are located on the Pacific plate, which is moving northwest. Considering how this island chain may have formed, where do you think the new volcanic island will be located? Explain your answer.

20 **Evaluating Hypotheses** What evidence could confirm the existence of mantle plumes?

INTERPRETING GRAPHICS

The graph below illustrates the average change in temperature above or below normal for a community over several years. Use the graph below to answer the questions that follow.

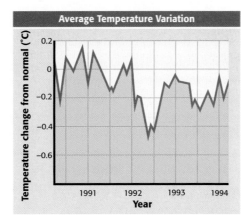

21 If the variation in temperature over the years was influenced by a major volcanic eruption, when did the eruption most likely take place? Explain.

22 If the temperature were measured only once each year (at the beginning of the year), how would your interpretation be different?

---

15. Cinder cones are made from eruptions of pyroclastic materials. They are small and have steep sides. Shield volcanoes are made of lava that spreads over large distances before it solidifies, making very large, gently sloped volcanoes. Composite volcanoes are made of both lava and pyroclastic material. Composite volcanoes have large, gently sloping bases and steep sides.

16. Sample answer: Volcanoes form new crust and help create fertile soil.

Critical Thinking

17. An answer to this exercise can be found at the end of this book.

18. You would be traveling toward the volcano because the larger the pyroclastic material is, the closer it will be to the vent. It takes more energy to move larger particles than it does to move smaller particles.

19. The new island will be located southeast of Hawaii because the Pacific plate is moving toward the northwest.

20. Answers may vary. Students may suggest studying the composition and temperature of rock in the area where a mantle plume is thought to be.

Interpreting Graphics

21. The eruption probably happened in 1992 because that year had the lowest below-normal temperature. The volcanic ash that erupted into the atmosphere blocked the sunlight and lowered the temperature.

22. If the temperature was measured once a year, the graph would indicate that 1991 had the lowest temperature. This would indicate that the eruptions happened in 1991 instead of 1992.

---

13. The presence of water in magma tends to cause explosive eruptions.

14. Earthquakes may indicate the movement of magma. Changes in the composition of volcanic gases may indicate changes in the magma chamber that may precede an eruption. Changes in the slope of a volcano may indicate that magma is rising. Finally, satellite data can reveal changes in surface temperature that may indicate that magma is rising.

CHAPTER RESOURCES

Chapter Resource File

- **Chapter Review** GENERAL
- **Chapter Test A** GENERAL
- **Chapter Test B** ADVANCED
- **Chapter Test C** SPECIAL NEEDS
- **Vocabulary Activity** GENERAL

Workbooks

Study Guide
- Assessment resources are also available in Spanish.

Standardized Test Preparation

Teacher's Note

To provide practice under more realistic testing conditions, give students 20 minutes to answer all of the questions in this Standardized Test Preparation.

MISCONCEPTION ALERT

Answers to the standardized test preparation can help you identify student misconceptions and misunderstandings.

READING

Passage 1

1. C
2. I
3. B

TEST DOCTOR

Question 1: Earthquakes can cause tsunamis, but earthquakes are not tsunamis. A shock wave was produced by the explosion, but a shock wave is not a tsunami. A tsunami is an ocean wave produced by an earthquake, volcanic explosion, or asteroid impact.

READING

Read each of the passages below. Then, answer the questions that follow each passage.

Passage 1 When the volcanic island of Krakatau in Indonesia exploded in 1883, a shock wave sped around the world seven times. The explosion was probably the loudest sound in recorded human history. What caused this enormous explosion? Most likely, the walls of the volcano ruptured, and ocean water flowed into the magma chamber of the volcano. The water instantly turned into steam, and the volcano exploded with the force of 100 million tons of TNT. The volcano ejected about 18 km³ of volcanic material into the air. The ash clouds blocked out the sun, and everything within about 80 km of the volcano was plunged into darkness for more than two days. The explosion caused a <u>tsunami</u> that was nearly 40 m high. Detected as far away as the English Channel, the tsunami destroyed almost 300 coastal towns. In 1928, another volcano rose from the caldera left by the explosion. This volcano is called <u>Anak</u> Krakatau.

1. In the passage, what does *tsunami* mean?
   - **A** a large earthquake
   - **B** a shock wave
   - **C** a giant ocean wave
   - **D** a cloud of gas and dust

2. According to the passage, what was the size of the Krakatau explosion probably the result of?
   - **F** pyroclastic material rapidly mixing with air
   - **G** 100 million tons of TNT
   - **H** an ancient caldera
   - **I** the flow of water into the magma chamber

3. What does the Indonesian word *anak* probably mean?
   - **A** father
   - **B** child
   - **C** mother
   - **D** grandmother

Passage 2 Yellowstone National Park in Montana and Wyoming contains three overlapping calderas and evidence of the <u>cataclysmic</u> ash flows that erupted from them. The oldest eruption occurred 1.9 million years ago, the second eruption happened 1.3 million years ago, and the most recent eruption occurred 0.6 million years ago. Seismographs regularly detect the movement of magma beneath the caldera, and the hot springs and geysers of the park indicate that a large body of magma lies beneath the park. The geology of the area shows that major eruptions occurred about once every 0.6 or 0.7 million years. Thus, a devastating eruption is long overdue. People living near the park should be evacuated immediately.

1. In the passage, what does *cataclysmic* mean?
   - **A** nonexplosive
   - **B** ancient
   - **C** destructive
   - **D** characterized by ash flows

2. Which of the following clues are evidence of an active magma body beneath the park?
   - **F** cataclysmic ash flows
   - **G** the discovery of seismoclasts
   - **H** minor eruptions
   - **I** seismograph readings

3. Which of the following contradicts the author's conclusion that an eruption is "long overdue"?
   - **A** Magma has been detected beneath the park.
   - **B** With a variation of 0.1 million years, an eruption may occur in the next 100,000 years.
   - **C** The composition of gases emitted indicates that an eruption is near.
   - **D** Seismographs have detected the movement of magma.

Passage 2

1. C
2. I
3. B

TEST DOCTOR

Question 2: The ash flows are not evidence of an active magma body beneath the park because they happened 0.6 million years ago. *Seismoclast* is not a word. There have been no recent eruptions in the park. However, seismograph readings indicate that magma is moving underneath the park.

Question 3: Remind students that this passage expresses an author's opinion and that being able to distinguish fact from opinion is an important skill. The author gives no evidence to substantiate the opinion that a devastating eruption is "long overdue."

The map below shows some of the Earth's major volcanoes and the tectonic plate boundaries. Use the map below to answer the questions that follow.

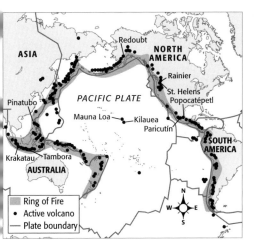

MATH

Read each question below, and choose the best answer.

1. Midway Island is 1,935 km northwest of Hawaii. If the Pacific plate is moving to the northwest at a rate of 9 cm per year, how long ago was Midway Island over the hot spot that formed the island?

   A 215,000 years

   B 2,150,000 years

   C 21,500,000 years

   D 215,000,000 years

2. In the first year that the Mexican volcano Paricutín appeared in a cornfield, it grew 360 m. The volcano stopped growing at about 400 m. What percentage of the volcano's total growth occurred in the first year?

   F 67%

   G 82%

   H 90%

   I 92%

3. A pyroclastic flow is moving down a hill at 120 km/h. If you lived in a town 5 km away, how much time would you have before the flow reached your town?

   A 2 min and 30 s

   B 1 min and 21 s

   C 3 min and 12 s

   D 8 min and 3 s

4. The Columbia River plateau is a lava plateau that contains 350,000 km^3 of solidified lava. The plateau took 3 million years to form. What was the average rate of lava deposition each century?

   F 0.116 km^3

   G 11.6 km^3

   H 116 km^3

   I 11,600 km^3

1. If ash from Popocatépetl landed on the west coast of the United States, what direction did the ash travel?

   A northeast

   B northwest

   C southeast

   D southwest

2. Why aren't there any active volcanoes in Australia?

   F Australia is not located on a plate boundary.

   G Australia is close to Krakatau and Tambora.

   H Australia is near a plate boundary.

   I Australia is near a rift zone.

3. If a scientist traveled along the Ring of Fire from Mt. Redoubt to Krakatau, which of the following most accurately describes the directions in which she traveled?

   A west, southeast, east

   B west, southeast, west

   C west, southwest, east

   D west, southwest, west

Standardized Test Preparation

CHAPTER RESOURCES

Chapter Resource File

• Standardized Test Preparation GENERAL

State Resources

For specific resources for your state, visit **go.hrw.com** and type in the keyword **HSMSTR**.

Weird Science

Background

According to native Hawaiian mythology, Pele lives in the active crater of Kilauea. If Pele is angered, she stamps her feet, causing earthquakes and lava flows. Hawaiian myth states that she appears as an old woman just before an eruption. To prevent eruptions, villagers sometimes made sacrifices to appease her. Typically they sacrificed a pig, but if no pigs were available, a thick skinned fish called *Humu-humu-nuku-nuku-a-puaa* (which grunts like a pig) would suffice. Have students research myths about volcanoes and share their findings with the class.

Science, Technology, and Society

Background

The villagers in Heimaey lost about a third of their village to the Eldfell eruption but succeeded in protecting their harbor. If the eruption had flowed its course, lava would have filled in the harbor of one of Iceland's most profitable fishing communities. After the eruption was over, villagers constructed a geothermal power plant to take advantage of the thermal energy of the lava flow.

Science in Action

Weird Science

Pele's Hair

It is hard to believe that the fragile specimen shown below is a volcanic rock. This strange type of lava, called *Pele's hair,* forms when volcanic gases spray molten rock high into the air. When conditions are right, the lava can harden into strands of volcanic glass as thin as a human hair. This type of lava is named after Pele, the Hawaiian goddess of volcanoes. Several other types of lava are named in Pele's honor. Pele's tears are tear-shaped globs of volcanic glass often found at the end of strands of Pele's hair. Pele's diamonds are green, gemlike stones found in hardened lava flows.

Language Arts ACTIVITY

Volcanic terms come from many languages. Research some volcanic terms on the Internet, and create an illustrated volcanic glossary to share with your class.

Science, Technology, and Society

Fighting Lava with Fire Hoses

What would you do if a 60 ft wall of lava was advancing toward your home? Most people would head for safety. But when an eruption threatened to engulf the Icelandic fishing village of Heimaey in 1973, some villagers held their ground and fought back. Working 14-hour days in conditions so hot that their boots would catch on fire, villagers used fire-hoses to spray sea water on the lava flow. For several weeks, the lava advanced toward the town, and it seemed as if there was no hope. But the water eventually cooled the lava fast enough to divert the flow and save the village. It took 5 months and about 1.5 billion gallons of water to fight the lava flow. When the eruption stopped, villagers found that the island had grown by 20%!

Social Studies ACTIVITY

WRITING SKILL To try to protect the city of Hilo, Hawaii, from an eruption in 1935, planes dropped bombs on the lava. Find out if this mission was successful, and write a report about other attempts to stop lava flows.

Answer to Language Arts Activity
Answers may vary.

Answer to Social Studies Activity
B-3 and B-4 bombers tried to stop the flow of lava into the city of Hilo. The mission was unsuccessful. Ground-based explosives have been more successful. In 1996, the Italian army detonated 15,000 pounds of explosives to stop a lava flow. They also built earthen walls to dam the lava.

Careers

Tina Neal

Volcanologist Would you like to study volcanoes for a living? Tina Neal is a volcanologist at the Alaska Volcano Observatory in Anchorage, Alaska. Her job is to monitor and study some of Alaska's 41 active volcanoes. Much of her work focuses on studying volcanoes in order to protect the public. According to Neal, being near a volcano when it is erupting is a wonderful adventure for the senses. "Sometimes you can get so close to an erupting volcano that you can feel the heat, hear the activity, and smell the lava. It's amazing! In Alaska, erupting volcanoes are too dangerous to get very close to, but they create a stunning visual display even from a distance."

Neal also enjoys the science of volcanoes. "It's fascinating to be near an active volcano and become aware of all the chemical and physical processes taking place. When I'm watching a volcano, I think about everything we understand and don't understand about what is happening. It's mind-boggling!" Neal says that if you are interested in becoming a volcanologist, it is important to be well rounded as a scientist. So, you would have to study math, geology, chemistry, and physics. Having a good understanding of computer tools is also important because volcanologists use computers to manage a lot of data and to create models. Neal also suggests learning a second language, such as Spanish. In her spare time, Neal is learning Russian so that she can better communicate with research partners in Kamchatka, Siberia.

Math ACTIVITY

The 1912 eruption of Mt. Katmai in Alaska could be heard 5,620 km away in Atlanta, Georgia. If the average speed of sound in the atmosphere is 342 m/s, how many hours after the eruption did the citizens of Atlanta hear the explosion?

go hrw .com

To learn more about these Science in Action topics, visit go.hrw.com and type in the keyword **HZ5VOLF.**

Current Science

Check out Current Science® articles related to this chapter by visiting go.hrw.com. Just type in the keyword **HZ5CS09.**

Answer to Math Activity

342 m/s × 60 s/min × 60 m/h = 1,231,200 m/h

1,231,200 m/h ÷ 1000 m/km = 1231 km/h

5620 km ÷ 1231 km/h = 4.6 h

Homework ——— ADVANCED

USAID Between 1999 and 2000, Neal served a two-year detail with the United States Agency for International Development (USAID) in Washington, D.C. Through USAID, Neal worked with the Office of U.S. Foreign Disaster Assistance to help other nations prevent or cope with natural disasters. In this role, Neal visited Nepal, Colombia, Ecuador, Kazakhstan, and other countries. Have students find out more about how USAID employs Earth scientists in international programs.

Skills Practice Lab

Mysterious Minerals

Teacher's Notes

Time Required

One 45-minute class period

Lab Ratings

EASY ——————————→ HARD

Teacher Prep
Student Set-Up
Concept Level
Clean Up

MATERIALS

The materials listed on the student page are sufficient for each student. Students may also work in groups of 3 to 4. You will need one streak plate per student or group. A class should be able to share 3 to 5 streak plates.

Safety Caution

Remind students to review all safety cautions and icons before beginning this lab activity. Students need to be careful with glass microscope slides. Broken slides are likely to have sharp edges. Caution students not to taste the mineral samples.

Skills Practice Lab

Mysterious Minerals

Imagine sitting on a rocky hilltop, gazing at the ground below you. You can see dozens of different types of rocks. How can scientists possibly identify the countless variations? It's a mystery!

In this activity, you'll use your powers of observation and a few simple tests to determine the identities of rocks and minerals. Take a look at the Mineral Identification Key on the next page. That key will help you use clues to discover the identity of several minerals.

MATERIALS

- gloves, protective
- iron filings
- minerals, samples
- slides, microscope, glass
- streak plate

SAFETY

Procedure

1. On a separate sheet of paper, create a data chart like the one below.

2. Choose one mineral sample, and locate its column in your data chart.

3. Follow the Mineral Identification Key to find the identity of your sample. When you are finished, record the mineral's name and primary characteristics in the appropriate column in your data chart. **Caution:** Put on your safety goggles and gloves when scratching the glass slide.

4. Select another mineral sample, and repeat steps 2 and 3 until your data table is complete.

Analyze the Results

1. Were some minerals easier to identify than others? Explain.

2. A streak test is a better indicator of a mineral's true color than visual observation is. Why isn't a streak test used to help identify every mineral?

3. On a separate sheet of paper, summarize what you learned about the various characteristics of each mineral sample you identified.

Mineral Summary Chart						
Characteristics	**1**	**2**	**3**	**4**	**5**	**6**
Mineral name						
Luster						
Color						
Streak			DO NOT WRITE IN BOOK			
Hardness						
Cleavage						
Special properties						

Preparation Notes

Explain to students that they are not determining the absolute hardness of the mineral samples. Instead, they are comparing the hardness of the samples with that of glass.

Your sample minerals should include pyrite, galena, hematite, magnetite, orthoclase (feldspar), quartz, muscovite, gypsum, hornblende (amphibole), garnet, biotite, and graphite.

Lab Notes

Each test in this lab tells the student more about the sample and narrows the possibilities. For example, the fact that a particular mineral sample does not have a streak eliminates hematite as a possibility but indicates that quartz is a possibility.

- It is possible for minerals that are softer than glass to leave a mark on glass. If the glass wipes clean and no scratch remains, then students will know that the mineral is softer than glass.

- Garnet is typically red, but it can also be pale green.

Mineral Identification Key

1. a. If your mineral has a metallic luster, **GO TO STEP 2.**
b. If your mineral has a nonmetallic luster, **GO TO STEP 3.**

2. a. If your mineral is black, **GO TO STEP 4.**
b. If your mineral is yellow, it is **PYRITE.**
c. If your mineral is silver, it is **GALENA.**

3. a. If your mineral is light in color, **GO TO STEP 5.**
b. If your mineral is dark in color, **GO TO STEP 6.**

4. a. If your mineral leaves a red-brown line on the streak plate, it is **HEMATITE.**
b. If your mineral leaves a black line on the streak plate, it is **MAGNETITE.** Test your sample for its magnetic properties by holding it near some iron filings.

5. a. If your mineral scratches the glass microscope slide, **GO TO STEP 7.**
b. If your mineral does not scratch the glass microscope slide, **GO TO STEP 8.**

6. a. If your mineral scratches the glass slide, **GO TO STEP 9.**
b. If your mineral does not scratch the glass slide, **GO TO STEP 10.**

7. a. If your mineral shows signs of cleavage, it is **ORTHOCLASE FELDSPAR.**
b. If your mineral does not show signs of cleavage, it is **QUARTZ.**

8. a. If your mineral shows signs of cleavage, it is **MUSCOVITE.** Examine this sample for twin sheets.
b. If your mineral does not show signs of cleavage, it is **GYPSUM.**

9. a. If your mineral shows signs of cleavage, it is **HORNBLENDE.**
b. If your mineral does not show signs of cleavage, it is **GARNET.**

10. a. If your mineral shows signs of cleavage, it is **BIOTITE.** Examine your sample for twin sheets.
b. If your mineral does not show signs of cleavage, it is **GRAPHITE.**

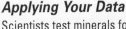
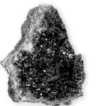

Applying Your Data

Using your textbook and other reference books, research other methods of identifying different types of minerals. Based on your findings, create a new identification key. Give the key and a few sample minerals to a friend, and see if your friend can unravel the mystery!

Analyze the Results

1. Students will find that some minerals required fewer steps to identify than others. For example, pyrite and galena are identified in two steps. Students may also find that they recognize some of the minerals and that the identification key is there merely to verify the identity.

2. For a mineral to leave a streak on the streak plate, the plate must be harder than the mineral. Therefore, extremely hard minerals do not leave a streak. Also, some minerals that are softer than a streak plate leave behind a colorless streak.

3. Answers will vary.

Applying Your Data

Scientists test minerals for their density, crystal form, reaction to acids, optical properties, fluorescence, and radioactivity. Students should create an identification key that is very similar to the one provided in the lab, but their key should include different characteristics.

CHAPTER RESOURCES

Chapter Resource File
- Datasheet for LabBook
- Lab Notes and Answers

Crystal Growth

Teacher's Notes

Time Required

Two 45-minute class periods

Lab Ratings

EASY ──────────────→ HARD

Teacher Prep 🧪🧪
Student Set-Up 🧪🧪🧪
Concept Level 🧪🧪
Clean Up 🧪🧪

MATERIALS

The materials listed are enough for a group of 4 to 5 students working cooperatively. Using a higher proportion of magnesium sulfate crystals to water will take significantly longer.

Safety Caution

Remind students to review all safety cautions and icons before beginning this lab activity.

Preparation Notes

Samples of igneous rocks may be obtained locally or through various science supply catalogs.

Crystal Growth

Magma forms deep below the Earth's surface at depths of 25 km to 160 km and at extremely high temperatures. Some magma reaches the surface and cools quickly. Other magma gets trapped in cracks or magma chambers beneath the surface and cools very slowly. When magma cools slowly, large, well-developed crystals form. But when magma erupts onto the surface, it cools more quickly. There is not enough time for large crystals to grow. The size of the crystals found in igneous rocks gives geologists clues about where and how the rocks formed.

In this experiment, you will demonstrate how the rate of cooling affects the size of crystals in igneous rocks by cooling crystals of magnesium sulfate at two different rates.

Ask a Question

1 How does temperature affect the formation of crystals?

Form a Hypothesis

2 Suppose you have two solutions that are identical in every way except for temperature. How will the temperature of a solution affect the size of the crystals and the rate at which they form?

Test the Hypothesis

3 Put on your gloves, apron, and goggles.

4 Fill the beaker halfway with tap water. Place the beaker on the hot plate, and let it begin to warm. The temperature of the water should be between 40°C and 50°C. **Caution:** Make sure the hot plate is away from the edge of the lab table.

5 Examine two or three crystals of the magnesium sulfate with your magnifying lens. On a separate sheet of paper, describe the color, shape, luster, and other interesting features of the crystals.

6 On a separate sheet of paper, draw a sketch of the magnesium sulfate crystals.

MATERIALS

- aluminum foil
- basalt
- beaker, 400 mL
- gloves, heat-resistant
- granite
- hot plate
- laboratory scoop, pointed
- magnesium sulfate (MgSO$_4$) (Epsom salts)
- magnifying lens
- marker, dark
- pumice
- tape, masking
- test tube, medium-sized
- thermometer, Celsius
- tongs, test-tube
- watch (or clock)
- water, distilled
- water, tap, 200 mL

SAFETY

7 Use the pointed laboratory scoop to fill the test tube about halfway with the magnesium sulfate. Add an equal amount of distilled water.

8 Hold the test tube in one hand, and use one finger from your other hand to tap the test tube gently. Observe the solution mixing as you continue to tap the test tube.

9 Place the test tube in the beaker of hot water, and heat it for approximately 3 min. **Caution:** Be sure to direct the opening of the test tube away from you and other students.

10 While the test tube is heating, shape your aluminum foil into two small boatlike containers by doubling the foil and turning up each edge.

11 If all the magnesium sulfate is not dissolved after 3 min, tap the test tube again, and heat it for 3 min longer. **Caution:** Use the test-tube tongs to handle the hot test tube.

12 With a marker and a piece of masking tape, label one of your aluminum boats "Sample 1," and place it on the hot plate. Turn the hot plate off.

13 Label the other aluminum boat "Sample 2," and place it on the lab table.

14 Using the test-tube tongs, remove the test tube from the beaker of water, and evenly distribute the contents to each of your foil boats. Carefully pour the hot water in the beaker down the drain. Do not move or disturb either of your foil boats.

15 Copy the table below onto a separate sheet of paper. Using the magnifying lens, carefully observe the foil boats. Record the time it takes for the first crystals to appear.

Crystal-Formation Table

Crystal formation	Time	Size and appearance of crystals	Sketch of crystals
Sample 1		DO NOT WRITE IN BOOK	
Sample 2			

Lab Notes

Some volcanic rocks contain both large and small crystals because the magma cooled for a period of time before erupting. This period of time was long enough for some minerals to crystallize but too short for other minerals to form.

CHAPTER RESOURCES

Chapter Resource File

- Datasheet for LabBook
- Lab Notes and Answers

Analyze the Results

1. Answers may vary. A correct prediction would state that a cool solution will produce crystals more quickly than a warm solution. A correct prediction would also state that the crystals produced in a warm solution will be much larger than those produced in a cool solution.

2. Because the original crystals were small, students may conclude that they formed quickly.

Draw Conclusions

4. Accept all reasonable sketches.

5. See the chart at the bottom of this page.

Communicating Your Data

Volcanic rocks that form in the air as the result of a violent volcanic eruption would cool quickly and have small crystals. Volcanic rocks that form from lava oozing out of a volcano would cool more slowly and have larger crystals.

16 If crystals have not formed in the boats before class is over, carefully place the boats in a safe place. You may then record the time in days instead of in minutes.

17 When crystals have formed in both boats, use your magnifying lens to examine the crystals carefully.

Analyze the Results

1 Was your prediction correct? Explain.

2 Compare the size and shape of the crystals in Samples 1 and 2 with the size and shape of the crystals you examined in step 5. How long do you think the formation of the original crystals must have taken?

Draw Conclusions

3 Granite, basalt, and pumice are all igneous rocks. The most distinctive feature of each is the size of its crystals. Different igneous rocks form when magma cools at different rates. Examine a sample of each with your magnifying lens.

4 Copy the table below onto a separate sheet of paper, and sketch each rock sample.

5 Use what you have learned in this activity to explain how each rock sample formed and how long it took for the crystals to form. Record your answers in your table.

Igneous Rock Observations			
	Granite	**Basalt**	**Pumice**
Sketch			
How did the rock sample form?		*DO NOT WRITE IN BOOK*	
Rate of cooling			

Communicating Your Data

Describe the size and shape of the crystals you would expect to find when a volcano erupts and sends material into the air and when magma oozes down the volcano's slope.

Igneous Rock Obsevations			
	Granite	**Basalt**	**Pumice**
How did the rock sample form?	the slow cooling of magma beneath the Earth's surface	the quick cooling of lava on the Earth's surface	ejected magma from a volcano during a violent eruption
Rate of cooling	cools slowly; large crystals	cools quickly; small crystals	cools very quickly; very small or no crystals

Model-Making Lab

Metamorphic Mash

Metamorphism is a complex process that takes place deep within the Earth, where the temperature and pressure would turn a human into a crispy pancake. The effects of this extreme temperature and pressure are obvious in some metamorphic rocks. One of these effects is the reorganization of mineral grains within the rock. In this activity, you will investigate the process of metamorphism without being charred, flattened, or buried.

Procedure

1. Flatten the clay into a layer about 1 cm thick. Sprinkle the surface with sequins.

2. Roll the corners of the clay toward the middle to form a neat ball.

3. Carefully use the plastic knife to cut the ball in half. On a separate sheet of paper, describe the position and location of the sequins inside the ball.

4. Put the ball back together, and use the sheets of cardboard or plywood to flatten the ball until it is about 2 cm thick.

5. Using the plastic knife, slice open the slab of clay in several places. Describe the position and location of the sequins in the slab.

Analyze the Results

1. What physical process does flattening the ball represent?

2. Describe any changes in the position and location of the sequins that occurred as the clay ball was flattened into a slab.

Draw Conclusions

3. How are the sequins oriented in relation to the force you put on the ball to flatten it?

4. Do you think the orientation of the mineral grains in a foliated metamorphic rock tells you anything about the rock? Defend your answer.

Applying Your Data

Suppose you find a foliated metamorphic rock that has grains running in two distinct directions. Use what you have learned in this activity to offer a possible explanation for this observation.

MATERIALS

- cardboard (or plywood), very stiff, small pieces
- clay, modeling
- knife, plastic
- sequins (or other small flat objects)

SAFETY

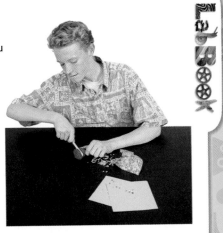

Metamorphic Mash

Teacher's Notes

Time Required

One 45-minute class period

Lab Ratings

🔺	🔺🔺	🔺🔺🔺	🔺🔺🔺🔺
EASY			→ HARD

Teacher Prep 🔺

Student Set-Up 🔺🔺

Concept Level 🔺🔺

Clean Up 🔺🔺

MATERIALS

The materials listed on the student page are enough for 1 student.

Safety Caution

Remind students to review all safety cautions and icons before beginning this lab activity.

Procedure

3. The sequins should be lying in a random pattern. Any layering is the result of rolling the ball.

5. The sequins are all horizontal.

Analyze the Results

1. It represents the pressure that creates metamorphic rock.

2. Before the ball was flattened, the sequins were in a random pattern. Once the ball was flattened, they lined up perpendicular to the pressure.

CHAPTER RESOURCES

Chapter Resource File

- Datasheet for LabBook
- Lab Notes and Answers

Dwight Patton
Carrol T. Welch Middle School
Horizon City, Texas

Draw Conclusions

3. The sequins are aligned perpendicular to the force.

4. Because the grains line up at right angles to the pressure, they are perpendicular to the strongest stress.

Applying Your Data

Answers may vary. Sample answer: Two pressures acting on the rock at different times must have pushed on the rock in different directions.

Model-Making Lab

Oh, the Pressure!

Teacher's Notes

Time Required
One 45-minute class period

Lab Ratings

🍶	🍶🍶	🍶🍶🍶	🍶🍶🍶🍶
EASY			HARD

Teacher Prep 🍶🍶🍶
Student Set-Up 🍶🍶
Concept Level 🍶🍶🍶
Clean Up 🍶🍶🍶

MATERIALS
The materials listed on the student page are enough for a group of 3 to 4 students.

Safety Caution
Remind students to review all safety cautions and icons before beginning this lab activity.

Lab Notes
Homemade modeling dough may be substituted for modeling clay in this activity. In step 6, students may find it easier to trim each layer of clay with the plastic knife before stacking the layers together.

Model-Making Lab

Oh, the Pressure!

When scientists want to understand natural processes, such as mountain formation, they often make models to help them. Models are useful in studying how rocks react to the forces of plate tectonics. A model can demonstrate in a short amount of time geological processes that take millions of years. Do the following activity to find out how folding and faulting occur in the Earth's crust.

MATERIALS

- can, soup (or rolling pin)
- clay, modeling, 4 colors
- knife, plastic
- newspaper
- pencils, colored
- poster board, 5 cm × 5 cm squares (2)
- poster board, 5 cm × 15 cm strip

SAFETY

Ask a Question

① How do synclines, anticlines, and faults form?

Form a Hypothesis

② On a separate piece of paper, write a hypothesis that is a possible answer to the question above. Explain your reasoning.

Test the Hypothesis

③ Use modeling clay of one color to form a long cylinder, and place the cylinder in the center of the glossy side of the poster-board strip.

④ Mold the clay to the strip. Try to make the clay layer the same thickness all along the strip; you can use the soup can or rolling pin to even it out. Pinch the sides of the clay so that the clay is the same width and length as the strip. Your strip should be at least 15 cm long and 5 cm wide.

Daniel Bugenhagen
Yutan Jr.–Sr. High
Yutan, Nebraska

5 Flip the strip over on the newspaper your teacher has placed across your desk. Carefully peel the strip from the modeling clay.

6 Repeat steps 3–5 with the other colors of modeling clay. Each person should have a turn molding the clay. Each time you flip the strip over, stack the new clay layer on top of the previous one. When you are finished, you should have a block of clay made of four layers.

7 Lift the block of clay, and hold it parallel to and just above the tabletop. Push gently on the block from opposite sides, as shown below.

8 Use the colored pencils to draw the results of step 6. Use the terms *syncline* and *anticline* to label your diagram. Draw arrows to show the direction that each edge of the clay was pushed.

9 Repeat steps 3–6 to form a second block of clay.

10 Cut the second block of clay in two at a 45° angle as seen from the side of the block.

Preparation Notes

Homemade Modeling Dough (optional) The night before the activity, prepare enough modeling dough for each class, using the recipe below. The recipe provides enough dough for each group. Combine the following ingredients in a large saucepan over low heat in the order that they are listed:

- 2 cups cold water
- $\frac{1}{3}$ cup cooking oil
- 1 cup salt
- 4 tsp cream of tartar
- 2 cups flour
- food coloring

Constantly stir the mixture until the modeling dough forms a ball. Turn the modeling dough out onto a floured surface. Use a ruler to divide the dough into fourths. When the dough cools slightly, add 15–20 drops of food coloring to each quarter. Fold and knead to evenly distribute the color throughout the dough. Place the dough in an airtight container, such as an 8 oz yogurt container. If you freeze it, the modeling dough will last for months.

Just before the activity, cover all workspaces with newspaper, and secure the newspapers in place. If the dough gets dry, rinse your hands and continue to mold the dough.

CHAPTER RESOURCES
Chapter Resource File
• Datasheet for LabBook
• Lab Notes and Answers

Lab Notes

Students should realize that stress is equivalent to pressure or force. Explain to them that rocks can undergo stress without deforming. When the stress becomes too great, the rocks become folded or faulted. This deformation is also called *strain*. Stress and the result of stress (strain) are two different concepts.

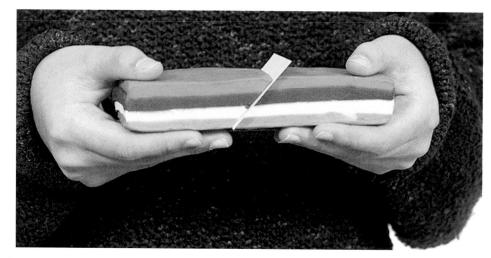

⑪ Press one poster-board square on the angled end of each of the block's two pieces. The poster board represents a fault. The two angled ends represent a hanging wall and a footwall. The model should resemble the one in the photograph above.

⑫ Keeping the angled edges together, lift the blocks, and hold them parallel to and just above the tabletop. Push gently on the two blocks until they move. Record your observations.

⑬ Now, hold the two pieces of the clay block in their original position, and slowly pull them apart, allowing the hanging wall to move downward. Record your observations.

Analyze the Results

❶ What happened to the first block of clay in step 7? What kind of force did you apply to the block of clay?

❷ What happened to the pieces of the second block of clay in step 12? What kind of force did you apply to them?

❸ What happened to the pieces of the second block of clay in step 13? Describe the forces that acted on the block and the way the pieces of the block reacted.

Draw Conclusions

❹ Summarize how the forces you applied to the blocks of clay relate to the way tectonic forces affect rock layers. Be sure to use the terms *fold, fault, anticline, syncline, hanging wall, footwall, tension,* and *compression* in your summary.

Analyze the Results

1. The first block got shorter and taller. The layers of clay became folded due to compression.

2. One of the pieces (the hanging wall) slid above the other piece (the footwall) due to compression.

3. One of the pieces (the footwall) moved up relative to the other piece (the hanging wall) as tension was released.

Draw Conclusions

4. The conclusion should be a complete summary of this activity, indicating the direction of pressure at each step. Any diagrams should be correctly labeled, and students should demonstrate a good understanding of the terms *fold, fault, anticline, syncline, hanging wall, footwall, tension,* and *compression.*

Skills Practice Lab

Earthquake Waves

The energy from an earthquake travels as seismic waves in all directions through the Earth. Seismologists can use the properties of certain types of seismic waves to find the epicenter of an earthquake.

P waves travel more quickly than S waves and are always detected first. The average speed of P waves in the Earth's crust is 6.1 km/s. The average speed of S waves in the Earth's crust is 4.1 km/s. The difference in arrival time between P waves and S waves is called *lag time.*

In this activity, you will use the S-P-time method to determine the location of an earthquake's epicenter.

MATERIALS

• calculator (optional)
• compass
• ruler, metric

SAFETY

Procedure

1 The illustration below shows seismographic records made in three cities following an earthquake. These traces begin at the left and show the arrival of P waves at time zero. The second set of waves on each record represents the arrival of S waves.

Seismographic Records

Austin

Bismarck

Portland

| 0 | 50 | 100 | 150 | 200 |

Time scale (seconds)

2 Copy the data table on the next page.

3 Use the time scale provided with the seismographic records to find the lag time between the P waves and the S waves for each city. Remember that the lag time is the time between the moment when the first P wave arrives and the moment when the first S wave arrives. Record this data in your table.

4 Use the following equation to calculate how long it takes each wave type to travel 100 km:

100 km ÷ *average speed of the wave* = time

CHAPTER RESOURCES

Chapter Resource File

• **Datasheet for LabBook**
• **Lab Notes and Answers**

CLASSROOM TESTED & APPROVED

Janel Guse
West Central Middle School
Hartford, South Dakota

Earthquake Waves

Teacher's Notes

Time Required

One 45-minute class period

Lab Ratings

| △ | △△ | △△△ | △△△△ |
EASY ————————————→ HARD

Teacher Prep △
Student Set-Up △
Concept Level △△△
Clean Up △

MATERIALS

The materials listed on the student page are enough for 2 students.

Safety Caution

Remind students to review all safety cautions and icons before beginning this lab activity.

Preparation Notes

Be sure that students understand in step 6 how to calculate the distance from each city to the epicenter of the earthquake. These distances must be correct to accurately determine the epicenter of the earthquake on the map.

Emphasize to students that the circles on the map must intersect or come very close to intersecting in order to determine the epicenter of the earthquake. If the circles do not come close to intersecting, tell students that they must check their calculations.

Procedure

3. Austin: 150 s
Bismarck: 168 s
Portland: 120 s

6. Austin: 1,875 km; Bismarck: 2,100 km; Portland: 1,500 km

Analyze the Results

1. San Diego, California

Draw Conclusions

2. Sample answer: Seismologists require at least three intersecting circles to determine the epicenter of an earthquake. The first two circles intersect in two places. When a third circle is used, all three circles intersect in only one place near the epicenter.

5 To find lag time for earthquake waves at 100 km, subtract the time it takes P waves to travel 100 km from the time it takes S waves to travel 100 km. Record the lag time.

6 Use the following formula to find the distance from each city to the epicenter:

$$distance = \frac{measured\ lag\ time\ (s) \times 100\ km}{lag\ time\ for\ 100\ km\ (s)}$$

In your data table, record the distance from each city to the epicenter.

7 Trace the map below onto a separate sheet of paper.

8 Use the scale to adjust your compass so that the radius of a circle with Austin at the center is equal to the distance between Austin and the epicenter of the earthquake.

Epicenter Data Table		
City	Lag time (seconds)	Distance to the epicenter (km)
Austin, TX		
Bismarck, ND	*DO NOT WRITE IN BOOK*	
Portland, OR		

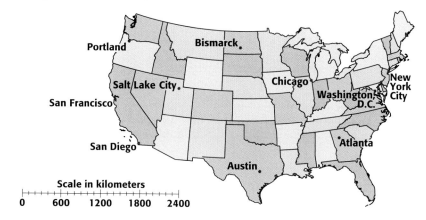

Scale in kilometers
0   600   1200   1800   2400

9 Put the point of your compass at Austin on your copy of the map, and draw a circle.

10 Repeat steps 8 and 9 for Bismarck and Portland. The epicenter of the earthquake is located near the point where the three circles meet.

Anayze the Results

1 Which city is closest to the epicenter?

Draw Conclusions

2 Why do seismologists need measurements from three different locations to find the epicenter of an earthquake?

Skills Practice Lab

Some Go "Pop," Some Do Not

Volcanic eruptions range from mild to violent. When volcanoes erupt, the materials left behind provide information to scientists studying the Earth's crust. Mild, or nonexplosive, eruptions produce thin, runny lava that is low in silica. During nonexplosive eruptions, lava simply flows down the side of the volcano. Explosive eruptions, on the other hand, do not produce much lava. Instead, the explosions hurl ash and debris into the air. The materials left behind are light in color and high in silica. These materials help geologists determine the composition of the crust underneath the volcanoes.

MATERIALS

- paper, graph (1 sheet)
- pencils (or markers), red, yellow, and orange
- ruler, metric

Procedure

1 Copy the map below onto graph paper. Take care to line the grid up properly.

2 Locate each volcano from the list on the next page by drawing a circle with a diameter of about 2 mm in the proper location on your copy of the map. Use the latitude and longitude grids to help you.

3 Review all the eruptions for each volcano. For each explosive eruption, color the circle red. For each quiet volcano, color the circle yellow. For volcanoes that have erupted in both ways, color the circle orange.

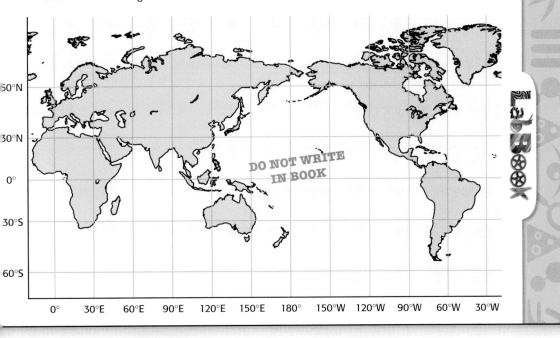

DO NOT WRITE IN BOOK

C. John Graves
Monforton Middle School
Bozeman, Montana

Lab Notes

In a very simple way, this lab models how the composition of magma can evolve. For example, basaltic (mafic) magma can evolve into granitic (felsic) magma through chemical differentiation processes. Scientists often use measurements of trace elements in the resulting rock to "fingerprint" the source of magma from which volcanic rocks formed.

Skills Practice Lab

Some Go "Pop," Some Do Not

Teacher's Notes

Time Required

One 45-minute class period

Lab Ratings

EASY			HARD

Teacher Prep 🧪🧪
Student Set-Up 🧪
Concept Level 🧪🧪🧪
Clean Up 🧪

MATERIALS

The materials listed on the student page are enough for 1 student. Students may wish to use tracing paper in step 1.

Preparation Notes

Students should be aware that volcanoes with a high water and silica content tend to erupt explosively. They should use this information to analyze the data in this activity. You may also wish to inform students that, in general, quietly erupting volcanoes are derived from basaltic magma, and explosively erupting volcanoes are derived from granitic magma. Remind students that oceanic crust is basaltic and low in silica, and continental crust is granitic and high in silica.

Students may need some practice finding locations by using latitude and longitude. If necessary, guide them through the steps needed to locate the first volcano on the chart.

Analyze the Results

1. Nonexplosive volcanoes are usually located on oceanic crust.

2. Explosive volcanoes are usually located on continental crust.

3. Volcanoes that erupt in both ways are usually located near boundaries between oceanic and continental crusts.

4. The crust under the oceans must be low in silica. Students may also know that the crust is likely to be made of basalt.

5. Continental crust is generally high in silica. Students may also know that the crust is likely to be made of granite.

Draw Conclusions

6. The volcanoes that erupt in both ways must be near the boundary between the oceanic crusts and the continental crusts. The crust must have both basalt and granite.

7. The volcanoes that erupt in both ways are located near the boundaries between continents and oceans. Students should understand that two different crusts must meet in these areas and that both granitic (felsic) and basaltic (mafic) magma is generated.

Volcanic Activity Chart

Volcano name	Location	Description
Mount St. Helens	46°N 122°W	An explosive eruption blew the top off the mountain. Light-colored ash covered thousands of square kilometers. Another eruption sent a lava flow down the southeast side of the mountain.
Kilauea	19°N 155°W	One small eruption sent a lava flow along 12 km of highway.
Rabaul caldera	4°S 152°E	Explosive eruptions have caused tsunamis and have left 1–2 m of ash on nearby buildings.
Popocatépetl	19°N 98°W	During one explosion, Mexico City closed the airport for 14 hours because huge columns of ash made it too difficult for pilots to see. Eruptions from this volcano have also caused damaging avalanches.
Soufriere Hills	16°N 62°W	Small eruptions have sent lava flows down the hills. Other explosive eruptions have sent large columns of ash into the air.
Long Valley caldera	37°N 119°W	Explosive eruptions have sent ash into the air.
Okmok	53°N 168°W	Recently, there have been slow lava flows from this volcano. Twenty-five hundred years ago, ash and debris exploded from the top of this volcano.
Pavlof	55°N 161°W	Eruption clouds have been sent 200 m above the summit. Eruptions have sent ash columns 10 km into the air. Occasionally, small eruptions have caused lava flows.
Fernandina	42°N 12°E	Eruptions have ejected large blocks of rock from this volcano.
Mount Pinatubo	15°N 120°E	Ash and debris from an explosive eruption destroyed homes, crops, and roads within 52,000 km^2 around the volcano.

Analyze the Results

1. According to your map, where are volcanoes that always have nonexplosive eruptions located?

2. Where are volcanoes that always erupt explosively located?

3. Where are volcanoes that erupt in both ways located?

4. If volcanoes get their magma from the crust below them, what can you say about the silica content of Earth's crust under the oceans?

5. What is the composition of the crust under the continents? How do we know?

Draw Conclusions

6. What is the source of materials for volcanoes that erupt in both ways? How do you know?

7. Do the locations of volcanoes that erupt in both ways make sense, based on your answers to questions 4 and 5? Explain.

Applying Your Data

Volcanoes are present on other planets. If a planet had only nonexplosive volcanoes on its surface, what would we be able to infer about the planet? If a planet had volcanoes that ranged from nonexplosive to explosive, what might that tell us about the planet?

Applying Your Data

Answers should reflect the idea that the crust on planets with nonexplosive volcanoes must be low in silica compared to the crust on Earth. Students may also realize that planets that have only nonexplosive volcanoes must have basaltic crust. If a planet has all three types of volcanoes, it must have both basaltic and granitic crusts.

CHAPTER RESOURCES

Chapter Resource File

- **Datasheet for LabBook**
- **Lab Notes and Answers**

Contents

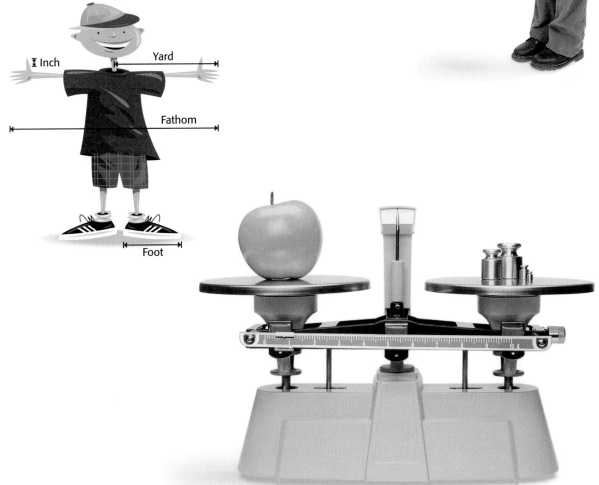

Appendix

✓ Reading Check Answers

Chapter 1 Minerals of the Earth's Crust

Section 1

Page 5: An element is a pure substance that cannot be broken down into simpler substances by ordinary chemical means. A compound is a substance made of two or more elements that have been chemically bonded.

Page 6: Answers may vary. Silicate minerals contain a combination of silicon and oxygen; nonsilicate minerals do not contain a combination of silicon and oxygen.

Section 2

Page 9: A mineral's streak is not affected by air or water, but a mineral's color may be affected by air or water.

Page 10: Scratch the mineral with a series of 10 reference minerals. If the reference mineral scratches the unidentified mineral, the reference mineral is harder than the unidentified mineral.

Section 3

Page 15: Surface mining is used to remove mineral deposits that are at or near the Earth's surface. Subsurface mining is used to remove mineral deposits that are too deep to be removed by surface mining.

Page 17: Sample answer: Gemstones are nonmetallic minerals that are valued for their beauty and rarity rather than for their usefulness.

Chapter 2 Rocks: Mineral Mixtures

Section 1

Page 28: Types of rocks that have been used by humans to construct buildings include granite, limestone, marble, sandstone, and slate.

Page 32: Rock within the Earth is affected by temperature and pressure.

Page 33: The minerals that a rock contains determine a rock's composition.

Page 34: Fine-grained rocks are made of small grains, such as silt or clay particles. Medium-grained rocks are made of medium-sized grains, such as sand. Coarse-grained rocks are made of large grains, such as pebbles.

Section 2

Page 37: Felsic rocks are light-colored igneous rocks rich in aluminum, potassium, silicon, and sodium. Mafic rocks are dark-colored igneous rocks rich in calcium, iron, and magnesium.

Page 39: New sea floor forms when lava that flows from fissures on the ocean floor cools and hardens.

Section 3

Page 41: Halite forms when sodium and chlorine ions in shallow bodies of water become so concentrated that halite crystallizes from solution.

Page 43: Ripple marks are the marks left by wind and water waves on lakes, seas, rivers, and sand dunes.

Page 45: Regional metamorphism occurs when pressure builds up in rock that is buried deep below other rock formations or when large pieces of the Earth's crust collide. The increased pressure can cause thousands of square miles of rock to become deformed and chemically changed.

Page 46: An index mineral is a metamorphic mineral that forms only at certain temperatures and pressures and therefore can be used by scientists to estimate the temperature, pressure, and depth at which a rock undergoes metamorphosis.

Page 49: Deformation causes metamorphic structures, such as folds.

Chapter 3 The Rock and Fossil Record

Section 1

Page 61: Catastrophists believed that all geologic change occurs rapidly.

Page 62: A global catastrophe can cause the extinction of species.

Section 2

Page 65: Geologists use the geologic column to interpret rock sequences and to identify layers in puzzling rock sequences.

Page 67: An unconformity is a surface that represents a missing part of the geologic column.

Page 68: A disconformity is found where part of a sequence of parallel rock layers is missing. A nonconformity is found where horizontal sedimentary rock layers lie on top of an eroded surface of igneous or metamorphic rock. Angular unconformities are found between horizontal sedimentary rock layers and rock layers that have been tilted or folded.

Section 3

Page 71: A half-life is the time it takes one-half of a radioactive sample to decay.

Page 72: strontium-87

Section 4

Page 74: An organism is caught in soft, sticky tree sap, which hardens and preserves the organism.

Page 76: A mold is a cavity in rock where a plant or an animal was buried. A cast is an object created when sediment fills a mold and becomes rock.

Page 78: To fill in missing information about changes in organisms in the fossil record, paleontologists look for similarities between fossilized organisms or between fossilized organisms and their closest living relatives.

Page 79: *Phacops* can be used to establish the age of rock layers because *Phacops* lived during a relatively short, well-defined time span and is found in rock layers throughout the world.

Section 5

Page 81: approximately 2 billion years

Page 82: The geologic time scale is a scale that divides Earth's 4.6 billion-year history into distinct intervals of time.

Page 84: The Mesozoic era is known as the *Age of Reptiles* because reptiles, including the dinosaurs, were the dominant organisms on land.

Chapter 4   Plate Tectonics
Section 1

Page 97: The crust is the thin, outermost layer of the Earth. It is 5 km to 100 km thick and is mainly made up of the elements oxygen, silicon, and aluminum. The mantle is the layer between the crust and core. It is 2,900 km thick, is denser than the crust, and contains most of the Earth's mass. The core is the Earth's innermost layer. The core has a radius of 3,430 km and is made mostly of iron.

Page 98: The five physical layers of the Earth are the lithosphere, asthenosphere, mesosphere, outer core, and inner core.

Page 101: Although continental lithosphere is less dense than oceanic lithosphere is, continental lithosphere has a greater weight and will displace more asthenosphere than oceanic lithosphere.

Page 102: Answers may vary. A seismic wave traveling through a solid will go faster than a seismic wave traveling through a liquid.

Section 2

Page 104: Similar fossils were found on landmasses that are very far apart. The best explanation for this phenomenon is that the landmasses were once joined.

Page 107: The molten rock at mid-ocean ridges contains tiny grains of magnetic minerals. The minerals align with the Earth's magnetic field before the rock cools and hardens. When the Earth's magnetic field reverses, the orientation of the mineral grains in the rocks will also change.

Section 3

Page 109: A transform boundary forms when two tectonic plates slide past each other horizontally.

Page 110: The circulation of thermal energy causes changes in density in the asthenosphere. As rock is heated, it expands, becomes less dense, and rises. As rock cools, it contracts, becomes denser, and sinks.

Section 4

Page 112: Compression can cause rocks to be pushed into mountain ranges as tectonic plates collide at convergent boundaries. Tension can pull rocks apart as tectonic plates separate at divergent boundaries.

Page 114: In a normal fault, the hanging wall moves down. In a reverse fault, the hanging wall moves up.

Page 116: Folded mountains form when rock layers are squeezed together and pushed upward.

Chapter 5   Earthquakes
Section 1

Page 131: During elastic rebound, rock releases energy. Some of this energy travels as seismic waves that cause earthquakes.

Page 133: Earthquake zones are usually located along tectonic plate boundaries.

Page 135: Surface waves travel more slowly than body waves but are more destructive.

Section 2

Page 137: Seismologists determine an earthquake's start time by comparing seismograms and noting differences in arrival times of P and S waves.

Page 138: Each time the magnitude increases by 1 unit, the amount of ground motion increases by 10 times.

Section 3

Page 141: With a decrease of one unit in earthquake magnitude, the number of earthquakes occurring annually increases by about 10 times.

Page 142: Retrofitting is the process of making older structures more earthquake resistant.

Page 144: You should crouch or lie face down under a table or desk.

Chapter 6   Volcanoes
Section 1

Page 157: Nonexplosive eruptions are common, and they feature relatively calm flows of lava. Explosive eruptions are less common and produce large, explosive clouds of ash and gases.

Page 158: Because silica-rich magma has a high viscosity, it tends to trap gases and plug volcanic vents. This causes pressure to build up and can result in an explosive eruption.

Page 160: Volcanic bombs are large blobs of magma that harden in the air. Lapilli are small pieces of magma that harden in the air. Volcanic blocks are pieces of solid rock erupted from a volcano. Ash forms when gases in stiff magma expand rapidly and the walls of the gas bubbles shatter into tiny glasslike slivers.

Section 2

Page 162: Eruptions release large quantities of ash and gases, which can block sunlight and cause global temperatures to drop.

Page 164: Calderas form when a magma chamber partially empties and the roof overlying the chamber collapses.

Section 3

Page 167: Volcanic activity is common at tectonic plate boundaries because magma tends to form at plate boundaries.

Page 169: When a tectonic plate subducts, it becomes hotter and releases water vapor. The water lowers the melting point of the rock above the plate, causing magma to form.

Page 170: According to one theory, a rising body of magma, called a mantle plume, causes a chain of volcanoes to form on a moving tectonic plate. According to another theory, a chain of volcanoes forms along cracks in the Earth's crust.

Study Skills

FoldNote Instructions

Have you ever tried to study for a test or quiz but didn't know where to start? Or have you read a chapter and found that you can remember only a few ideas? Well, FoldNotes are a fun and exciting way to help you learn and remember the ideas you encounter as you learn science!

FoldNotes are tools that you can use to organize concepts. By focusing on a few main concepts, FoldNotes help you learn and remember how the concepts fit together. They can help you see the "big picture." Below you will find instructions for building 10 different FoldNotes.

Pyramid

1. Place a sheet of paper in front of you. Fold the lower left-hand corner of the paper diagonally to the opposite edge of the paper.

2. Cut off the tab of paper created by the fold (at the top).

3. Open the paper so that it is a square. Fold the lower right-hand corner of the paper diagonally to the opposite corner to form a triangle.

4. Open the paper. The creases of the two folds will have created an X.

5. Using scissors, cut along one of the creases. Start from any corner, and stop at the center point to create two flaps. Use tape or glue to attach one of the flaps on top of the other flap.

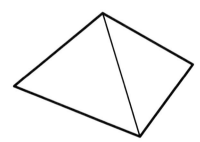

Double Door

1. Fold a sheet of paper in half from the top to the bottom. Then, unfold the paper.

2. Fold the top and bottom edges of the paper to the crease.

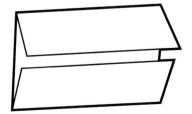

196 Appendix

Booklet

1. Fold a sheet of paper in half from left to right. Then, unfold the paper.

2. Fold the sheet of paper in half again from the top to the bottom. Then, unfold the paper.

3. Refold the sheet of paper in half from left to right.

4. Fold the top and bottom edges to the center crease.

5. Completely unfold the paper.

6. Refold the paper from top to bottom.

7. Using scissors, cut a slit along the center crease of the sheet from the folded edge to the creases made in step 4. Do not cut the entire sheet in half.

8. Fold the sheet of paper in half from left to right. While holding the bottom and top edges of the paper, push the bottom and top edges together so that the center collapses at the center slit. Fold the four flaps to form a four-page book.

Layered Book

1. Lay one sheet of paper on top of another sheet. Slide the top sheet up so that 2 cm of the bottom sheet is showing.

2. Hold the two sheets together, fold down the top of the two sheets so that you see four 2 cm tabs along the bottom.

3. Using a stapler, staple the top of the FoldNote.

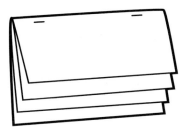

Key-Term Fold

1. Fold a sheet of lined notebook paper in half from left to right.

2. Using scissors, cut along every third line from the right edge of the paper to the center fold to make tabs.

Four-Corner Fold

1. Fold a sheet of paper in half from left to right. Then, unfold the paper.

2. Fold each side of the paper to the crease in the center of the paper.

3. Fold the paper in half from the top to the bottom. Then, unfold the paper.

4. Using scissors, cut the top flap creases made in step 3 to form four flaps.

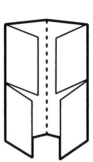

Three-Panel Flip Chart

1. Fold a piece of paper in half from the top to the bottom.

2. Fold the paper in thirds from side to side. Then, unfold the paper so that you can see the three sections.

3. From the top of the paper, cut along each of the vertical fold lines to the fold in the middle of the paper. You will now have three flaps.

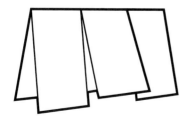

Table Fold

1. Fold a piece of paper in half from the top to the bottom. Then, fold the paper in half again.

2. Fold the paper in thirds from side to side.

3. Unfold the paper completely. Carefully trace the fold lines by using a pen or pencil.

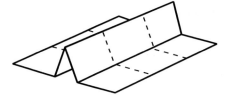

Two-Panel Flip Chart

1. Fold a piece of paper in half from the top to the bottom.

2. Fold the paper in half from side to side. Then, unfold the paper so that you can see the two sections.

3. From the top of the paper, cut along the vertical fold line to the fold in the middle of the paper. You will now have two flaps.

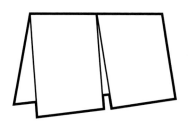

Tri-Fold

1. Fold a piece a paper in thirds from the top to the bottom.

2. Unfold the paper so that you can see the three sections. Then, turn the paper sideways so that the three sections form vertical columns.

3. Trace the fold lines by using a pen or pencil. Label the columns "Know," "Want," and "Learn."

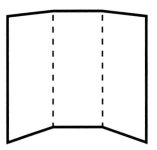

Graphic Organizer Instructions

Have you ever wished that you could "draw out" the many concepts you learn in your science class? Sometimes, being able to *see* how concepts are related really helps you remember what you've learned. Graphic Organizers do just that! They give you a way to draw or map out concepts.

All you need to make a Graphic Organizer is a piece of paper and a pencil. Below you will find instructions for four different Graphic Organizers designed to help you organize the concepts you'll learn in this book.

Spider Map

1. Draw a diagram like the one shown. In the circle, write the main topic.

2. From the circle, draw legs to represent different categories of the main topic. You can have as many categories as you want.

3. From the category legs, draw horizontal lines. As you read the chapter, write details about each category on the horizontal lines.

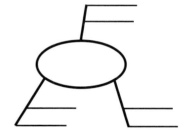

Comparison Table

1. Draw a chart like the one shown. Your chart can have as many columns and rows as you want.

2. In the top row, write the topics that you want to compare.

3. In the left column, write characteristics of the topics that you want to compare. As you read the chapter, fill in the characteristics for each topic in the appropriate boxes.

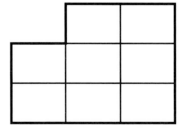

Chain-of-Events-Chart

1. Draw a box. In the box, write the first step of a process or the first event of a timeline.

2. Under the box, draw another box, and use an arrow to connect the two boxes. In the second box, write the next step of the process or the next event in the timeline.

3. Continue adding boxes until the process or timeline is finished.

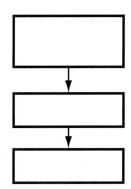

Concept Map

1. Draw a circle in the center of a piece of paper. Write the main idea of the chapter in the center of the circle.

2. From the circle, draw other circles. In those circles, write characteristics of the main idea. Draw arrows from the center circle to the circles that contain the characteristics.

3. From each circle that contains a characteristic, draw other circles. In those circles, write specific details about the characteristic. Draw arrows from each circle that contains a characteristic to the circles that contain specific details. You may draw as many circles as you want.

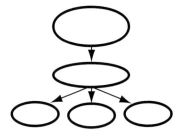

SI Measurement

The International System of Units, or SI, is the standard system of measurement used by many scientists. Using the same standards of measurement makes it easier for scientists to communicate with one another.

SI works by combining prefixes and base units. Each base unit can be used with different prefixes to define smaller and larger quantities. The table below lists common SI prefixes.

SI Prefixes

Prefix	Symbol	Factor	Example
kilo-	k	1,000	kilogram, 1 kg = 1,000 g
hecto-	h	100	hectoliter, 1 hL = 100 L
deka-	da	10	dekameter, 1 dam = 10 m
		1	meter, liter, gram
deci-	d	0.1	decigram, 1 dg = 0.1 g
centi-	c	0.01	centimeter, 1 cm = 0.01 m
milli-	m	0.001	milliliter, 1 mL = 0.001 L
micro-	μ	0.000 001	micrometer, 1 μm = 0.000 001 m

SI Conversion Table

SI units	From SI to English	From English to SI
Length		
kilometer (km) = 1,000 m	1 km = 0.621 mi	1 mi = 1.609 km
meter (m) = 100 cm	1 m = 3.281 ft	1 ft = 0.305 m
centimeter (cm) = 0.01 m	1 cm = 0.394 in.	1 in. = 2.540 cm
millimeter (mm) = 0.001 m	1 mm = 0.039 in.	
micrometer (μm) = 0.000 001 m		
nanometer (nm) = 0.000 000 001 m		
Area		
square kilometer (km^2) = 100 hectares	1 km^2 = 0.386 mi^2	1 mi^2 = 2.590 km^2
hectare (ha) = 10,000 m^2	1 ha = 2.471 acres	1 acre = 0.405 ha
square meter (m^2) = 10,000 cm^2	1 m^2 = 10.764 ft^2	1 ft^2 = 0.093 m^2
square centimeter (cm^2) = 100 mm^2	1 cm^2 = 0.155 in.^{2}	1 in.^{2} = 6.452 cm^2
Volume		
liter (L) = 1,000 mL = 1 dm^3	1 L = 1.057 fl qt	1 fl qt = 0.946 L
milliliter (mL) = 0.001 L = 1 cm^3	1 mL = 0.034 fl oz	1 fl oz = 29.574 mL
microliter (μL) = 0.000 001 L		
Mass		
kilogram (kg) = 1,000 g	1 kg = 2.205 lb	1 lb = 0.454 kg
gram (g) = 1,000 mg	1 g = 0.035 oz	1 oz = 28.350 g
milligram (mg) = 0.001 g		
microgram (μg) = 0.000 001 g		

Appendix

Measuring Skills

Using a Graduated Cylinder

When using a graduated cylinder to measure volume, keep the following procedures in mind:

1. Place the cylinder on a flat, level surface before measuring liquid.

2. Move your head so that your eye is level with the surface of the liquid.

3. Read the mark closest to the liquid level. On glass graduated cylinders, read the mark closest to the center of the curve in the liquid's surface.

Using a Meterstick or Metric Ruler

When using a meterstick or metric ruler to measure length, keep the following procedures in mind:

1. Place the ruler firmly against the object that you are measuring.

2. Align one edge of the object exactly with the 0 end of the ruler.

3. Look at the other edge of the object to see which of the marks on the ruler is closest to that edge. (Note: Each small slash between the centimeters represents a millimeter, which is one-tenth of a centimeter.)

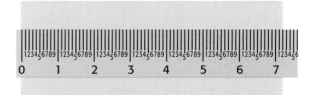

Using a Triple-Beam Balance

When using a triple-beam balance to measure mass, keep the following procedures in mind:

1. Make sure the balance is on a level surface.

2. Place all of the countermasses at 0. Adjust the balancing knob until the pointer rests at 0.

3. Place the object you wish to measure on the pan. **Caution:** Do not place hot objects or chemicals directly on the balance pan.

4. Move the largest countermass along the beam to the right until it is at the last notch that does not tip the balance. Follow the same procedure with the next-largest countermass. Then, move the smallest countermass until the pointer rests at 0.

5. Add the readings from the three beams together to determine the mass of the object.

6. When determining the mass of crystals or powders, first find the mass of a piece of filter paper. Then, add the crystals or powder to the paper, and remeasure. The actual mass of the crystals or powder is the total mass minus the mass of the paper. When finding the mass of liquids, first find the mass of the empty container. Then, find the combined mass of the liquid and container. The mass of the liquid is the total mass minus the mass of the container.

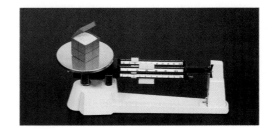

Scientific Methods

The ways in which scientists answer questions and solve problems are called **scientific methods.** The same steps are often used by scientists as they look for answers. However, there is more than one way to use these steps. Scientists may use all of the steps or just some of the steps during an investigation. They may even repeat some of the steps. The goal of using scientific methods is to come up with reliable answers and solutions.

Six Steps of Scientific Methods

1 Ask a Question

Good questions come from careful **observations.** You make observations by using your senses to gather information. Sometimes, you may use instruments, such as microscopes and telescopes, to extend the range of your senses. As you observe the natural world, you will discover that you have many more questions than answers. These questions drive investigations.

Questions beginning with *what, why, how,* and *when* are important in focusing an investigation. Here is an example of a question that could lead to an investigation.

Question: How does acid rain affect plant growth?

2 Form a Hypothesis

After you ask a question, you need to form a **hypothesis.** A hypothesis is a clear statement of what you expect the answer to your question to be. Your hypothesis will represent your best "educated guess" based on what you have observed and what you already know. A good hypothesis is testable. Otherwise, the investigation can go no further. Here is a hypothesis based on the question, "How does acid rain affect plant growth?"

Hypothesis: Acid rain slows plant growth.

The hypothesis can lead to predictions. A prediction is what you think the outcome of your experiment or data collection will be. Predictions are usually stated in an if-then format. Here is a sample prediction for the hypothesis that acid rain slows plant growth.

Prediction: If a plant is watered with only acid rain (which has a pH of 4), then the plant will grow at half its normal rate.

3 Test the Hypothesis

After you have formed a hypothesis and made a prediction, your hypothesis should be tested. One way to test a hypothesis is with a controlled experiment. A **controlled experiment** tests only one factor at a time. In an experiment to test the effect of acid rain on plant growth, the **control group** would be watered with normal rain water. The **experimental group** would be watered with acid rain. All of the plants should receive the same amount of sunlight and water each day. The air temperature should be the same for all groups. However, the acidity of the water will be a variable. In fact, any factor that is different from one group to another is a **variable.** If your hypothesis is correct, then the acidity of the water and plant growth are *dependant variables.* The amount a plant grows is dependent on the acidity of the water. However, the amount of water each plant receives and the amount of sunlight each plant receives are *independent variables.* Either of these factors could change without affecting the other factor.

Sometimes, the nature of an investigation makes a controlled experiment impossible. For example, the Earth's core is surrounded by thousands of meters of rock. Under such circumstances, a hypothesis may be tested by making detailed observations.

4 Analyze the Results

After you have completed your experiments, made your observations, and collected your data, you must analyze all the information you have gathered. Tables and graphs are often used in this step to organize the data.

5 Draw Conclusions

After analyzing your data, you can determine if your results support your hypothesis. If your hypothesis is supported, you (or others) might want to repeat the observations or experiments to verify your results. If your hypothesis is not supported by the data, you may have to check your procedure for errors. You may even have to reject your hypothesis and make a new one. If you cannot draw a conclusion from your results, you may have to try the investigation again or carry out further observations or experiments.

6 Communicate Results

After any scientific investigation, you should report your results. By preparing a written or oral report, you let others know what you have learned. They may repeat your investigation to see if they get the same results. Your report may even lead to another question and then to another investigation.

Scientific Methods in Action

Scientific methods contain loops in which several steps may be repeated over and over again. In some cases, certain steps are unnecessary. Thus, there is not a "straight line" of steps. For example, sometimes scientists find that testing one hypothesis raises new questions and new hypotheses to be tested. And sometimes, testing the hypothesis leads directly to a conclusion. Furthermore, the steps in scientific methods are not always used in the same order. Follow the steps in the diagram, and see how many different directions scientific methods can take you.

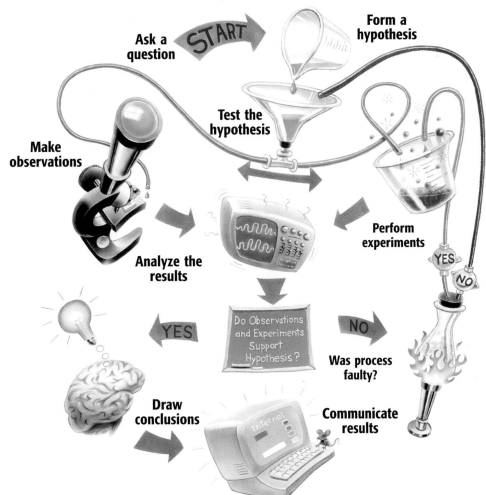

Appendix

Math Refresher

Science requires an understanding of many math concepts. The following pages will help you review some important math skills.

Averages

An **average,** or **mean,** simplifies a set of numbers into a single number that *approximates* the value of the set.

Example: Find the average of the following set of numbers: 5, 4, 7, and 8.

Step 1: Find the sum.
$$5 + 4 + 7 + 8 = 24$$

Step 2: Divide the sum by the number of numbers in your set. Because there are four numbers in this example, divide the sum by 4.

$$\frac{24}{4} = 6$$

The average, or mean, is **6.**

Ratios

A **ratio** is a comparison between numbers, and it is usually written as a fraction.

Example: Find the ratio of thermometers to students if you have 36 thermometers and 48 students in your class.

Step 1: Make the ratio.
$$\frac{36 \text{ thermometers}}{48 \text{ students}}$$

Step 2: Reduce the fraction to its simplest form.
$$\frac{36}{48} = \frac{36 \div 12}{48 \div 12} = \frac{3}{4}$$

The ratio of thermometers to students is **3 to 4,** or $\frac{3}{4}$. The ratio may also be written in the form 3:4.

Proportions

A **proportion** is an equation that states that two ratios are equal.
$$\frac{3}{1} = \frac{12}{4}$$

To solve a proportion, first multiply across the equal sign. This is called *cross-multiplication*. If you know three of the quantities in a proportion, you can use cross-multiplication to find the fourth.

Example: Imagine that you are making a scale model of the solar system for your science project. The diameter of Jupiter is 11.2 times the diameter of the Earth. If you are using a plastic-foam ball that has a diameter of 2 cm to represent the Earth, what must the diameter of the ball representing Jupiter be?

$$\frac{11.2}{1} = \frac{x}{2 \text{ cm}}$$

Step 1: Cross-multiply.
$$\frac{11.2}{1} \diagup\!\!\!\!\diagdown \frac{x}{2}$$
$$11.2 \times 2 = x \times 1$$

Step 2: Multiply.
$$22.4 = x \times 1$$

Step 3: Isolate the variable by dividing both sides by 1.
$$x = \frac{22.4}{1}$$
$$x = 22.4 \text{ cm}$$

You will need to use a ball that has a diameter of **22.4** cm to represent Jupiter.

Percentages

A **percentage** is a ratio of a given number to 100.

  Example: What is 85% of 40?

Step 1: Rewrite the percentage by moving the decimal point two places to the left.
$$0.85$$

Step 2: Multiply the decimal by the number that you are calculating the percentage of.
$$0.85 \times 40 = 34$$
85% of 40 is **34.**

Decimals

To **add** or **subtract decimals,** line up the digits vertically so that the decimal points line up. Then, add or subtract the columns from right to left. Carry or borrow numbers as necessary.

  Example: Add the following numbers: 3.1415 and 2.96.

Step 1: Line up the digits vertically so that the decimal points line up.
$$\begin{array}{r} 3.1415 \\ + 2.96 \\ \hline \end{array}$$

Step 2: Add the columns from right to left, and carry when necessary.
$$\begin{array}{r} {\scriptstyle 1\ \ 1} \\ 3.1415 \\ + 2.96 \\ \hline 6.1015 \end{array}$$

The sum is **6.1015.**

Fractions

Numbers tell you how many; **fractions** tell you *how much of a whole.*

  Example: Your class has 24 plants. Your teacher instructs you to put 5 plants in a shady spot. What fraction of the plants in your class will you put in a shady spot?

Step 1: In the denominator, write the total number of parts in the whole.
$$\frac{?}{24}$$

Step 2: In the numerator, write the number of parts of the whole that are being considered.
$$\frac{5}{24}$$

So, $\frac{5}{24}$ of the plants will be in the shade.

Reducing Fractions

It is usually best to express a fraction in its simplest form. Expressing a fraction in its simplest form is called *reducing* a fraction.

  Example: Reduce the fraction $\frac{30}{45}$ to its simplest form.

Step 1: Find the largest whole number that will divide evenly into both the numerator and denominator. This number is called the *greatest common factor* (GCF).

Factors of the numerator 30:
  1, 2, 3, 5, 6, 10, **15,** 30

Factors of the denominator 45:
  1, 3, 5, 9, **15,** 45

Step 2: Divide both the numerator and the denominator by the GCF, which in this case is 15.
$$\frac{30}{45} = \frac{30 \div 15}{45 \div 15} = \frac{2}{3}$$

Thus, $\frac{30}{45}$ reduced to its simplest form is $\frac{2}{3}$.

Adding and Subtracting Fractions

To **add** or **subtract fractions** that have the **same denominator,** simply add or subtract the numerators.

Examples:

$$\frac{3}{5} + \frac{1}{5} = ? \text{ and } \frac{3}{4} - \frac{1}{4} = ?$$

Step 1: Add or subtract the numerators.

$$\frac{3}{5} + \frac{1}{5} = \frac{4}{} \text{ and } \frac{3}{4} - \frac{1}{4} = \frac{2}{}$$

Step 2: Write the sum or difference over the denominator.

$$\frac{3}{5} + \frac{1}{5} = \frac{4}{5} \text{ and } \frac{3}{4} - \frac{1}{4} = \frac{2}{4}$$

Step 3: If necessary, reduce the fraction to its simplest form.

$\frac{4}{5}$ cannot be reduced, and $\frac{2}{4} = \frac{1}{2}$.

To **add** or **subtract fractions** that have **different denominators,** first find the least common denominator (LCD).

Examples:

$$\frac{1}{2} + \frac{1}{6} = ? \text{ and } \frac{3}{4} - \frac{2}{3} = ?$$

Step 1: Write the equivalent fractions that have a common denominator.

$$\frac{3}{6} + \frac{1}{6} = ? \text{ and } \frac{9}{12} - \frac{8}{12} = ?$$

Step 2: Add or subtract the fractions.

$$\frac{3}{6} + \frac{1}{6} = \frac{4}{6} \text{ and } \frac{9}{12} - \frac{8}{12} = \frac{1}{12}$$

Step 3: If necessary, reduce the fraction to its simplest form.

The fraction $\frac{4}{6} = \frac{2}{3}$, and $\frac{1}{12}$ cannot be reduced.

Multiplying Fractions

To **multiply fractions,** multiply the numerators and the denominators together, and then reduce the fraction to its simplest form.

Example:

$$\frac{5}{9} \times \frac{7}{10} = ?$$

Step 1: Multiply the numerators and denominators.

$$\frac{5}{9} \times \frac{7}{10} = \frac{5 \times 7}{9 \times 10} = \frac{35}{90}$$

Step 2: Reduce the fraction.

$$\frac{35}{90} = \frac{35 \div 5}{90 \div 5} = \frac{7}{18}$$

Dividing Fractions

To **divide fractions,** first rewrite the divisor (the number you divide by) upside down. This number is called the *reciprocal* of the divisor. Then multiply and reduce if necessary.

Example:

$$\frac{5}{8} \div \frac{3}{2} = ?$$

Step 1: Rewrite the divisor as its reciprocal.

$$\frac{3}{2} \rightarrow \frac{2}{3}$$

Step 2: Multiply the fractions.

$$\frac{5}{8} \times \frac{2}{3} = \frac{5 \times 2}{8 \times 3} = \frac{10}{24}$$

Step 3: Reduce the fraction.

$$\frac{10}{24} = \frac{10 \div 2}{24 \div 2} = \frac{5}{12}$$

Scientific Notation

Scientific notation is a short way of representing very large and very small numbers without writing all of the place-holding zeros.

Example: Write 653,000,000 in scientific notation.

Step 1: Write the number without the place-holding zeros.

653

Step 2: Place the decimal point after the first digit.

6.53

Step 3: Find the exponent by counting the number of places that you moved the decimal point.

6.53000000

The decimal point was moved eight places to the left. Therefore, the exponent of 10 is positive 8. If you had moved the decimal point to the right, the exponent would be negative.

Step 4: Write the number in scientific notation.

$$\mathbf{6.53 \times 10^8}$$

Area

Area is the number of square units needed to cover the surface of an object.

Formulas:

area of a square = side × side
area of a rectangle = length × width
area of a triangle = $\frac{1}{2}$ × base × height

Examples: Find the areas.

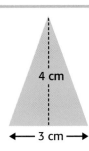

Triangle
area = $\frac{1}{2}$ × base × height
area = $\frac{1}{2}$ × 3 cm × 4 cm
*area = **6 cm²***

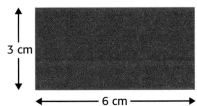

Rectangle
area = length × width
area = 6 cm × 3 cm
*area = **18 cm²***

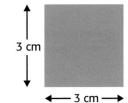

Square
area = side × side
area = 3 cm × 3 cm
*area = **9 cm²***

Volume

Volume is the amount of space that something occupies.

Formulas:

volume of a cube = side × side × side

volume of a prism = area of base × height

Examples:

Find the volume of the solids.

Cube
volume = side × side × side
volume = 4 cm × 4 cm × 4 cm
*volume = **64 cm³***

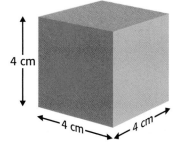

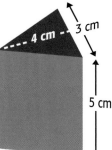

Prism
volume = area of base × height
volume = (area of triangle) × height
volume = ($\frac{1}{2}$ × 3 cm × 4 cm) × 5 cm
volume = 6 cm² × 5 cm
*volume = **30 cm³***

Properties of Common Minerals

<table>
<tr><th>Mineral</th><th>Color</th><th>Luster</th><th>Streak</th><th>Hardness</th></tr>
<tr><td colspan="5">Silicate Minerals</td></tr>
<tr><td>Beryl</td><td>deep green, pink, white, bluish green, or yellow</td><td>vitreous</td><td>white</td><td>7.5–8</td></tr>
<tr><td>Chlorite</td><td>green</td><td>vitreous to pearly</td><td>pale green</td><td>2–2.5</td></tr>
<tr><td>Garnet</td><td>green, red, brown, black</td><td>vitreous</td><td>white</td><td>6.5–7.5</td></tr>
<tr><td>Hornblende</td><td>dark green, brown, or black</td><td>vitreous</td><td>none</td><td>5–6</td></tr>
<tr><td>Muscovite</td><td>colorless, silvery white, or brown</td><td>vitreous or pearly</td><td>white</td><td>2–2.5</td></tr>
<tr><td>Olivine</td><td>olive green, yellow</td><td>vitreous</td><td>white or none</td><td>6.5–7</td></tr>
<tr><td>Orthoclase</td><td>colorless, white, pink, or other colors</td><td>vitreous</td><td>white or none</td><td>6</td></tr>
<tr><td>Plagioclase</td><td>colorless, white, yellow, pink, green</td><td>vitreous</td><td>white</td><td>6</td></tr>
<tr><td>Quartz</td><td>colorless or white; any color when not pure</td><td>vitreous or waxy</td><td>white or none</td><td>7</td></tr>
<tr><td colspan="5">Native Elements</td></tr>
<tr><td>Copper</td><td>copper-red</td><td>metallic</td><td>copper-red</td><td>2.5–3</td></tr>
<tr><td>Diamond</td><td>pale yellow or colorless</td><td>adamantine</td><td>none</td><td>10</td></tr>
<tr><td>Graphite</td><td>black to gray</td><td>submetallic</td><td>black</td><td>1–2</td></tr>
<tr><td colspan="5">Carbonates</td></tr>
<tr><td>Aragonite</td><td>colorless, white, or pale yellow</td><td>vitreous</td><td>white</td><td>3.5–4</td></tr>
<tr><td>Calcite</td><td>colorless or white to tan</td><td>vitreous</td><td>white</td><td>3</td></tr>
<tr><td colspan="5">Halides</td></tr>
<tr><td>Fluorite</td><td>light green, yellow, purple, bluish green, or other colors</td><td>vitreous</td><td>none</td><td>4</td></tr>
<tr><td>Halite</td><td>white</td><td>vitreous</td><td>white</td><td>2.0–2.5</td></tr>
<tr><td colspan="5">Oxides</td></tr>
<tr><td>Hematite</td><td>reddish brown to black</td><td>metallic to earthy</td><td>dark red to red-brown</td><td>5.6–6.5</td></tr>
<tr><td>Magnetite</td><td>iron-black</td><td>metallic</td><td>black</td><td>5.5–6.5</td></tr>
<tr><td colspan="5">Sulfates</td></tr>
<tr><td>Anhydrite</td><td>colorless, bluish, or violet</td><td>vitreous to pearly</td><td>white</td><td>3–3.5</td></tr>
<tr><td>Gypsum</td><td>white, pink, gray, or colorless</td><td>vitreous, pearly, or silky</td><td>white</td><td>2.0</td></tr>
<tr><td colspan="5">Sulfides</td></tr>
<tr><td>Galena</td><td>lead-gray</td><td>metallic</td><td>lead-gray to black</td><td>2.5–2.8</td></tr>
<tr><td>Pyrite</td><td>brassy yellow</td><td>metallic</td><td>greenish, brownish, or black</td><td>6–6.5</td></tr>
</table>

Silicate Minerals

Nonsilicate Minerals

Appendix

Density (g/cm³)	Cleavage, Fracture, Special Properties	Common Uses
2.6–2.8	1 cleavage direction; irregular fracture; some varieties fluoresce in ultraviolet light	gemstones, ore of the metal beryllium
2.6–3.3	1 cleavage direction; irregular fracture	
4.2	no cleavage; conchoidal to splintery fracture	gemstones, abrasives
3.0–3.4	2 cleavage directions; hackly to splintery fracture	
2.7–3	1 cleavage direction; irregular fracture	electrical insulation, wallpaper, fireproofing material, lubricant
3.2–3.3	no cleavage; conchoidal fracture	gemstones, casting
2.6	2 cleavage directions; irregular fracture	porcelain
2.6–2.7	2 cleavage directions; irregular fracture	ceramics
2.6	no cleavage; conchoidal fracture	gemstones, concrete, glass, porcelain, sandpaper, lenses
8.9	no cleavage; hackly fracture	wiring, brass, bronze, coins
3.5	4 cleavage directions; irregular to conchoidal fracture	gemstones, drilling
2.3	1 cleavage direction; irregular fracture	pencils, paints, lubricants, batteries
2.95	2 cleavage directions; irregular fracture; reacts with hydrochloric acid	no important industrial uses
2.7	3 cleavage directions; irregular fracture; reacts with weak acid; double refraction	cements, soil conditioner, whitewash, construction materials
3.0–3.3	4 cleavage directions; irregular fracture; some varieties fluoresce	hydrofluoric acid, steel, glass, fiberglass, pottery, enamel
2.1–2.2	3 cleavage directions; splintery to conchoidal fracture; salty taste	tanning hides, salting icy roads, food preservation
5.2–5.3	no cleavage; splintery fracture; magnetic when heated	iron ore for steel, pigments
5.2	no cleavage; splintery fracture; magnetic	iron ore
3.0	3 cleavage directions; conchoidal to splintery fracture	soil conditioner, sulfuric acid
2.3	3 cleavage directions; conchoidal to splintery fracture	plaster of Paris, wallboard, soil conditioner
7.4–7.6	3 cleavage directions; irregular fracture	batteries, paints
5	no cleavage; conchoidal to splintery fracture	sulfuric acid

Glossary

A

absolute dating any method of measuring the age of an event or object in years (70)

asthenosphere the soft layer of the mantle on which the tectonic plates move (98)

C

caldera a large, semicircular depression that forms when the magma chamber below a volcano partially empties and causes the ground above to sink (164)

cast a type of fossil that forms when sediments fill in the cavity left by a decomposed organism (76)

catastrophism a principle that states that geologic change occurs suddenly (61)

cleavage the splitting of a mineral along smooth, flat surfaces (9)

composition the chemical makeup of a rock; describes either the minerals or other materials in the rock (33)

compound a substance made up of atoms of two or more different elements joined by chemical bonds (5)

compression stress that occurs when forces act to squeeze an object (112)

continental drift the hypothesis that states that the continents once formed a single landmass, broke up, and drifted to their present locations (104)

convergent boundary the boundary formed by the collision of two lithospheric plates (109)

core the central part of the Earth below the mantle (97)

crater a funnel-shaped pit near the top of the central vent of a volcano (164)

crust the thin and solid outermost layer of the Earth above the mantle (96)

crystal a solid whose atoms, ions, or molecules are arranged in a definite pattern (5)

D

deformation the bending, tilting, and breaking of the Earth's crust; the change in the shape of rock in response to stress (131)

density the ratio of the mass of a substance to the volume of the substance (10)

deposition the process in which material is laid down (29)

divergent boundary the boundary between two tectonic plates that are moving away from each other (109)

E

elastic rebound the sudden return of elastically deformed rock to its undeformed shape (131)

element a substance that cannot be separated or broken down into simpler substances by chemical means (4)

eon (EE AHN) the largest division of geologic time (83)

epicenter the point on Earth's surface directly above an earthquake's starting point, or focus (136)

epoch (EP uhk) a subdivision of a geologic period (83)

era a unit of geologic time that includes two or more periods (83)

erosion the process by which wind, water, ice, or gravity transports soil and sediment from one location to another (29)

extinction the death of every member of a species (83)

extrusive igneous rock rock that forms as a result of volcanic activity at or near the Earth's surface (39)

F

fault a break in a body of rock along which one block slides relative to another (114)

focus the point along a fault at which the first motion of an earthquake occurs (136)

folding the bending of rock layers due to stress (113)

foliated describes the texture of metamorphic rock in which the mineral grains are arranged in planes or bands (47)

fossil the remains or physical evidence of an organism preserved by geological processes (74)

fracture the manner in which a mineral breaks along either curved or irregular surfaces (9)

G

gap hypothesis a hypothesis that is based on the idea that a major earthquake is more likely to occur along the part of an active fault where no earthquakes have occurred for a certain period of time (141)

geologic column an arrangement of rock layers in which the oldest rocks are at the bottom (65)

geologic time scale the standard method used to divide the Earth's long natural history into manageable parts (82)

H

half-life the time needed for half of a sample of a radioactive substance to undergo radioactive decay (71)

hardness a measure of the ability of a mineral to resist scratching (10)

hot spot a volcanically active area of Earth's surface far from a tectonic plate boundary (170)

I

index fossil a fossil that is found in the rock layers of only one geologic age and that is used to establish the age of the rock layers (78)

intrusive igneous rock rock formed from the cooling and solidification of magma beneath the Earth's surface (38)

isotope an atom that has the same number of protons (or the same atomic number) as other atoms of the same element do but that has a different number of neutrons (and thus a different atomic mass) (70)

L

lava plateau a wide, flat landform that results from repeated nonexplosive eruptions of lava that spread over a large area (165)

lithosphere the solid, outer layer of the Earth that consists of the crust and the rigid upper part of the mantle (98)

luster the way in which a mineral reflects light (8)

M

magma chamber the body of molten rock that feeds a volcano (158)

mantle the layer of rock between the Earth's crust and core (97)

mesosphere the strong, lower part of the mantle between the asthenosphere and the outer core (99)

mineral a naturally formed, inorganic solid that has a definite chemical structure (4)

mold a mark or cavity made in a sedimentary surface by a shell or other body (76)

N

nonfoliated describes the texture of metamorphic rock in which the mineral grains are not arranged in planes or bands (48)

nonsilicate mineral a mineral that does not contain compounds of silicon and oxygen (6)

O

ore a natural material whose concentration of economically valuable minerals is high enough for the material to be mined profitably (14)

P

paleontology the scientific study of fossils (63)

period a unit of geologic time into which eras are divided (83)

plate tectonics the theory that explains how large pieces of the Earth's outermost layer, called *tectonic plates,* move and change shape (108)

P wave a seismic wave that causes particles of rock to move in a back-and-forth direction (134)

R

radioactive decay the process in which a radioactive isotope tends to break down into a stable isotope of the same element or another element (70)

radiometric dating a method of determining the age of an object by estimating the relative percentages of a radioactive (parent) isotope and a stable (daughter) isotope (71)

reclamation the process of returning land to its original condition after mining is completed (15)

relative dating any method of determining whether an event or object is older or younger than other events or objects (64)

rift zone an area of deep cracks that forms between two tectonic plates that are pulling away from each other (168)

rock a naturally occurring solid mixture of one or more minerals or organic matter (28)

rock cycle the series of processes in which a rock forms, changes from one type to another, is destroyed, and forms again by geological processes (28)

S

sea-floor spreading the process by which new oceanic lithosphere forms as magma rises toward the surface and solidifies (106)

seismic gap an area along a fault where relatively few earthquakes have occurred recently but where strong earthquakes have occurred in the past (141)

seismic wave a wave of energy that travels through the Earth and away from an earthquake in all directions (134)

seismogram a tracing of earthquake motion that is created by a seismograph (136)

seismograph an instrument that records vibrations in the ground and determines the location and strength of an earthquake (136)

seismology (siez MAHL uh jee) the study of earthquakes (130)

silicate mineral a mineral that contains a combination of silicon, oxygen, and one or more metals (6)

strata layers of rock (singular, *stratum*) (40)

stratification the process in which sedimentary rocks are arranged in layers (43)

streak the color of the powder of a mineral (9)

subsidence (suhb SIED'ns) the sinking of regions of the Earth's crust to lower elevations (118)

superposition a principle that states that younger rocks lie above older rocks if the layers have not been disturbed (64)

S wave a seismic wave that causes particles of rock to move in a side-to-side direction (134)

T

tectonic plate a block of lithosphere that consists of the crust and the rigid, outermost part of the mantle (100)

tension stress that occurs when forces act to stretch an object (112)

texture the quality of a rock that is based on the sizes, shapes, and positions of the rock's grains (34)

trace fossil a fossilized mark that is formed in soft sediment by the movement of an animal (76)

transform boundary the boundary between tectonic plates that are sliding past each other horizontally (109)

U

unconformity a break in the geologic record created when rock layers are eroded or when sediment is not deposited for a long period of time (67)

uniformitarianism a principle that states that geologic processes that occurred in the past can be explained by current geologic processes (60)

uplift the rising of regions of the Earth's crust to higher elevations (118)

V

vent an opening at the surface of the Earth through which volcanic material passes (158)

volcano a vent or fissure in the Earth's surface through which magma and gases are expelled (156)

Glossary

Spanish Glossary

A

absolute dating/datación absoluta cualquier método que sirve para determinar la edad de un suceso u objeto en años (70)

asthenosphere/astenosfera la capa blanda del manto sobre la que se mueven las placas tectónicas (98)

C

caldera/caldera una depresión grande y semicircular que se forma cuando se vacía parcialmente la cámara de magma que hay debajo de un volcán, lo cual hace que el suelo se hunda (164)

cast/molde un tipo de fósil que se forma cuando un organismo descompuesto deja una cavidad que es llenada por sedimentos (76)

catastrophism/catastrofismo un principio que establece que los cambios geológicos ocurren súbitamente (61)

cleavage/exfoliación el agrietamiento de un mineral en sus superficies lisas y planas (9)

composition/composición la constitución química de una roca; describe los minerales u otros materiales presentes en ella (33)

compound/compuesto una substancia formada por átomos de dos o más elementos diferentes unidos por enlaces químicos (5)

compression/compresión estrés que se produce cuando distintas fuerzas actúan para estrechar un objeto (112)

continental drift/deriva continental la hipótesis que establece que alguna vez los continentes formaron una sola masa de tierra, se dividieron y se fueron a la deriva hasta terminar en sus ubicaciones actuales (104)

convergent boundary/límite convergente el límite que se forma debido al choque de dos placas de la litosfera (109)

core/núcleo la parte central de la Tierra, debajo del manto (97)

crater/cráter una depresión con forma de embudo que se encuentra cerca de la parte superior de la chimenea central de un volcán (164)

crust/corteza la capa externa, delgada y sólida de la Tierra, que se encuentra sobre el manto (96)

crystal/cristal un sólido cuyos átomos, iones o moléculas están ordenados en un patrón definido (5)

D

deformation/deformación el proceso de doblar, inclinar y romper la corteza de la Tierra; el cambio en la forma de una roca en respuesta a la tensión (131)

density/densidad la relación entre la masa de una substancia y su volumen (10)

deposition/deposición el proceso por medio del cual un material se deposita (29)

divergent boundary/límite divergente el límite entre dos placas tectónicas que se están separando una de la otra (109)

E

elastic rebound/rebote elástico ocurre cuando una roca deformada elásticamente vuelve súbitamente a su forma no deformada (131)

element/elemento una substancia que no se puede separar o descomponer en substancias más simples por medio de métodos químicos (4)

eon/eón la mayor división del tiempo geológico (83)

epicenter/epicentro el punto de la superficie de la Tierra que queda justo arriba del punto de inicio, o foco, de un terremoto (136)

epoch/época una subdivisión de un período geológico (83)

era/era una unidad de tiempo geológico que incluye dos o más períodos (83)

erosion/erosión el proceso por medio del cual el viento, el agua, el hielo o la gravedad transporta tierra y sedimentos de un lugar a otro (29)

extinction/extinción la muerte de todos los miembros de una especie (83)

extrusive igneous rock/roca ígnea extrusiva una roca que se forma como resultado de la actividad volcánica en la superficie de la Tierra o cerca de ella (39)

fault/falla una grieta en un cuerpo rocoso a lo largo de la cual un bloque se desliza respecto a otro (114)

focus/foco el punto a lo largo de una falla donde ocurre el primer movimiento de un terremoto (136)

folding/plegamiento fenómeno que ocurre cuando las capas de roca se doblan debido a la compresión (113)

foliated/foliada término que describe la textura de una roca metamórfica en la que los granos de mineral están ordenados en planos o bandas (47)

fossil/fósil los restos o las pruebas físicas de un organismo preservados por los procesos geológicos (74)

fracture/fractura la forma en la que se rompe un mineral a lo largo de superficies curvas o irregulares (9)

G

gap hypothesis/hipótesis del intervalo una hipótesis que se basa en la idea de que es más probable que ocurra un terremoto importante a lo largo de la parte de una falla activa donde no se han producido terremotos durante un determinado período de tiempo (141)

geologic column/columna geológica un arreglo de las capas de roca en el que las rocas más antiguas están al fondo (65)

geologic time scale/escala de tiempo geológico el método estándar que se usa para dividir la larga historia natural de la Tierra en partes razonables (82)

H

half-life/vida media el tiempo que tarda la mitad de la muestra de una substancia radiactiva en desintegrarse por desintegración radiactiva (71)

hardness/dureza una medida de la capacidad de un mineral de resistir ser rayado (10)

hot spot/mancha caliente un área volcánicamente activa de la superficie de la Tierra que se encuentra lejos de un límite entre placas tectónicas (170)

I

index fossil/fósil guía un fósil que se encuentra en las capas de roca de una sola era geológica y que se usa para establecer la edad de las capas de roca (78)

intrusive igneous rock/roca ígnea intrusiva una roca formada a partir del enfriamiento y solidificación del magma debajo de la superficie terrestre (38)

isotope/isótopo un átomo que tiene el mismo número de protones (o el mismo número atómico) que otros átomos del mismo elemento, pero que tiene un número diferente de neutrones (y, por lo tanto, otra masa atómica) (70)

L

lava plateau/meseta de lava un accidente geográfico amplio y plano que se forma debido a repetidas erupciones no explosivas de lava que se expanden por un área extensa (165)

lithosphere/litosfera la capa externa y sólida de la Tierra que está formada por la corteza y la parte superior y rígida del manto (98)

luster/brillo la forma en que un mineral refleja la luz (8)

M

magma chamber/cámara de magma la masa de roca fundida que alimenta un volcán (158)

mantle/manto la capa de roca que se encuentra entre la corteza terrestre y el núcleo (97)

mesosphere/mesosfera la parte fuerte e inferior del manto que se encuentra entre la astenosfera y el núcleo externo (99)

mineral/mineral un sólido natural e inorgánico que tiene una estructura química definida (4)

mold/molde una marca o cavidad hecha en una superficie sedimentaria por una concha u otro cuerpo (76)

N

nonfoliated/no foliada término que describe la textura de una roca metamórfica en la que los granos de mineral no están ordenados en planos ni bandas (48)

nonsilicate mineral/mineral no-silicato un mineral que no contiene compuestos de sílice y oxígeno (6)

O

ore/mena un material natural cuya concentración de minerales con valor económico es suficientemente alta como para que el material pueda ser explotado de manera rentable (14)

P

paleontology/paleontología el estudio científico de los fósiles (63)

period/período una unidad de tiempo geológico en la que se dividen las eras (83)

plate tectonics/tectónica de placas la teoría que explica cómo se mueven y cambian de forma las placas tectónicas, que son grandes porciones de la capa más externa de la Tierra (108)

P wave/onda P una onda sísmica que hace que las partículas de roca se muevan en una dirección de atrás hacia delante (134)

R

radioactive decay/desintegración radiactiva el proceso por medio del cual unlos isótopos radiactivos tienden a desintegrarse y formar un isótopos estables del mismo elemento o de otros elementos (70)

radiometric dating/datación radiométrica un método para determinar la edad de un objeto estimando los porcentajes relativos de un isótopo radiactivo (precursor) y un isótopo estable (hijo) (71)

reclamation/restauración el proceso de hacer que la tierra vuelva a su condición original después de que se terminan las actividades de explotación minera (15)

relative dating/datación relativa cualquier método que se utiliza para determinar si un acontecimiento u objeto es más viejo o más joven que otros acontecimientos u objetos (64)

rift zone/zona de rift un área de grietas profundas que se forma entre dos placas tectónicas que se están alejando una de la otra (168)

rock/roca una mezcla sólida de uno o más minerales o de materia orgánica que se produce de forma natural (28)

rock cycle/ciclo de las rocas la serie de procesos por medio de los cuales una roca se forma, cambia de un tipo a otro, se destruye y se forma nuevamente por procesos geológicos (28)

S

sea-floor spreading/expansión del suelo marino el proceso por medio del cual se forma nueva litosfera oceánica a medida que el magma se eleva hacia la superficie y se solidifica (106)

seismic gap/brecha sísmica un área a lo largo de una falla donde han ocurrido relativamente pocos terremotos recientemente, pero donde se han producido terremotos fuertes en el pasado (141)

seismic wave/onda sísmica una onda de energía que viaja a través de la Tierra y se aleja de un terremoto en todas direcciones (134)

seismogram/sismograma una gráfica del movimiento de un terremoto elaborada por un sismógrafo (136)

seismograph/sismógrafo un instrumento que registra las vibraciones en el suelo y determina la ubicación y la fuerza de un terremoto (136)

seismology/sismología el estudio de los terremotos (130)

silicate mineral/mineral silicato un mineral que contiene una combinación de sílice, oxígeno y uno o más metales (6)

strata/estratos capas de roca (40)

stratification/estratificación el proceso por medio del cual las rocas sedimentarias se acomodan en capas (43)

streak/veta el color del polvo de un mineral (9)

subsidence/hundimiento del terreno el hundimiento de regiones de la corteza terrestre a elevaciones más bajas (118)

superposition/superposición un principio que establece que las rocas más jóvenes se encontrarán sobre las rocas más viejas si las capas no han sido alteradas (64)

S wave/onda S una onda sísmica que hace que las partículas de roca se muevan en una dirección de lado a lado (134)

T

tectonic plate/placa tectónica un bloque de litosfera formado por la corteza y la parte rígida y más externa del manto (100)

tension/tensión estrés que se produce cuando distintas fuerzas actúan para estirar un objeto (112)

texture/textura la cualidad de una roca que se basa en el tamaño, la forma y la posición de los granos que la forman (34)

trace fossil/fósil traza una marca fosilizada que se forma en un sedimento blando debido al movimiento de un animal (76)

transform boundary/límite de transformación el límite entre placas tectónicas que se están deslizando horizontalmente una sobre otra (109)

Spanish Glossary

U

unconformity/disconformidad una ruptura en el registro geológico, creada cuando las capas de roca se erosionan o cuando el sedimento no se deposita durante un largo período de tiempo (67)

uniformitarianism/uniformitarianismo un principio que establece que es posible explicar los procesos geológicos que ocurrieron en el pasado en función de los procesos geológicos actuales (60)

uplift/levantamiento la elevación de regiones de la corteza terrestre a elevaciones más altas (118)

V

vent/chimenea una abertura en la superficie de la Tierra a través de la cual pasa material volcánico (158)

volcano/volcán una chimenea o fisura en la superficie de la Tierra a través de la cual se expulsan magma y gases (156)

Index

Boldface page numbers refer to illustrative material, such as figures, tables, margin elements, photographs, and illustrations.

Index

Index

Index

Index

W

water
  density of, 10
  in volcanic eruptions, 158, 169,
    169
waxy luster, **8**
weathering, in the rock cycle, 29,
  29, 31
Wegener, Alfred, 104–105, 127
Wieliczka salt mine, 24
Williamson, Jack, 24
woolly mammoths, 75, **75,** 92

Y

Yellowstone National Park, 164
Yoho National Park, **77**

Credits

Abbreviations used: **(t)** top, **(c)** center, **(b)** bottom, **(l)** left, **(r)** right, **(bkgd)** background

PHOTOGRAPHY

Front Cover Doug Scott/Age Fotostock

Skills Practice Lab Teens Sam Dudgeon/HRW

Connection to Astrology Corbis Images; **Connection to Biology** David M. Phillips/Visuals Unlimited; **Connection to Chemistry** Digital Image copyright © 2005 PhotoDisc; **Connection to Environment** Digital Image copyright © 2005 PhotoDisc; **Connection to Geology** Letraset Phototone; **Connection to Language Arts** Digital Image copyright © 2005 PhotoDisc; **Connection to Meteorology** Digital Image copyright © 2005 PhotoDisc; **Connection to Oceanography** © ICONOTEC; **Connection to Physics** Digital Image copyright © 2005 PhotoDisc

Table of Contents iv (yellow), E. R. Degginger/Color–Pic, Inc.; iv (purple), Mark A. Schneider/Photo Researchers, Inc.; (green), Dr. E.R. Degginger Bruce Coleman Inc.; iv (bl), The G.R. "Dick" Roberts Photo Library; v (b), ©National Geographic Image Collection/Robert W. Madden; x (bl), Sam Dudgeon/HRW; xi (tl), John Langford/HRW; xi (b), Sam Dudgeon/HRW; xii (tl), Victoria Smith/HRW; xii (bl), Stephanie Morris/HRW; xii (br), Sam Dudgeon/HRW; xiii (tl), Patti Murray/Animals, Animals; xiii (tr), Jana Birchum/HRW; xiii (b), Peter Van Steen/HRW

Chapter One 2–3, Terry Wilson; 4, Sam Dudgeon/HRW; 5, Dr. Rainer Bode/Bode–Verlag Gmb; 6 (tr), Victoria Smith/HRW; 6 (bc), Sam Dudgeon/HRW; 6 (tl), Sam Dudgeon/HRW; 7, (copper), E. R. Degginger/Color–Pic, Inc.; 7, (calcite), E. R. Degginger/Color–Pic, Inc.; 7, (fluorite), E. R. Degginger/Color–Pic, Inc.; 7, (corundum), E. R. Degginger/Color–Pic, Inc.; 7, (gypsum), SuperStock; 7, (galena), Visuals Unlimited/Ken Lucas; 8, (vitreous), Biophoto Associates/Photo Researchers, Inc.; 8, (waxy), Biophoto Associates/Photo Researchers, Inc.; 8, (silky), Dr. E.R. Degginger/Bruce Coleman Inc.; 8, (submetallic), John Cancalosi 1989/DRK Photo; 8 (bl), Kosmatsu Mining Systems; 8, (resinous), Charles D. Winters/Photo Researchers, Inc.; 8, (pearly), Victoria Smith/HRW; 8, (metallic), Victoria Smith/HRW; 8, (earthy), Sam Dudgeon/HRW; 9 (tr, c, bl), Sam Dudgeon/HRW; 9, Tom Pantages; 10, (1), Visuals Unlimited/Ken Lucas; 10, (3), Visuals Unlimited/Dane S. Johnson; 10, (7), Carlyn Iverson/Absolute Science Illustration and Photography; 10, (8), Mark A. Schneider/Visuals Unlimited; 10, (9), Charles D. Winters/Photo Researchers, Inc.; 10, (10), Bard Wrisley; 10, (5), Biophoto Associates/Photo Researchers, Inc.; 10, (6), Victoria Smith/HRW; 10, (4), Mark A. Schneider/Photo Researchers, Inc.; 10, (2), Sam Dudgeon/HRW; 11 (tc), Sam Dudgeon/HRW; 11 (tr), Sam Dudgeon/HRW, Courtesy Science Stuff, Austin, TX; 11 (br), Tom Pantages Photography; 11 (bc), Sam Dudgeon/HRW; 11 (tl), Mark A. Schneider/Photo Researchers, Inc.; 11 (tl), Mark A. Schneider/Photo Researchers, Inc.; 11 (bl), 12 (t), Sam Dudgeon/HRW; 12 (bl), Victoria Smith/HRW Photo, Courtesy Science Stuff, Austin, TX; 12 (c), Breck P. Kent; 13 (br), Sam Dudgeon/HRW; 13 (c), Breck P. Kent; 13 (t), Visuals Unlimited/Ken Lucas; 14 (br), Wernher Krutein; 15, Stewart Cohen/Index Stock Photography, Inc.; 16, Digital Image copyright © 2005 PhotoDisc; 17, Historic Royal Palaces; 18 (c), Russell Dian/HRW; 18 (b), 19 (r), Sam Dudgeon/HRW; 20, Digital Image copyright © 2005 PhotoDisc; 21 (b), E. R. Degginger/Color–Pic, Inc.; 24 (t), Stephan Edelbroich; 25 (t), Will & Dennie McIntyre/McIntyre Photography; 25 (b), Mark Schneider/Visuals Unlimited

Chapter Two 26–27, Tom Till; 28 (bl), Michael Melford/Getty Images/The Image Bank; 28 (br), Joseph Sohm; Visions of America/CORBIS; 29, CORBIS Images/HRW; 32 (t), Joyce Photographics/Photo Researchers, Inc.; 32 (l), Pat Lanza/Bruce Coleman Inc.; 32 (r), Sam Dudgeon/HRW ; 32 (b), James Watt/Animals Animals/Earth Scenes; 32 (l), Pat Lanza/Bruce Coleman Inc.; 33, (granite), Pat Lanza/Bruce Coleman Inc.; 33, (mica), E. R. Degginger/Color–Pic, Inc.; 33, (aragonite), Breck P. Kent; 33, (limestone), Breck P. Kent; 33, (calcite), Mark Schneider/Visuals Unlimited; 33, (feldspar), Mark Schneider/Visuals Unlimited; 33, (quartz), Digital Image copyright © 2005 PhotoDisc; 34 (tl), Sam Dudgeon/HRW; 34 (tc), Dorling Kindersley; 34 (tr, br), Breck P. Kent; 34 (bl), E. R. Degginger/Color–Pic, Inc.; 35, Joseph Sohm; Visions of America/CORBIS; 36 (l), E. R. Degginger/Color–Pic, Inc.; 37 (tr, tl, bl), Breck P. Kent; 37 (br), Victoria Smith/HRW; 39, J.D. Griggs/USGS; 40, CORBIS Images/HRW; 41, (conglomerate), Breck P. Kent; 41, (siltstone), Sam Dudgeon/HRW; 41, (sandstone), Joyce Photographics/Photo Researchers, Inc.; 41, (shale), Sam Dudgeon/HRW; 42 (tl), Stephen Frink/Corbis; 42 (br), Breck P. Kent; 42 (bc), David Muench/CORBIS; 43, Franklin P. OSF/Animals Animals/Earth Scenes; 44, George Wuerthner; 46, (calcite), Dane S. Johnson/Visuals Unlimited; 46, (quartz), Carlyn Iverson/Absolute Science Illustration and Photography; 46, (hematite), Breck P. Kent; 46, (garnet), Breck P. Kent/Animals Animals/Earth Scenes; 46, (chlorite), Sam Dudgeon/HRW; 46, (mica), Tom Pantages; 47, (shale), Ken Karp/HRW; 47, (slate), Sam Dudgeon/HRW; 47, (phyllite), Sam Dudgeon/HRW; 47, (gneiss), Breck P. Kent; 47, (schist), Sam Dudgeon/HRW; 48 (tl), E. R. Degginger/Color–Pic, Inc.; 48 (bl), Ray Simmons/Photo Researchers, Inc; 48 (tr), The Natural History Museum, London; 48 (br), Breck P. Kent; 49, Jim Wark/Airphoto; 51 (t), Sam Dudgeon/HRW; 51 (b), James Tallon; 56 (l), Wolfgang Kaehler/CORBIS; 56 (tr), Dr. David Kring/Science Photo Library/Photo Researchers, Inc.; 57 (r), James Miller/Courtesy Robert Folk, Department of Geological Sciences, University of Texas at Austin; 57 (l), Dr. Philppa Uwins, Whistler Research PTY/SPL/Photo Researchers, Inc.

Chapter Three 58, National Geographic Image Collection/Jonathan Blair, Courtesy Hessian Regional Museum, Darmstadt, Germany; 61, GeoScience Features Picture Library; 63, Museum of Northern Arizona; 64 (l), Sam Dudgeon/HRW; 64 (r), Andy Christiansen/HRW; 66 (tl), Fletcher & Baylis/Photo Researchers, Inc.; 66 (tr), Ken M. Johns/Photo Researchers, Inc.; 66 (bl), Glenn M. Oliver/Visuals Unlimited; 66 (br), Francis Gohier/Photo Researchers, Inc.; 71, Sam Dudgeon/HRW; 72, Tom Till/DRK Photo; 73, Courtesy Charles S. Tucek/University of Arizona at Tucson; 74, Howard Grey/Getty Images/Stone; 75, Francis Latreille/Nova Productions/AP/Wide World Photos; 76 (b), The G.R. "Dick" Roberts Photo Library; 76 (t), © Louie Psihoyos/psihoyos.com; 77 (l), Brian Exton; 77 (r), Chip Clark/Smithsonian; 78 (l), ; 79, Thomas R. Taylor/Photo Researchers, Inc.; 80, James L. Amos/CORBIS; 81 (tl), Tom Till Photography; 81 (fish), Tom Bean/CORBIS; 81 (leaf), James L. Amos/CORBIS; 81 (turtle), Layne Kennedy/CORBIS; 81 (fly), Ken Lucas/Visuals Unlimited; 83, Chip Clark/Smithsonian; 84 (t), Neg. no. 5793 Courtesy Dept. of Library Services., American Museum of Natural History; 84 (b), Neg. no. 5799 Courtesy Department of Library Services., American Museum of Natural History; 85, Neg. no. 5801 Courtesy Department of Library Services, American Museum of Natural History; 86, Jonathan Blair/CORBIS; 88 (b), The G.R. "Dick" Roberts Photo Library; 89 (fly), Ken Lucas/Visuals Unlimited; 92 (tl), Beth A. Keiser/AP/Wide World Photos; 92 (tr), Jonathan Blair/CORBIS; 93, Courtesy Kevin C. May

Chapter Four 94–95, James Balog/Getty Images/Stone; 97 (t), James Wall/Animals Animals/Earth Scenes; 100, Bruce C. Heezen and Marie Tharp; 111 (tc), ESA/CE/Eurocontrol/Science Photo Library/Photo Researchers, Inc.; 111 (tr), NASA; 112 (bl, br), Peter Van Steen/HRW; 113 (bc), Visuals Unlimited/SylvesterAllred; 113 (br), G.R. Roberts Photo Library; 115 (tl), Tom Bean; 115 (tr), Landform Slides; 116, Jay Dickman/CORBIS; 117 (b), Michele & Tom Grimm Photography; 118, Y. Arthus–B./Peter Arnold, Inc.; 119, Peter Van Steen/HRW; 121, Sam Dudgeon/HRW; 126 (bl), NASA/Science Photo Library/Photo Researchers, Inc.; 126 (c), Ron Miller/Fran Heyl Associates; 126 (tr), Photo by S. Thorarinsson/Solar–Filma/Sun Film–15/3/courtesy of Edward T. Baker, Pacific Marine Environmental Laboratory, NOAA; 127 (r), Bettman/CORBIS

Chapter Five 128–129, Robert Patrick/Sygma/CORBIS; 131, Roger Ressmeyer/CORBIS; 137, Earth Images/Getty Images/Stone; 139, Bettmann/CORBIS; 142, Michael S. Yamashita/CORBIS; 144, Paul Chesley/Getty Images/Stone; 146, NOAA/NGDC; 147, Sam Dudgeon/HRW; 149, Bettmann/CORBIS; 152, Sam Dudgeon/HRW; 152 (t), Courtesy Stephen H. Hickman, USGS; 153 (t), Todd Bigelow/HRW; 153 (b), Corbis Images

Chapter Six 154–155, Carl Shaneff/Pacific Stock; 156 (bl), National Geographic Image Collection/Robert W. Madden; 156 (br), Ken Sakamoto/Black Star; 157 (b), Breck P. Kent/Animals Animals/Earth Scenes; 157, Joyce Warren/USGS Photo Library; 159 (tl), Tui De Roy/Minden Pictures; 159 (bl), B. Murton/Southampton Oceanography Centre/Science Photo Library/Photo Researchers, Inc.; 159 (tr), Visuals Unlimited/Martin Miller; 159 (br), Buddy Mays/CORBIS; 160 (tr), Tom Bean/DRK Photo; 160 (tl), Francois Gohier/Photo Researchers, Inc.; 160, (tlc), Visuals Unlimited Inc./Glenn Oliver; 160, (tlb), E. R. Degginger/Color–Pic, Inc.; 161 (tr), Alberto Garcia/SABA/CORBIS; 161, Robert W. Madden/National Geographic Society; 162, Images & Volcans/Photo Researchers, Inc.; 163 (br), SuperStock; 163 (cr), SuperStock; 163 (tr), Roger Ressmeyer/CORBIS; 164 (tl), Yann Arthus–Bertrand/CORBIS; 165, Joseph Sohm; ChromoSohm Inc./CORBIS; 170 (bl), Robert McGimsey/USGS Alaska Volcano Observatory; 174 (tr), Alberto Garcia/SABA/CORBIS; 178 (bl), CORBIS; 178 (tr), Photo courtesy of Alan V. Morgan, Department of Earth Sciences, University of Waterloo; 178 (tc), © Sigurgeir Jonasson; Frank Lane Picture Agency/CORBIS; 179 (bl), Courtesy Christina Neal; 179 (r), Courtesy Alaska Volcano Observatory

Lab Book/Appendix "LabBook Header", "L", Corbis Images; "a", Letraset Phototone; "b", and "B", HRW; "o", and "k", images ©2006 PhotoDisc/HRW; 181 (tr), Victoria Smith/HRW, Courtesy of Science Stuff, Austin, TX; 181, (galena), Ken Lucas/Visuals Unlimited; 181 (cr), Charlie Winters/HRW; 181, 182, 183 (hematite, br), Sam Dudgeon/HRW; 184 (all), Andy Christiansen/HRW; 185, Sam Dudgeon/HRW; 186, Tom Bean; 187, 188, Sam Dudgeon/HRW; 189, Andy Christiansen/HRW; 193 (tr) Sam Dudgeon/HRW

TEACHER EDITION CREDITS

1E (bl), Mark A. Schneider/Photo Researchers, Inc.; 1E (br), Mark A. Schneider/Photo Researchers, Inc.; 1F (tr), Breck P. Kent; 1F (bl), Stewart Cohen/Index Stock Photography, Inc.; 1F (tl), Historic Royal Palaces; 25E (r), J.D. Griggs/USGS; 25E (aragonite), Breck P. Kent; 25E (limestone), Breck P. Kent; 25E (calcite), Mark Schneider/Visuals Unlimited; 25E (siltstone), Sam Dudgeon/HRW; 25E (sandstone), Dorling Kindersley; 25E (conglomerate), Breck P. Kent; 25F (tl), CORBIS Images/HRW; 25F (mica), Tom Pantages; 25F (chlorite), Sam Dudgeon/HRW; 25F (mica), Tom Pantages; 57E (br), Tom Till/DRK Photo; 57F (t), © Louie Psihoyos/psihoyos.com; 57F (br), Ken Lucas/Visuals Unlimited; 127E (b), Michael S. Yamashita/CORBIS; 127F (tr), Paul Chesley/Getty Images/Stone; 153E (bl), ©National Geographic Image Collection/Robert W. Madden; 153E (tl), E. R. Degginger/Color–Pic, Inc.; 153F (l), Alberto Garcia/SABA/CORBIS; 153F (r), Roger Ressmeyer/CORBIS

Answers to Concept Mapping Questions

The following pages contain sample answers to all of the concept mapping questions that appear in the Chapter Reviews. Because there is more than one way to do a concept map, your students' answers may vary.

CHAPTER 1 Minerals of the Earth's Crust

15.
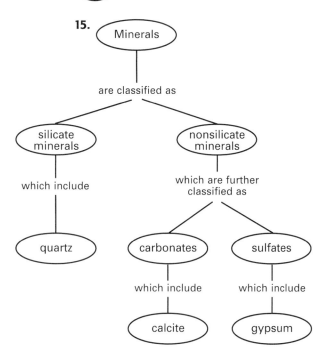

CHAPTER 2 Rocks: Mineral Mixtures

17.
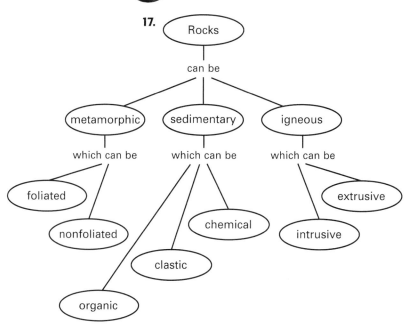

CHAPTER 3   The Rock and Fossil Record

18.

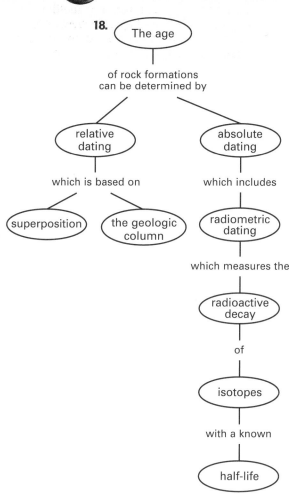

The age

of rock formations
can be determined by

relative dating — which is based on → superposition, the geologic column

absolute dating — which includes → radiometric dating

which measures the

radioactive decay

of

isotopes

with a known

half-life

CHAPTER 4   Plate Tectonics

17.

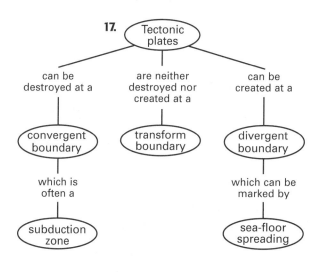

Tectonic plates

can be destroyed at a → convergent boundary → which is often a → subduction zone

are neither destroyed nor created at a → transform boundary

can be created at a → divergent boundary → which can be marked by → sea-floor spreading

CHAPTER 5   Earthquakes

16.

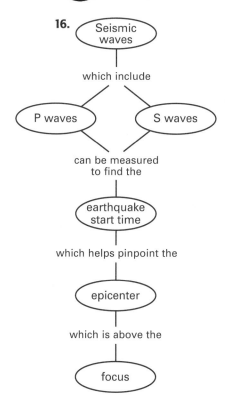

Seismic waves

which include

P waves, S waves

can be measured to find the

earthquake start time

which helps pinpoint the

epicenter

which is above the

focus

CHAPTER 6   Volcanoes

17.

Volcanoes

produce

lava — such as → aa, pahoehoe

pyroclastic material — such as → volcanic bombs, lapilli